POOR GAL

POOR GAL

The Cultural History of Little Liza Jane

Dan Gutstein

University Press of Mississippi / Jackson

The University Press of Mississippi is the scholarly publishing agency of
the Mississippi Institutions of Higher Learning: Alcorn State University,
Delta State University, Jackson State University, Mississippi State University,
Mississippi University for Women, Mississippi Valley State University,
University of Mississippi, and University of Southern Mississippi.

www.upress.state.ms.us

The University Press of Mississippi is a member
of the Association of University Presses.

Transcribed lyrics for recordings of Wilson "Stavin' Chain" Jones
"Li'l Liza Jane" (1934); Aunt Molly Jackson "Liza Jane" (1939);
Bessie Jones "Steal Miss Liza" (1961); and Sam Chatmon "Little Liza Jane" (1978)
are printed with permission *From the Alan Lomax Collection
at the American Folklife Center, Library of Congress.*

Transcribed lyrics for the John and Ruby Lomax recording of the
traditional folk song "Steal Miss Liza" (sometimes called "Steal Liza Jane")
by Johnny Mae Medlock, Gussie Slater, and Ruth Hines are printed
with acknowledgment of *John and Ruby Lomax 1939 southern states recording
trip (AFC 1939/001), American Folklife Center, Library of Congress.*

Library of Congress Cataloging-in-Publication Data

Names: Gutstein, Daniel, author.
Title: Poor gal : the cultural history of Little Liza Jane / Dan Gutstein.
Other titles: American made music series.
Description: Jackson : University Press of Mississippi, 2023. | Series: American made
music series | Includes bibliographical references and index.
Identifiers: LCCN 2023033213 (print) | LCCN 2023033214 (ebook) | ISBN 9781496849342
(hardback) | ISBN 9781496849359 (trade paperback) | ISBN 9781496849366 (epub) |
ISBN 9781496849373 (epub) | ISBN 9781496849380 (pdf) | ISBN 9781496849397 (pdf)
Subjects: LCSH: Folk songs, English—United States—History and criticism. |
Folk music—United States—History and criticism. | African Americans—Music—
History and criticism. | Work songs—United States—History and criticism. |
Slavery—United States—Songs and music—History and criticism.
Classification: LCC ML3551 .G88 2023 (print) | LCC ML3551 (ebook) |
DDC 782.42162/13—dc23/eng/20230802
LC record available at https://lccn.loc.gov/2023033213
LC ebook record available at https://lccn.loc.gov/2023033214

British Library Cataloging-in-Publication Data available

To Emily Cohen

The World's Only
Fiddler Illustrator Supernumerary.
My Friend, My Colleague.
& A Poor Gal Enthusiast Herself.

To WPA Respondents

Marshall Butler, Lawrence Evans, Dosia Harris,
Bryant Huff, Lina Hunter, Alice Hutcheson,
Hannah Jameson, Lydia Jefferson, Lucy Thurston,
and Anda Woods.

CONTENTS

APOLOGIA

I present *Poor Gal* to you with goodness in my heart. The book required more than five years to complete, during very trying times. It is not perfect, however, and I would like to address one of its shortcomings.

I apologize for the presence of difficult language in these pages. The book's narrative arc travels through slavery, minstrelsy, and the Jim Crow era, all of which perpetuated cruelty and racism. To say "barbaric and shameful" does not approach the deep well of sadness I have felt when studying decades and decades of brutality that runs contrary to the basic tenets of decency.

This language can be found in some song titles, lyrics, narratives of formerly enslaved people, cultural studies, and literary works. While these inclusions may be vital to representing the full voyage of "Little Liza Jane" and its sibling songs, the vocabulary may be occasionally painful. I am sorry. My great hope would be for readers to witness how "Little Liza Jane" has outlasted a reprehensible environment.

Despite this imperfection, I urge you to read *Poor Gal* to the last word. Spread the story. Tell children about the "Liza Jane" family of songs. And sing (or play) one of these bright melodies every single day.

ACKNOWLEDGMENTS

First and foremost, I would like to express deep gratitude to David Evans for an astonishing amount of encouragement and guidance. Without his mentorship, this book would never have been completed.

Thank you to Craig Gill and the team at University Press of Mississippi for bringing this project to life.

I am much obliged to Nathan Salsburg at the Association for Cultural Equity for enlightening conversation and permission to transcribe lyrics recorded by John Lomax and Alan Lomax.

Many thanks to Chris O'Leary for instructive conversation and sharing his "Little Liza Jane" research.

Thanks for key assists from Tucker Nance (music notation), Brandon Fitzgerald (review of a rare source), and John Minton (expertise on WPA narratives).

Thanks to Rachel Morris, from the Rare Book Collections of the Center for Popular Music, Middle Tennessee State University, for forwarding the 1866 version of "Eliza Jane," found in Billy Emerson's *Nancy Fat Songster*.

Conversations and/or interviews with Tim Brooks, Bill Ferris, Dom Flemons, Shennette Garrett-Scott, Kyra Gaunt, Tammy Kernodle, Eric Lott, and Phil Wiggins were incredibly helpful and motivational. Thank you for your time and insights.

Much appreciation to Wayne "Dr. B." Brumfield, Heather Fuller, Ruth and Martin Gutstein, Phyllis Rosenzweig and Alan Wallach, Casey Smith, Rod Smith, Ms. S. R. Stewart, Terence Winch, Michael Zito, and Ted Zook, for encouragement, advice, friendship, logistical support, and/or singing during the completion of this book.

Much gratitude to Melissa Houghton at Women in Film & Video for her enthusiasm related to this project. WIFV is the fiscal sponsor for a forthcoming documentary film about "Liza Jane." Stay tuned!

Finally, I would like to remember my long-term mentor, Faye Moskowitz, who loved to sing "Liza Jane" and passed away before this book could be published. Her wise words, sense of humor, and passion for folk music have contributed enormously to this effort. Not a day goes by when I do not think about Faye singing, "If you love me Liza Jane / Put your little hand in mine / You won't lack for no cornbread / As long as the sun do shine."

POOR GAL

SLUDGE AND THEORY

This book chronicles the extraordinary voyages of "Little Liza Jane" and a suite of closely related folk songs that likely originated among enslaved people during celebratory dances or "frolics" on southern plantations. In its early days, "Little Liza Jane" and its sibling songs were probably not intoned the same way twice, with interchangeable bits of folk lyrics attached to the name Liza Jane. From the Civil War years onward, various mechanisms acted upon the songs to propel them across multiple boundaries, including the color line, geographical regions, performance traditions, musical genres, and historical milestones. Eventually, "Little Liza Jane" itself would become one of the most beloved, widely adopted, and widely recorded folk songs to enter the popular canon. Through the study of "Little Liza Jane" and related songs, *Poor Gal* narrates a uniquely transcendent American story. Consider, for example, the plights of two opposing Civil War regiments: a Union outfit comprised of Black soldiers and the other unit fighting for the Confederacy. Both marched toward a sprawling battle at Spotsylvania Courthouse in the spring of 1864. Separated by the colors of their skins and the colors of their uniforms, the two regiments may have even taken aim at one another. But they had something in common. They were both singing related "Liza Jane" songs built almost certainly from African American folk melodies.

Devotees of American folk music will recognize a head-swimming number of song titles and refrains that feature the character Liza Jane, such as "Little Liza Jane" or "Li'l Liza Jane," "Goodbye Liza Jane," "Steal Miss Liza," "Oh! Liza, Poor Gal," and simply enough, "Liza Jane" or "Eliza Jane." There are many more titles. There can be dozens of renditions within a variant branch, as well as hybrid forms, and there is an additional suite of songs—including "Whoa Mule" and "Run, Mollie, Run"—into which the Liza Jane character "intrudes." This book will demonstrate the relationships among these songs as well as their developmental pathways, but for efficiency's sake, the discussion will at times refer to this group as the "Liza Jane" family of songs, or simply, "Liza Jane." To extend this construct a little bit farther, the discussion will center on the largest branches, as noted above, yet not to the exclusion of some very telling lesser limbs.

The "Liza Jane" family of songs is not diagrammable the way one might plat out a conventional family tree. In all probability, several early variants existed at once without a clear sense of which one might have come first. Moreover, many early details—revealed in Works Progress Administration (WPA) narratives of previously enslaved people, Civil War regimental histories, and other reminiscences that appear decades after the events they document—may instill some doubt, despite their rich founts of information and their uncoordinated corroboration of one-another. To be sure, the study of these songs will require the navigation of some historical "sludge." Introducing the word "sludge" should not impeach the singularity of the first people to perform "Little Liza Jane" and its variants. To the contrary, the songs exhibit a vibrant cultural history, and by acknowledging the presence of sludge, this study is merely admitting the simple truth. Namely, complete certainty does not exist regarding the budding moments in the "Liza Jane" family.

More technically, "sludge" may equate to (1) a collection of reminiscences that might challenge timelines or a sense of believability; and (2) when specifically focusing on date-stamped sources, the sudden appearance of a phrase, lyric, or verse that seems to emerge "out of thin air" and therefore implies the existence of other, undiscovered materials. In this context, the word "sludge" thereby acknowledges an element of uncertainty. It would be most desirable, of course, to present a sequence of information that would eliminate every ambiguity, but in the end, the quest to situate the "Liza Jane" family of songs, especially in its earliest years, may resemble other ancestral quests for which definitive answers are unavailable. To help explain the formation of these songs, therefore, this book will depend upon a basic theoretical framework.

In his autobiography, *Father of the Blues*, musician and composer W. C. Handy writes that his blues "[were] built around, or suggested by [. . .] snatches, phrases, cries, and idioms."[1] He additionally describes this inspiration as a "snatch of folk melody."[2] Interestingly enough, in his WPA narrative, respondent Anda Woods mentions the phrase "snotches of songs" when relating performance details about "Miss Liza Jane."[3] Woods and other enslaved people appear to have been the earliest performers of the "Liza Jane" family, with ten WPA narratives referring to "snotches" as well as performance rituals related to "Liza Jane." For himself, W. C. Handy offers the example of "a Negro plowman" whose overheard "snatch of song" resonated with the composer at a young age. In addition to a simple melody and other vocalizations (given as "A—O—OO—A—O—OO"), the plowman's song consisted of a single line: "I wouldn't live in Cairo-oo."[4]

The sociologist Howard Odum refers to such tunes as "one-verse songs" in his 1911 article "Folk-Song and Folk-Poetry as Found in the Secular Songs of the Southern Negroes."[5] Writing in the *Journal of American Folklore*, Odum defines the one-verse form as "a single line, repeated again and again, constituting the entire song."[6] He describes the formation of such a song as "simple and natural"[7] and taking inspiration from "common scenes of everyday life."[8] To illustrate his point, Odum cites a sample lyric—"The wind sho' do blow"—that might have been repeated several times as a fully-realized piece.[9] Another line may have been added—for example, "Ain't goin' to rain no mo'"—to form a rhyming couplet.[10] According to Odum, the one-verse form prevailed among African American folk singers in the early years of the twentieth century, or as he words it, "[the] great majority of Negro songs which are current now are 'one-verse songs,' and almost all have arisen and developed along the one-verse method."[11] It would follow that the one-verse form prevailed in the nineteenth century as well. There may be a relationship between what Odum observed ("one-verse songs") and the melodies that inspired W. C. Handy, namely, the "snatches of folk melody" that led him to compose masterpieces like "St. Louis Blues." Whether or not Odum and Handy were describing the very same mechanisms can be debated, but either way, the articulation of their ideas informs the nascent states of the "Liza Jane" family of songs. It is entirely possible that a single line or a rhyming couplet may have constituted an entire song at such a formative stage.

These spare forms—"snotches" of folk material or one-verse songs—may have origins in Africa. In his 1974 book, *The Music of Africa*, ethnomusicologist J. H. Kwabena Nketia refers to strophic forms of solo singing, or what he describes as "a single verse repeated, often with slight variations, for the desired number of stanzas."[12] Nketia's observations are amplified by two musicologists, V. Kofi Agawu and A. M. Jones, both of whom offer examples of Ghanaian forms that approximate one-verse songs. As part of his 1987 article "The Rhythmic Structure of West African Music," Agawu presents a traditional Ewe lament—"I have worked for nothing / My life's work amounts to nothing"[13]—in a couplet, with minor variation from the first to the second line. Among other examples, Agawu also renders a "Ewe Funeral Dirge" as a five-line piece that departs very little from its core phrasing:

> Counsellor
> Call the counsellor
> Call the counsellor to come and see (bear witness)
> Something very painful has happened to me today
> Call the counsellor to come and see![14]

Similarly, in his 1959 book, *Studies in African Music*, A. M. Jones depicts a host of children's play-songs and fishing songs in both the original Ewe language and in English translation, with several of them resembling one-verse songs. For instance, one of the play-songs, a Ghanaian lullaby, appears as a couplet: "A naughty child is usually rocked to and fro / Swing! swing! he is usually rocked to and fro."[15] This humorous and tender "snotch" is accompanied by an optimistic fishing song, also in couplet form: "The fish are coming, the fish are coming from afar / They are coming all higgledy-piggledy."[16] Neither Agawu nor Jones establishes these brief songs as the dominant example of African vocal music, but the prevalence of these forms in their two texts, and among other studies of African singing, raises the possibility that songs of this basic structure traveled to the Americas during the horror and disgrace of the slave trade.

With dozens and dozens of names to choose between, why would enslaved people have chosen Liza Jane to begin with and kept with it? The answer may not be terribly complicated. A statesman of American music, Duke Ellington, might supply the answer. During an interview for a televised 1966 ABC music documentary, *Anatomy of Pop: The Music Explosion*, Ellington stresses how, by the 1960s, categories were not necessary to distinguish between songs. In effect, he was allowing for newer forms, such as rock 'n' roll, to be weighed (as equals) against his own genre, jazz, which had previously reigned as America's popular music. As a coiner and proponent of the phrase "beyond category," Ellington remarks that "music is either agreeable to the ear or not," and therefore, one agreeable piece (whatever its "category") should compare favorably to another agreeable piece.[17] Simply put, the name Liza Jane may have been agreeable to the ear, therefore enabling its vast transcendence. "Li'l Liza Jane" alliterates powerfully, with "li'l" emphasizing the adorable youthfulness of a young woman. Variant titles, including "Goodbye Liza Jane" and "Steal Miss Liza," catch the ear with the intrigue of a lover's rift and the promise of a dancing game, respectively.

Ample evidence indicates that the "Liza Jane" family of songs arose as a woman's name affixed to "snotches" of folk melodies or as several "one-verse songs" among enslaved people on plantations in several states. During the Civil War, some of these variants migrated to regiments from both sides of the conflict before being absorbed, organized, and transformed extensively by the inherently racist institution of minstrelsy, which served as one bridge—but hardly the only one—between the Civil War years and the advent of the recording era, the gate, as it were, to the musical paradises of the twentieth century. Though some of its sibling songs were performed on the minstrel stage, the best-known variant, "Little Liza Jane," does not seem to have been embraced by minstrel troupes and instead leaped from folk tradition into popular culture through influential sheet music publication. Even though a minstrel song may have been titled, for example, "My Little Old Liza Jane," it did not include, in all probability, the classic "Little Liza Jane" chorus or melody. "Liza Jane" songs

likely existed in the repertoire of enslaved people for some time before emancipation and probably spilled out here and there, perhaps spurring some regional
adoption. That said, "Little Liza Jane" and its family members have never been
fully organized, as there is no single text, tune, or published version that can
account for all subsequent "Liza Jane" songs. Folklorists operating in the late
nineteenth and early twentieth centuries never pointed to a fully organized,
ultimate ancestor.

Music historian and David Bowie authority, Chris O'Leary, portrays "Little
Liza Jane" as a "musical weed" in *Rebel Rebel*, the first of his two-volume set
that definitively examines the pop icon's studio recordings.[18] His meaning:
the song grows everywhere. As it happens, an adaptation of "Little Liza Jane"
became Bowie's first single in 1964. He cut the record as a teenager in a London
studio positively buzzing with guitar and saxophone, mistaking the song for
an African American spiritual.[19] Besides crossing the Atlantic Ocean, "Little
Liza Jane" journeyed more than one hundred years for it to become Bowie's
first A-side, and tracking this astonishing progression will require a somewhat
fractal approach in addition to a linear examination. The narrative will proceed
apace, double back, veer down some new-cut roads and some lanes, go up on
the mountaintop to give its horn a blow, and disclose some rather stupendous
details in the process.

I.

_____

SNOTCHES OF SONGS

The WPA *Slave Narrative Collection*

ANTEBELLUM SOUTH / THE LATE 1930s

While many American narratives of enslaved people have been collected and published, some dating back to the eighteenth century, the WPA *Slave Narrative Collection*, numbering more than 2,300 interviews, continues to be the broadest and most important such compilation brought to press. Interviewers employed by a subsidiary agency of the WPA, the Federal Writers' Project (FWP), gathered these firsthand accounts from formerly enslaved African Americans in the late 1930s. Taken together, the elderly respondents portray a wide range of eye-opening situations, from appalling brutality at the hands of their enslavers to wild breakdowns during Saturday night frolics, yet not without controversy. Historians would initially register a slate of reasons to distrust the narratives, questioning, for example, the memories of the respondents. In the last few decades, however, interest has grown in the contents of the *Slave Narrative Collection*. Writing in the March 2021 issue of *The Atlantic*, poet-scholar Clint Smith indicates that historians have revisited these stories in order to "see our shared past with new eyes."[1] In his article "We Mourn for All We Do Not Know," Smith underscores the enduring importance of these accounts. "The FWP narratives afford us the opportunity," he contends, "to understand how slavery shaped this country through the stories of those who survived it."[2] Indeed, the narratives present a rich trove of essential details, with many respondents illuminating the matters of song, music, and dance.

Norman Yetman, in his 1967 article "The Background of the *Slave Narrative Collection*," establishes the basic information regarding the men and women who were interviewed:

[O]ver two-thirds were over eighty [years old] when interviewed. Almost all had experienced slavery within the states of the Confederacy and still resided there. The major categories of slave occupations were all adequately represented. The slave holdings of the ex-slave's owner varied considerably, ranging from over a thousand slaves to situations in which the informant was the only slave owned by the master. The treatment these individuals received ran the gamut from the most harsh, impersonal and exploitative to the extremely indulgent, intimate and benevolent.[3]

At the time of emancipation in 1865, according to Yetman, 16 percent of the informants were five years old or younger; 27 percent were six to ten years of age; 24 percent were between eleven and fifteen years old; and the remainder, roughly 33 percent, were sixteen years or older. The number of people interviewed for the WPA collection represented roughly 2 percent of the total population of previously enslaved people still living in the United States at that time.[4]

Editors Ira Berlin, Marc Favreau, and Steven F. Miller identify and discuss the potential textual problems with the *Slave Narrative Collection* (and related collections) in the introduction to their book *Remembering Slavery*. They begin with an extreme figure, the historian Ulrich B. Phillips, who regarded slavery as a benevolent institution, and who deemed "politicians, pamphleteers, and aged survivors [as] hopelessly tainted" by their relationship to it.[5] Even as time went on, the editors write, "most historians treated the narratives with disdain."[6] Some cited "the unreliable memories of elderly informants," while others "questioned the statistical representativeness of the informants."[7] By the late 1970s, however, "The narratives, once dismissed as historical ephemera, had moved to the center of the study of slavery."[8] New scholars, however, advanced different concerns. Given that the FWP interviewers were mostly white southerners, these next-generation historians "suspected that ex-slaves had not told what had actually happened but what their interviewers wanted to hear."[9] Moreover, the FWP interviewers displayed a range of faults, from referring to the respondents in patronizing terms to extensive editing of the responses.[10] With respect to the latter, interviewers may have "altered the dialect as well as the words of their informant—sometimes to make them conform to popular caricatures of 'authentic' Black speech, sometimes to make them conform to standard English. [. . .] Most of the narratives might best be considered fair summaries."[11]

Despite these and other potential limitations, the editors of *Remembering Slavery* conclude that many of the interviews "evoked compelling remembrances of slavery of the sort it is impossible to fabricate."[12] The elderly status of the respondents, "and the respect traditionally granted elderly people in Southern society, often provided an opportunity for [previously enslaved people] to speak openly and forcefully."[13] Berlin, Favreau, and Miller place the narratives among any other historical sources, citing their strengths and weaknesses. "The best scholars of slavery have used them critically and cautiously," they argue, "carefully evaluating the quality of each narrative, verifying the ex-slave's memory against other sources."[14]

Folk music scholar Robert B. Winans came to a similar, if nuanced, conclusion while studying the African American musical traditions of the mid-nineteenth century. He relied exclusively on the WPA material for his 1990 article "Black Instrumental Music Traditions in the Ex-Slave Narratives." In it, he evaluates the prevalence of instrumentation referred to by the WPA respondents, with fiddle being the most common, followed by banjo, percussion instruments (tin pans, buckets, bones, drums, tambourine, and jawbone), and quills.[15] Winans also lists a partial repertoire of songs and tunes, including references to the "Liza Jane" family.[16] "For non-controversial matters of slave life, such as their musical traditions," he writes, "the [WPA] narratives are a rich source of quite reliable information."[17] The key phrase might be "non-controversial matters of slave life," which calls to mind the sorts of limitations discussed in the introduction to *Remembering Slavery*. Here, Winans implies that revelations involving song, musical instruments, and performance rituals might have been given at face value, with respondents, for instance, not seeking to slant their answers for the benefit of white interviewers, who may have been perceived as agents of the government. (In fact, they were.) The scholar John Blassingame concurred. In his 1975 article "Using the Testimony of Ex-Slaves: Approaches and Problems," Blassingame reasons, "On certain topics, the WPA interviews are incomparable sources. They probably contain, for example, more religious and secular songs than any other single source."[18] Seeing as how many respondents were young at the time of emancipation and elderly when interviewed, it would be important, as the editors of *Remembering Slavery* point out, to evaluate each narrative independently, comparing it to others.

At least ten men and women, who were not enslaved on the same plantations, referenced the "Liza Jane" family of songs during their WPA narratives: Marshall Butler, Lawrence Evans, Dosia Harris, Bryant Huff, Lina Hunter, Alice Hutcheson, Hannah Jameson, Lydia Jefferson, Lucy Thurston, and Anda Woods. Owing to the brutality of slavery, these narratives could be painful to read, but at the same time, they display a wealth of cultural information and contain precious details about the "Liza Jane" family of songs. The most salient particulars provided by these respondents can be found below, including ages, locations, song titles, lyrics, performance rituals, and any other information that might be helpful to understanding the earliest performances involving "Liza Jane."

Marshall Butler was interviewed at an unspecified location in Georgia and enslaved in Wilkes County, Georgia. He was eighty-eight years old at the time of his WPA interview. Butler indicates that he attended Saturday night frolics when the enslaved people on his plantation celebrated time off by drinking lemonade and whiskey and singing songs like "Little Liza Jane." He did not offer lyrics. He remarks, "Dat wuz our day to howl and we howled." According to Butler, musicians played songs on a fiddle and a tin can; in particular, one of the musicians would beat the strings of the fiddle with broom straws, creating an effect akin to the sound of a banjo.[19]

Lawrence Evans was interviewed in Star, Mississippi and enslaved in Rankin County, Mississippi, but his age was not given. He, too, refers to frolics, in which enslaved people would build fires in the woods and play ring games, holding hands, in the firelight. He does not title his version of the song, but offers the following lyrics, adding that people would "sing some ole song dat dey would make up, lak dis:

> Run Liza Jane an' take her home,
> Run Liza Jane an' take her home,
> Run Liza Jane an' take her home,
> Run, run, run."[20]

Dosia Harris was seventy-eight years old at the time of her WPA interview. She was interviewed in Athens, Georgia, and enslaved in Greene County, Georgia. During her narrative, she refers to the young people on her plantation: "Young folks never had nothin' but good times on deir minds. Dey danced, frolicked, and cut de buck in gen'ral. Dey didn't have no sho' 'nough music, but dey sho' could sing it down. One of de dance songs went somepin' lak dis:

> Oh! Miss Liza, Miss Liza Jane!
> Axed Miss Liza to marry me.
> Guess what she said?
> She wouldn't marry me
> If de last Nigger was dead."[21]

While "Oh! Miss Liza, Miss Liza Jane!" might look to be the refrain, Harris does not offer a title for the song.

Bryant Huff was interviewed at an unspecified location in Georgia and enslaved in Warren County, Georgia, but his age was not given. Entitled "Old Slave Story," his narrative was rendered in the interviewer's voice without including much vernacular. As part of the narrative, Huff and other enslaved people on his plantation "sang their troubles away." No title was given, but the interviewer relates these lyrics: "I went down a new cut road / She went down the lane / I turned my back upon her / And 'long come Liza Jane."[22]

Lina Hunter was about ninety years old at the time of her WPA interview, which took place in Athens, Georgia. She was enslaved in Oglethorpe County, Georgia. In her narrative, Hunter refers to the workers having "finished pickin' out de cotton, and den lots of drinkin' and dancin'. 'Bout dat dancin', Honey, I could sho cut dem corners. Dancin' is one thing I more'n did lak to do, and I wish I could hear dat old dance song again. Miss Liza Jane, it was, and some of de words went lak dis, 'Steal 'round dem corners, Miss Liza Jane / Don't slight none, Miss Liza Jane / Swing your partner, Miss Liza Jane.' Dere was heaps and lots more of it, but it jus' won't come to me now."[23]

Alice Hutcheson was seventy-six years old at the time of her WPA interview; she indicates that she was born in 1862. She was interviewed in Athens, Georgia, and enslaved in Monroe County, Georgia. While she recalls singing "Old Liza Jane" and "Susan Jane" (perhaps a related song) during "cornshuckin'" harvests, it would have been a very early memory. After the corn-shucking, everyone ate supper, and then, she conveys, "dey started up playin' dem fiddles and banjoes, and de dancin' begun. White folkses danced da twistification up at de big house, but us had reg'lar old breakdowns in a house what Marstar let us have to dance in."[24]

Hannah Jameson was about eighty-six years old at the time of her WPA narrative. She was born into slavery in Bright Star, Arkansas and was thirteen years old in 1863 when her enslaver moved to Hughes Springs, Texas, where she was interviewed. In her response, Jameson describes a celebration that followed a corn harvest in Arkansas. "After the corn was all husked and all the white folks was gone to bed they danced the rabbit dance and sing like this, early one morning, on my Massa's farm:

> Cut that pigeon wing, Lizy Jane
> I heard dem chickens a-givin the alarm
> Shake yo feet, Miss Lizy Jane
> Shake yo feet, Niggers
> It'll soon be day
> Skoot along lively, Miss Lizy Jane
> Massa ketch us dancin', there'll be hell to pay
> We got taters to dig and hoe dat corn
> Hit dat duffle-shiffle, Lizy Jane
> You'd better be a-humpin, coz it'll soon be morn
> Shake dat balmoral, Lizy Jane."[25]

Lydia Jefferson was eighty-six years old at the time of her WPA interview. She was enslaved in Avoyelles Parish, Louisiana, and interviewed in Houston, Texas; her enslaver had moved to a rural area of Texas during the Civil War. She recalls the formal need to address "de white folk's chillen 'young Marse' or 'young Mis' 'pending iffen it was a boy or girl, but we plays ring games with 'em like 'Choose Your Partner' and 'Catch Liza Jane,' and sociates with 'em every day." While she mentions the title, "Catch Liza Jane," she does not mention any lyrics. She recalls how "freedom sunshine" came out at the moment she was freed and indicates that she was "'bout fourteen year old" at that time.[26]

Lucy Thurston was 101 years old at the time of her WPA interview. She was born into slavery in Flemingsburg, Kentucky, sold to an enslaver in Covington, St. Tammany Parish, Louisiana and interviewed in Lincoln County, Mississippi. Before she was brought to a plantation in Louisiana, she and her mother were both placed on the auction block in New Orleans. She recalls how "Marster Dickey bid on Mammy, but some other man out bid him an my Mammy was sol away frum me. I cried an cried, but twarnt' no use. Marster Dickey took me to Covington, La. an I wuk out in the fiels. Finally I got happy an sang wid de res'. I member one song us used to sing mos' of all was:

> Ohooooooooo lil Liza, lil Liza Jane,
> Ohoooooooooooooooo lil Liza, lil Liza Jane.
> Hair as blak as coal in de mi—ine,
> Lil Liza Jane,
> Eyes so large an' big an' fin'
> Lil Liza Jane.
> OHoooooooo lil Liza, lil Liza Jane,
> OHoooooooo lil Liza, lil Liza Jane.
> Mouse in de hol and de cats' gwine get it,
> Lil Liza Jane,
> Cats in de' tree an' de dawg gwine get it,
> Lil Liza Jane.
> Ohoooooooooo lil Liza, lil Liza Jane,
> Ohhhhhhhh lil Liza, lil Liza Jane."[27]

Anda Woods was ninety years old (or potentially older) at the time of his WPA interview. He was born in Perry County, Alabama and was enslaved either there or in Hinds County, Mississippi, where he was interviewed. During his reminiscences, he reflects on his teenage years: "When I was 'bout sixteen an' seventeen I was still a slave. We was 'lowed to go to dances. If dey was on a 'nother plantation us had to git a pass to go from old Marse. A slave warn't 'lowed to leave wid-out one. Dem dances was grand. Ev'y body would be enjeyin' dey se'ves den. I can hear 'em yet hollerin', 'swing yo' pardner,' on over in a co'ner de fiddles a playin' de ole rag times an' dem singin' snotches of songs lak dis: 'You go down de new cut road / I'll go down de lane / If yo' git deir befo' I does / Kiss Miss Liza Jane.'" He does not formally state a title for the song. His characterization of the revelers singing "snotches of songs" echoes the recollections of W. C. Handy.[28]

If 1937 is adopted as the uniform year when these interviews took place, and then seventy-two years are subtracted from that starting point, then the ages of these ten respondents—at the end of the Civil War—are estimated to be three, six, fourteen, fourteen, sixteen, eighteen, eighteen, and twenty-nine years old, with the ages of two people unknown. It is reasonable to assume that at least six of the respondents were old enough to recall details of their lives prior to being freed, although nobody can definitively vouch for the accuracy of these recollections. By the time these interviews were conducted, "Liza Jane" songs had appeared on the radio and in recorded form; "Li'l Liza Jane" had been a hit in the World War I era, and by the mid-1930s, many songs from the "Liza Jane" family had been part of minstrel and community repertoire for decades. Respondents may have heard the songs in a variety of ways as they grew older, and yet, as much as memories and eras might have been conflated in the minds of these elderly men and women, there is no obvious reason to doubt them, no obvious reason to discredit the collective weight of their recollections.

Three titles were given outright in the WPA material: "Little Liza Jane," "Old Liza Jane," and "Catch Liza Jane." Other titles can be deduced from the lyrics recited by the informants: "Miss Liza Jane" (four times, one of which could be dubbed "Miss Lizy Jane"), "Run Liza Jane," "Liza Jane," and "Li'l Liza Jane." Two of the titles—one given as "Catch Liza Jane" and one deduced from lyrics as "Run Liza Jane"—were described as ring games played by children ("Catch") and adults ("Run"); neither appears as a title or a refrain in commercial recordings.

Five of these "Liza Jane" versions were said to have been sung by enslaved people on Georgia plantations, while two were apparently known in Mississippi, two in Louisiana, and one version was noted in Arkansas. A question might arise as to how these versions might have been so geographically dispersed from one another, especially during an era when the movements and external contacts of African Americans were so institutionally restricted. In terms of cultural sharing that may have transpired locally, the narrative of Anda Woods establishes a "pass system," in which enslaved people could visit other plantations so long as they had written permission.[29]

In her dissertation, *Geographies of Freedom*, historian Alisha Hines argues that "Historians interested in gender and travel in the nineteenth century" should consider the neglected "experiences of women on steamboats, especially black women."[30] According to Hines, steamboats offered Black women "access to mobility. In addition, work on the river allowed enslaved black women to evade the violent intimacy of the mistress' household and earn wages for the same kind of labor performed by domestic slaves."[31] Hines comments extensively on the Mississippi River and its tributaries, which comprised a transportation network "that carried over one million enslaved men and women from tobacco and cotton fields in the Old South to cotton and sugar plantations in the Mississippi River valley."[32] Enslaved Black women worked on steamboats up and down this transportation network, sometimes seizing the opportunity to escape slavery. The story of "Celeste," from 1855, is just one of many examples given by Hines. "A twenty-four-year-old bright mulatto woman, [she] hired herself out on the *Reindeer*, a steamboat that plied the western rivers. Although a slave, she had done so many times before. Her owner, Stephen Ridgley, allowed the French and English-speaking woman the freedom to 'make her own bargains with boats.'" Ridgley returned from a trip to discover that Celeste had fled when the *Reindeer* docked in Illinois.[33]

Arguably, some enslavers allowed even greater latitude to those they had enslaved. According to Marion Lucas, author of *A History of Blacks in Kentucky*, general passes were given to some enslaved people, such as:

> Milton Clarke, who worked on steamboats that stopped at Ohio River Valley cities, [and] obtained a pass to visit his sister in New Orleans. From New Orleans Clarke journeyed to Galveston, Texas, before returning to Cincinnati. It was Clarke's pass which ultimately allowed him to flee to Canada.[34]

While Lucas's accounts of "slave mobility" may not be unusual, he also identifies "Eliza Jane" as a popular marching song among enslaved people in Kentucky.[35] Although the source material cited by Lucas does not offer conclusive verification of this claim, it is possible that "Liza Jane" variants did circulate in Kentucky before and during the Civil War, and if so, they may have traveled along with the enslaved people who were granted passes.

Numerous African American men joined the Union Army, a circumstance that will be developed in the next chapter, and will demonstrate how a song might have traveled from plantations to regiments and beyond. Some enslaved people, however, accompanied their enslavers to the Confederate lines. Dosia Harris's WPA narrative contains the following passage about her father, who had traveled to the front lines:

> When Marse William went to de War, he tuk my pappy wid him. Dey come back home on one of dem flyloughs, (furloughs) or somepin lak

dat, end you jus' ought to have seed de way us chillun crowded 'round pappy when he got dar. One of his fingers had done got shot off in de fightin', and us chillun thought it was one of de funniest lookin' things us had ever seed, a man wid a short finger.[36]

Surely, the Civil War offered the opportunity for songs to travel from planta-tions to the front lines, yet beforehand, if anybody who knew a "Liza Jane" song was issued a local pass or a broader pass, the "Liza Jane" family could have been transmitted from plantation to plantation, or from state to state. Lydia Jefferson's narrative referenced a move, by the enslaver, from Louisiana to Texas, during which he brought along those he had enslaved. As part of a horrifying recollection, Lucy Thurston was sold on an auction block in New Orleans. In these ways—through the movement of the landowner himself or by an enslaver selling his human property—a song could have traveled from one area to another. And once there, it could have been modified to suit the customs of a new environment. One wonders if the WPA had interviewed not *two* percent but *twenty* percent of the country's previously enslaved people, then would there have been *one hundred* narratives to include mentions of the "Liza Jane" family of songs?

Notably, dance terminology courses through many of these ten narratives. Perhaps the most exotic WPA response radiates from Hannah Jameson, who refers to several dance steps, including the "duffle shiffle" (or double shuffle) and the "pigeon wing." These moves may date back to the eighteenth century, according to Jean Stearns and Marshall Stearns, authors of *Jazz Dance*. The Stearns explain how the dancer John Durang executed both dance steps as part of his blackface minstrelsy role as "Friday" at Philadelphia's Southwark Theatre in 1789. The "Double shuffle down, do" and "Pigeon wing going around" were steps two and six of a twenty-two-part routine known as "The Hornpipe," which featured Durang in a pantomime of *Robinson Crusoe, or Harlequin Friday*.[37] Durang's adoption of these dances, as the Stearns point out, indicates that he "knew something about Negro dances" or at least purported to know something about them, and implies these dances were adapted from the slave culture of his era.[38] Step four in Durang's routine was entitled "Cut the buckle down, finish the shuffle,"[39] and perhaps Dosia Harris refers to a version of this step when remarking that young people on her plantation "cut de buck, in gen'ral."

Still other phrases from the WPA *Slave Narrative Collection* might refer to square dancing, which some people mistake for the sole province of Appala-chian whites. On the contrary, African Americans played a formative role in the development of square dance calls, steps, and music. Per the scholarship of Philip Jamison, enslaved Black fiddlers played music at white dances in the late 1600s and throughout the tens of decades of their servitude.[40] In his article "Square Dance Calling: The African-American Connection," Jamison describes the arrival of European dances and dance figures—allemande, quadrille, dos-a-dos, cotillion, promenade, and others—in the early years of the fledgling republic.[41] Enslaved people not only served as musicians for these dances but began to dance these steps themselves, alongside their own traditions.[42]

Jamison notes how cotillions, quadrilles, the Virginia Reel, and African dances "co-existed at plantation 'frolics' during the first half of the nine-teenth century," and many were performed in "squares."[43] In fact, Jamison establishes the unique aspects of square dance calls and their Black roots, averring that:

> Calling did not arrive with the early European settlers, but it originated and developed in this country and came into the Appalachian region sometime during the nineteenth century. Early accounts of dancing in Appalachia from the late 1700s and early 1800s predate the practice of calling, and refer only to contra dances, reels, and jigs, dances which were performed without the aid of a caller. Written evidence from the nineteenth century suggests that the first callers were African-American musicians and that dance calling was common in the black culture throughout the country before it was adopted by whites, and became an integral part of the Appalachian dance tradition.[44]

When Anda Woods reports he "can hear 'em yet hollerin', 'swing yo' pard-ner,'" and when Lina Hunter recalls "some of de words went lak dis, 'Steal 'round dem corners, Miss Liza Jane / Don't slight none, Miss Liza Jane / Swing your partner, Miss Liza Jane,'" both might be referring to square dance rituals that originated among enslaved people before they migrated to white traditions.

Many decades after the Civil War ended, storied musicologist John Lomax recorded an African American musician, Pete Harris, performing a song dubbed "Square Dance Calls (Little Liza Jane)."[45] This Richmond, Texas field recording from 1934 offers additional evidence that "Little Liza Jane" and other variants were part of a Black dance-calling tradition, and yet, about forty years later, in 1977, the fiction writer James Alan McPherson wrote, "No one will believe that I like country music" in the very first sentence of his Pulitzer Prize-winning collection of short stories, *Elbow Room*.[46] It may have seemed unlikely for a Black person in the 1970s to have preferred tra-ditional country music, a sense not lost on McPherson. One page later, he adds, "But most of all I like square dancing—the interplay between fiddle and caller, the stomping, the swishing of dresses, the strutting, the proud turnings, the laughter."[47] These kinds of "breakdowns," as Alice Hutcheson noted in her narrative, may have resembled McPherson's description and vice versa. But as McPherson illustrates, by the latter half of the twentieth century, it may have been normal to conclude that square dancing had been a white province and to regard a Black man's interest in "the proud turnings" as unusual.

In addition to square dance language, the "snotches" of songs reported in the WPA material present a distinctive "word hoard" that would be built upon as the various "Liza Jane" family members evolved. Words like "little" and "li'l" may evoke the preciousness of a love interest. "Catch," "run," and "steal" are indicative of adult dance games and children's ring games. While differing, of course, from square dance calls, these words nonetheless offer powerful instructions to the participants. Some of the "snotches" commented on the rigors and excitement of courtship: a man asking for a hand in marriage and the resulting humiliation of being refused; the sudden appearance of a girl; perhaps even a competition to kiss Liza Jane. Though not entirely unique to "Liza Jane" songs, the twin routes of the "new cut road" and "the lane" create opportunities for the characters to separate from one another, and this construct will be developed in the chapters to come. The heartbreaking rendition described by Lucy Thurston, the song which helped her tamp down the anguish at seeing her own mother sold to another enslaver, was the only WPA example given of a work song. Noteworthy in her rendition are the phrases—"Mouse in de hol and de cats' gwine get it" and "Cats in de' tree an' de dawg gwine get it"—which may refer to game song language. The way singers attached spare phrases or improvised lyrics to the girl's name would represent important devices for the musicians who inherited these songs.

One such musician, blues singer and guitar player Sam Chatmon, learned "Little Liza Jane" from his father, Henderson Chatmon, who may have performed it as a work song while enslaved. Sam Chatmon attributed his rendition of "Little Liza Jane" more than once to his father's experiences "playing the fiddle in slavery time,"[48] yet scholarship by T. DeWayne Moore suggests that Henderson Chatmon may have been too young to toil in the fields or as a musician prior to the onset of the Civil War.[49] Sam Chatmon played the song not only during a filmed 1978 interview with musicologist Alan Lomax but also for authors Margaret McKee and Fred Chisenhall. The former can be found on the website of the Association for Cultural Equity, an organization that Lomax himself founded. Meanwhile, the latter resulted in transcribed lyrics that McKee and Chisenhall included in their 1993 book, *Beale Black and Blue*. But a crucial thing happened between the two versions. Both times, Chatmon credited the song to his father, and yet both versions were strikingly different from each other, save the refrain:

Little Liza Jane

Sam Chatmon (Lomax version)

Hey Liza, Little Liza Jane
Oh Liza, Little Liza Jane

Steal that gal with the red dress on, Little Liza Jane
Don't just hide what shows you more, Little Liza Jane

Oh Liza, Little Liza Jane
Oh Liza, Little Liza Jane

You get there before I do, Little Liza Jane
Tell Li'l Liza I'm coming through, Little Liza Jane
Steal that gal with the red dress on, Little Liza Jane
Don't just hide what shows you more, Little Liza Jane

Oh Liza, Little Liza Jane
Run Liza, Little Liza Jane[50]

Little Liza Jane

Sam Chatmon (McKee and Chisenhall version)

Hey, Liza, Little Liza Jane,
Oh, Liza, Little Liza Jane.
Can't get the saddle on the old grey mule,
Can't get the saddle on the old grey mule,
Whoa, whoa, mule, can't get the saddle on the old grey mule.[51]

Nobody can verify whether these lyrics originated in "slavery time," but the Lomax film recalls the language of ring games through words like "steal," "hide," and "run," and evokes Lawrence Evans's narrative: "Run, Liza Jane, an' take her home." The McKee and Chisenhall "snotch" may fuse together the refrain from "Little Liza Jane" as well as language from a related song, "Whoa Mule," which will be discussed in the pages to come. Chatmon's titling reinforces the reminiscences of Marshall Butler and Lucy Thurston, who sang the song at Saturday night frolics and during forced labor, respectively. That is, they sang a variant they referred to as "Little Liza Jane" or "Li'l Liza Jane," but in Thurston's case, the lyrics are much different than Chatmon's versions, even as the refrains do approximate one another. By comparing Thurston's and Chatmon's renditions, a conclusion could be drawn that none of the early songs in the "Liza Jane" family originated through a single, organized rendition, but rather by "snotches" of folk material attached in varying forms, cadences, and perhaps through local traditions, to the girl's name. In fact, an inspection of Chatmon's very own performances could result in the same conclusion: no two renditions were ever the same save the refrain. Multiple versions of a single variant offer powerful commentary on improvisational music making among enslaved people, and in particular, the formation of the "Liza Jane" family of folk songs.

None of the WPA respondents claimed to be the original singer of the "Liza Jane" song she or he recollected in the *Slave Narrative Collection*. Sam Chatmon did not claim that his father invented the tune. It is possible that the "Liza Jane" family existed in the repertoire of enslaved musicians for many years before the transmission of certain variants, first to Civil War regiments and then to minstrelsy troupes at the conclusion of the war. Additional corroboration of this custody may be traced to folk music collector Dorothy Scarborough, who presented a white informant from Texas, Judge W. R. Boyd, as part of her 1925 study, *On the Trail of Negro Folk Songs*. As Scarborough reports, "Boyd remembers much of the slave-life in the South and recalls vividly the songs the Negroes on the plantations used to sing."[52]

At sunset, according to Boyd, "the Negroes on the plantation, before the war, would sing as follows:

> Oh, Miss Liza, oh, mah darlin' !—hoo ah hoo
> Gwine away to leave you—hoo ah hoo
> Gwine away to-morrow—hoo ah hoo
> Ain't you mighty sorry?—hoo ah hoo!
>
> Oh, Miss Liza, oh, mah honey!—hoo ah hoo!
> Comin' back to see you—hoo ah hoo
> Won't you be mah honey?—hoo ah hoo
> Gives you all mah money— hoo ah hoo!
>
> Oh, Miss Liza, oh, mah lovie !—hoo ah hoo
> Don't you know ah lub you?—hoo ah hoo!
> Come to me, mah baby !—hoo ah hoo
> Don't you want to marry?—hoo ah hoo!"[53]

While it is possible that Judge Boyd is referring to a member of the "Liza Jane" family, these lyrics lack the second half of the girl's name. He might have forgotten to mention it, or this may represent a half-sibling in the "Liza Jane" family. There are some similarities, however, between this recollection and the WPA materials; for example, the references to "Miss Liza" as well as the question of marriage. This version also conjures the postwar minstrelsy hit "Goodbye Liza Jane" in Boyd's inclusion of the line "Gwine away to leave you." While absent from the *Slave Narrative Collection*, the "Goodbye Liza Jane" variant appears in newspaper articles before the conclusion of the Civil War and one of the regimental histories that will be presented below. It is eminently possible that a "Liza Jane" song was swirling around a Texas plantation, where, for instance, Hannah Jameson had moved with her enslaver. Curiously, the refrain—"hoo ah hoo!"—approximates the vocalizations that W. C. Handy observed, as sung by the Negro plowman: "A—O—OO—A—O—OO."

For a family of songs that may have been widespread among enslaved Black people on numerous southern plantations, no record of its variants can be found in printed materials prior to 1864 and 1865. If there is an undiscovered, printed, formally organized version out there that predates the earliest known newspaper appearances (1864 to 1865), the earliest known songster appearance (1866), and the earliest known minstrelsy performances (1865 to 1867), then such a version was not likely to have been a popular hit and was not adopted widely by performance troupes. Even if such a version does exist, it certainly did not prefigure the many variants that likely sprang out of American slavery and were eventually recounted in the WPA responses. In fact, the evidence points to a cluster of songs that developed among enslaved people from Georgia, Mississippi, Louisiana, Arkansas, and perhaps elsewhere. As Clint Smith emphasizes in *The Atlantic*, these accounts "might reveal the humanity of those who were enslaved, and show that despite circumstances predicated on their physical and psychological exploitation, they were still able to laugh, play, celebrate, and find joy."[54] The songs featured "snotches" of folk material joined to the name "Liza Jane," that itself may have been, to recall the heroic Duke Ellington, "agreeable to the ear." Their voyages as songs were only beginning.

"LIZA JANE," YOU LITTLE ROGUE

Dr. Adonis and the Regiments

1864 TO 1865 / THE LATE NINETEENTH CENTURY

On February 23, 1864, a war correspondent with the *nom de plume* "Dr. Adonis" published a front-page column in the *Louisville Daily Journal* (Kentucky), where it was categorized as "Special Correspondence."[1] Reporting from Tullahoma, Tennessee, Dr. Adonis begins a detailed report by lamenting his recent departure from Murfreesboro, calling the town a "pleasant little place" before issuing several affectionate flourishes. Showing a propensity for the ladies, he addresses all the young women of the town by writing, "Dear girls of Murfreesboro, farewell. May heaven shower its blessings upon you as I did my blarney." The war correspondent's fondness for women and his flair for "the poetic" may predict his stunning relationship to the "Liza Jane" family of songs, and furthermore, his placement of the word "blarney" offers a clue as to the man's identity. He was, in fact, an Irishman with ties to the *Chicago Tribune* and a Wisconsin newspaper.

Dr. Adonis goes on to describe the Union military presence headquartered in Tullahoma under the leadership of Major General [Henry Warner] Slocum, and a host of other situations, including formidable "bushwhackers and guerrillas," below-freezing temperatures, difficulties in locating whiskey, and the arrival of "poor whites" from surrounding areas. With respect to the latter, Dr. Adonis refers to these arrivals as having been robbed "by the armies" of everything and who are "suffering for the necessaries of life." Many of these "poor whites" were women since Dr. Adonis remarks that "Most of them have husbands or brothers in the rebel army." In short, women were arriving in Tullahoma with no means of supporting themselves any longer. After describing an appointment to the position of "Provost Marshal," the correspondent launches a slim final paragraph, in which he bemoans:

"I might write of a thousand other interesting things, but at present I must say. Good bye, 'Liza Jane.' DR. ADONIS."[2]

This may represent the first date-stamped reference to any member of the "Liza Jane" family, although not the only one to be printed in newspapers before the Civil War concluded. While not likely, it is possible that Dr. Adonis was referring to a specific girl named Liza Jane. By placing the name in quotes, however, the correspondent was likely referring to a song named "Liza Jane," and perhaps, by wrestling it out of his mind as the final stroke of his column, he unwittingly invented the title "Goodbye Liza Jane." That possibility cannot be conclusively ruled out, given his choice to place the girl's name in quotes but not the words "Good bye." Nonetheless, a song with the chorus "Goodbye Liza Jane" may have been circulating at that point, even if the song itself was referred to as "Liza Jane." Given the relatively limited scope of the WPA *Slave Narrative Collection*, the variant may not have been captured during those interviews, but the scenario of a song "leaking out" from the repertoire of enslaved people is perhaps the likeliest explanation for Dr. Adonis overtaking a "snotch" of its refrain.

The Tullahoma report was not the only instance, however, when Dr. Adonis mentioned "Liza Jane" in the *Louisville Daily Journal*. Scant weeks later, the same correspondent had relocated to Chattanooga, Tennessee, where he reported, once again, as "Special Correspondence of the Louisville Journal." His front-page article appeared on March 15, 1864, and begins with "Facts and Fancies from the Sunny South." As part of his opening, Dr. Adonis waxes:

The good book tells us that "the wicked flee when none pursueth," and experience teaches that it is best to take things easy, since the world isn't much to man when his wife is a widow. So much of a preface is necessary to prove that I am not a wicked youth, and that I profit by experience, from the fact that I took the world easy and enjoyed life pleasantly in making a march from Louisville to this theatre of great events, in the unparalleled time of five weeks and a month. But then there were a great many springs along the way, in the tasting of whose limpid waters, one's heart was bathed in bliss, and the world's great sorrow wasted away. Then, too, there were pretty, very pretty flowers springing up on either side, as I advanced, and the beautiful in my nature would fain dwell in rapturous delight upon the loving and the living beauty before me. How heavenly is the thought that brings one back to those elysian delights which were as pure as the touches of angels. Ah, "Liza Jane," you little rogue, you must not woo me from writing about mules and military matters, puddings and politics, marriage and madness, fools and philosophers, and so on. And now for a change of programme.[3]

Upon which, Dr. Adonis sallies forth to describe "The Looks of Chattanooga." The correspondent would seem to mix proverb, the poetic, and personal detail in this excerpt, perhaps indicating just how long—"five weeks and a month"— he had been corresponding from the theater of battle. Does his mention of "Liza Jane" (again in quotes) reference an actual girl or a song? Given that Dr. Adonis adds "you little rogue," and given the gentlemanly way he tended to conduct himself in print, it is hard to believe that he would be characterizing an actual person, however seriously or lightheartedly. The phrase "you little rogue" suggests affection; the word "little" will eventually become the most important modifier in the song's lengthy arc. Even the word "woo" matters. It already conjures a blithe, if fictional, courtship scenario set amongst the rigors of chronicling the war. Most signs point toward a song.

Nevertheless, about twelve days earlier, on March 2, 1864, Dr. Adonis weighed-in with "special correspondence" from Huntsville, Alabama. Among other matters, he reports the necessity for some Union officers to occupy a mansion otherwise inhabited by female relatives of a fellow who had traveled to the front lines in service of the Confederacy. Having accompanied the officers in this endeavor, Dr. Adonis apparently "intercepted" a few "love letters" penned by the women to their romantic interests and vice versa. He relates a few examples, but nothing more relevant than an earnest letter penned, ostensibly, by a barely literate young woman who intended to reach a private in the rebel ranks.

In its entirety, without correction, this letter reads:

DARE SOLOMING: i write to you To dalting. Uncle jake says there's a right smart uv you boys that i know yull Not forget yur Liza Jane. good By. God Bless You sol. We had A dance To widow johnsings the other night. my Old bow Bill harding Wanted me to dance With him but i Inclined. When you Left sol i promised not To dance with Ery a young man or sit upon his knee until you got back or killed. O sol The yanks are Cutting up Mightily. I hard that you was killed on the pikit lyn, but my Heart don't feel it, and sol it Feels mightily for you sometimes. i Kiss your picture before the yanks To make them mad. Thar's a curly headed Yank with blue eyes, thats a saying he'll kiss me if i keep A doing of it. i wouldn't care if He did, But for your sake dare sol. Get a furlow And come to me. cross over the river At caperton's ferry, near stevingson, And I'll give the curly headed yank a kiss to Let ye over. good by sol. i must go. Mother says The Yanks are A hunting down the chickens And goin to the smoke house. the hom guards on tother side of The tennessee and sum of the confederate cavalry stole all the chickens from the Union folks Thar. cousing Jane had A offer to marry a Yank last week, but lord me she'll do it. Thers hapes uv Our girls a marry on em. i won't never du it, no Never, if I can du better. i hait Them wurz than i love u. o dare come To see me just wonst. if u knew How i suffer for you And A little snuff yud come. the weather is right Bad and so is my colde dare sol. Sol i love u as i Never loved no wone. right to me sol At caperton's ferry. Yur Ever loving and affectionate, LIZA JANE[4]

That "Liza Jane" bids "Sol" good bye, even as she instructs him to write a response, represents the emotionally bruising center of this (unmailed) correspondence. To be fair, it is impossible to verify the authenticity of the letter, which may have been, for whatever reason, a fabrication. Notably, some "short" words are misspelled, while some "long" words are rendered correctly. And yet, Dr. Adonis wrote the phrase "Good bye, 'Liza Jane'" around the very same time and even referred to the Liza Jane character on a second occasion, dubbing her a "little rogue." Not only does the unusual phrase "Liza Jane. good By" surface in this letter, but duplicate syntax ("Liza Jane, good bye") would emerge about nine months later in a Kansas newspaper, which printed a couplet of "Liza Jane" lyrics in the early days of January 1865. This twist will be developed early in the next chapter and cannot be ignored. Did Liza Jane's letter to Sol influence a song already in circulation?

More will be learned about Dr. Adonis's rather swashbuckling life at the conclusion of this chapter, including his presence on the funeral train that bore the body of Abraham Lincoln. More than a year before he boarded the funeral train, the correspondent twice referred to "Liza Jane" as a likely character within a song while, at approximately the same juncture, printing a searching love letter written by a woman he identified as Liza Jane. The "rebel love letter" would make appearances in other newspapers as well, such as the *Chicago Daily Tribune* (March 5, 1864),[5] the *Portland Daily Press* (Maine, March 28, 1864),[6] and the *Fremont Journal* (Ohio, November 11, 1864).[7] Even if the letter had been a forgery, numerous people nevertheless encountered the phrasing, "Liza Jane. good By."

Here the sludge thickens. It is most plausible that the war correspondent encountered a version of the song "Goodbye Liza Jane" and simply referred to the lyrics and the girl in the song as part of the two columns in which he did not print love letters. There may be no relationship whatsoever between the Liza Jane who purportedly wrote to her boyfriend, Sol, and the character "Liza Jane," who Dr. Adonis twice addressed on separate occasions; that is, the fictional "Liza Jane" of the song would be the "rogue" and not the southerner who feared for Sol's death. In any event, it is implausible that the gentleman reporter would mock an ailing young woman, especially given his predilection to praise the ladies of Murfreesboro. It is even possible that the "rebel love letter" supplied a phrase to a song that was already in circulation, seeing as how the letter was printed in newspapers from Illinois to Kentucky, from Ohio to Maine. But how would Dr. Adonis have come across "Liza Jane" lyrics in the first place, which almost certainly had origins in slavery?

As a war correspondent traveling throughout the South, Dr. Adonis could have encountered the song in a few different ways. Given that "Liza Jane" songs make their way into regimental histories, it is possible he encountered a variant in his dealings with soldiers. His writings, after all, refer to an abiding knowledge of officers and enlisted men from both sides of the conflict. And while it is unknown if he visited any contraband camps, there, too, he may have spoken with or overheard formerly enslaved people, who could have sung "Liza Jane" lyrics after they had defected to the Union lines. In a column published on February 29, 1864, Dr. Adonis notes:

> One hundred and fifty negroes from about Huntsville and beyond passed through here yesterday for Nashville. Large numbers pass through almost daily. The contrabands about here are also being sent to Nashville. Those remaining are employed by the government, and their families are furnished comfortable huts in a portion of the village by themselves.[8]

Moreover, as discussed earlier, Dosia Harris's father went to aid the Confederate war effort with his enslaver. He may have taught whichever "Liza Jane" variant he knew to other soldiers and, by extension, anybody who might have overheard a regiment singing while it marched or camped. It is distantly possible that Dr. Adonis encountered a printed version of the song, but no such publication has been discovered.

The opportunities for cultural transmission undoubtedly multiplied as the Civil War progressed, with more and more enslaved people defecting to Union encampments. These defectors were regarded as "seized property" as if they were possessions first and people second. This classification resulted from a policy emplaced by Major General Benjamin Butler, and in time, as historian Adam Goodheart notes, "the fugitives had a new name: *contrabands*."[9] His book, *1861: The Civil War Awakening*, explores the many "awakenings" of the conflict, including the lack of civility with which escaped enslaved people were treated. Goodheart poses uncomfortable questions: "Were these blacks people, or property? Free, or slave?"[10] In some cases, the "contrabands" were paid for labor and given rations, but many struggled as the liberating side did not entirely know how to treat them or even refer to them. In *The Music of Black Americans*, musicologist Eileen Southern writes, "Life in the contraband camp was in many ways similar to life on the plantation.

Black people lived in special quarters under supervision of the whites and worked at jobs that would aid in the war effort."[11] They suffered through shortages of clothing and food. Nevertheless, noting how "freedom was in the air," Southern also indicates that singing and music was in the air as well, "night and day."[12]

African Americans not only wound up in contraband camps during the Civil War but also, as noted above, in active military units. As part of his book *A History of the Eleventh New Hampshire Regiment*, Captain Leander W. Cogswell describes an unexpected group of soldiers who he encountered during his chapter, "Camp Life at Annapolis," which narrates a restful interlude in April and May 1864. About a half mile from where he had been stationed "was the encampment of the colored troops, a division of whom had just been added to the Ninth Corps."[13] Cogswell devotes some of this narrative to the "monkey-shines and oddities" of the Black troops.[14] For example, he illustrates some of the punishments the Black soldiers had received but mostly in a way that conveys the soldiers' witty reactions to these forms of disciplinary measures.[15] Then he turns towards some of the women who visited them in camp. "It was very amusing to watch the dashing colored girls flock to the camp to see their lovers dressed in army blue at 'Uncle Sam's' expense, and drilling 'for sojers.' Of course 'Liza' blubbered a little, and slopped over at the eyes, as 'Clim' chucked her under the chin and sang—

> Oh! I's gwine away fur to leab you,
> Oh, good-bye, good-bye!
> Oh! I's gwine away fur to leab you,
> Oh, good-bye, Liza Jane!"[16]

Cogswell further depicts the African American soldiers as proud to be in the service and valiant. The notion that they fought nobly "had more truth than many people suppose."[17] He clearly felt a passion for the war's ultimate mission, in how he differentiated between Confederate soldiers and the African American soldiers serving in the Ninth Army Corps. Cogswell writes, "When the Confederate soldiers were questioned as to why they were fighting against the old flag, they usually replied by saying, 'We are fighting for our rights,' but were unable to tell what rights had been denied them. Could not the colored troops use the same words with far more truthfulness?"[18] As it turns out, this regimental history (published in 1891) was not Cogswell's only book. About ten years earlier, he published *History of the Town of Henniker, Merrimack County, New Hampshire*, among some additional works published at other times.[19] Clearly at home in a historical framework, he presents a vivid, detailed portrait of his regiment's history during the war.

It appears as if Cogswell was referring to soldiers of the Forty-Third United States Colored Troops (USCT) Regiment. Its chaplain, Jeremiah Marion Mickley, penned his own regimental history, *The Forty-Third Regiment United States Colored Troops*. In it, he indicates that the Forty-Third Regiment was organized in March 1864 at Camp William Penn in Philadelphia and traveled to Annapolis on April 18 to join the Ninth Army Corps.[20] According to Mickley, the Forty-Third Regiment took up its march to join the Army of the Potomac on April 23 and, en route, marched through Washington, DC, where it was reviewed by Abraham Lincoln himself.[21] Mickley establishes the importance of this moment: "As these were the first colored troops destined to the Potomac Army, their soldierly appearance and movements were closely scanned."[22] Cogswell himself notes, "these troops were the subject of much comment by the newspapers throughout the country."[23] The timeline established for the movements of the Forty-Third Regiment would have given Captain Cogswell several days to have observed the Black soldiers in Annapolis. Once the Forty-Third USCT Regiment reached Virginia, its soldiers guarded a railroad, reinforced the "right flank of the army," and fought the enemy.[24] "In these engagements," Mickley writes, "they manifested great steadiness and intrepidity under severe fire and immediately proved themselves a reliable troop."[25] The chaplain describes the multiple combat experiences of the regiment, including its participation in the siege of Richmond. Later in the war, the Forty-Third Regiment traveled to Texas, where "it camped, finally, on the bank of the Rio Grande River, opposite the city of Matamoros, Mexico."[26] In this capacity, the soldiers disrupted trade between the French and the Confederacy.[27] The Forty-Third Regiment was discharged in Philadelphia on November 30, 1865, and by that time, many of its men had been killed or wounded.[28]

While most of the soldiers who fought in the Forty-Third USCT Regiment were recruited in Pennsylvania, it is likely that many of them had origins elsewhere. In *Making and Remaking Pennsylvania's Civil War*, historian William Blair explains how "Recruiting stations for conscripting African Americans were set up across Pennsylvania."[29] In one example, fifty-four African American men attended a meeting, and many of them had escaped from the South.[30] Still, there is evidence that several of the Black soldiers who served in the Forty-Third Regiment came from other states. For example, the book *Men of Color, To Arms!* indicates as many as seven soldiers from Vermont served in the Forty-Third Regiment.[31] Of course, it is widely documented that formerly enslaved people and those that had escaped enslavement served in Union regiments, often with distinction. The "Liza Jane" song overheard by Captain Cogswell in Annapolis, therefore, could have originated in a couple of dozen states; many of the soldiers had fled the South or joined the unit from afar.

The intersection of the Eleventh New Hampshire Regiment and the Forty-Third United States Colored Troops Regiment is meaningful in several ways. To begin, Cogswell documents the recitation of a "Liza Jane" song by the African American enlisted men of the Forty-Third Regiment. They were singing what, today, would be classified as the refrain to "Goodbye Liza Jane" but may have had a different title in 1864—or rather, no title at all. These lyrics may have been, pursuant to W. C. Handy or Howard Odum, "snatches" of folk material or variations on a one-verse song. With the Ninth Army Corps about to "move out," the Black soldiers were likely singing about their departure and addressing their song to the women gathered around them. Cogswell does seem to indicate that one of the "dashing colored girls" may have been weeping, as one of the soldiers "chucked her under chin," a gesture implying some "tough love." In this encounter, the African American women could have learned the song and the white men of the Eleventh New Hampshire Regiment could have learned this "Liza Jane" tune as well. Many of the men who served in the Ninth Army Corps could have eventually adopted these lyrics. Just as with the WPA *Slave Narrative Collection*, one must take a skeptical approach when considering a recollection published decades after the events may have transpired, but the dates and places of Cogswell's reminiscences are, at the very least, supported by the chaplain of the Forty-Third USCT Regiment. Moreover, Cogswell would have had no special incentive to fabricate details about the recitation of a simple folk song. It is true that "Goodbye Liza Jane" had been a "hit" in minstrelsy for decades prior to the publication of this regimental history. Therefore, Captain Cogswell may have substituted some of the "hit" lyrics for singing he might have barely recalled, but on the other hand, there is no obvious reason to discredit his reminiscence. He is not, for example, exaggerating his own bravery, or the heroism of his troops, in the presentation of this scene.

The Forty-Third Regiment participated in the major battle fought between the Union and the Confederacy near Spotsylvania, Virginia. In his history, Mickley indicates that the regiment saw action there from May 7 to May 15, with a sizeable number of its officers, fifteen of them, participating.[32] Often called the Battle of Spotsylvania Courthouse (formerly spelled "Spottsylvania"), the clash lasted nearly two weeks in the middle of May 1864. Collectively, according to *The Virginia Campaign of '64 and '65*, written by military historian Andrew Atkinson Humphreys, more than 150 thousand soldiers contested the inconclusive battle, with the Union troops outnumbering the Confederate troops and thousands of casualties plaguing both sides.[33] Among the Confederate ranks was one H. C. Wall, whose book *Historical Sketch of the Pee Dee Guards, Co. D, 23rd North Carolina Regiment*, places the unit in the vicinity at the time of the hostilities. Wall narrates:

It was about the 7th of May, 1864, that the Brigade, after a most delight-
ful season of recreation while on *detach* duty in the vicinity of Hanover
and at Taylorsville, received orders to rejoin the army at the Wilderness, near Spottsylvania Court House, in the direction of which point
the enemy was advancing. The march was taken up accordingly; and in
the series of engagements that took place—known as the battles of the
Wilderness—our boys had a part to perform.[34]

Wall initially describes skirmishes but then illustrates the "thrilling" and "hor-
rid" sensations of "the 12th of May, 1864, at Spottsylvania Court House, [when]
the *full strength* of these two armies was joined in battle."[35] The fighting resulted
in wounded, dead, and captured Pee Dee Guards.[36] As part of the battle details,
however, Wall depicts a moment when Company D had been resupplied with
"hard tack and bacon" and moreover, "from lungs strengthened by full stom-
achs, an inspiring chorus rang out to the tune of 'g'lang Liza Jane.'"[37] Wall
then details how Company D—with the song prevailing—chased a unit of
Yankee cavalry.[38]

A while later, Company D apparently engaged in the lengthy pursuit of a
Union force said to be in retreat. Both armies, the one advancing and the one
retreating, "moved slowly for a number of days as if their commanders had
determined on no particular programme."[39] In Wall's recollections, the soldiers
were "marching each day not enough to fatigue them, and having no enemy
to annoy them, recuperated rapidly from the past 'hard times' and could sing
out 'Liza Jane' with greater relish than ever."[40] Based upon Wall's recollections,
Company D sang "Liza Jane" when well-fed, on the front foot, and in good
spirits. They sang it often. "G'lang" or "get along" may have represented a dance
call, and in all probability, "G'lang Liza Jane" constituted a portion of the song's
chorus. Since there were no more lyrics given, there is nothing to suggest a
lengthy, organized song. There is no information given as to how the members
of Company D came to know the song or for how long they had been singing
"Liza Jane." H. C. Wall, or Henry Clay Wall, was not listed among the unit's officers and instead, to his credit, seems to have been a rather articulate everyday
soldier. In that capacity, he was probably well-versed in the songs of the rank
and file. He published this history in 1876, about eleven years after the Civil
War concluded, and while skepticism must be applied to all recollections of
this nature, there does not seem to be anything controversial surrounding the
revelation of these memories. Wall indicates that Company D battled up until
the time of its surrender, April 9, 1865.[41]

Taking both the Cogswell and Wall regimental histories into account, there
is evidence that an African American unit and a Confederate unit were both
singing "Liza Jane" songs in the vicinity of one another between April and

May 1864, as they were eventually arrayed on opposite sides of the battle at Spotsylvania Courthouse. It is not inconceivable that they shot at one another. By this point, the songs would have already been transmitted from the domain of their likely origins among the repertoire of enslaved people. Black soldiers fighting for the Union might have known those "Goodbye Liza Jane" lyrics intrinsically, whereas it could be anybody's guess how the Pee Dee Guards came into possession of "G'lang Liza Jane" lyrics. They might have learned the song from enslaved people or other soldiers.

If nothing else, the presence of "Liza Jane" songs among the soldiers of the Forty-Third USCT Regiment and the soldiers of the Pee Dee Guards contains powerful symbolism of "common threads" despite the obvious divisiveness at hand: the two units separated by race, ideology, politics, and the colors of their uniforms. Since the two songs seem to feature somewhat different refrains, there is no evidence that a single, authoritative ancestor would have prefigured them. This cluster of observations, beginning with Dr. Adonis and including the two warring sides at Spotsylvania Courthouse, emerges in early to mid-1864. And yet, there are other Civil War histories that refer to the "Liza Jane" family, involving additional recollections and actions among the soldierly ranks.

The Indiana Sixty-Seventh Regiment endured great hardship upon entering the Civil War. In his regimental narrative, *The History of the 67th Regiment Indiana Infantry Volunteers*, Colonel Reuben B. Scott describes the unit's participation in the Battle of Munfordville, Kentucky, in September 1862, with grim outcomes. "The severity of this battle," he writes, "is attested by our flag and staff being struck one hundred and forty-six times."[42] He references the "horrible sights" that the regiment beheld, "not being inured to the horrors of battle."[43] The soldiers witnessed many of their schoolmates buried in graves "far away from home and friends."[44] The Sixty-Seventh Regiment surrendered, was paroled, exchanged for Confederate prisoners, and sent back to Indiana, where it regrouped.[45] Eventually, the regiment reentered the conflict and, after a second surrender in 1863, became attached to the Army of the Gulf, a command that operated along the Gulf States. It remained in this role until the end of the war.[46] Having given an overview of the regiment's successes and failures, Scott's survey of the Regiment's major activities concludes with the words, "And here we now disband forever."[47]

Yet a curious addendum commences on the very next page. Here, Scott relates "A Secret Voyage on the Lower Mississippi and Gulf Coast."[48] In the early months of 1864, Colonel Scott and other members of the Sixty-Seventh Regiment remained in a lower New Orleans parole camp, a holding area where former prisoners-of-war loitered or served in noncombat roles until they were formally exchanged for Confederate soldiers who were, themselves, placed in similar parole camps.[49] Colonel Scott and his men had become restless when "Just about this time an incident did occur that offered a few of us an opportunity for a little diversion."[50] Eight soldiers were told to venture across the river to Algiers, where they would find a small ship, the "Liza Jane," which they would sail into channels, inlets, and bayous, noting the depths, widths, and directions of currents. Ostensibly, this information would help the Army of the Gulf prevent local Confederate sympathizers from smuggling supplies. Colonel Scott portrays the onset of the adventure, referring to the Liza Jane as a "pretty good hull" and narrating the exploits of sailing hither and yonder.[51] At one point in the reminiscence, he refers to the craft as "our little Liza Jane," and before long, the men are singing a tune they refer to as "Get Along Liza Jane" as the "main sail caught the wind and we sped out upon the water."[52] The men of the Sixty-Seventh attach lyrics to the refrain—i.e., "How glorious her gallant course she goes / Her white wings flying never from her foes"[53]—that are martial and courageous but do not otherwise suggest a relationship to typical "Liza Jane" word hoards. Colonel Scott mentions the song by name, "Get Along Liza Jane," three times in the course of his "Secret Voyage" addendum.[54]

If nothing more, this regimental history adds ballast to the probability that "Liza Jane" songs were in circulation by winter-spring 1864. Though the lyrics reported by Colonel Scott do not overlap with traditional "Liza Jane" lyrics, the family of "Liza Jane" songs likely began as "snotches" of folk material and, to that point in 1864, may not have had any organized verses. To reiterate some earlier speculation, the refrains may have been songs unto themselves and may have invited the improvisation of additional lyrics. Seeing as two of the ten WPA narratives placed the song in antebellum Louisiana and another two in antebellum Mississippi, it is entirely possible that these soldiers may have encountered a version of the song before they went sailing on a ship conveniently named the "Liza Jane." The word "conveniently" is applied here with opposing perspectives. On the one hand, this could all be a "fish story" with little basis in reality. On the other hand, there have been several boats throughout nautical history named "Liza Jane" or "Eliza Jane," and the title of the boat may have inspired the crew to sing a refrain they had coincidentally learned. As with any narrative to appear years after the events it narrates, the history of the Sixty-Seventh Indiana Regiment, published in 1892, must be regarded with typical caution; and yet, a regimental history that admits to the unit's defeats, captures, and paroles does not seem overly gilded. It would not win Colonel Scott any plaudits to recollect a song, particularly one without roots in military traditions. In fact, the name of the boat and the refrain of the song are obviously secondary to the mission, which was, itself, a "lightly heroic" noncombat adventure, given the "paroled" status of the eight infantrymen.

At least two additional regimental histories mention "Liza Jane," but with abiding brevity to render the context blurry. Members of the Eleventh Indiana Battery reportedly exclaimed, "get along Liza Jane," when freeing a stuck cannon during the Battle of Chickamauga in 1863.[55] The regiment's historian, Lieutenant John Otto, relates the detail in *History of the 11th Indiana Battery During the War of the Rebellion* while narrating a retreat from Confederate forces. Even as the soldiers may have briefly uttered the song's refrain upon freeing the artillery piece, there is no reference to singing or music. In fairness, this exclamation may have been applied retrospectively by Lieutenant Otto, whose account came to press in 1894.

Similarly, in the *History of the Fifteenth Regiment, Iowa Veteran Volunteer Infantry*, soldiers were said to have encountered merrymaking in which the revelers "whooped up Liza Jane" near Duckport, Louisiana, in 1863.[56] The phrase is not linked to a song or singing; it is likely that the author applied the phrase retrospectively. By 1887, the time of the book's publication, the phrase "whooped up Liza Jane" may have stood for "celebrated raucously" or even "made moonshine," although, as demonstrated later in this book, the words "whoop," "hoop," "hoopo," "hoopty," and so forth, do get attached to the "Liza Jane" family of songs.

These final two regimental histories do not specifically mention singing, unlike the examples of the Eleventh New Hampshire Regiment (when encountering the Forty-Third United States Colored Troops Regiment), the Pee Dee Guards, and the Sixty-Seventh Indiana Infantry Regiment. The dates of these three examples—the singing examples—tend to correlate with the timeline initiated by Dr. Adonis in his February–March 1864 proclamations. It is possible these regimental historians not only encountered one-verse "Liza Jane" songs during the Civil War but also witnessed organized "Liza Jane" songs in popular performance long after the war had concluded, all before publishing their wartime reminiscences. This may have influenced how they titled or described the "Liza Jane" songs they and their fellow soldiers initially observed in 1864.

Speaking of Dr. Adonis, the Civil War ambled onward for him, and he followed the scoop. He filed a report from New Orleans entitled "Department of the Gulf," which appeared in the *Chicago Tribune* on March 30, 1865.[57] Among other details, he related examples of "turned tables" as the war slugged toward inevitable Union victory. "Humanity is progressing—humanity is retrograding," he begins. "I am reminded of this double progressive state by seeing a number of rebel prisoners and deserters, passing along the street, guarded by colored soldiers." This calls to mind the Forty-Third Regiment, which was stationed relatively nearby in Texas. In response to some Mexican agitation, Dr. Adonis printed the words of another correspondent, who wrote, "Affairs in Mexico do not look promising for Maximillian." Indeed, the monarch, an Austrian archduke, would be toppled by assassination two years later, but tragically for the United States, it was President Lincoln who was shot to death by John Wilkes Booth just two weeks after this column appeared. On April 22, 1865, the *Chicago Tribune* published a complete list of people who accompanied the remains of President Lincoln on his funeral train as it departed Washington, DC, one day earlier. There, among the many relatives of Lincoln and representatives of government, was the name "Dr. Adonis," who represented the Chicago newspaper. He and the others would travel along with the body of the slain president as the train wended its way, ultimately, toward Springfield, Illinois.[58]

According to a front-page article in the *Sunday Call* (San Francisco), on May 1, 1892, Dr. Adonis died in the same California city a week earlier, on Monday, April 25, 1892.[59] As noted by the uncredited author, the reporter's name was Stephen Byron Donahue, an Irishman who had passed away at fifty-five years of age. (He would have been about twenty-seven years old as he accompanied the body of President Lincoln back to Illinois.) Donahue, also known as Byron Adonis, "was a very tall individual with rather sharp features, who wore a reddish mustache and sometimes an imperial, and who always wore his hair, a light brown, down to his shoulders." The author further describes the man as having bright eyes and an intellectual face but that he kept his past hidden. Readers might have chuckled as he was labeled "at times a pleasant companion"—as well as an eccentric and an enigma. His past would have involved a stint in Milwaukee, where in 1863, the *Semi-Weekly Wisconsin* referred to him as "Byron O'Donohoe, a compositor." After announcing he and two of his colleagues had been drafted, the short blurb then clarifies his identity as "the well-known correspondent 'Dr. Adonis,' who will write some valuable and interesting letters from the army."[60] Dr. Adonis may have been conscripted but did not end up as a soldier.

Roughly six years before Dr. Adonis passed away, a newly minted regimental history mentioned the correspondent. The *"Twentieth Connecticut"* by John W. Storrs relates an incident during which Dr. Adonis may have revealed some sensitive military information during his wartime reporting.[61] To avenge this transgression, the unit invented an unflattering song about the reporter, which begins "Och! Dr. Adonis came out from Killarney / To blather the gin'rals and peddle his blarney."[62] The song further describes Dr. Adonis as having "weedy flax hair" and weighing "half a stone."[63] Though penned in jest, the song seems to confirm some of the details—Irish lineage and longish, light-brown hair—put forward by the obituary. Clearly, Dr. Adonis led an adventurous life, charming some and provoking others. Several of his exploits were presented by the *Sunday Call* for admiration, including swimming frigid waters upon the annexation of Alaska, for the sake of delivering a story ahead of his competitors. He nearly fought a duel there, too, with an irate Russian.

Having fallen ill, without any hope of salvation, Dr. Adonis gave instructions that his body be cremated in the Buddhist tradition. His ashes were scattered "to the winds." There were no surviving family members referred to, and there was no wife, although the article did mention a love interest from many years earlier. Adherents of a certain poor gal will insist he first swooned for that little rogue, "Liza Jane."

1865

The scene switches to Kansas, a state not often associated with the Civil War but one that had been known as "Bleeding Kansas" in the years leading up to the North-South conflict. Notably, hostilities would rage there during the war itself. As recounted by historian James Monaghan in *Civil War on the Western Border*, the two sides fought one of the largest mounted cavalry battles of the entire Civil War near Fort Scott on October 25, 1864.[1] It would be "the first [battle] to be waged between regular troops on Kansas soil."[2] A decisive win for the Union, the Battle of Mine Creek generated the noteworthy captures of "Brigadier General Cabell, four colonels, a thousand men, and ten pieces of artillery."[3] A private by the name of James Dunlavy famously captured Confederate Major General John Marmaduke.[4] More battles would ensue nearby, with the Union forces generally outmaneuvering the Confederate ranks, but much bloodshed ensued, some of it Union, some of it Confederate, and some of it Native American.[5]

Scarcely ten weeks after these hostilities raged in the Trans-Mississippi Theater, the *Daily Monitor* (Topeka, Kansas) published a rather pacific article entitled "Happy New Year" on the second page of its Wednesday, January 4, 1865 edition. Above the text sits a firing cannon and a rippling American flag. In its entirety, the article reads:

> By an order from the mayor, Monday the 2d, was set aside as a day of festivity, and was celebrated in due and ancient form. Quite a number of the nimrods from Fort Scott spent the day shooting chicken, squirrels, quails, etc., whilst those of finer temperaments devoted their time to music and a general old-fashioned New Year's calling.—During the afternoon, we noticed Mr. Bruin figuring very conspicuously in the ciccillian circle, and adding much to the performance of the menagerie. After calling at the houses and paying their respects to many of our citizens, the procession brought up in front of the Wilder House; the band formed in a semi-circle and Mr. Bruin occupied the center, standing erect on his—eh—on

his hind feet, beating time with his paws, which was a great source of amusement to the small boys and guests of the House.

Mr. Charley, together with his worthy assistant just from the East, are deserving of much credit for the splendid manner in which they exhibited this wonderful animal.

At about half past 5 o'clock, the party dispersed by mutual consent, singing the 4th stanza of that new piece.—

"O, Liza Jane, good bye,

O, good bye Liza Jane."

Taking everything into consideration, it was a complete success, and all went home pleased with the re-union of the New Year. May they have many such during the year sixty-five.[6]

While the presence of the active cannon would remind readers that the Civil War had raged nearby, nevertheless, the tone of the article conveyed merry-making and optimism for the new year. Clearly, the most important creature in the newspaper piece would be "Mr. Bruin," a bear that danced in the "ciccillian [*sic*] circle," beat time with his paws, and otherwise entertained the revelers outside the Wilder House inn with the oddities of his stances. His handlers, one Mr. Charley and his assistant from the East, may have been traveling with Mr. Bruin in order to earn a living at facilitating events such as this one. A band played. The revelers sang not just any song but a couplet from what would now be titled "Goodbye Liza Jane."

Important clues abound regarding these lines, the earliest known date-stamped lyrics to appear in publication. This couplet is referred to as "the 4th stanza of that new piece," suggesting the song had been formally arranged and published recently enough to be considered new. The title is unknown, as are any of the other lyrics. "That new piece" is not tied to a singer, minstrel troupe, songwriter, or theatrical piece, suggesting, instead, some form of regional adoption or minor songbook publication. The revelers in Fort Scott knew and sang the couplet happily amidst joyousness that ushered in the hopeful prospects of 1865. Soldiers on both sides of the Civil War demonstrated a fondness for "Liza Jane" songs, and seeing as this celebration transpired in a town of military significance, perhaps the rank and file had transported it there to the Trans-Mississippi Theater. As noted previously, the syntax devised by the young woman, Liza Jane, in her sorrowful 1864 letter to her beau, Sol, a private in the Confederate army, comes to mind: "Liza Jane. good By." Her letter had appeared in newspapers across the country, and her phrasing is duplicated—however deliberately or coincidentally—in the first line of this couplet: "O, Liza Jane, good bye." The vast majority of "Goodbye Liza Jane" renditions to follow would not repeat this word order.

About six months later, in July 1865, and about three hundred miles north, workers began to lay rails, aiming westward for the transcontinental railroad. Nonfiction author David Bain notes in *Empire Express* the construction was not too distant from Fort Scott: "[With] a complete lack of fanfare, a small work gang standing on the Missouri mudflats above Omaha watched as several of their number unceremoniously hoisted the first rails of the Union Pacific onto the track bed and pounded the spikes home."[7] By October 1865, writes Steven Ambrose, "Graders were up to the Loup River (Columbus, Nebraska), and advance teams were rapidly making their way across the next hundred miles."[8] His book *Nothing Like It in the World* also describes the after-work traditions of the railroad workers who toiled in Nebraska at that time. In addition to playing cards, the men would sing songs, such as "Whoop Along Liza Jane."[9] This observation is not supported with a citation of source material, yet the presence of "Goodbye Liza Jane" lyrics at the January 2, 1865, Fort Scott celebration supports this timeline. The word "whoop" has also been presented in the history of the Iowa Fifteenth Regiment and will be further explored in the pages to come, noting that it does get attached to the "Liza Jane" family in a variety of ways. At the same time, "whoop" may be a mistranslation of African American folk dialect. If, however, these railroad workers were indeed singing "Liza Jane" on their track-laying route to the west, then they could have spread it wherever they sang. "Liza Jane" songs nevertheless scooted ahead and made their first appearances out west long before the intercontinental railroad joined them there. The *enfant terrible* Johnny Tuers shall materialize in the relatively new state of Nevada, but before he does, two newspaper articles in the eastern half of the country deserve attention.

The *Ashland Union* (Ohio) published a front-page article on October 25, 1865, penned by newspaperman Marcus M. "Brick" Pomeroy, then of the *La Crosse Democrat* (Wisconsin), concerning his efforts to intoxicate mosquitoes.[10] As part of this witty piece, Pomeroy relates numerous strategies to avoid puncture by mosquitoes at nighttime, including raw beef steak steeped in old rye whiskey, emplaced at the head of the bed. Ten minutes later, he notes, "Every mosquito was drunk as a blind fiddler." Pomeroy then renders the plights of many drunk mosquitoes, for instance, one "with a belly like Falstaff [. . .] dancing Juba on the bible." Yet another "lay on her back beating the devil's dream on an invisible tambourine with one leg." As if this was not enough, Pomeroy observes, "Another chap [who] was drilling a hole through a revolver handle, and singing 'Little Old Liza Jane.'" The surprising revelation of this title, plus the details of the article's authorship, effectively place "Little Old Liza Jane" in both Wisconsin and Ohio circa Autumn 1865. As with the Kansas newspaper on January 4, 1865, Pomeroy does not associate the song with a particular singer (other than a mosquito) or publication, and therefore, the revelation cannot offer clues as to its provenance or popularity. Noteworthy are the words "little" and "old" as affixed to the girl's name; they recall the WPA narratives of Marshall Butler and Lucy Thurston, who referenced "Little Liza Jane," as well as Alice Hutcheson, who referenced "Old Liza Jane." The song "Eliza Jane" turns up in a Billy Emerson songster in 1866; said to be an "Original," and discussed at more length below, its chorus nevertheless emphasizes "My little old Eliza Jane."[11] Had Mr. Pomeroy attended a performance by Emerson or another minstrel troupe that had by that juncture adopted the song in its repertoire? This is unknown. It is telling how, in addition to Dr. Adonis, another newspaperman of national repute had taken a fancy to a "Liza Jane" ditty and a comic ditty at that, given its association with drunken insects.

A couple of weeks later, on November 4, 1865, the *Weekly Review* of Crawfordsville, Indiana, was busy carrying onward within a national landscape decidedly altered from, say, Dr. Adonis's late-March reportage from New Orleans: that of a war ended and the unexpected presidency of Andrew Johnson negotiating a host of complexities. In addition to bemoaning the "fraud" of Johnson's presidency, editors replied to a hopeful poet identified only as "N. McC." Their response, without identifying the poet's submission, reads as follows: "We can not publish your verses. The first verse is passable, the others not good. We suggest for you the following metre:

> As I went down the new cut road
> She went down the lane,
> And all that I could say to her
> Was go along Liza Jane."[12]

Many poets before and since have felt the sting from editorial boards. On this day, editors suggested cadence and rhyme akin to what Bryant Huff and Anda Woods would relate many decades later in their WPA narratives. The line "I went down the new cut road" is not unique to "Liza Jane" songs but represents, rather, a verse that floats through antebellum minstrelsy. For instance, the song "Jinny Come Along," found in *Christy's Negro Songster*, 1856, contains the following couplet: "Dar was a Terrapin an a Toad / Both cum up de new cut road."[13] Another example can be found in the William Francis Allen collection, *Slave Songs of the United States*, originally published in 1867. A tune entitled "Charleston Gals" begins, "As I walked down the new-cut road / I met the tap and then the toad."[14] On the other hand, "She went down the lane" does not seem to exhibit a similar trajectory and may not have featured in antebellum minstrelsy. It may be another "snotch" of folk material that was added, potentially, because "lane" could be straight-rhymed with "Jane." Moreover, the road and the lane provide the genteel opportunity for a lover's rift, in which the character Liza Jane might reject the suitor by heading down the lane. (Or the road.) To be sure, the girl might also travel up the lane or the road, offering the suitor a new opportunity.

While this editorial decision may have disappointed "N. McC," it might nevertheless represent the first date-stamped appearance of "the road" and "the lane." Notably, "Go along Liza Jane" approximates the "Get along Liza Jane" chorus that the Sixty-Seventh Indiana Regiment reportedly sang while they sailed on the hull of the same name, as well as the "G'lang Liza Jane" refrain that the Pee Dee Guards belted out around the time they participated in the Battle of Spotsylvania Courthouse. Phrases like "get along," "git along," "g'lang," and "go along" may represent dance calls; another potential meaning may involve "moving on" from a challenging situation as if to "clap one's hands free of it." The editors did not associate these lines with a particular singer or a songbook. Instead, the lines might have transferred from soldiers of the Sixty-Seventh Indiana Regiment to the public and, therefore, may have been relatively novel to that point.

Not long thereafter, out west, the *enfant terrible* Johnny Tuers performed "My Little Ole Liza Jane" in the town of Gold Hill, Nevada, on consecutive nights. On November 23, 1865, the *Gold Hill Daily News* proclaimed: "Music Hall.—The 'Cure,' by Collins, was the principal feature at this place of amusement, last night. Johnny Tuers, Sheppard, Wallace, Ward, and Foster were on hand in 'My Little Ole Liza Jane,'—they can't be beat in that. Go and see them to-night."[15] Tuers would appear to be the star of this collective as his name comes first. Even though this represents the first known date-stamped professional performance of a "Liza Jane" song, it would be wrong to assume that it was the very first "Liza Jane" song to be performed for the theater-going public. With variants popping up all over the country, from Kansas to Ohio, from Nebraska to Nevada, paid performers were likely presenting them in a variety of spaces, such as the Music Hall in Gold Hill, and yet, this is the first known performance to be date-stamped. Johnny Tuers, the star, bore considerable gifts and also contended with inner demons.

Tuers is identified as a "trapeze artist as well as a champion clog dancer" by Mark Knowles in his study, *Tap Roots*, which describes how Tuers "once leapt 125 feet from a trapeze, from the dress circle to the back of the stage."[16] The WPA book *San Francisco Theatre Research, Vol. 13, Minstrelsy*, which focuses on the history of the theatre scene in San Francisco, portrays Tuers as "The champion flat-foot dancer of the Pacific Coast."[17] By citing the *Daily Alta California*, which published an account dated January 30, 1873, the WPA book recounts an incident in which Tuers had quarreled with another performer, Charles Howard, at the Snug Saloon on Washington Street. They wrestled, with Howard getting the better of Tuers, who drew his pistol and fired a shot. The bullet did not strike Howard, but rather the stage manager James Dowling, killing him.[18] A series of newspaper articles across different states then narrates the minstrel's surprising acquittal in 1875,[19] as well as the information that Howard had been assailing Tuers about "a variety actress usually billed as Josie Mansfield."[20] Tuers, the *enfant terrible*, had gotten in an argument over a love interest, taken a shot at one man, and struck another, wounding him mortally, before a jury conferred mercy on him.

The inner demons did not vanish, however, for a performer the *New York Herald* once welcomed by noting "first appearance in this city of the California Star, Johnny Tuers, the Champion Big Shoe Song and Dance Artist."[21] Tuers assaulted a woman named Lottie Livingstone, in San Francisco, on June 15, 1876. They had quarreled, and Tuers fired a shot at Livingstone, grazing her and inflicting a powder burn, as well, but the attack did not kill her.[22] Ensuing newspaper coverage discloses how "Johnny Tuers, the San Francisco minstrel, was fined $500 on Saturday for a murderous assault committed some time since on Lydia Livingston. [. . .] In case of failure to pay the fine, Judge Blake gave Tuers the privilege of going to the County Jail for 250 days."[23] Here, and for the better, Mr. Tuers seems to have drifted out of the public eye, with the newspaper coverage drying up, unable or unwilling to resuscitate him.

A champion flat-foot dancer, a trapeze artist, a minstrel singer, a man with inner rage, a killer. Even as the lyrics are unknown, be they comic or elegiac, Tuers was nevertheless the perfect sort of "celebrity scoundrel" to sing a "Liza Jane" song. Referred to as a "negro minstrel," he was not African American but a man who applied burnt cork makeup in the minstrel tradition and, in all probability, participated in grotesque characterizations of African American men and women during his performances. The trajectory of the "Liza Jane" family would soon change, with dozens of famous minstrel troupes adopting certain variants for decades to come. It is not clear what became of Johnny Tuers after paying his fine or going to the county jail, and it is equally unclear from which direction he arrived on the theatre scene. His last name may have made him Welsh, for example, but the transitive French verb "tuer" comes to mind, as well: "To murder."

INTERMISSION NUMBER ONE

The Potential Influences of Robert Burns, "Susan Jane," and Others

LATE EIGHTEENTH CENTURY TO
THE EARLY TWENTIETH CENTURY

The story of the "Liza Jane" family does not begin with a Scottish poet, or does it? The poetry of Robert Burns enjoyed widespread popularity in the United States throughout the period when "Little Liza Jane" and its variants might have formed: between the mid-1850s, potentially, and the Civil War years. An article penned by James M. Montgomery, "How Robert Burns Captured America," implies that carrying a collection of Burns poems was next to godliness, literally, as "Burns-and-the-Bible was a standard part of every nineteenth century traveling kit."[1] Montgomery's piece describes the formation of at least fifteen Burns Clubs, by 1859, across the United States. As a young man, Abraham Lincoln could quote much of Burns's oeuvre and cities across the country—including places like Natchez, Atlanta, and New Orleans—hosted noteworthy Burns events.[2] Politician and editor Horace Greeley referred to Burns as "the Peasant Poet" and further characterized him as the champion of "the unprivileged million."[3] Burns was celebrated by Henry Wadsworth Longfellow, Edgar Lee Masters, Robert Greenleaf Whittier, Walt Whitman, and Ralph Waldo Emerson; the latter proclaimed that he "[gave] voice to all the experiences of common life."[4]

Perhaps this working-class appeal can be demonstrated among old-time country musicians such as Fiddlin' John Carson and Bradley Kincaid, both of whom will be discussed in a later chapter, yet whose "Liza Jane" lyrics might echo a famous Burns line, "O my Luve is like a red, red rose." In their lyrics, the musicians first compare the Liza Jane character with the glossy properties of a cherry, then compare the cherry with a rose. Therefore, Carson and Kincaid associate the "love interest" (Liza Jane) with a rose, which, according to the implied redness of the cherry, would depict the "love" in the roseate hues of the flower:

Liza's like a cherry, cherry's like a rose
How I knew little Liza, goodness only knows

—Fiddlin' John Carson, from "Good-bye Liza Jane" (1926)[5]

Cheeks is like a cherry, the cherry's like a rose
How I like that pretty little girl, goodness gracious knows

—Bradley Kincaid, from "Liza Up In The 'Simmon Tree" (1929)[6]

And yet, another Burns poem aligns more closely with one of the largest branches of the "Liza Jane" family.

Known as "Farewell to Eliza" as well as "From Thee, Eliza, I Must Go" (its first line), the eighteenth-century poem importantly conjures a separation, which lies at the heart of many "Liza Jane" songs, but in particular, "Goodbye Liza Jane."

Farewell to Eliza
Robert Burns

From thee, Eliza, I must go,
And from my native shore;
The cruel fates between us throw
A boundless ocean's roar:
But boundless oceans, roaring wide,
Between my love and me,
They never, never can divide
My heart and soul from thee.

Farewell, farewell, Eliza dear,
The maid that I adore!
A boding voice is in mine ear,
We part to meet no more!
But the latest throb that leaves my heart,
While Death stands victor by,
That throb, Eliza, is thy part,
And thine that latest sigh!

—from *Grigg's Southern and Western Songster*, 1851.[7]

In particular, the repetition of "farewell" in the poem's ninth line—"Farewell, farewell, Eliza dear"—cements the rift. This departure places an "ocean's roar" between the speaker and his love. While Eliza is referred to in the present tense, the speaker does mention "Death" as a "victor" who "stands by."

Indeed, some "Liza Jane" variants refer to a "poor gal" who perishes on the train. Bradley Kincaid croons about this outcome in "Liza Up in the 'Simmon Tree," and notably, as part of the 1927 recording of "Run, Mollie, Run," the estimable Henry "Ragtime" Thomas sings: "Poor Liza / Poor Liza Jane / Poor Liza, poor girl / Died on the train."[8] The Liza Jane character "intrudes" into the Thomas song, which also includes a Burns-like comparison between love and the rose: "Cherry, cherry / Cherry like a rose / How I love that pretty yellow gal / God almighty knows." With respect to the "cherry and rose" construct, the three American musicians—Carson, Kincaid, and Thomas—easily resemble one another, thereby representing a potent example of "folk material" drifting between versions of related songs. Potentially, the influence of Robert Burns drifts between them as well.

In 1876, the journalist Lafcadio Hearn, who spent several years in New Orleans, reported overhearing the refrain—"Farewell 'Liza Jane! / Farewell 'Liza Jane! / Don't throw yourself away, for I / Am coming back again"—in a "Broadway saloon" on the levee.[9] This observation can be found in a compilation of his writings, *Lafcadio Hearn's America*, and suggests that "Farewell Liza Jane" had become a riverboat song by then. Hearn's presentation of the refrain recalls the Burns poem "Farewell to Eliza," and his report detailing the songs of roustabouts on the New Orleans levee will be described in the pages to come.

As previously identified, several sources establish the Civil War years as the era when the phrase "Goodbye Liza Jane" first appeared. African American Soldiers of the Forty-Third USCT Regiment were said to have sung the refrain while encamped in Annapolis in April 1864. Also in 1864, the correspondent Dr. Adonis proclaimed the phrase in an article published by the *Louisville Daily Journal*. By January 4, 1865, a Kansas newspaper, the *Daily Monitor*, published a couplet for an early version of "Goodbye Liza Jane." Beyond the name "Eliza" and the concept of parting, or farewell, only speculation can link the Burns verses to the "Liza Jane" family when judging what influence, if any, the Scotsman may have wielded on the first singers of the "Liza Jane" songs. Still, as Montgomery observes in his article, "Burns lives in public monuments in obscure and prominent spots of cities all over the nation," including many of the areas where ten WPA narratives established the presence of "Liza Jane" songs.[10] On top of travelers carrying collections of Burns's poetry, as well as numerous American songsters printing the bard's poems among their pages, "Farewell to Eliza" also showed up in newspapers of the era. For example, the *North Carolinian* (Fayetteville) published the poem on June 3, 1848.[11]

Even if Robert Burns partially inspired the song "Goodbye Liza Jane," he provided only half the girl's name. In theory, then, the minstrel song "Susan

Jane" could have provided the other half. Frank Williams published words and music to a version of "Susan Jane" in 1854, with performance attributed to Christy's Minstrels and bearing a subtitle, "Dis child is by his Lub Forsaken." The chorus emphasizes that Susan Jane has been sent down the river—presumably, horrifically sold to another enslaver—where the speaker cannot join her, thus establishing a rift. The final verse, rendered in minstrelsy dialect, reads as follows:

> De boat push'd off, and dat's the last
> Dat I hab see'd ob Suze:
> De tears run down her cheek so fast
> It gib this child the blues.[12]

While the Williams lyrics do not resemble the "Liza Jane" lyrics given by respondents in the WPA *Slave Narrative Collection*, one woman, Alice Hutcheson, did indicate that she sang both "Old Liza Jane" and "Susan Jane" while enslaved. The names "Liza" and "Susan" resemble each other, partially, with both containing "z" sounds in their middles and both containing two syllables; alternate spellings of both names, Lize and Suze, possess even greater interchangeability. Some renditions of "Goodbye Liza Jane" might approximate aspects of "Susan Jane" when considering the singers taking leave from their love interests, as may have been the case with the soldiers of the Forty-Third USCT Regiment, who were about to march in front of President Lincoln en route to the Virginia battlefields.

Performed by a widely known troupe, Christy's Minstrels, this version of "Susan Jane" could have been popular enough to spread among southern plantations in the years when the "Liza Jane" family might have been forming. This is, nevertheless, speculative, and there is no obvious tie between "Susan Jane" and the "Liza Jane" "snotches" that were described in the *Slave Narrative Collection*. At the same time, owing to the popularity of Burns and minstrelsy, it is possible that both "Farewell to Eliza" and "Susan Jane" were known to some plantation owners and their bondspeople. Adding the two titles together and subtracting "Susan" would yield "Farewell to Eliza Jane," which does resemble the language overheard by Lafcadio Hearn in New Orleans. Cleaning things up a bit and further substituting the more-folksy "goodbye" and "Liza" for the more-formal "farewell" and "Eliza" would yield "Goodbye Liza Jane."

Outside of their status as common women's names during the nineteenth century, Eliza, Liza, and Jane could have been supplied as the inspiration for improvisational singing via popular texts in a variety of ways. Numbers like "Jane Monroe" and "Jersey Jane" appeared in an 1854 minstrelsy songster—*Christy's Plantation Melodies*—that may tie the two songs to the same troupe which sang Frank Williams's version of "Susan Jane."[13] In 1848, the publication of *White's New Ethiopian Song Book No. 3* revealed the song "Peter Story," which contained a character dubbed "Little Lizzy," as well as the song "My Dear Eliza," which is a bit closer in substance than the Burns poem to various versions of "Goodbye Liza Jane."[14] In that piece, which is credited to W. B. Donaldson and sung by White's famous Band of Serenaders, the singer is in love with a "yaller charmer" named Eliza, who eventually becomes his lawful wife.[15] Nonetheless, Eliza's mother "wallop'd me wid a broom stick" when she overheard the singer professing his love to her daughter.[16] The convention of a suitor being chased off by a broom-wielding parent would be repeated several decades later when the Tenneva Ramblers recorded "Miss Liza Poor Gal" at the legendary Bristol Sessions, as will be described below. Yet in 1848, the singer of "My Dear Eliza" remarks that "I was gwine to leabe her," which somewhat prefigures the refrain of "Goodbye Liza Jane," as sung by the Forty-Third USCT Regiment in Annapolis.[17]

If this sludge was not thick enough, an uncredited poem entitled "Truly Affecting" was *not* rejected by the editorial staff of the *Iowa Republican* (Iowa City), gracing its pages on December 18, 1852.

Truly Affecting

'Twas on a moonlit side-walk,
'Neath the ailanthus tree,
That she leaned against my waistcoat,
And whispered—"Marry me."

Oh, that agonizing moment,
I never, never shall forget;
Her lips with nectar [laced*],
I think I [hast*] them yet.

Just as this little Eden
Approached reality—
A gruff voice uttered sternly—
"What is all this I see?"

And then I felt a pegged boot
Applied with might and main;
I fell upon the side-walk,
And off went Liza Jane![18]

*These words are difficult to make out.

Maddeningly, and with sludge aplenty, this poem echoes the minstrel piece "My Dear Eliza" when describing the intervention by another suitor or a gruff parent—the "pegged boot"—in warding off an admirer of the nectar-lipped Liza Jane. Its overarching narrative, that of a comically painful love affair, will repeat often as the "Liza Jane" family evolves. Not, however, a minstrel piece, "Truly Affecting" probably leaped into print briefly on a late autumn day in 1852 and exited without inspiring any members of the "Liza Jane" family to blossom. Similarly, a few months later, in winter-spring 1853, two people— one dubbed "Mountain Poet" and the other identified as both "Lizzy Jane" and "Lizzie Jane"—traded mildly amorous and mildly insulting poems in the *Loudon Free Press* (Tennessee). When the "Mountain Poet" professed love on March 5, the "Lizzie Jane" character responded with scorn on March 19, whereupon the "Mountain Poet" responded by likening the "Lizzy Jane" figure to a pasture animal on April 2.[19] In all likelihood, the "Liza Jane" family did not spring from this exchange, even if sludge prevailed.

These many examples of potential influences all matter. Just how much? It is unclear. Recalling the distant possibility that Dr. Adonis himself may have coined the phrase "Goodbye Liza Jane," his utterances and every one of these enticing threads must be acknowledged since they create sludge with their very existence; yet, even if Robert Burns and "Susan Jane" begat one member of the "Liza Jane" family, or if any single one of these texts effected the same outcome, their potential influence does not nearly account for the numerous "Liza Jane" variants that spawned (or coexisted) in a variety of idioms.

With this intermission now drawing to a close and with some initial details of—the shameful institution of—minstrelsy having entered the conversation, the arc of the "Liza Jane" universe now resumes.

V.

"LIZA JANE" MEETS THE MASSES

Postbellum Minstrelsy, Part First and Part Third

MID-NINETEENTH CENTURY / 1866 TO 1868

For a great number of decades, white male entertainers applied burnt cork makeup and performed songs, skits, comedy, and other material in grotesque caricatures of African Americans. Eventually, Black performers would participate as well. Known by its individual unit as the minstrel show, and more broadly as blackface minstrelsy, many performances were preposterous in their racist depictions, and yet, this format reigned as America's popular culture. The mid-1850s were not when minstrelsy began, but those years are a significant waypoint, according to scholar Robert Toll, in his book *Blacking Up*. "By the mid-1850s," he indicates, "minstrelsy had arrived at a basic three-part structure that it thereafter retained."[1] Jake Austen and Yuval Taylor, in their coauthored book, *Darkest America*, describe how a typical show of that era would begin:

> At the outset, the troupe would march onto the stage, perhaps singing a lively song, and parade around the chairs, arranged in a semicircle, until Mister Interlocutor said, "Gentlemen, be seated." Mister Interlocutor would stand in the middle, Tambo and Bones would sit on the ends, and at least a dozen other performers would be between them. The Interlocutor never laughed or used dialect; Tambo and Bones would play on his straight-faced manner by indulging in all manner of anarchic jokes and routines, punctuated with their rudimentary instruments and loud laughter. The first part was full of humorous songs, dances, jokes, and sentimental ballads.[2]

Camille Forbes, author of *Introducing Bert Williams*, further defines the endmen, who were also called "Brudder Tambo and Brudder Bones. [. . .]

Eventually, it became customary that Tambo was slim, whereas Bones was fat."[3] A layperson might successfully deduce that the character "Tambo" played the tambourine, whereas the character "Bones" played actual animal bones, castanets, or some other form of clackers. Additional musicians may have played the banjo or the fiddle; a wide range of singers might have also been present during part one, which was often described as "Part First" on a typical handbill. Toll points out, "The musical star of the first part was the romantic balladeer, usually a tenor, who sang sentimental love songs that provided an outlet for tender emotions and a chance for the ladies in the audience to sigh, to weep, or to do both."[4]

Part Two or Part Second presented the "variety section, or olio," as Toll explains; "[it] offered a wide range of entertainment to the audience and allowed time to put up the closing act's set behind the curtain."[5] Toll lists a number of specialists who might have performed in the olio section, such as "Song and dance men, acrobats, men playing combs, [quills], or glasses, and any number of other novelties."[6] Perhaps more importantly, this variety fare also involved the "stump speech," which Austen and Taylor define as an oration "full of malapropisms and delivered in a fake 'darkie' dialect, burlesquing anyone and anything that wasn't working class, from suffragettes to doctors."[7] Forbes delineates the "stump speech" as an absurd spectacle in the olio portion of the minstrel show, for the speech's deliverer "aspired to great wisdom and intelligence but always ultimately appeared foolish and ignorant."[8]

The show would conclude with Part Three or Part Third. Forbes writes, "A one-act play concluded the show, typically a vignette of carefree life on the plantation."[9] Toll adds that these one-act skits "were set on southern plantations with the entire troupe onstage in theatrical farm wear and concluded with a rousing song and dance number; they also included farces and slapstick comedies—inflated bladders, bombardments of cream pies, or fireworks explosions."[10] Austen and Taylor indicate that the concluding part of the minstrel show could also offer "a parody of a Shakespeare play, an Italian operetta, or something else well known to the audience. The whole [event] lasted a little less than two hours."[11] Minstrel shows varied widely, but many of them, from the 1850s onward, adhered to this format.

While some bits—romantic ballads, acrobatics, parodies of Shakespeare—may have been staged in a nonracial context, it is ultimately impossible to subtract the racism from burnt cork minstrelsy. Austen and Taylor, whose revisionist book follows "black minstrelsy from slavery to hip-hop," acknowledge how this entertainment form "did present black Americans primarily as figures of ridicule—submoronic, slothful, ugly, bestial—and undoubtedly the joys of racism were often essential to minstrelsy's success."[12] Leading up to this conclusion, they cite the historian Carl Frederick Wittke, who, in his 1930 book

Tambo and Bones, describes the typical character portrayed by minstrel troupes. Terming him "the stage negro," Wittke describes how this man:

> loved watermelons and ate them in a peculiar way. He turned out to be an expert wielder of the razor, a weapon which he always had ready for use on such special occasions as crap games, of which the stage negro was passionately fond [. . .] He always was distinguished by an unusually large mouth and a peculiar kind of broad grin; he dressed in gaudy colors and in a flashy style: he usually consumed more gin than he could properly hold; and he loved chickens so well that he could not pass a chicken-coop without falling into temptation [. . .] Moreover the negro's alleged love for the grand manner led him to use words so long that he not only did not understand their meaning, but twisted the syllables in the most ludicrous fashion in his futile efforts to pronounce them.[13]

In his preface, Wittke expresses "happy memories of the burnt cork semi-circle" as well as "a real love for the old-time minstrel show."[14] Clearly, he did not perceive the tragedy of white men "blacking up" and eating watermelon "in a peculiar way" or "falling into temptation" near a chicken-coop, among other humiliations. Wittke may have experienced minstrelsy in the late nineteenth and early twentieth centuries, as well as during his own "barnstorming student days,"[15] when representations of Blacks may have been particularly "submoronic, slothful, ugly, bestial."

Forbes carries the offensiveness of postwar minstrelsy into deeper water. In her estimation, minstrelsy mirrored the prevailing societal view of Black people as so substantially "lacking a history" that they might be considered fundamentally stateless, except for their "timeless" ownership by the southern plantation system: "Images ranged from artificially nostalgic representations of the lazy, childlike slave of the plantation to virulently derogatory characterizations of the free black, a menace to society."[16] Bizarrely, the requirement to "black up" also applied to African American performers who began to appear in minstrel shows after the Civil War. The subject of Forbes's book, Bert Williams, did as much in order to earn a living at the onset of his career. As Forbes illustrates, black minstrels "performed the traditional caricatures and donned burnt cork to blacken their often already dark skin in a hyperperformance of blackness staged for both white and black audiences alike."[17] The performer, while even being Black in some cases, nonetheless had to be blacker, as black as possible, by applying the minstrel mask of burnt cork. Minstrelsy's racism cannot be and should not be defended, yet troupes did popularize certain versions of "Liza Jane" songs while "blacking up."

By reading about "Johnny Tuers, the negro minstrel," a casual traveler through this subject matter might conclude that Tuers had African American roots, when in fact, the phrase conjures his specific métier, or rather, who he purported to emulate. It is possible that Tuers wore burnt cork makeup when singing "My Little Ole Liza Jane" at the Music Hall in Gold Hill, Nevada, in late November 1865. There is no handbill available for this performance; thus, the song cannot be placed within the three-part format that took hold in the mid-1850s. A related song, "Eliza Jane," appeared in Billy Emerson's *Nancy Fat Songster* the very next year, in 1866. This may represent the earliest appearance of a "Liza Jane" piece in a songbook publication. In typical songster fashion, the lyrics are presented without musical notation.

ELIZA JANE.
Original.

Oh, I went down to sheep-shuck town,
The water was wide and deep;
I put my foot right on a raft,
And scoot right across the creek.

Chorus.
My little old Eliza Jane,
My little old Eliza Jane,
Of all the gals I ever did love,
Is little old Eliza Jane,
Git back, my little old Eliza Jane.

How old are you my charming love,
How old are you my dear?
My mother says I am seventeen,
If I live to see next year.
Chorus—My little old Eliza Jane, &c.

Oh, twenty pound of meat a day,
And whiskey for to sell;
Oh, how can a young man stay in camp
When a pretty gal looks so well.
Chorus—My little old Eliza Jane, &c.[18]

The book's front matter reads "Billy Emerson's Nancy Fat Songster; being a collection of his Popular Ethiopian Lyrics, to which is added the Latest Comic and Sentimental Songs of the Day." By declaring the presence of "Ethiopian Lyrics," the songster establishes its place within the blackface minstrelsy tradition. These songbooks would typically be sold at minstrel shows; the theatergoers would remember the melody; thus, there would be no need for notated music. Here, too, "Eliza Jane" cannot be situated within the three-part format, but its relative straightforwardness and brevity might suggest the song-strewn Part First; it does not seem to correlate with a variety act or the lengthier requirements of a closing skit. While purporting to be an "Original," the song's refrain clearly turns up in the previous year with Tuers in Nevada.

As for the song's narrative, the boy leaves home for a "sheep-shuck town," and by crossing the creek, wide and deep, he seems to arrive in a camp where there are ample provisions of meat and whiskey; it could be a moonshine operation, given that the whiskey may be "for to sell." The publication date being so close to the Civil War, a word like "camp" might conjure a soldier's encampment. In an interesting turn, the singer inserts a playful interrogation by the Eliza Jane character, and as a result, gives his age as seventeen, "If I live to see next year." While many "Liza Jane" songs were advertised as comic ditties, the tone of this piece is difficult to decipher. Eliza Jane is classically described as "little," "old," and "pretty," and the boy singles her out from all the gals he ever did love. He is homesick. He may be a country white; the song does not appear to lampoon Blacks. There is a separation between a guy and his gal, and this unattainability of love will replay itself again and again as the "Liza Jane" family evolves. When the singer proclaims, "Git back, my little old Eliza Jane," he not only seems to underscore his country roots but might be repeating a dance call. Perhaps the song functioned as a dance number, as well. "Git back" also calls to mind the regimental and newspaper examples of similar phrases: "Go along Liza Jane," "Get along Liza Jane," and "G'lang, Liza Jane."

Beginning with performers like Tuers and Emerson from 1865 to 1866, songs from the "Liza Jane" family entered an industry that dominated American entertainment, according to John Strausbaugh, in the years from 1865 through the 1880s.[19] In his book *Black Like You*, Strausbaugh conjures "Giant minstrel troupes [roaming] the landscape the way the dinosaurs had ruled the Jurassic. All the big cities had their resident troupes; at one point, New York City had ten."[20] Newspaper advertisements and playbills, beginning around 1867 and rippling outward for at least three decades, began to establish the popularity of "Liza Jane" songs among these full-time companies, as well as troupes with fewer resources, and situate the songs within the minstrel show format. For instance, the *Daily Dramatic Chronicle* (a publication associated with the *San Francisco Chronicle*) and the *Chicago Tribune* demonstrated in 1867 that "Liza Jane" songs may have featured in Part Third in the initial days of their absorption by minstrel companies.

On Thursday, February 7, 1867, the *Daily Dramatic Chronicle* ran a front-page advertisement for Wilson & Wilson's New York Minstrels.[21] This represents one of the earliest date-stamped references to a "Liza Jane" song appearing in a high-capacity setting. Taking place at Platt's Music Hall in San Francisco, the event boasted "24 performers," including a brass band. With numerous songs slated for the first part and several oddities listed in the second part, the advertisement then reads, "Entertainment to conclude with Old Dan Smith's Walk-Around, 'LITTLE OLD LIZA JANE!' By the Entire Company," with the song title printed in large typeface. Tickets cost fifty cents, and the festivities likely ended around ten o'clock, which is when, according to the advertisement, carriages could be ordered. Clearly, the song was given special billing, and this may suggest its relatively fresh status as a minstrel piece. It would be the last thing that theatergoers would have heard, a melody they hummed as they stepped into carriages or walked home. Titled "Little Old Liza Jane," the song may have shared characteristics with the Johnny Tuers and Billy Emerson versions, but without lyrics to peruse, this is uncertain.

On Sunday, April 28, 1867, the *Chicago Tribune* listed a fourth-page advertisement for activities at Arlington Hall featuring a minstrel troupe of the same name, Arlington's Minstrels.[22] This troupe was led by Billy Arlington, according to *Burnt Cork and Tambourines*, by circus historian William L. Slout. Arlington, being a bona fide star, enjoyed a lengthy career in minstrelsy, and in this configuration, he served as an endman in his own troupe, as Slout indicates, which boasted at least sixteen performers.[23] Part I and Part II are strewn with songs and olio, respectively. The *Tribune* advertisement then describes "Part Third," which will "conclude with the Startling Ethiopian Operatic Romance, entitled HOME FROM THE WARS, or The Returned Veteran." The skit includes the "laughable incidents of:

The Detected Runaway!
The Soldier's Return!
The Story of the Wars!
And the Recognition of the Two Brothers!"

Of special pertinence to the "Liza Jane" family, however, would be "[the] company will conclude the Festivity of the Brothers meeting with a new, screaming Walk-around entitled LITTLE OLD 'LIZA JANE." General admission was fifty cents, with reserved seats going for seventy-five cents. As in San Francisco, carriages were available at ten o'clock. Here, the song would close a comedic skit that nevertheless hearkened back a couple of years to the end of the Civil War. As in the San Francisco example, "Little Old 'Liza Jane" would be the last thing theatergoers would have experienced that night. On May 1, 1867, the *Chicago*

Tribune ran another advertisement for Arlington Hall, proclaiming that "Little Old 'Liza Jane" would be in its first week, thereby reinforcing the sense that "Liza Jane" songs were just beginning to appear in large-scale minstrel repertoire.[24]

The writer Carl Sandburg would not be born for another ten years, but he would eventually commemorate Chicago through his eponymous poem, which begins:

> Hog Butcher for the World,
> Tool Maker, Stacker of Wheat,
> Player with Railroads and the Nation's Freight Handler;
> Stormy, husky, brawling,
> City of the Big Shoulders![25]

The people who attended Billy Arlington's show—the tool makers, the stackers of wheat, the stormy, husky, brawling Chicagoans—would have learned this minstrelsy version of "Liza Jane." Sizable audiences might have listed out into the city, singing the refrain. The rendition is unknown, and at the same time, it was probably rendered under the guise of minstrelsy's ugly racism, but the girl's name would have been circulating in the "City of the Big Shoulders."

Back in San Francisco, on June 7, 1868, a St. James Theatre *Play Bill* noted the performance, that very night, of Birch, Wambold & Backus' San Francisco Minstrels at the St. James Theatre.[26] The "Programme" listed the songs in "Part Premier," which included "Liza Jane," billed as a "Comic Song" performed by "Billy Burch," with his name misspelled. Birch was a widely known performer, and this rendition probably drew a large audience. The lyrics and performance details are otherwise unknown.

On Thursday, July 23, 1868, the well-known troupe of Emerson, Allen & Manning's Minstrels performed at Tony Pastor's Opera House in New York, where Billy Manning sang "Eliza Jane."[27] While the troupe's playbill lists the song as a "Comic Ditty" and the troupe includes Billy Emerson, there is no evidence that Emerson's version (from his 1866 *Nancy Fat Songster*) had anything in common with the version performed by his troupe-mate, Billy Manning. The lyrics and performance details are unknown. Here, too, New Yorkers would have learned a minstrelsy version of the song bearing the girl's name, as it was situated in "Part First," placed between "Annie o' the Banks o' Dee" and "There's no such Girl as mine."

In the bustling postwar cities of New York, Chicago, and San Francisco, among other locales, star minstrel performers sang "Liza Jane" songs in Part First and Part Third (but not the variety "olio" portion) of the standard minstrel show format. By this point, the tunes had undergone significant transformation from their likely origins among enslaved people. In place of one-verse songs or "snotches"—bits of folk lyrics that may have varied from one recitation to the next—there were several fixed stanzas that did not vary between performances. Moreover, "Liza Jane" songs were sung by white performers to emulate Black people through derogatory rituals such as the application of burnt cork makeup and unflattering onstage behavior. A title like "My Little Ole Liza Jane" may offer information regarding a possible refrain, and yet, the Billy Emerson variant simply entitled "Eliza Jane" contains similar lyrics. The absorption of "Liza Jane" variants by minstrelsy introduced the songs to crowds of theatergoers, but audiences at that juncture probably did not comprehend the string of interactions that had taken place for these "smoothed out" renditions to reach the minstrel stage.

Just how did these "Liza Jane" songs leap into the repertoire of minstrel troupes? John Strausbaugh addresses this question indirectly when writing, "One of the oddities of the minstrel show was the way it balanced its cruel, dehumanizing jokes at the expense of Black people with a fond, often tearjerking nostalgia for the South—a South few of the performers, and fewer of their audience members, knew anything about."[28] In all likelihood, the adoption of "Liza Jane" songs did not revolve around the troupes encountering enslaved people who had labored in the fields on southern plantations but instead depended on the unusual mechanisms specific to the Civil War era.

The case of the Lumbard Brothers, for example, deserves some attention in this context. Frank and Jules Lumbard were performers who, according to a 1931 article in the *DeKalb Chronicle* (Illinois), sang at recruiting drives during the Civil War and, as a result, swelled the Union ranks by as many as twenty thousand enlistees.[29] Both Lincoln and Grant acknowledged their contributions. As part of its reportage, the *DeKalb Chronicle* article also reprinted an earlier piece published by the *Chicago Record-Herald* in 1912. In the reprinted piece, an old soldier story portrays how the two brothers also visited the front lines: "It was on the road from Bull Run to Appomattox, in 1863 when the Lumbards were calling on Union friends. Someone had asked them to sing." As the tale unfolds, the Confederate soldiers and Union soldiers communicated with one another across the trenches and agreed to stop the hostilities so both sides could hear the two brothers. "And the story goes that the firing did cease while the Lumbards sang and that their last selection brought tears to the eyes of the soldiers on both sides, for they sang, 'Home Sweet Home.'" During the war, the brothers interacted with recruits as well as soldiers at the front lines, and after the conflict ended, they returned to performance. Notably, an advertisement for the Frank Lumbard Concert Troupe sits just underneath the previously described *Chicago Tribune* advertisement for Arlington's Minstrels, on April 28, 1867, in which Arlington's troupe performed "Little Old 'Liza Jane."[30] Performers, therefore, could have learned "Liza Jane" songs from soldiers during the war years and transported them to minstrelsy. Similarly, a minstrel troupe may have overheard railroad workers belting out "Whoop Along Liza Jane." A troupe may have simply learned the refrain to a "Liza Jane" song by encountering a war correspondent such as Dr. Adonis or the newspaperman Brick Pomeroy. Given the presence of "Liza Jane" variants—in 1865—from Ohio to Nevada, just about anybody could have mentioned the song to a minstrel bandleader.

In addition to the recent scholarship of Alisha Hines, as noted above, the musicologist Eileen Southern describes how enslaved Black watermen worked as stevedores, firemen, and laborers on the docks and often the boats themselves that traveled up and down the nation's waterways.[31] In her book *The Music of Black Americans*, she further asserts that many of the same workers also provided "shows of the vaudeville type for the boat passengers at the end of the day's labor and music for dancing afterward. Stevedores always sang as they worked."[32] To emphasize the scope of this activity, Southern establishes the vast geographical areas in which this cultural exchange may have taken place:

> Black watermen carried their special worksongs, along with other kinds of Negro folksongs, up and down the rivers—from Wheeling, West Virginia, and Cincinnati on the Ohio River, from Omaha, Nebraska, Kansas City and St. Louis on the Missouri River, to the towns on the Mississippi itself, Cairo, Illinois, Memphis, Tennessee, and finally, to New Orleans. The same songs or similar ones could be heard on the Gulf Coast in Mobile, Alabama, and on the Atlantic Coast in Savannah, Georgia; Charleston, South Carolina; Norfolk, Virginia; and in northern ports. The watermen were truly itinerant musicians, and may have been responsible, more than any other single force, for the spread of Negro folksongs from one community to another, white as well as black.[33]

The previously cited scholarship of Alisha Hines might otherwise add the example of enslaved women who also labored on the waterways. Through the writings of Lafcadio Hearn, there is further evidence that the "Liza Jane" family was present among New Orleans watermen in the 1870s, and it is not difficult to imagine catchy, bouncy songs about Liza Jane transferring from watermen to white minstrels, who could have overheard singing and music on riverboats. Other Black people could have learned these folksongs in the same manner, Southern indicates, hence spreading the tunes from the waterways to plantations.

John Strausbaugh notes how some minstrel performers—to underscore the authenticity of their material—claimed to be emulating enslaved people, while others, perhaps hoping to enhance their careers, seemed intent on claiming ownership of songs and dances for themselves. Employing a bit of an over-worn pun, he declares that the ultimate truths regarding the origins of song material are not so black-and-white. Influence came from both sides.[34] No minstrel activity has been unearthed, however, that would have preceded the "Liza Jane" recollections established in the WPA *Slave Narrative Collection.* While indirect sources such as Robert Burns or the popular song "Susan Jane" may have played a secondary role in the formation of some "Liza Jane" titles or refrains, Eileen Southern underscores the likelihood of songs trading hands back and forth by averring:

> The minstrel songs, originally inspired by genuine slave songs, were altered and adapted by white minstrels to the taste of white America in the nineteenth century, and then were taken back again by black folk for further adaptation to Negro musical taste. Thus the songs passed back into the folk tradition from which they had come.[35]

Shortly after the United States exited the destructive decade of the 1860s, white versions of "Goodbye Liza Jane" would surface in the sheet music, songsters, and minstrel playbills of the years to follow before the first African American recording star, George W. Johnson, would demonstrate Southern's analysis by becoming the first performer of any race to record similar "Liza Jane" lyrics.

In particular, Johnson would repurpose a "Goodbye Liza Jane" variant that had developed over decades of blackface minstrel shows, which were, according to writer Amiri Baraka/LeRoi Jones, "at their best, mere parodies of Negro life, though I do not think that the idea of 'the parody' was always present."[36] In *Blues People,* Baraka/Jones observes how audiences must have found it amusing for "a white man with a painted face to attempt to reproduce some easily identifiable characteristic of 'the darky.'"[37] When adding, "There was room for artistic imprecision in the minstrel show," Baraka/Jones indicates that the individual performances may not have mattered to the audience as much as "the very idea of the show itself: 'Watch these Niggers.'"[38] Baraka/Jones also speaks of cycles in which one group steals the other's group music, then the original music-maker steals back the imitation, and so forth, concluding, somewhat in lamentation: "The hopelessly interwoven fabric of American life where blacks and whites pass so quickly as to become only grays!"[39]

FROM THE *BOLD SOLDIER BOY'S SONGBOOK* TO THE CYLINDERS OF GEORGE W. JOHNSON

"Oh, Goodbye Liza Jane"

1868 TO 1898

On February 16, 1868, the editors of the *Daily Press and Herald* (Knoxville, Tennessee), published a couplet whose provenance they could not establish, citing the author's undeservedly obscure status:

> Oh she went up the new-cut road and I went up the lane—
> Oh! Who's dat heel a burnin'? Oh! good bye Liza Jane![1]

The context is vague, but the couplet was presented in response to a reader (dubbed a "remorseless scribbler") who had forwarded the flowery sighs of an equally obscure love poem. The formula of going up the new cut road while the love interest goes up the lane not only enables the straight rhyme with "Liza Jane" but also allows the rift between the guy and his gal, Liza Jane, to inhabit a simple, vivid structure. A burning heel might suggest the girl's haste to escape the encounter; both the comic possibilities of a lover's pell-mell flight and the obvious placement of dialect might lend themselves to minstrel routines.

In her book *Spirituals and the Birth of a Black Entertainment Industry*, musicologist Sandra Jean Graham briefly describes Eddie Fox as a violinist and orchestra leader for Simmons and Slocum's Minstrels in 1870.[2] A survey of performers published in 1911, *Monarchs of Minstrelsy*, written by minstrel show producer Edward Le Roy Rice, provides some additional information on Fox, who was born in Glens Falls, New York, in 1848.[3] After the Civil War, he spent time with Newcomb & Arlington's Minstrels in 1867, thereby developing a relationship with Billy Arlington, whose own troupe sang "Little Old 'Liza

Jane" in Chicago around the same time.[4] A few years later, Fox journeyed to Philadelphia, where the Arch Street Opera House had been built expressly for Simmons and Slocum's Minstrels.[5] Fox directed the house orchestra and stayed with the popular troupe—organized by Lew Simmons and E. N. Slocum—for several seasons before finishing his career with a few additional troupes.[6] Rice claims that Fox had been the highest salaried bandleader in minstrelsy and also lists some of his greatest compositions, including, in 1871, sheet music for "Good Bye Liza Jane."[7] This continues to be the earliest known sheet music publication in the "Liza Jane" family.

Printed by Lee & Walker in Philadelphia, "Good Bye Liza Jane" is presented as a "Comic Song by Eddie Fox, as Sung by Lew Simmons, at the Arch Street Opera House."[8] At the top of the cover page, the song is dedicated to R. Hughes, who, according to *Monarchs of Minstrelsy*, may have been Ruey Hughes, an entertainer who fell ill and passed away in 1871.[9] Though unidentified on the cover, two large portraits seem to depict Simmons and Slocum, the two leaders of the Philadelphia-based minstrel troupe. On the first page of the music, Fox is additionally identified as having arranged the song; nowhere, overtly, does the publication credit the writer of the words. With the refrain and lyrics for one or more versions of "Goodbye Liza Jane" already in circulation, clearly, Fox did not invent the entire song, and the omission of a lyricist may acknowledge the unclear provenance of the words, some of which, in any event, derived from other minstrel songs. Chances are, he popularized a song he learned elsewhere and modified it to suit Simmons and Slocum's troupe. At the very least, elements of the refrain appeared years earlier in Kansas and Tennessee newspapers, and there is also some distant possibility the Irish newspaperman, "Dr." Stephen Byron "Adonis" Donahue, coined the title in 1864.

It is unknown how many phrases or melodic elements Fox may have borrowed from unidentified originals. In its entirety, Fox's version reads as follows:

Good Bye Liza Jane.
Comic Song.

The time has come, I must go
I must play on the old banjo
Walk dad Lew Oh Mister Lew [*]
Ehe ! Ehe ! he ! hear me now [*]
The time has come I do declare
I want a lock of my girl's hair
Walk dad Lew Oh Mister Lew
Ehe ! Ehe ! he ! hear me now.

[2d Chorus:]
I'm going away to leave you good bye good bye
I'm going away to leave you good bye Liza Jane
I'm going away to leave you I'm going down to Lynchburg town
If you get there before I do it's good bye Liza Jane.

Behind the hen-house on my knees
I thought I heard a chicken sneeze
Walk dad Lew Oh Mister Lew
Ehe ! Ehe ! he ! hear me now
Twas nothing but a rooster saying his pray'rs
And giving out a hymn Such a getting upstairs
Walk dad Lew Oh Mister Lew
Ehe ! Ehe ! he ! hear me now.

[2d Chorus]

Chickens and hens have gone to roost,
A hawk flew down and bit an old goose
Walk dad Lew Oh Mister Lew
Ehe ! Ehe ! he ! hear me now
Bit a young duck in the middle of the back
Make the old drake go quack, quack, quack
Walk dad Lew Oh Mister Lew
Ehe ! Ehe ! he ! hear me now.

[2d Chorus]

[*This couplet is identified as "Chorus" in the sheet music.]

In many ways, the song agitates against the convention of "making sense" as a narrative and instead may present itself as a vehicle for racial parody and onstage clowning. There are two choruses, including a couplet nestled among the verses—"Walk dad Lew Oh Mister Lew / Ehe ! Ehe ! he ! hear me now"—and the second chorus, which hearkens back to the Forty-Third USCT Regiment in Annapolis. Given that Lew Simmons is identified as the singer of "Good Bye Liza Jane," obviously, the first chorus refers to him and was likely addressed to him through the singing of other performers. The curious "Ehe ! Ehe ! he !" may simulate laughter, and importantly, George W. Johnson might have emphasized this facet when he repackaged fragments of the song in the 1890s.

Silliness abounds. The most unusual line of the song may refer to the singer pining for a lock of his girl's hair. From that point, much of the language outside the choruses conjures plantation environs, replete with a hen house, chickens, roosters, a hawk, and a duck. The chicken sneezing and the rooster saying his "pray'rs" may be secondary to the singer loitering behind the hen-house on his knees. This image recalls the observation of Wittke, noted earlier, who comments on "the stage Negro" loving chickens so much, "he could not pass a chicken-coop without falling into temptation." The audience at the Arch Street Opera House probably understood this convention, and after all, these lyrics could not be separated from Simmons and his troupe appearing onstage in burnt cork makeup. In other words, Simmons probably presented the image of the "lazy, childlike slave of the plantation," as Forbes observes, by strumming his banjo and sneaking around the hen-house. Yet, with hawks biting geese and ducks "[going] quack, quack, quack," the piece does veer into slapstick cacophony. Arguably, the song has been "whitened" a bit. Gone is a word like "gwine" that the Forty-Third Regiment may have voiced; gone is a word like "leab." In their place, the more proper "going" and "leave" have been installed but lost is the character of the song's likely earliest singers. Of course, white authors, such as Leander Cogswell of the Eleventh New Hampshire Regiment, made these representations of vernacular but nevertheless estimated what they had overheard.

Some of Fox's words could be termed "floating lyrics" because they drift from one song to the next. For instance, a piece dubbed "Git Along, John" appeared in *The New Negro Forget-Me-Not Songster*, published in 1859, with the following couplet: "Behind de hen house on my knee / Tinks I hear de chicken sneeze."[10] Fox adopts the phrase "Such a getting upstairs" from a popular song of nearly the same title; "Sich A Gittin Up Stairs" and other related songs materialized in numerous nineteenth-century songbooks, including, for example, the 1853 *Jenny Lind Forget-Me-Not Songster*.[11] The reference to "Lynchburg town" likely refers to a minstrel song of the same title, written by Frank Spencer and found in numerous antebellum songsters, such as *White's New Illustrated Melodeon Songbook*, from 1851. In this song, billed as "The Original" version of "Lynchburg Town," the singers "play de ole banjo," and as part of the chorus, aver that "we're gwine long down to Lynchburg town" where they will entertain the white folks down there about fun and glee.[12] Through these references, it is obvious that Fox deliberately drew from older minstrel material in addition to one or more variants of "Goodbye Liza Jane" when arranging his song. In effect, he attached bits of "performative material" to the refrain, which may have been a one-verse song originally created by enslaved people.

After Simmons and Slocum's Minstrels began to perform "Good Bye Liza Jane" in 1871, numerous entertainers and troupes sang it throughout the country and around the world in the ensuing years. A sampling of this activity would include:

1871	Advertisement in the *New York Clipper.* "A Young Gentleman of Dramatic Ability wishes to engage with a dramatic troupe. Can play several pieces. Sings 'Good Bye Liza Jane.' Managers Address W. R. Torrence, Xenia, Ohio."[13]
1873	Credited to a person identified as "Crockett," a version of "Good-Bye Liza Jane" associated with a carpetbagger theme appears in the *Staunton Spectator and General Advertiser*, Virginia[14]
1874	Mr. Harry Kelly sings the "Comic Ballad—Good-Bye, Luiza Jane" for the Great California Minstrels in Auckland, New Zealand[15]
1874	John Williams sings "Good Bye 'Liza Jane" for the New York Minstrels in West Scituate, Massachusetts[16]
1876	Mr. Harry Talbott sings the "Comic Song, Good-Bye Eliza Jane" for Moore & Burgess Minstrels in London, England[17]
1871–1876 (estimated)	Duprez & Benedict's Minstrels perform "Good-bye Liza Jane" in an unknown location[18]
1876	The *Columbus Courier*, Kansas, reprints "Good bye, 'Liza Jane" lyrics from the *Cincinnati Commercial.* Though uncredited, these lyrics were, in fact, reported by journalist Lafcadio Hearn in New Orleans[19]
1877	Luke Schoolcraft sings "Good Bye Liza Jane" for Schoolcraft & Coes' Minstrels at the Howard Athenaeum in Boston, Massachusetts[20]
1879	Lew Simmons (formerly of Simmons and Slocum's Minstrels) sings "Good Bye, Liza Jane" with the London Minstrels in Durban, South Africa[21]
1883	Luke Schoolcraft sings "Comic Song Good Bye, Liza Jane" for Billy Birch's San Francisco Minstrels at the San Francisco Minstrels Opera House in New York[22]
1883	A person identified as "Kalawaia" sings "Good-bye, Eliza Jane" in the New Music Hall, Honolulu, for the Hawaiian Amateur Minstrel Troupe[23]

| 1887 (estimated) | Luke Schoolcraft sings "Good bye, Liza Jane" for Schoolcraft and Coes' Minstrels at the Howard Athenaeum in Boston, Massachusetts[24] |
| 1889 | Mr. T. E. Stutson sings "Good Bye Liza Jane" for the Madagascar Minstrels at the Music Hall in Boston, Massachusetts. Additional text indicates that the song is "Specially composed by the Poet Laureate of the retiring City Democracy"[25] |

"Goodbye Liza Jane," therefore, develops a national and global presence as numerous large minstrel troupes and newspapers carry renditions of the song to substantial audiences and readership in the United States, New Zealand, South Africa, England, and the Territory of Hawaii. Luke Schoolcraft demonstrated much fondness for the song, which he sang as part of his own troupe's activities as well as for at least one other troupe. Writing in *Monarchs of Minstrelsy*, Edward Le Roy Rice describes Schoolcraft's early activities as a butcher, and a Dutch comedian before his first engagement with Newcomb's Minstrels found him "sitting on the end" in 1872. A short while later, he formed an enduring partnership with George Coes. Throughout his career, he associated with many performers who have already been introduced, such as Simmons and Slocum's Minstrels and different troupes led by Billy Emerson. Schoolcraft grew up in New Orleans, having been born there in 1847.[26]

In circulation, feasibly wide circulation, from 1868 until it folded in 1882, *Henry De Marsan's New Comic and Sentimental Singer's Journal* contained "all the popular Songs of the day."[27] Sociologist Paul Charosh indicates, in his article "Studying Nineteenth Century Popular Song," the De Marsan journal eventually reached two hundred issues, "with each issue [including] the texts of about fifty songs sung in the 'Theatres, Opera-Houses, and Concert-Rooms of the United States and Great Britain.'"[28] Charosh likens each issue to a songster, given the "multiple pages and song texts."[29] Along the sidebar of each cover page, the De Marsan journal lists distribution agents in seven cities: Boston, Philadelphia, Cincinnati, Newark, Rochester, Detroit, and Albany, yet Charosh also mentions presences in New York City, New Bedford, and London (Canada) as other distribution outlets.[30] According to Charosh, De Marsan maintained a print shop in New York City, on Chatham Street, in the area known as Park Row, where he stocked valentines, toy books, paper dolls, and other ephemera among his inventory.[31] Charosh points out that this type of songbook production, which included De Marsan's contemporaries, such as publishers Robert DeWitt and Oliver Ditson, made "popular song available, in text-only form, and as sheet music, for pennies, nickels, and dimes."[32] Based on these observations, coupled with a lengthy publication run, De Marsan's songbooks likely reached a substantial number of people. According to a dissertation, *Sounding Sentimental: American Popular Song from Nineteenth-Century Ballads to 1970s Soft Rock*, by Emily Margot Gale, De Marsan did not date his issues, which typically ran eight pages, but produced them approximately on a monthly basis.[33] Thus, the dates of individual issues can be estimated by assuming a June 1868 start and counting forward by one month per issue.

As it turns out, *Henry De Marsan's New Comic and Sentimental Singer's Journal* featured "Liza Jane" variants as well as other pieces that may have simply included "intrusions" of the girl's name. In terms of the former, Volume II, Number 137, estimated to have appeared in 1879 or 1880, contained "Hoop 'em up 'Liza Jane." This variant did not credit its author and concluded both stanzas with the line "My sweet ole Liza Jane."[34] On the other hand, Volume I, Number 65, estimated to have appeared in 1873 or 1874, contained the song "Golden Showers," with credit to "Jas. Maas, the well known comedian." According to the journal, the song was "sung in all the Minstrels' Theatres in New-York City." Here, the Liza Jane character intrudes. The piece refers to her as "Miss Liza," who's "got a baby, baby, baby." While not obviously a refrain, the following couplet—"Golden showers are falling down: / Liza Jane has come to town"— occurs twice.[35] She does not materialize elsewhere in the piece. This might have been notoriety enough for the "Liza Jane" family but for an appearance of another "Goodbye Liza Jane" variant.

Volume I, Number 86 of the De Marsan journal contained a version of "Good-Bye, Liza Jane," with additional prefatory information, "As sung by Frank Lum, the great Sensation Comic Singer, with immense applause." The publication does not credit a writer; thus, for all intents and purposes, the rendition can be attributed to Lum. Estimating the date of publication as 1875 to 1876, the song's full text appears as follows:

Good-Bye, Liza Jane

Away down south where I was born,
I husk the wood, and chop the corn,
Walk that loo, oh ! miss loo,
Ah ! Ah ! Ah ! hear me now:
A roasted ear to the house I bring.
The overseer cotch me and made me sing.

Chorus.
Walk that loo, oh ! miss loo,
Ah ! Ah ! Ah ! hear me now:
For I am going away to leave you, good-bye, good-bye:

I am going away to leave you, good-bye, Liza Jane.
Oh ! I am going away to leave you, oh ! I am going down to Lynchburg
    town
If you get there before I do, oh ! good-bye, Liza Jane.

Ducks play cards and chickens drink wine,
And monkeys grow upon grape vines:
Walk that loo, oh ! miss loo,
Ah ! Ah ! Ah ! hear me now:
Corn-starch pudding and tapioca pie,
Oh ! the gray cat picked out the black cat's eye.

[Chorus.]

The old cow in the young cow's shed,
Fell over a corn and broke off her head :
Walk that loo, oh ! miss loo,
Ah ! Ah ! Ah ! hear me now:
And when the jackass heard the row,
He stabbed himself with the tail of a cow.

[Chorus.]

A nigger came from Arkansas,
The worst old fool I ever saw :
Walk that loo, oh ! miss loo, [*]
He went some water for to get,
And he carried it home in a corn basket.

[Chorus.]³⁶

[*] This line is given without its typical partner in the couplet.

Not to be confused with the singer Frank Lumbard, who evidently effected
a cease-fire with his singing, Frank Lum performed within a minstrelsy and
circus context. Though scant information can be found regarding him, William Slout indicates that Lum "accompanied the R Sands Circus in the summer of 1863."³⁷ The Library of Congress lists three publications—"Flip flap,"
"Jeremy Diddler," and "Hop lite loo"—generated by Henry De Marsan as song
sheets, with attribution to Lum as a singer; Lum is further described in these
songsheets as "celebrated comic vocalist" or "celebrated Ethiopian comedian."³⁸

They are not dated by the Library of Congress, but other online sources such as Google Books suggest a range of dates from 1860 to 1864, and "Flip flap," in particular, contains Civil War imagery. Moreover, in May 1873, the *New York Clipper*, a weekly entertainment newspaper, posted an advertisement by Lum. He writes, "Comedian, Comic Singer, Bill Writer and Newspaper Advertiser, is open for engagements after May 14, Address Frank Lum, Stage Manager, 198 Spring Street, New York."[39] As an aid in confirming the estimated publication date of Lum's appearance in the De Marsan journal, a song sheet for "Good-Bye, Liza Jane" materialized in Scotland, published by Poet's Box, 80 London Street, Glasgow, with nearly identical lyrics; it is dated Saturday, November 24, 1877.[40] The song sheet does not credit Lum, instead claiming to be an "Original."

Lum's version of "Good-Bye, Liza Jane" more than resembles Fox's version in the refrains. There, it largely preserves the original language, except for replacing the reference to Lew Simmons with a feminine slant, "Walk that loo, oh ! miss loo." Moreover, the laughter of Fox's rendition is changed slightly to "Ah ! Ah ! Ah ! hear me now." Thus, Lum focuses more of the repeating elements on the girl (the "miss") and removes the paternalistic references—"Walk dad Lew"—which Fox had built into his version. This later version expands upon the agrarian setting as well as the derogatory racial elements. In Lum's rendition of "Good-Bye, Liza Jane," the singer approximates a simpleton by reversing the chores of chopping wood and husking corn. He is obviously enslaved since he is stopped by an overseer and compelled to sing. As in Fox's version, silliness overcomes the song, with ducks playing cards and chickens getting drunk off wine. Monkeys grow like grapes, in Lum's estimation. The cows and jackasses would seem to tumble all over each other. The last stanza, however, plays more obviously upon racial hatred than the Fox version, when the singer—presumably Lum in blackface makeup—identifies someone even more foolish than himself: "[a man who] came from Arkansas" went "some water for to get / And carried it home in corn basket."

This last stanza, however, floated toward Lum from earlier minstrel songs and is not the only example of Lum borrowing stock phrases or "floating verses" from previous singers, remembering, of course, Fox did the same in his variant. One example of this derogatory mocking can be found in *Buckley's Song Book for the Parlor*, an 1855 songster, which contains the lines as part of the song "I'se Going Far Away."

> A niggar came from Arkansas (line 1)
> De biggest fool I eber saw (line 3)
> He went some water for to git (line 11)
> And carried it in a corn basket (line 12)[41]

The New Negro Forget-Me-Not Songster, from which Eddie Fox may have borrowed a few lines, may have also supplied some lines to Lum. In "Git Along, John," one couplet approximates some of Lum's silliness: "Turkey playin on de punkin vine / Goose chaw backer and duck drink wine."[42] The ultimate source of these and many other lyrics may never be known, but more importantly, they were traveling between performers and troupes for many decades and being attached to many different songs.

Another such scenario accounts for Lum's opening lines in "Good-Bye, Liza Jane." At the very least, these lines can be located in *The Bold Soldier Boy's Song Book*, likely printed in Richmond, Virginia, for Confederate soldiers, between 1861 and 1865. Therein, a version of the song "Kemo Kimo" begins:

> Away down south, where I was born,
> Sing song, Kitty, Kitty Kimeo,
> I chop de wood and husk de corn,
> And sing all day of Kitty Kimeo.[43]

In "Kemo Kimo," the chopping and husking duties may be rendered appropriately, but the specter of burnt cork minstrelsy hovers. At this juncture, the sludge gets rather thick. A variant of the "Liza Jane" family, "Goodbye Liza Jane," with likely origins among enslaved people, transfers to the racist institution of minstrelsy, wherein a series of renditions evolves over time, including one variation which installs a couple of lines that had materialized in a Confederate songster. The singer George W. Johnson would repossess "Goodbye Liza Jane" lyrics about twenty-two years after the Lum publication, incorporating some of the very same lines from "Kemo Kimo" that had appeared in *The Bold Soldier Boy's Song Book*. Johnson thus demonstrates Eileen Southern's notion of Black musicians reclaiming folk material from minstrelsy, but not without the added counterweight, in Johnson's case, of singing some lines embraced by Confederate soldiers more than thirty years earlier.

Media historian Tim Brooks has become, in essence, George W. Johnson's biographer, creating an important, durable record of his life and development as a musician. Brooks devotes the first three chapters of his book, *Lost Sounds*, to Johnson, who was likely born into slavery in Virginia during the mid-1840s.[44] His parents were said to be teenagers at the time of his birth, with his father maybe fifteen years old and his mother even younger.[45] "Shortly after he was born," "[Johnson] was placed as the companion of the young son of a prosperous white farmer," whose neighbor may have "owned Johnson's father at the time."[46] In this arrangement, Johnson studied flute and became literate. He also "learned how to get along in the white world," according to Brooks, a skill that would benefit him later in New York. Johnson gained his freedom as a boy and, as a young teenager, began working for white families as a house servant.[47]

He would have been about fifteen or sixteen years old when the Civil War erupted in Virginia, a state known for the comings and goings of both armies. As mentioned above, two units that sang "Liza Jane" songs—the Forty-Third USCT Regiment and the Twenty-Third North Carolina Regiment, or Pee Dee Guards— participated in the Battle of Spotsylvania Court House, about seventy miles from Johnson's home. Loudoun County, where he lived, saw "forty-six battles and skirmishes [. . .] between 1861 and 1865," according to Brooks.[48] Johnson did his best during and after the war, but with conditions oppressive for Black people anywhere in the South, he relocated to New York sometime between 1873 and 1876. Brooks reports Johnson's addresses as situating him in the Tenderloin or Hell's Kitchen sections of New York City during that period, beloved by neighbors as a street musician who could whistle notes as perfectly as those on a flute.[49]

In 1890, a man who represented the New Jersey Phonograph Company overheard Johnson whistling near the Hudson River ferryboat terminal. The man, Victor Emerson, convinced Johnson to make some recordings and paid him for the work.[50] Johnson knew the popular songs of the day, but Emerson convinced him to record a "coon song."[51] Akin to the situation that resembled Camille Forbes's narrative about Bert Williams, who applied burnt cork makeup to his already dark skin in order to hold employment as a performer, Johnson obliged and recorded a self-deprecating piece, "The Whistling Coon," featuring his flute-like whistles.[52] In those days, recordings were made onto "little brown wax cylinders" that could be played for a nickel on portable "talking machines," which enabled customers to listen through "rubber ear tubes."[53] Since there was no way to duplicate a recording, except by singing, Johnson would have spent an entire afternoon, or presumably a series of afternoons, singing the same song over and over into as many as six recording devices at a time, until Emerson had enough copies he could sell to vendors.[54] Simultaneously, Brooks writes, Johnson was making cylinder recordings for the New York Phonograph Company in Manhattan.[55] Johnson is widely regarded as being the first African American recording star, with his second trademark number, "The Laughing Song," also distributed in 1890. Johnson's whistling and laughing "quickly became the rage on coin machines around New York" and eventually outside New York.[56] By all accounts, George W. Johnson negotiated this part of his life as a street musician, musical whistler, and laughter artist with buoyancy and conviviality. The new technology—the "talking machines"—must have been miraculous for the public, which in turn, made Johnson's recordings some of the best-selling cylinders of the decade.

By the time an opportunity developed to record some new material at the Edison studio—1897, according to Brooks, and as late as 1898, according to

Craig Martin Gibbs[57]—Johnson's cylinders had reportedly sold more than fifty thousand copies, which may have been hyperbole, but either way, his intense popularity ensured that any new material would likely reach thousands of listeners.[58] Johnson, in turn, opted to record a "Liza Jane" song. Entitled "The Laughing Coon," Johnson's version of the song will immediately recall Fox and Lum, whose published versions allowed space for laughter. This song also resembles yet another variant, "Good-by, Liza Jane," that was published in the popular *Delaney's Song Book* in 1896.[59] The title, "The Laughing Coon," was probably designed to spark an association with Johnson's earlier hits, "The Whistling Coon" and "The Laughing Song." Although not every version of the cylinder recordings would be exactly alike, given the recording process of the era, virtually every recording would seem to include the following lyrics:

The Laughing Coon
George W. Johnson

Away down south, where I was born
We used to hoe and weed that corn
Always low, walking slow, ha ha ha, do you hear me now?

Chorus:
I'se gwine away to leave you, goodbye, goodbye
I'se gwine away to leave you, oh goodbye Liza Jane
I am the happy laughing coon, ha ha ha ha ha
Come out in the valley and look for the moon, ha ha ha ha ha (&c.)

The ducks play cards, the chickens drink wine
The monkeys doze on a large grapevine
Walk down low, always slow, ha ha ha, do you hear me now?

[Chorus][60]

In the earliest versions, dated 1897 or 1898, Johnson is accompanied only by a pianist, who may have been Frank Banta, according to Brooks.[61] Later versions of the song add an additional stanza—"We went to walk, you and me / You got stung by a bumblebee / [Unknown] sting me too, I'll not walk with you anymore"—before the final chorus. Still other ensuing versions involve a full, rowdy orchestra.[62] Some renditions appear on ten-inch wax.[63]

The nucleus of the song, the refrain, incorporates elements that Leander Cogswell may have observed in the Forty-Third USCT Regiment ("I'se gwine away fur to leab you") as well a snippet of the couplet published by the *Daily*

Monitor in January 1865: "O, good bye Liza Jane." A phrase such as "I'se gwine away to leave you" or "I'se gwine away fur to leab you" may have been a perfectly natural dialect for Johnson, but previous iterations can also be traced to minstrelsy. Johnson may have been familiar with those songs, for example, "Whats de matter, Susey," from *White's New Illustrated Melodeon Songbook* (1851), where the line "I'm gwine away to leab you" comprises part of the chorus.[64] As noted above, a version of the song "Kemo Kimo," published in a Confederate songster, contains the first two lines of Johnson's song. The third line of Johnson's song—"Always low, walking slow"—had blurred into the strangeness of low, slow traipsing, but still resembles Eddie Fox's "Walk dad Lew" and Frank Lum's "Walk that loo" via the slant rhymes of "low," "slow," "Lew," and "loo." Johnson's first burst of laughter corresponds to Fox's placement of "Ehe ! Ehe ! he !" and Frank Lum's "Ah ! Ah ! Ah !" All three men incorporate the "hear me now" phrase, which is either an assertion or a question meant, however distantly, for Liza Jane herself. As for the ducks playing cards, the chickens drinking wine, and the monkeys dozing on the grapevine, either Frank Lum's version supplied these lines, or they derived, as noted, from Christy's Minstrels or perhaps other sources. The melody of George W. Johnson's song resembles the Fox melody, and yet, Johnson's reclamation of the song emphasizes his boisterous laughter, which effectively repurposes the minstrel lyrics for the benefit of his own garrulous skills.

Johnson not only became the first African American recording star but the first entertainer, Black or white, to record "Liza Jane" lyrics. Undoubtedly, thousands of people listened to Johnson's singing, laughter, and "Goodbye Liza Jane" refrain after depositing their nickels. While Johnson would not eclipse his earliest recordings in terms of popularity, Brooks indicates that "The Laughing Coon" remained in the catalogs of Edison and Columbia for many years.[65] Nevertheless, Johnson's career may have peaked by this point. Brooks describes Johnson's colorful life after he recorded "The Laughing Coon," which would include a wide spectrum of events, ranging from performative matters to a murder trial, in which Johnson would be acquitted of the charge of killing his common-law wife.[66] Eventually, Johnson drifted away from his musical career altogether. His final years were unpleasant, with his songs dropping out of record catalogs and his income evaporating. He died of complications related to pneumonia and myocarditis in 1914 and was buried in an unmarked grave.[67] George W. Johnson did more, however, than attach his celebrity to the "Liza Jane" family. His booming version of the song fills the air with his gregarious character in the early days of the talking machine era. Johnson's recording continues to be an important milestone in the extensive travels of the "Liza Jane" family, with special emphasis placed upon the plight of African American musicians in his day. There were not many opportunities to earn a living, never mind the type of material that a Black musician had to record if he or she wanted to earn that elusive living, but Johnson did produce records, and he sang about "Liza Jane" in the process.

Around the time that Johnson recorded his "Liza Jane" song, the poet Daniel Webster Davis published his second collection of verse, *'Weh Down Souf and other Poems*.[68] The phrase "'weh down souf" or "away down south" does conjure the middle of the middle of that peculiar institution, slavery, and its plantation system; that is, not just *down* south, but *way* down south. Davis presents the phrase as dialectal. George W. Johnson sang it a bit "cleaner" but full of his enthralling voice. It does hearken back to the Civil War, at the very least, way down south in Virginia, where Davis, like Johnson, was born. An insightful 1973 article written by Joan R. Sherman, "Daniel Webster Davis: A Black Virginia Poet in the Age of Accommodation," describes the clashing forces faced by African Americans like Davis and Johnson, both born into slavery, and both rising into notoriety through their professional and creative spheres. Sherman writes that Davis's poems "are denounced by modern Afro-Americans [in 1973] as historically and sociologically unsound portraits which degrade the race and suppress the horrors of enslavement,"[69] and yet she also establishes Davis as "an unsentimental pragmatist and far less accommodating as he seemed."[70] Davis left behind "a rich store of imaginative poetry and forceful prose, and the image of a dedicated, race-proud man who rose 'up from slavery'" to become a leader in the Richmond, Virginia area.[71]

Why refer to Davis? A bit of leafing through *'Weh Down Souf* might take the reader to the character "little Liza" who had been "married off, / so menny years ago"[72] or even to the verses for "Miss Liza's Banjer."[73] But amidst the collection, Davis situates the poem "Ol' Virginny Reel" and, amid the poem, offers instructions for the dance of the same name.

> Ef you nebber seed de moshun, I will tell yo' how it goes;
>   'Tis a-bobbin' up an' down a hop an' jump,
> An' a-turnin' ebry lady ez yo' kum back down de line,
>   Jes' like a bobtail moc'sin roun' de stump.
> "Miss Liza Jane" is lubly, an' "Balmoral" is fin',
>   An' "Wipe dem Di'mon Winders" makes you feel;
> But not "Bounce Aroun' My Sugar Lump," nor "Turnin' Good Ol' Man,"
>   Ken 'gin to tetch de ol' Virginny reel.[74]

This vivid passage connects to the WPA respondent Hannah Jameson, whose narrative not only mentioned "Miss Lizy Jane" but seemed to "call" a series of dance instructions, including "Shake dat balmoral, Lizy Jane." Furthermore, lyrics reported in an 1897 Illinois newspaper article echo both Jameson (nearly word for word) and Davis. Ostensibly written about the singing of a formerly enslaved person, the *Albion Journal* piece references the Lizy Jane character as well as several dance moves, for instance: "Shake dat balmoral, Lizy Jane!"[75] Here, in the Davis poem, "Miss Liza Jane" may be a lovely girl or a "lubly" dance move, and "Balmoral" may refer to a boot, a hat, or a dance step, but either way, Davis's poetry demonstrates similarities with first-generation song performance in the "Liza Jane" family. This would include not only Hannah Jameson but Dosia Harris, Lina Hunter, and Anda Woods, all of whom referred to "Miss Liza Jane."

Hannah Jameson, George W. Johnson, and Daniel Webster Davis: all three endured terrible hardship. They told their stories through narrative, cylinder recording, and poetry. And while telling their stories, up came the girl. Her name. Miss Liza Jane.

FROM THE NEW ORLEANS LEVEE
TO THE HAMPTON INSTITUTE

"Little Liza Jane" *ad infinitum*

1873 TO 1893 / EARLY TWENTIETH CENTURY

The jolly editors of the *Thomaston Herald* (Georgia) published a warm and humorous blurb entitled "Personal" in their March 15, 1873 issue. Aimed toward a townsman, "Mr. J. N. Webb," the little piece reads:

> PERSONAL.—Our buoyant friend and fellow townsman Mr. J. N. Webb, returned home, during the week from the New Orleans Carnival, where he "saw the eliphant," he says, in all his undisguised magnificence. Being a gay and festive widow-(wooer), 'twas expected he would fling his circumventing *Webbing* round some stubborn "Liza Jane"; wrapping up the gal within its silken meshes; "bear her home in joyous triumph" &c. But it seems that,—
> "She took down the new cut road;
> He took down the lane—
> Git along thar, my Liza Jane,
> Little Old Liza Jane."[1]

While poking some good-natured fun at their friend, this blurb represents yet another powerful indication that "Liza Jane" lyrics continued to spread, presumably through mass adoption by minstrel troupes, with the convention of the "new cut road" and "the lane" attracting a variety of concluding lines. As noted earlier, the editors of the *Daily Press and Herald* in Knoxville, Tennessee, associated the "new cut road" and "the lane" with "Goodbye Liza Jane" in 1868, while in 1865, the *Weekly Review* in Crawfordsville, Indiana published what is thought to be the first date-stamped reference to "new cut road" and "the lane," with the lovelorn speaker uttering the only phrase he could muster: "Go along Liza Jane."

These examples inform several matters. In addition to the rhyming opportunity—lane and Jane—and the dichotomy of taking opposite paths, there is also "git along" and "go along," which could signify a dance call, a sour grapes utterance to a "Liza Jane" who will not accept a proposal, or even (and more crudely) a misapplied yelp otherwise aimed at a mule or another beast of burden. The Georgia newspaper's final line also links to several earlier titles, including Johnny Tuers's "My Little Ole Liza Jane," Brick Pomeroy's "Little Old Liza Jane," and the refrain from Billy Emerson's "Eliza Jane," all of which emanate from the middle of the previous decade. Continued popularity demonstrates that the "Liza Jane" family had not vanished, and to the contrary, kept popping up, especially in bright, lighthearted ways, such as this neighborly ribbing of the man who "saw the eliphant [sic]." The editors consider Liza Jane "stubborn," for indeed, she tends to resist amorous advances.

Also of interest would be Mr. J. N. Webb's travel to New Orleans, a city that bears more than a passing relationship to "Little Liza Jane" and its related variants. Unusual hybrid versions of the song were developing there, owing to a report from world citizen Lafcadio Hearn. According to the article "Lafcadio Hearn, American Folklorist" by historian W. K. McNeil, Hearn was born in Greece of English-Irish-Greek parentage, spent an unhappy childhood in the English isles, emigrated to America in his late teens, and eventually became a naturalized Japanese citizen in his mid-forties.[2] During his American years, he worked as a journalist for the Cincinnati-based *Enquirer* but was fired for engaging in a common-law marriage with a mulatto woman. A competitor paper, the Cincinnati *Commercial*, paid him to report from New Orleans on the political conditions in that city, and off he went, living there for several years.[3] As noted in the previous chapter, Hearn's 1876 report from New Orleans appeared in not only the *Commercial* but also other newspapers at the time, including the *Columbus Courier* in Kansas. McNeil categorizes Hearn as a folklorist and, in reference to his 1876 writings, suggests this was the first publication of his collecting efforts.[4] "From blacks on the city's levee waterfront," writes McNeil, "[Hearn] gathered a number of roustabout songs. These included slave songs, worksongs with alternating lines and chorus, as well as verse and refrain songs with an Anglo-Scots origin." McNeil lists "Liza Jane" among the songs gathered by Hearn but does not categorize the song within his framework.[5]

In *Lafcadio Hearn's America*, folklorist Simon J. Bronner reprints the writings of the journalist, wanderer, and music collector. Entitled "Levee Life: Haunts and Pastimes of the Roustabouts," Chapter I contains the 1876 narrative that materialized in the *Commercial* and other newspapers, and therein, Hearn describes the "negro" workers as being "the best roustabouts and unrivaled as firemen."⁶ Indicating that Black roustabouts account for nearly two-thirds of the total number of stevedores and longshoremen, Hearn goes on to portray the boat traffic which might originate in New Orleans and unload on the Cincinnati levee. As part of defining the prowess of the roustabouts, the work conditions, and the lives of the characters who worked—and sang—on the New Orleans waterfront, Hearn writes:

> Roustabout life in the truest sense is, then, the life of the colored popula-
> tion of the Rows, [. . .] blacks and mulattoes from all parts of the States,
> but chiefly from Kentucky and Eastern Virginia, where most of them
> appear to have toiled on the plantations before Freedom; and echoes
> of the old plantation life still live in their songs and their pastimes.
> You may hear old Kentucky slave songs chanted nightly on the steam-
> boats, [. . .] you may see the old slave dances nightly performed to the
> air of some ancient Virginia-reel in the dance houses of Sausage Row or
> the "ball rooms" of Bucktown.⁷

The Black workers may have been suspicious of a man approaching them with a pad and pencil; thus, Hearn describes a system of plying some of the roustabouts with drinks and cigars in order to hear their river songs. The locales of these transactions included "a popular roustabout haunt on Broad-way, near Sixth" as well as a "dingy frame cottage near the corner of Sixth and Culvert Streets."⁸

Alluding to the raw nature of these river songs, Hearn informs his reader-ship that some of them "are not of a character to admit of publication in the columns of a daily newspaper."⁹ He then goes on to present lyrics for several songs, including one of a "somewhat livelier description. It has, we believe, been printed in somewhat different form in certain songbooks. We give it as it was sung to us in a Broadway saloon:

> I come down the mountain,
>   An' she come down the lane,
> An' all that I could say to her
>   Was, "Good Bye, 'Liza Jane."
>
> [Chorus]
> Farewell, 'Liza Jane!
>   Farewell, 'Liza Jane!
> Don't throw yourself away, for I
>   Am coming back again.

I got up on a house-top,
   An' give my horn a blow;
Thought I heerd Miss Dinah say,
   "Yonder comes your beau."

[Chorus]

Ef I'd a few more boards,
   To build my chimney higher,
I'd keep aroun' the country gals,
   Chunkin' up the fire.

[Chorus][10]

Hearn's collection of this variant may give evidence to the interrelationship between different "Liza Jane" traditions. A few years earlier, "Goodbye Liza Jane" became a minstrelsy hit and may have been widely adopted, and yet, this version is decidedly not "Goodbye Liza Jane," with that phrase only sung once. Or perhaps it is not "Goodbye Liza Jane" alone. As noted earlier, the refrain "Farewell, 'Liza Jane" may connect to the Robert Burns poem "Farewell to Eliza." The first verse follows the established convention of the dual pathways, in this case, the singer coming down the mountain and Liza Jane taking the lane. By the time Hearn's article appeared in newspapers, the old-time country fiddler Uncle Am Stuart was a young man in his teens or twenties; he would record "Old Liza Jane" almost fifty years later, including a related passage: "I went up on the mountain / I give my horn a blow / I thought I heard my Liza say / yonder comes my beau." By 1924, when Stuart committed the old-time piece to wax, these lines may have become stock phrases, but in 1876, they may have represented a relatively fresh tradition. The horn blow, as interpreted by Miss Dinah, may signify that a male admirer (a "beau") is arriving for Liza Jane. It need not make sense of course. It need not be scrutinized for a discernible through-action. The final stanza, though hard to interpret firmly, does not project triumph. The wistful lyrics indicate resignation, and the image of the "country gals / Chunkin' up the fire" does not sound very romantic. A humorous despair may prevail.

    Though Hearn does not link this version overtly to the traditions of enslaved people, it does proffer little bits of folk material attached to the girl's name. Hearn introduces it as being lively and remembering that he was interviewing longshoremen, the piece could have been sung extensively as a boat song boomed out by roustabouts while performing manual labor. This evokes the writings of Eileen Southern and Alisha Hines, who indicate just how enslaved men and women worked the waterways, with singing and music likely following them wherever they sailed. Hearn's introduction to his New Orleans collection acknowledges the origins of the workers as well, many of whom apparently hailed from plantations in Kentucky and Virginia. According to Hearn, the untitled song likely had been printed "in certain songbooks," but which songbooks and in which form? "Goodbye Liza Jane" may be the easiest answer, but the "new cut road" and "the lane" had also been circulating for several years. This may be, however, the earliest known date-stamped example of the singer climbing up a structure (a house top) to give his horn a blow, with the idea that Liza Jane or another person might consider the horn-wielding chap her suitor.

As noted earlier, *Henry De Marsan's Comic and Sentimental Singers' Journal* published an uncredited version of "Hoop 'em up 'Liza Jane" in its undated Volume II, Number 137 issue, estimated to have appeared in 1879 or 1880. This version builds upon the burgeoning country lyrics Lafcadio Hearn noted earlier in New Orleans.

Hoop 'em up 'Liza Jane

Goin' across de mountain,
I gave my horn a blow,
Thought I heard Miss 'Liza
Yonder comes my beau.
She's nicer than the roses,
That grow down on the plain,
I lub dat little yaller gal—
My sweet ole 'Liza Jane

If you want to buy a horse,
Don't buy a horse dat's lame;
But if you want to buy a mule,
Buy ole 'Liza Jane.
She's sweeter dan de 'lasses,
Dat drops from sugar cane;
She is de darlin' ob my heart—
My sweet ole 'Liza Jane.[11]

The title "Hoop 'em up 'Liza Jane" may contain white misapprehension of Black dialect. None of the WPA narratives make mention of "hoop" or "whoop," and it is possible that the word may be a substitute for "Oh po' Liza" or "Oo po' Liza." If said quickly, the sound "oop," "hoop," or even "hoopo" can emerge.

Nevertheless, words like "whoop" and "hoop" were attached to the girl's name, and a small tradition did materialize, perhaps beginning with intercontinental railroad workers. While basically nonsensical on its face, the title suggests an activity, but the implication is ultimately unclear. The initial action of the song involves the singer blowing his horn on the mountain, at which point he may overhear "Miss Liza" referring to him, or yet another man, as her sweetheart. "Roses" begin to enter the vocabulary of "Liza Jane" songs and will continue into the next century, with recordings by Fiddlin' John Carson, Henry "Ragtime" Thomas, and Bradley Kincaid, among others, comparing Liza Jane to the rouge of the thorny flowers. "Hoop 'em up 'Liza Jane" contains a perplexing mixture of proper English and minstrel dialect, with phrases like "I gave my horn a blow" set against "I lub dat little yaller gal," which references a light-skinned Black woman. In this number, the character Liza Jane is yaller, sweet, ole, and little, and the refrain connects to versions that began popping up as early as 1865, such as Johnny Tuers's "My Little Ole Liza Jane."

Many "Liza Jane" songs were billed as "comic ditties," and thus, the turn toward farm animals in the second stanza may correlate to humorous depictions of the girl being stubborn in the matter of love. In the first stanza, Liza Jane is clearly a "yaller gal" who recognizes her beau, but in the second stanza, she may be a mule or, more likely, a reluctant girl compared to a mule. Sense, of course, does not matter, and it may be folly to expect comprehensible arcs from song lyrics. Mercifully, the stanza returns to the language of sweetness, introducing words like "lasses" (for molasses) and "cane," both of which will continue to appear in subsequent country versions. For example, the great Mississippi John Hurt would record a "Liza Jane" snotch in 1963 with the following lyrics:

> I'm going up on the mountain
> To get me a load of cane
> Gonna make me a barrel of molasses
> Gonna sweeten ole Liza Jane[12]

Hurt's song is part of a medley entitled "Liza Jane (God's Unchanging Hand)." In many ways, the De Marsan and the Mississippi John Hurt versions correspond. The speaker in Hurt's version goes up on the mountain; he refers to harvesting cane and making molasses in order to sweeten Liza Jane, who, apparently, lacks warmth; Hurt, too, familiarizes the girl by employing the modifier "ole" as in "well known." These two versions are separated by more than eighty years, yet the traditional lyrics survive the journey. Given that De Marsan's songbook incorporated minstrel numbers, such as Frank Lum's variation of "Goodbye Liza Jane," it would be reasonable to assume this

uncredited variant had some relationship to postbellum minstrelsy. Lafcadio Hearn's report of the roustabout version in New Orleans preceded the
De Marsan publication by a few years, confirming that the language was already
in circulation among longshoremen traveling up and down the Mississippi
River area.

   Two or three years after the De Marsan songbook publication of "Hoop 'em
up 'Liza Jane," a man named Angus S. Hibbard published a peculiar three-act
"medley operetta" titled *Chic or Birds of a Feather*. The unpaginated front matter from 1883 describes the dramatis personae —a variety of plough boys, city
girls, dairy maids, city swells, et al.—and the setting; the operetta transpires
in gardens, a door yard, and "fence and roadway in rear." *Chic* may emulate
dramatic texts from antiquity as it contains ample verses to be sung in unison
and ample parts for choruses. It also peddles an air of gaiety as the "Plough
Boys" revel in their status as hayseeds: "Hurrah for the Country Boy," they
sing after crooning about their dead snail.[13] The "City Girls" enter before long,
and even when not singing, they deliver lines in sing-song verse: "And then
we'll try, without their feelings hurting / To show these boys what we know
about flirting."[14] And so Act I springs forward, in song and verse, until a dance
number brings down the curtain. As Act II gets underway, the audience can
hear the "City Boys—behind scenes." They are Black and are carrying on about
"de debbil [. . .] cutting down my apple tree" before remonstrating with one
another, "alla, alla, alla, alla lu yah!"[15] After a pause, however, one of the City
Boys changes the tone, promising to "lick" a rival over competition for the same
girl. He then sings or recites:

   Oh, Hoopo Liza, poor gal, Oh Hoopo Liza Jane,
   Oh, Hoopo Liza, poor gal, and she died on the train.[16]

The text then refers to the "City Boys" with a slur, and the operetta moves gaily
onward, but not before the glimpse of these lyrics, with the odd word "Hoopo"
capitalized as if it is part of Liza Jane's name. It is also unusual to sound out
"Hoopo" in the same line as "Oh" and "poor" since the word "Hoopo" sounds
like "oh poor" or "ooh po' Liza." In effect, it is like saying, "Oh, oh poor Liza,
poor gal, Oh oh poor Liza Jane." Since the author situates this little song with
the operetta's Black characters (who were likely played by whites), he may
be assigning them some dialectical soup that he, himself, could not fathom.
(Incidentally, "poor Liza, poor gal" may resemble the title of a song "Poor Rosy,
Poor Gal" that may date to 1862 or earlier.) Nonetheless the date stamp matters
greatly when tracing the progression of "Liza Jane" lyrics. *Chic* gives the earliest known references to the phrase "poor gal" as well as the notion of the Liza
Jane character dying on the train. Both conventions will be applied widely in

twentieth-century recordings, by musicians such as Bradley Kincaid and Pete Seeger, among many others.

While unlikely to be the ultimate source of these lines, *Chic* nevertheless stamps them 1883, thus establishing them as traditional lyrics well before the turn of the century. Nothing is known of the operetta's history, but the book was published in San Francisco and contained a goodly number of advertisements at the back for going concerns in San Francisco and Oakland, suggesting a well-financed local production in the San Francisco Bay Area. It might be reasonable to conclude that these lyrics were imported from a songster or from Bay Area minstrel shows, but no link has been discovered. According to the *Evening Star* (Washington, DC), Angus S. Hibbard may have been an A. T. & T. executive and an inventor. A brief obituary dated October 22, 1945, describes Hibbard as a pioneer engineer who was a native of Milwaukee.[17]

Just as the "Goodbye Liza Jane" variant rocketed around the minstrel stage, the pages of songbooks, and newspaper publications in the latter half of the nineteenth century, so did other members of the "Liza Jane" family, either as full songs or through the intrusion of the Liza Jane character into the refrains and stanzas of other ditties. Here are some selected appearances in the United States and abroad.

1870	*Cedar Falls Gazette* (Iowa), declares "Git along 'Liza Jane" beneath a drawing of a large rooster, upon completion of Burlington, Cedar Rapids, and Minnesota Railroad[18]
1870	*The Mercury*, Hobart, Tasmania, Australia, publishes advertisement for American Excelsior Minstrels appearing at Town Hall; included will be "My Little Old Eliza Jane"[19]
1871	Billy Birch sings "Liza Jane" for Birch, Wambold, Bernard & Backus San Francisco Minstrels, at 585 Broadway in New York[20]
1872	*The Mercury*, Hobart, Tasmania, Australia, publishes advertisement for Hobart Town Amateur Christy Minstrels; included will be "Negro Walk Around and Breakdown entitled 'Little Old Eliza Jane'"[21]
1873	Billy Birch sings "Comic Song—Liza Jane" for the San Francisco Minstrels at Hooley's Opera House in Brooklyn[22]
1873	*Daily Beacon* (Wichita, Kansas), advertisement for Wichita Theatre Variety Show includes mention of Johnny Reddeu singing "Liza Jane, My Liza"[23]

1874	Sam Howe sings "'Liza Jane" for the Ethiopian Dramatic Society, location unknown[24]
1874	Jimmy Mack sings "Eliza Jane" for Washington Minstrels at Beacon Hall in Somerville, Massachusetts[25]
1874	*South Australian Register*, Adelaide, advertisement for Great Barlow Troupe at Theater Royal; included will be "Plantation Festival of 'Little Old 'Liza Jane'"[26]
1874	*The Mercury*, Hobart, Tasmania, Australia, reviews performance by Nubian Minstrels at the Working Men's Club; included was "Little Old Liza Jane"[27]
1875	*Sydney Morning Herald*, Australia, advertisement for Monster Magnet Variety Troupe; included will be "plantation walk-around 'Ole 'Liza Jane'"[28]
1875	The character "Miss Liza Jane" appears in the song "Big Eye Rabbit," as published in *Harper & Stansill's Sweet June Rose Songster*[29]
1872–1876 (estimated)	Luke Schoolcraft sings "'Liza Jane" for Emerson's California Minstrels at the Olympic Theatre in New York[30]
1877	Billy Birch sings "Comic Song, Liza Jane" for San Francisco Minstrels at the San Francisco Minstrels' Opera House in New York[31]
1878–1879 (estimated)	The character "Miss Liza Jane" appears in the song "The Briar" as published in *Henry De Marsan's Comic & Sentimental Singers' Journal*, credited to James Mass[32]
1880	Luke Schoolcraft sings "'Liza Jane" for Megatherian Minstrels at Hooley's Theatre in Boston, Massachusetts[33]
Undated	Eph Horn Jr. sings "'Liza Jane" as part of the Female Minstrels at the Avenue Variety Theatre in Philadelphia[34]

The "Liza Jane" family appealed to troupes throughout Australia, who often situated the songs in "Part Third" of the minstrel show format. In the United States, the minstrel Luke Schoolcraft demonstrated a continued fondness for a range of "Liza Jane" songs; it is unknown whether these versions included any "Goodbye Liza Jane" lyrics, but Schoolcraft is documented as having performed various renditions of "Liza Jane" songs with different blackface minstrel troupes across many years. According to *Monarchs of Minstrelsy*, Billy Birch enjoyed a long onstage career from the 1840s until 1890. In 1857, he survived a shipwreck off the coast of South Carolina but eventually found his way to New York, where he spent the bulk of his career. As part of the San Francisco Minstrels, Birch performed at 585 Broadway from 1865 until 1872. From that point forward, he entered partnerships with other performers, including Birch, Wambold & Backus' Minstrels.[35] Clearly, he demonstrated a fondness for "Liza Jane." Collectively, the performances and publications of "Goodbye Liza Jane" and other branches of the "Liza Jane" family reached large audiences all over the country and the world, and this is well before the most popular variant—"Little Liza Jane"—fully entered the public sphere. As shall be seen, it was indeed spreading, in the background, as a beloved dance game. In the background, yes, but not quietly!

In 1918 and 1919, the musicologist Natalie Curtis Burlin published a four-book sequence entitled *Hampton Series, Negro Folk-Songs*, which she collected at Hampton Normal and Agricultural Institute. Located in southeastern Virginia on the Atlantic coast, Hampton Institute was founded in 1868 as a "pioneer industrial school for Negroes and Indians" in the wake of the Civil War.[36] As part of her foreword to *Book I*, Curtis Burlin explains, "These notations of Negro folk-songs are faithful efforts to place on paper an exact record of the old traditional plantation songs *as sung by Negroes*. The harmonies are the Negroes' own."[37] She seems to have spent considerable time on the campus, learning these songs from the students and the staff, but notes, "Nobody teaches Negro songs [at Hampton]."[38] Thus, she describes the singing as "spontaneous and natural" and portrays the campus as abuzz with song:

> All around the grounds at Hampton the visitor comes across little groups of students singing together under the trees, or humming harmonies to one another's songs as they go to their work at the shops or in the fields. Music is literally "in the air."[39]

Curtis Burlin presents the Hampton version of "'Liza-Jane" in *Book IV* of her series, which appeared in 1919. It plainly connects to the version of "Li'l Liza Jane," popularized by 1916 sheet music publication, but Curtis Burlin indicates that "harmonies for the old melodies have been more or less traditional at Hampton throughout the fifty years of the life of the school."[40] Her version follows below, but evidence to confirm the song's extensive history on campus can be found when flashing back to Hampton Normal and Agricultural Institute in 1886 for the annual report of General Samuel C. Armstrong, principal.[41]

First addressing enrollment, Armstrong notes, "Numbers have slightly increased, but are still close upon six hundred. Nearly one-fourth are Indians, and two-fifths are young women. All but twenty-three (day scholars) are boarders from abroad, representing thirteen States and territories; average age, eighteen years."[42] General Armstrong concentrates on the Black students when discussing the plights of those who have graduated: "Of the negro race, 576 have, since 1868, taken the full course, of whom 522 are now living. Of these over 90 per cent have taught school."[43] About half the teachers had been residing in Virginia; all the teachers, combined, had been teaching about "25,000 negro children"; other professions that Black graduates entered would include government service, farming, trades, ministry, law, medicine, and editing.[44] Owing to the presence of men and women on campus, many students married one another. Moreover, Armstrong observes, "The great majority have acquired property."[45]

General Armstrong describes a typical day in which "the boys fall into their military companies for inspection, and the girls go to some house hold work, which is to help pay their school bill. From 8:40 to 12 they are passing constantly from one class to another."[46] Of course, Curtis Burlin could not have known, having visited the school more than twenty-five years later, but Armstrong indicates that singing had been taught, at least during his tenure at the school: "The noon recess, which lasts from 12 to 1:30, has during the winter been the only time found available for classes [for those] who were anxious to learn to sing by note, and these gave readily twenty minutes of their recess for this purpose."[47] The Hampton schedule was relatively grueling, with additional courses, military drills, cooking lessons (for the girls), chapel prayers, and study hours concluding by 9:00 p.m., shortly before the "retiring bell" sounded, at which point, judging from Armstrong's account, most of the students probably fell into bed exhausted.[48]

The principal details the curricula of Hampton's divisions—the Normal School (the main school), the Night School, the Indian School, and the Butler School (for young children)—before turning to "Home and Social Life."[49] As a former military man, he continues to make reference to inspections and cleanliness of rooms, drilling, and the like, but also describes the establishment of libraries and "base ball" contests between "the Normal School nine and neighboring clubs."[50] In all, Armstrong portrays a very regimented system. This would have left little time for other diversions, but the principal does elaborate upon eagerly anticipated social evenings: "At such times surprising articles of finery are brought out of mysterious places, the poorest student looks neat in his clean linen, and on some extraordinary occasions a dress coat even has been seen."[51] There, General Armstrong turns to renditions of songs and reveals precious information, writing:

The old time plays of "Little Liza Jane" and "Rain a Little, Snow a Little," have decreased in popularity of late, and have given way to what are considered more genteel games or to the aristocratic promenade. The chief characteristics of these old games was the singing of a weird refrain—"Rain a little, snow a little; ain't goin' to rain no more"; or, "O, little Liza, little Liza Jane, come with me across the sea, little Liza Jane"—repeated *ad infinitum*, and accompanied by a great clapping of hands and shuffling of feet and snatching of partners. Oddly enough the Indians have adopted these discarded games of their colored brothers and sisters, and play them with great zest and enjoyment.[52]

By introducing them as "plays," Armstrong probably classifies these two pieces as "game songs" or as "play party songs"; the latter category will be developed in a future chapter. If, in 1886, he refers to "Little Liza Jane" as an "old time" song, then the song's presence probably dates back many years at the school. General Armstrong is widely acknowledged by many sources, including historian Robert Francis Engs, as being the school's founder and first principal and, therefore, in possession of firsthand institutional knowledge. While Armstrong refers to each of these two old singing games as having "a weird refrain," these songs seem to have grown on him and left him perhaps a bit disappointed in their fluctuating popularity among the Black students. Notably, the Native American students, with "great zest and enjoyment," adopted the tunes and may have contributed to their preservation, even as the African American students (at the time) might have regarded them as passé.

Yet Armstrong's writings allow substantial insights into performance rituals, lyrics, and potential origins. To begin, "Little Liza Jane" was enacted as a stealing partners dance game, with "great clapping of hands and shuffling of feet and snatching of partners." Virtually all the WPA respondents mentioned similarities in title or performance rituals, including, for instance, Marshall Butler ("Little Liza Jane"—title), Lucy Thurston ("Little Liza Jane"—title), Lawrence Evans ("Run Liza Jane"—dance game), and Lydia Jefferson ("Catch Liza Jane"—ring game). The title is given plainly, without words that minstrelsy might have affixed to it, such as "my" and "ole." By mentioning the line "come with me across the sea," Armstrong creates another compelling link to Robert Burns, whose eighteenth-century poem "Farewell to Eliza" conjures "boundless oceans, roaring wide" between the speaker and his love, Eliza. It is humorous to imagine General Armstrong being irritated by the refrains repeating *ad infinitum*; he is careful to italicize that Latinate phrase to emphasize his miffed reaction, but ultimately, the man also would seem to be longing for those clapping and dancing games, as he observed the students having high-spirited fun. Armstrong may have observed a pure version of the tune, a rendition that appears to be a "snotch" of folk material or what might be considered a one-verse song. Of course, "Little Liza Jane" was not the only song the General observed in this context, but also "Rain a Little, Snow a Little," which also presents with one-verse properties.

According to Engs's biographical work, *Educating the Disfranchised and Disinherited*, the General first served as an officer "in the 125th New York Regiment, and then in the 8th and 9th Regiments of the United States Colored Troops."[53] Eventually promoted to the rank of colonel and then in command of the Eighth United States Colored Troops Regiment, Armstrong and his men were present at the surrender of the Confederate army on April 9, 1865, at Appomattox Court House.[54] In 1866, at the conclusion of his wartime service, Armstrong was "confirmed in his rank of brevet brigadier general and forever thereafter would be known as 'the General.'"[55] On April 6, 1868, the General opened Hampton Normal and Agricultural Institute. It consisted of "an old army barracks, the remnants of Chesapeake Army Hospital, and the decrepit mansion house of the former Little Scotland Plantation."[56]

In fact, as Engs illustrates, the grounds of the Hampton Institute were situated near the "Grand Contraband Camp," a large site housing freed or runaway enslaved people. As Engs points out, "A significant portion of the early student body were the offspring of the 'contraband' at wartime Hampton."[57] Thus, it is always possible that the "Liza Jane" family came into the General's orbit through the young adult children of "contrabands" who camped nearby the grounds of what would become the Hampton Institute. Other Virginians, such as poet Daniel Webster Davis and singer George W. Johnson wrote of or sang a "Liza Jane" song; Lafcadio Hearn also mentioned Virginia as the source of many roustabouts who toiled and sang a "Liza Jane" song on the New Orleans levee. The Pee Dee Guards and the Forty-Third USCT Regiment marched to Spotsylvania Court House with "Liza Jane" songs in their repertory; thus, the family of folk songs may have been known to many Virginians before arriving at Hampton Institute. Officially, General Armstrong's date-stamped recollection places "Little Liza Jane" in Virginia in 1886, well before the variant enjoyed mainstream popularity. It is anybody's guess how long General Armstrong had been forced to hear the refrain *ad infinitum*, yet by categorizing the song as an "old time play," Armstrong suggests quite a while.

As if to confirm General Armstrong's remarks about singing at Hampton Institute, the very next year saw the publication of *Lend a Hand: A Journal of Organized Philanthropy*, edited by Edward E. Hale and dated January 1887. In this issue, a report is made from Hampton, where "Our Indian Lend a Hand Club is just entering upon its third year."[58] The report refers to "the Indian school," which would suggest the club members and the Native American students at Hampton Institute may have represented an overlapping population.[59] Either way, the report makes special mention of one Saturday, during which "the boys are invited to Winona (Elder Sisters' Lodge) and entertained by the girls and teachers."[60] Quiet students could find diversions with games like checkers and dominoes, while the more outgoing students take up livelier games.[61] The uncredited author notes that dancing is forbidden at the club but that the "more frisky members of the club have a game called 'Steal Pardners,' learned from the colored people, in which the clapping of hands and the lively singing of a jingle, the burden of which is,

> O, Eliza, little 'Liza Jane,
> Come my love and go with me,
> Little 'Liza Jane,

takes the place of more conventional music. After singing these words a few hundred times, they break off into another strain—Rain little, snow little, / 'Taint gwine to rain no mo', / O rain little, snow little, / 'Taint gwine to rain no mo',—until they are tired out and then they want to 'march.'"[62] And the festivities continue. The author confirms the General's account of "Little Liza Jane" lyrics and performance rituals but offers slightly different lyrics and emphasizes a rowdy recital without dancing. "Rain Little, Snow Little" pops up again, as well. It is possible that Armstrong himself is the uncredited author.

Given his appointment as an officer among two regiments of United States Colored Troops and his interactions with hundreds of African American students, it would seem unlikely for General Armstrong to have misapprehended any of these lyrics, such as mistaking "Little Liza" for "Eliza." It is possible, even likely, "Eliza" and "little Liza" were regular substitutes for one another, especially if "little Liza" was condensed to "li'l Liza," thereby matching the syllabic beat of the name "Eliza." Similarly, it is likely "Come my love and go with me" could have substituted for "Come with me across the sea," although the former was a stock line; a version of its phrasing dates to at least 1845 as part of the minstrelsy standard "Going Ober de Mountain."[63] The line also turned up in the song "Kemo Kimo" from *The Bold Soldier Boy's Songbook*.[64] Indeed, Armstrong might be forgiven for his "*ad infinitum*" remark if the lyrics were traditionally sung, as indicated in the Native American account, a few hundred times! While it may be an exaggeration to suggest a little three-line song was recited hundreds of times, this offers additional evidence that the song was performed in a one-verse or "snotch" format. The repetition would be enjoyable to the singer and the listener alike, per the sage Duke Ellington, if the lines were agreeable to the ear. The Lend a Hand report confirms Armstrong's information of the song being transmitted from the African American students to the Native American students, thereby documenting another cultural boundary crossed by the "Liza Jane" family.

Roughly seven years later, Volume XXII, Number 5 of the *Southern Workman and Hampton School Record* came out dated May 1894. It describes itself as a "sixteen page monthly" with additional information that it is "Printed on the Normal School Steam Press by Negro and Indian students trained in the office."[65] The *Workman* and the *Record* appear together and "report work for and progress of the Black and Red races of our country."[66] In this issue, the editors refer to May being the "anniversary month of General Armstrong's departure [and how] it will give tender pleasure to many to find once more in our columns, one of his characteristic talks to his students."[67] By "departure," the writer would have meant death, as the General had passed away in May 1893. In his book, Engs relates the onset and seriousness of Armstrong's illness: "A stroke in 1891 had left him paralyzed on one side. His third attack, in May 1893, had killed him."[68]

The General seems to have enjoyed strong rapport among the student body, and upon the one-year anniversary of his death, the school publication eventually turns to one of Armstrong's favorite topics, namely folk music, and in particular, the full printing of "Mrs. Spennie's paper on games, read before the April meeting of the Folk-Lore Society."[69] Indeed, Mrs. Spennie's paper establishes, foremost, the popularity of "Miss Liza Jane, Miss Liza Jane, / Where did you get your money?"[70] And if this were not enough, the very next game mentioned would be "Rain little bit, snow little bit / 'Taint going rain no more."[71] The "Liza Jane" song differs from the variant first reported at Hampton Institute by the General, but continued references imply a strong tradition of "Liza Jane" songs known at the school. Even as the variants reported at Hampton and Lend a Hand Club may have attached some stock phrasing, they do not resemble the lengthier, organized trademarks of minstrelsy songs. Instead, it is almost certain they were being put forward with singing and dancing rituals in the estimation of their original formats, with "snotches" and single verses being attached to the girl's name, Little Liza Jane, Eliza Jane, or Miss Liza Jane.

Natalie Curtis Burlin created her *Hampton Series* for the benefit of the school, stating, at the bottom of each cover, "All royalties from the sale of these books go to Hampton Institute, Virginia, for the benefit of Negro education."[72] African American song obviously stirred her, and in her exuberance, she may have attributed certain musical powers, almost supernatural, to the singers she encountered. Her critics would, according to historian Michelle Wick Patterson, "accuse her of racial essentialism, which clouded her accomplishments as a folk music collector."[73] Curtis Burlin's death at a relatively young age precluded an opportunity "to refine her viewpoints or publicly reflect on her career or its meanings."[74] Writing in the biographical work *Natalie Curtis Burlin*, Patterson rightly asserts that the musicologist cannot be dismissed "as a minor figure in the history of ethnomusicology and American thought."[75] On the contrary, her *Hampton Series* represents a remarkable achievement in documenting African American folk songs at an institution with a close connection to the people of the Civil War era. This folk music collection may have fulfilled, more broadly speaking, "her search for an identity as an American,"[76] as Patterson writes, or in Curtis Burlin's own words, from the introduction to *Book III*, the need to be called back to "that youth of natural poetry and song."[77]

Book I and *Book II* present nonsecular songs such as "Go Down, Moses" and "O Ev'ry Time I Feel de Spirit." Curtis Burlin switches to work songs in *Book III*, focusing on three pieces related to cotton harvest and another related to corn shucking. The first three volumes were published in 1918, while *Book IV* appeared in 1919 and devoted itself to a mixture of work, folk, and play songs. Its table of contents contains "Peanut-Pickin' Song," "Hammerin' Song," "Lullaby," and a vibrant trio—"Chicka-Hanka," "Hyah Rattler!" and "Old Rags, Bottles, Rags!"—featuring sounds, animals, and objects, before concluding with "'Liza-Jane."[78] In the Foreword to *Book IV*, Curtis Burlin remarks on the illumining properties of African American song, and in associating these properties with the Ralph Waldo Emerson essay "The Over-Soul," proposes a question: "The Negro 'Over-Soul'—is it Music?"[79]

Curtis Burlin establishes "'Liza-Jane" as a dance game and a "stealin' partners" ring game, confirming the details reported by General Armstrong and the Lend a Hand Club. The game depends upon there being an extra male dancer who dances by himself in the middle of a circle. Couples dance around him, and as part of the game, he "steals" a partner from one of the men in the circle. The odd man, now deprived of a mate, becomes the solo dancer in the middle of the ring, whose performance "is adorned with elaborate, loose-jointed pattering steps, while stamps, turns and flings add emphasis to the throbbing accentuation of the music."[80] Curtis Burlin establishes the song as being old but notes that recent additions—such as Brussels carpets and silver door-plates—have modernized its lyrics.[81] These updated lyrics may derive from sheet music publications in the twentieth century as well as the contributions of African American soldiers who served in World War I, some of whom joined in the singing. Curtis Burlin delineates the backgrounds of the singers by writing:

> The "Peanut-Pickin' Song" and the "Hammerin' Song" were sung for me by Ira Goodwin, Joseph Barnes, William Cooper and Timothy Carper, all Hampton students; but in the singing of the "Lullaby" and "'Liza-Jane" the quartet was augmented by James E. Scott, Page Lancaster, Benjamin Davis and other young men who "dropped in" during recreation hours at the school to add their voices and their sunny laughter to this work of record. Most of these "boys" who sang so gaily and lightheartedly and danced as they sang, answered their country's call and went singing into the service of the United States Army.[82]

In fact, a version of "Li'l Liza Jane" was included in the 1918 *Army Song Book*.[83] More on the World War I thread will be explored in a future chapter, but suffice it to say the "Liza Jane" song Curtis Burlin experienced at Hampton Institute had been updated from the form reported by General Armstrong. She cites "the fantasy and extravaganza of loosened high spirits, verses improvised," and "the shouted chorus" as components that influence "the hilarious fun of the song."[84] Even as she presents organized lyrics and musical notation, Curtis Burlin acknowledges the improvisational elements of singing and dancing which accompany the ring game.

The following lyrics appear in *Book IV* of Curtis Burlin's *Hampton Series*, with a 1919 publication date.

'LIZA-JANE
Dance-Game Song
("Stealin' Partners")

Come ma love an' go wid me, L'il' 'Liza-Jane,
Come ma love an' go wid me, L'il' 'Liza-Jane,

    O Eliza, L'il' 'Liza-Jane,
      O Eliza, L'il' 'Liza-Jane.

I got a house in Baltimo', L'il' 'Liza-Jane,
Street-car runs right by ma do', L'il' 'Liza-Jane.

    O Eliza, L'il' 'Liza-Jane,
      O Eliza, L'il' 'Liza-Jane.

I got a house in Baltimo', L'il' 'Liza-Jane,
Brussels carpet on de flo', L'il' 'Liza-Jane.

    O Eliza, L'il' 'Liza-Jane,
      O Eliza, L'il' 'Liza-Jane.

I got a house in Baltimo', L'il' 'Liza-Jane,
Silver door-plate on de do', L'il' 'Liza-Jane.

    O Eliza, L'il' 'Liza-Jane,
      O Eliza, L'il' 'Liza-Jane.[85]

"O Miss 'Liza" sometimes substitutes, according to Curtis Burlin, for "O Eliza."[86] The line "Come ma love an' go wid me" reappears; its association with the "Liza Jane" family had been first reported in the Lend a Hand Club narrative from 1887. Yet by this point, newfangled lyrics had been adopted by singers, reflecting the song's growing popularity and adoption by Black soldiers in World War I. These lyrics additionally emphasize home ownership, which may be a reason for the young woman to follow the suitor, and they also describe an urban existence in Baltimore, which acknowledges the great migration of poor Blacks (and whites) from small-town environs to population centers. Additionally, the word "Baltimore" offers straight rhyme destinations for the words "door" and "floor." Therefore, the addition of "Baltimore" may have been agreeable to the ear.

Inevitably, the two original "old time plays" first identified by General Armstrong in 1886—"Rain a Little, Snow a Little" and "Little Liza Jane"—had been joined together by Hampton students, and Curtis Burlin prints this version as well (along with musical notation).

> I got a house in Baltimo'—'Tain't gwineter rain no mo'
> Silver plate on de do'—'Tain't gwineter rain no mo'.
> O Eliza, L'il' 'Liza-Jane,
> O Eliza, L'il' 'Liza-Jane!
> Steadfast, lady, steadfast, 'Tain't gwineter rain no mo'.
> Steadfast, lady, steadfast, 'Tain't gwineter rain no mo'.
> O Eliza, L'il' 'Liza-Jane,
> O Eliza, L'il' 'Liza-Jane![87]

This would seem like a natural outcome for two songs with such a lengthy, side-by-side record of performance, or perhaps it had always been the case—namely, these two "snotches" may have drifted together on social nights at Hampton Institute by clapping, shouting students who had been stealing dance partners all evening. Though untitled, Curtis Burlin associates the hybrid version with "'Liza-Jane," and its appearance further cements the sense of "Liza Jane" songs as proliferating or branching at every opportunity. They incorporate the lyrics of other songs, restlessly improvising and evolving alongside the energy of the singers, musicians, and dancers who exult boisterously in their refrains. Here, the somewhat fractal examination of the "Liza Jane" family has leaped forward a couple of decades, with the purpose of connecting most of the extensive history of "Li'l Liza Jane" at Hampton Institute—and will return to Hampton before long—but now the lens returns to the nineteenth century.

In 1890, a New Englander named Mary Olmsted Clarke published a short article in the *Journal of American Folklore* entitled "Song-Games of Negro Children in Virginia." Recounted by "a colored servant, born in Virginia [. . .]

These games," Clarke writes, "are played by as many children as possible in some open field or common, and generally towards the close of day."[88] The singing players would form a circle, with one or more children located in the center, "and as far as possible suiting the action of the body to the words."[89] Only introducing it by writing, "The following seems to be a curious medley:—," Clarke offers lyrics for a song that might be otherwise titled "Go on, Liza Jane." The lyrics, in their entirety, are given as:

> Go on, Lize,
> Go on, Liza Jane,
> The funniest thing I ever saw,
> Buffalo kick off bell-cow's horn;
> Go on, Liza Jane.
>
> Go on, Lize,
> Go on, Lize,
> Go on, Liza Jane,
> The funniest thing I ever saw,
> The black cat skipping chine-e-o;
> Go on, Liza Jane.
>
> Go on, Lize,
> Go on, Lize,
> Go on, Liza Jane,
> I'll tell my mother when I get home,
> The boys won't let the girls alone;
> Go on, Liza Jane.[90]

The inclusion of a "Liza Jane" variant in Clarke's article adds emphasis to the state of Virginia as enjoying a rich tradition with the "Liza Jane" family of songs. Appearing only four years after General Armstrong's annual report to the State of Virginia, Clarke's transcription of the song, coupled with the reported performance rituals, suggests sturdy linkage to the "Git Along, Liza Jane" (or "Get along") songs.

Through the hijinks of cow and buffalo, the song refers to an agrarian environment, and through its reference to "The black cat skipping chine-e-o," the song may echo the phrase "Kitty Kimeo," from a version of the antebellum song "Kemo Kimo." Even as the piece is rendered in standard English and not in dialect, Clarke differentiates between "Lize" and "Liza." Many "Liza Jane" songs employ more than one variation of the girl's name, perhaps commenting on regional variances of speech or even the prevalence of nicknames. The specific mention of game songs, as well as the establishment of a circle, underscores the likelihood of "go on"—as well as "go along," "get along," "git along," and "g'lang"—as emblematic of dance calls or dance instructions. To be sure, the song depends upon snatches of folk matter. It presents only three couplets outside the refrain structure, and even one of those lines repeats.

Three years later, the *Journal of American Folklore* published a short article by Lila W. Edmands titled "Songs from the Mountains of North Carolina," which also purports to represent the mountaineers of Tennessee. In this 1893 piece, Edmands provides a glimpse into the folk music traditions of people who are isolated by their habitat. The musicians would turn toward these songs, according to her, "during long winter evenings and stormy days" when there was little else to accomplish, not even gossip.[91] Edmands indicates that the musicians picked homemade banjos, and the singers delivered the lyrics in "nasal tones." She also describes performances in which the musical interlude between stanzas "sometimes exceeds the length of the measures sung."[92] Her first example of this music cites a member of the "Liza Jane" family, and its lyrics are presented, in their entirety, as follows:

'Liza Jane

1.
When I go a ridin',
I take the railroad train;
But when I go a courtin',
I take sweet 'Liza Jane.

2.
When I go a fishin',
I take my hook and line;
But when I go a courtin',
I take that gal o' mine.

3.
You climb up the oak tree,
I'll climb up the gum,—
I never see a pretty gal
But what I love her some.

4.
I wish I had a needle and thread
As fine as I could sew,

I'd sew my true love to my side,
And down the road we'd go.

    5.

You go ride the old gray horse,
I'll go ride the roan;
You hug and kiss your gal,
I'll hug and kiss my own.

    6.

The jay bird and the "sparrer,"
They both came down together,
They flew through the briar patch,
And never lost a feather.

    7.

I wish I was in heaven,
Sittin' in the big arm "chere,"
With one arm round a whiskey barrel,
And t' other round my dear.

    8.

She went down the new cut road,
I went down the lane,
A heavy load and a sorry team
To drive out 'Liza Jane.[93]

An early source of Appalachian folk music tradition, Edmands presents a "Liza Jane" song with a lengthier run of lyrics than the few prior country versions, including Lafcadio Hearn's levee song. This rendition offers eight quatrains with no refrain. In fact, Edmands references the Liza Jane character only twice, except when her presence is conjured by words—"gal," "love," and "dear"— somewhat maddening in their lack of specificity. This decentralized form presages the formation of other like-minded forms, even Uncle Am Stuart's 1924 recording of "Old Liza Jane." His song, discussed below, more obviously devotes itself to the namesake character even though it, too, operates outside the realm of stanza-refrain regularity.

    Differing from Mary Olmsted Clarke's report involving ring games, Edmands relates performance rituals unintended for outdoor dance games but for entertainment during bleak periods of isolation due to harsh weather. The lyrics depend upon some familiar phrases and formulas, with reverberations from earlier traditions rippling through the song. Perhaps the greatest such "ripple" will involve the "new cut road" and "the lane," although the formula of "you do this" and "I'll do that" also applies to "You climb up the oak tree, / I'll climb up the gum" as well as "You go ride the old gray horse, / I'll go ride the roan." If the mention of an "old gray horse" does not evoke Sam Chatmon singing about the "old grey mule," then perhaps the "heavy load and a sorry team" will recall the mule for sale in the uncredited ditty, "Hoop 'em up 'Liza Jane," from Henry De Marson's journal. At its center, the Edmands "Liza Jane" variant represents a courtship piece touching on the "railroad train," sweetness, and whiskey, common themes that will multiply during the next century. The North Carolina (and Tennessee) singers follow numerous predecessors when concluding the song with disappointment; in the eighth stanza, Liza Jane is being driven out. This decidedly unromantic result clashes with the hopeful vision of the speaker sewing his true love to his side, "and down the road we'd go." One wonders about the tone of those final lines. With the wintry Appalachian winds whipping the shutters of mountaintop homes, would the singers carouse with garrulous humor or underscore the failed courtship with a sage appraisal of life's sobering cruelties?

The Edmands version introduces some words—the hook and line of fishing; the oak tree and the gum; the needle and thread of sewing; the jaybird and the "sparrer"; and the mention of sitting in heaven—not otherwise associated with the nineteenth century "Liza Jane" songs. Sludge may prevail when attempting to divine the origins of this word hoard. To paraphrase Amiri Baraka / LeRoi Jones: there may be no way of unpacking the hopelessly gray fabric of these lyrics, with some suggestion of minstrel influence (which may be both Black and white), some suggestion of African American input, and ultimately, white performance on lonely mountaintops. Organized and reported by a white woman, these lyrics undoubtedly have been shaped by many cultural forces.

Minstrelsy carried many "Liza Jane" songs into large auditoriums, popularizing the refrains often through a comic presentation. As noted, especially with respect to "Goodbye Liza Jane" variants, the reach of this activity extended to at least four continents, with demonstrable saturation in large American cities. Yet other variants enjoyed similar fanfare, with some famed singers such as Luke Schoolcraft developing a specialty with a range of songs in the "Liza Jane" family. Quite importantly, the family of songs maintained discernible traditions offstage as well, outside the standard three-part format of the minstrel show.

African American students at Hampton Institute performed "Little Liza Jane" for decades, with relentless repetition that impressed their principal, both irking and charming him. Native Americans at the same institution adopted the tune, and eventually, a modernized version appeared in Natalie Curtis Burlin's survey of folklore, the *Hampton Series*, which even demonstrated how two different tunes—"Li'l Liza Jane" and "Rain a Little, Snow a Little"—merged together. Curtis Burlin chronicled just one institution, in one state, one town, and one group of buildings, where young people had clapped, shouted, and stolen dance partners. There were likely other such places.

In any event, the improvisational dance game rituals of "Little Liza Jane" may have been poorly suited for the "organized burlesque" of minstrelsy. While some titles of minstrel numbers—"My Little Ole Liza Jane," for instance—contain the same words, there is scant evidence that they were, in fact, preserving the characteristics reported by General Armstrong, the Lend a Hand Club, and Curtis Burlin. To the contrary, the essential character of "Little Liza Jane" appears to have traveled intact toward the twentieth century as a one-line folk tune, with heavy dependence on "snatches of folk material" and improvised performance rituals. A minstrel song such as "My Little Ole Liza Jane" may have derived from a related "snotch," but clearly, as exemplified by Billy Emerson's 1866 songster rendition of "Eliza Jane," it would have been distinctly altered from its source material. With likely roots among enslaved people, "Little Liza Jane" or "Li'l Liza Jane" may have transferred to the Hampton Institute through students who had arrived from the "Grand Contraband Camp" just outside the school's grounds.

Importantly, Lila Edmands checked in from Appalachia in the early 1890s, where a "Liza Jane" variant had associated itself with a relatively new suite of country lyrics. In the mid-1870s, a New Orleans roustabout song had begun to adopt similar qualities, and as these boatmen traveled the waterways, singing loudly, they could have easily influenced travelers on a variety of tributaries far to the north. Lafcadio Hearn's report from the levee gave evidence of a peculiar "mongrel" version of the song, captured halfway between "Goodbye Liza Jane" and what today might be known as old-time lyrics. Undoubtedly, at the time Edmands published her article, many "Liza Jane" songs must have been swirling around in the stormy Appalachian Mountains. Mostly though, her report demonstrates how the "Liza Jane" family persevered in a harsh climate among a few hardy souls far from the flickering minstrel spotlight.

INTERMISSION NUMBER TWO

The Literary "Liza Jane" of Charles Chesnutt, Jean Toomer, and Margaret Walker

1898 / 1923 / 1966

As the nineteenth century wore on, "Liza Jane" songs materialized in widely circulated songbooks, such as the 1882 Oliver Ditson collection, *Minstrel Songs, Old and New.*[1] Someone lingering at the bookshelf might wonder if "Goodbye Liza Jane" or another variant enjoyed any kind of special relationship to other suites of thick publications, namely, works of fiction. Had a character from an American novel become the girl in the song? On the other hand, what if a variant or its namesake character drifted *into* a work of literature? What more could be learned about the "poor gal" if she became a fictional character or if "Liza Jane" lyrics were sung in a fictional setting?

To begin, the "Liza Jane" family of songs does not look to have origins in American fiction. Speculation could be focused on Harriet Beecher Stowe's 1852 antislavery novel, *Uncle Tom's Cabin*, which features a character named Eliza. There is even a brief mention of a character named "Eliza Jane" who was "taken" by a cough, an observation made to emphasize the beginnings of an illness in the young child, Eva.[2] Deep into the plot, the character Eliza, who has run away from the plantation, meets up with her husband, George. When Eliza remarks that the couple is within twenty-four hours of the Canadian border, George draws her towards himself, exclaiming, "O, Eliza!"[3] On its face, this exclamation resembles the shouted beginning of the "Little Liza Jane" chorus. Such examples are tantalizing and represent a small portion of the primordial "sludge" orbiting the "Liza Jane" family, but it is important to observe that none of these details involves the revelation of lyrics or singing. It is more likely the Robert Burns poem "Farewell to Eliza" and the minstrel standard "Susan Jane" influenced the formation of "Liza Jane" songs since their lyrics were in wide circulation as *lyrics*, as opposed to character names (and exclamations thereof) in a book of prose.

Minstrel troupes also staged plays or musicals in addition to song and dance. Among them could be found endless ill-fitting adaptations of *Uncle Tom's Cabin*. The cultural historian Eric Lott devotes a chapter, "Uncle Tomitudes," to this phenomenon in his study of minstrelsy, *Love & Theft*. Lott describes the "improbable political geometry" of the performer T. D. Rice, who played the celebrated, stereotypical Jim Crow persona, yet later in his career, the sympathetic role of Uncle Tom.[4] No doubt, the character Eliza would have been seen by large audiences over the course of numerous productions. Yet the names Eliza, Liza, and Jane in antebellum fictional works, plays, and even songs do not demonstrably cross from white literary and minstrel efforts to the culture of enslaved people and reemerge reformulated as an entire suite of folk songs. As noted above, if one source—such as the Scottish poet Robert Burns—did contribute the name "Eliza," with the other half of the name supplied from the minstrel song "Susan Jane," this fusion would not suddenly generate lyrics, performance rituals, dance steps, clapping, finger snapping, instrumentation choices, and melody for a tune sung by enslaved people. It would not generate multiple variants.

While nothing obvious connects antebellum American literary works to the formation of "Liza Jane" lyrics, the reverse is a different story. Characters named Liza Jane did turn up in pieces of fiction after the family of songs had developed and spread. A close reading of the text would be required to differentiate between, simply, a character named Liza Jane and one who may have displayed traits of the often-stubborn gal whose name populates so many songs. For example, Charles Chesnutt's widely studied short story, "The Wife of His Youth," first published in 1898 as part of a collection, *The Wife of His Youth And Other Stories of the Color Line*, situates a man named Mr. Ryder in a "Northern city" that may resemble Chesnutt's native Cleveland.[5] The fictional Ryder leads a group known as the Blue Vein Society, whose membership "consisted of individuals who were, generally speaking, more white than black." Or, in other words, "white enough to show blue veins."[6] A stationery clerk for a railroad company, Ryder maintains a well-furnished residence "containing among other things a good library, especially rich in poetry, a piano, and some choice engravings."[7] The through-action of the story involves Ryder throwing a ball in honor of his sweetheart, a wealthy young widow named Mrs. Molly Dixon, who had taught school in Washington, DC. During the ball, which would be given for members of the Blue Veins, Ryder would propose marriage.[8]

The afternoon of the ball, a woman arrives at Ryder's residence. She is described in unflattering terms, being less than five feet tall, having a face "crossed and recrossed with a hundred wrinkles," and being "very black—so black that her toothless gums" were not red but blue.[9] Chesnutt adds, "She looked like a bit of the old plantation life."[10] She has approached Ryder, she indicates, because she heard he was a "big man" and had lived in the area for a long time. Speaking in a thick dialect, the woman asks if Ryder knows her husband, a "merlatter man by de name er Sam Taylor," and gives her name as 'Liza Jane.[11] At Ryder's invitation, 'Liza Jane tells her life story. She describes the hardships of slavery, including an episode in which she helps her husband, Sam Taylor, escape the threat of being sold into slavery; he, as a free man to begin with, promised to return and help 'Liza Jane escape her actual enslavement. This had been twenty-five years earlier.[12] "I'se be'n lookin' fer 'im eber sence," the woman says, "an' I knows he's be'n lookin' fer me."[13] A great contrast has been set up by Chesnutt to this point in the story: the very Black woman, battered by slavery, set against the light-skinned members of the Blue Vein Society, who will attend a well-appointed ball during which the vibrant, attractive Molly Dixon will presumably accept an offer of marriage from the main character.

Ryder tries to convince 'Liza Jane that her husband may be dead or married to another woman, but the visitor rejects these possibilities, insisting upon Taylor's morality.[14] She has been searching for him in many cities, supporting herself as a cook.[15] 'Liza Jane shows Ryder a daguerreotype of the man and gives Ryder her address before she departs. After she departs, Ryder "went upstairs to his bedroom, and stood for a long time before the mirror of his dressing-case, gazing thoughtfully at the reflection of his own face."[16] It is thus implied that Ryder is 'Liza Jane's husband, Sam Taylor, from twenty-five years earlier. The ball goes forward, with the dancing getting underfoot at half past nine and supper scheduled for eleven o'clock. During the festivities, Ryder makes an important, if brief, disappearance.[17] Later, when a guest speaker calls upon him to address the gathering, and in particular, to celebrate "the ladies," Ryder unexpectedly describes 'Liza Jane's search and conjures the potential differences between the husband she seeks and herself—social standing, skin color—as well as the nonbinding status of their slave marriage.[18] Ryder continues to move the speech toward his own circumstances, "absolutely safe from recognition or discovery, unless he chose to reveal himself."[19] Finally, Ryder asks the attendees if, in this hypothetical situation, the man should reveal himself to the woman who sought him. The Blue Veins are moved by his talk, but none perhaps more than Molly Dixon, who "had listened with parted lips and streaming eyes."[20] She is the first person to answer him and declares, "He should have acknowledged her," while the other attendees agree.[21] At this point, Ryder leads 'Liza Jane into the ballroom, with her wearing "the white cap of an elderly woman." He then introduces her to everyone as "the wife of his youth."[22]

In some ways, the narrative arc of the story runs contrary to the basic narrative of the standard "Liza Jane" song, in which a woman of courtship age refuses to give her hand in marriage or displays other sassy, obstinate, comically unsweet behavior. The man pursues her, not the other way around. More than one scholarly appraisal of the story deems that Ryder conclusively accepts 'Liza Jane as his wife as if she proposed to him. Janet Mohr, in her article "Charles Chesnutt's Women," writes that "[Ryder] feels guilty for not having searched longer for her and accepts her as his legal wife."[23] In Mohr's estimation, "'Liza Jane thus gains the status of the black bourgeoisie through her persistence and her unwillingness to accept a lower social status."[24] Another take can be found in Tanfer Emin Tunc's article "The De(con)struction of Black/White Binaries: Critiques of Passing in Charles Waddell Chesnutt's *The Wife of His Youth and Other Stories of the Color Line*." In his analysis, Tunc weighs the relative luxury of Mr. Ryder emulating white people against an acknowledgment of plantation blackness. "While Ryder could have lived the rest of his life benefitting from the comforts and privileges of near-white existence, he fulfills his moral duty and honorably acknowledges the wife of his youth."[25]

Were the story to continue, Ryder might forfeit his status among the Blue Veins, a group Chesnutt obviously satirizes in "The Wife of His Youth." By closing, however, with Ryder leading 'Liza Jane into the ball and giving the other attendees no opportunity to acknowledge their own relationship to blackness, Chesnutt dooms them to their "white-face" existence, trapped in a cycle of attempting to appear as white as possible, as if they were minstrel performers in reverse. And what of the possibility that Chesnutt may have chosen the character name 'Liza Jane after encountering a "Liza Jane" variant? The story does involve a separation tale, and the name may have been, on the one hand, agreeable to the ear, but on the other hand, the character does display a good bit of distinctive obstinacy in her lengthy quest to recapture the relationship with her husband. In some "Liza Jane" renditions, the singer humorously portrays the "poor gal" in physically halting terms. For instance, this excerpt from Sandburg's *The American Songbag* likens the "Liza Jane" character to domestic items:

> Head Is like a coffee pot,
> Nose is like a spout,
> Her mouth is like an old fire-place,
> With the ashes all raked out.[26]

Ryder's initial appraisal of 'Liza Jane, while not crass, does focus on ideals of beauty that the woman cannot meet, being somewhat broken-down by her age and her station in life. Moreover, if Chesnutt had acquired any special knowledge of the song's origins, then he did associate the background of the woman, 'Liza Jane, and perhaps the song with slavery "down in ole Missoura."[27]

There is good reason to suspect Chesnutt's choice of a name in connection to the "Liza Jane" family of songs, especially as he adds the apostrophe before the "L." That subtle clue, rendered in eye English, would only be known by the reader since the woman's name, pronounced aloud, would be no different whether spelled Liza Jane or 'Liza Jane. The Blue Vein Society would not have known either way, but often enough, as has already been demonstrated, nineteenth-century song titles frequently contained the same apostrophe before the "L." Had her name been Eliza Jane and not the folksier 'Liza Jane, the connection to the song would have been less obvious, as "Goodbye Liza Jane" was probably the most popular variant in the late 1890s.

If "The Wife of His Youth" was indeed set in Cleveland, then the "Bona and Paul" vignette in Jean Toomer's 1923 novel *Cane* does not take place too far away, amid the "Hurtling, Loop-jammed L trains" of Chicago.[28] The Chesnutt and Toomer stories are linked through the racial "passing" of their light-skinned male leads, albeit in different ways. Unlike the choice that Mr. Ryder needs to make, Paul can pursue the affection he feels for a white woman, even as he grapples with finding a place of relative comfort in an oppressive world. "Bona and Paul" swings hard. It does not settle into the ebbs and flows of conventional sentences and punctuation, but it smashes the drums and scats and circles around the rooftops of Chicago in the deep swerve of a bass clarinet. Bona, the white girl, imagines Paul as "a candle that dances in a grove swung with pale balloons."[29] She likens him to a harvest moon. "He is an autumn leaf," she thinks, "He is a nigger. Bona! But dont all the dorm girls say so?"[30] Bona observes Paul in the gymnasium of their school. She insists on playing basketball, even though she is ill. "Bona, in center, is jumping against Paul." He outmaneuvers her, scoring not one but two goals, before they clash, with Paul giving her "a sharp crack on the jaw. She whirls. He catches her."[31] After this cringeworthy incident:

> He has a swift illusion that it is himself who has been struck. He looks at Bona. Whir. Whir. They seem to be human distortions spinning tensely in a fog. Spinning . . . dizzy . . . spinning. Bona jerks herself free, flushes a startling crimson, breaks through the bewildered teams, and rushes from the hall.[32]

Later, "Paul is in his room of two windows. Outside, the South-Side L track cuts them in two. Bona is one window. One window, Paul."[33] Within this framework, the romance is kindled, working on Paul's psyche, and is helped along by Paul's white roommate, Art, who has arranged a date for him, thereby bestowing upon the vignette its own destination, or through-action: a trip to the Crimson Gardens nightclub. "Whatdoysay, Paul? Get a wiggle on." Art wonders what is getting into Paul. "Christ, but he's getting moony. Its his blood. Dark blood: moony."[34]

Art and Paul wait for the girls to come down from their dormitory rooms. Before long, the girls arrive, with Bona at first projecting umbrage. "She resents Paul. She flares at him. She flares to poise and security."[35] Toomer's swing-swang narration propels Art and his date, Helen, and Paul and his date, Bona, toward Crimson Gardens. On the way, Bona professes her love for Paul, but Paul replies that he "cant talk love. Love is a dry grain in my mouth unless it is wet with kisses."[36] The two embrace, but Bona resists. She faults Paul for not returning her amorous words. Since she has declared her love, Paul must do the same. When he fails to do so, she hurries away from him to join Art and Helen. Once inside Crimson Gardens, the foursome attracts attention from people who cannot determine Paul's ethnicity: ". . . a Spaniard, an Indian, an Italian, a Mexican, a Hindu, or a Japanese?"[37] By this point, the elements for a complicated conflict have assembled, with Paul's skin dark enough to arouse suspicion from the bigoted Chicagoans in Crimson Gardens and with the trajectory of the date revealing imperfections in the attraction felt between Bona and Paul.

The moony Paul, the jittery Art, the two pretty girls Helen and Bona, the Crimson Gardens nightclub:

> Hurrah! So one feels. The drinks come. Four highballs. Art passes cigarettes. A girl dressed like a bare-back rider in flaming pink, makes her way through tables to the dance floor. All lights are dimmed till they seem a lush afterglow of crimson. Spotlights the girl. She sings. "Liza, Little Liza Jane."[38]

At the onset of "Little Liza Jane," Paul drifts into his thoughts. In them, he imagines "A negress [chanting] a lullaby beneath the mate-eyes of a southern planter."[39] The nightclub song works on Paul. He dreams of a comforting tune from the South.

In his article "Unacknowledged Familiarity: Jean Toomer and Eugene O'Neill," Robert Cooperman describes this exact moment as "symbolic of Paul's possible identity as a mulatto; he identifies with the music of both racial groups."[40] Cooperman adds that "Toomer's use of music, in every instance, serves to explore racial or sexual identity; it is never used merely to establish mood or atmosphere."[41] If this is true, then Toomer placed "Little Liza Jane" in the story for a good reason, and if that assumption is correct, then he probably recognized the song's archaeology. As Paul, a man who has "moony" African American blood, attempts to navigate the prejudices of white society, he attends a nightclub show in which a tune with origins in slavery emanates from the mouth of a singer whose "flaming pink" appearance may suggest whiteness, although Toomer does not conclusively establish her race.

The song continues, with pieces of the refrain—"O Eliza" / "Little Liza Jane" / "Liza"—interspersed among Paul's thoughts.[42] Paul and Bona dance together. "Their eyes meet. Both contemptuous. The dance takes blood from their minds and packs it, tingling, in the torsos of their swaying bodies."[43] They leave together, but Bona abandons Paul when he darts back to converse, a bit poetically, with the doorman.[44] The date fails owing to the gal's fickleness and the guy's inability to connect with her; both traits resemble the basic courtship narrative of the "Liza Jane" family. Toomer may have selected "Little Liza Jane" for those properties, or, understanding the hardships of the song's likely origins, Toomer may have chosen it so Paul could imagine the negress singing a lullaby on a southern plantation. This could potentially link Paul to his roots, much in the same way that the arrival of 'Liza Jane elicited the moral decision from Mr. Ryder in "The Wife of His Youth."

Margaret Walker's 1966 novel *Jubilee* does not have to look backward in time toward slavery days. It begins on a Georgia plantation in advance of the Civil War. Similar to Chesnutt and Toomer, Walker establishes a main character, Vyry, who has mixed parentage. In blunt terms, her mother, Sis Hetta, had been raped by the enslaver Marse John:

> Vyry was two years old. Mammy Sukey had been keeping her as she kept all Marster's bastards till they were big enough to work. She and Brother Ezekiel had nearly a two-mile walk bringing Vyry to see her dying mother, Hetta.[45]

During an interview published in *Frontiers: A Journal of Women's Studies*, Walker revealed the inspiration for the character: "Vyry was really Margaret, my great-grandmother. [. . .] My grandmother was a part of my raising, my rearing. She told me the story."[46] From 1936 to 1939, Walker also participated in the Illinois Writers' Project, a program sponsored by the WPA.[47] While it is uncertain whether she ever interviewed any previously enslaved people, she and her cohort may have encountered stories, folklore, and "snotches" of song in their work; this experience, as well, may have led Walker to overtake additional details of the slavery experience.

During the novel's early moments, Walker narrates a friendship between Vyry and her half-sister, Miss Lillian, the enslaver's daughter with his wife, Big Missy. As part of the novel's first section, "Sis Hetta's child—The Ante-Bellum Years," Walker writes that the two had begun to spend less time together, a development that distressed both children. Vyry's responsibilities on the plantation meant that the two girls could not play games together as frequently as in the past, "and so young Missy in the Big House frequently stole away to

the Quarters to play with the slave children in the late afternoon and early
twilight hours:

> Steal Miz Liza, steal Liza Jane.
> Steal Miz Liza, steal Liza Jane.
>
> That old man ain't got no wife,
> Steal Liza Jane.
> Can't get a wife to save his life,
> Steal Liza Jane."[48]

A few other game songs are given, but "Steal Miss Liza" is the first one rendered
as part of young Miss Lillian's interval playing with the enslaved children in
the Quarters. Walker does not attach any performance rituals or any other
details about the song, save its lyrics, as well as the notion that white and Black
children played the game together. Importantly, this calls to mind the WPA
response from Lydia Jefferson, whose narrative about playing "Catch Liza Jane"
and other ring games with "de white folk's chillen" could not have mirrored
this passage more aptly. In whichever way Walker learned the song—family
oral history, WPA connection, and/or another source—she precisely recreates
the conditions under which the game would be played, even allowing for the
daughter of the enslaver to participate, even citing the "late afternoon and
early twilight hours." The latter detail recalls Mary Olmsted Clarke's report of
when African American children in Virginia would play game songs: "generally
towards the close of day."

The game-playing diversion is not the main character's moment but that
of her playmate and half-sibling. Its authenticity matters. Not only does it
demonstrate the rituals of enslaved children, but it also shows how these rituals
transferred to white children. Walker offers powerful commentary about the
affection the children may have felt for one another when stating Vyry's and
Lillian's distress at not being able to play together as frequently as they had in
the past. Children may stand above bigotry before learning it from adults. Or
perhaps Lillian felt loneliness at the Big House and knew she would be accepted
in the Quarters, where she would have fun playing "Steal Miss Liza" and other
games. Miss Lillian's favorite game began, "Here comes a gentleman just from
Spain," and while playing it, the Black children:

> always chose Miss Lillian to be the pretty maiden and the fairest in the
> land. But one evening in the midst of the laughter and fun, the old black
> people sitting in their doorways, smoking and watching the young ones

play, Big Missy came down mad as a hornet and snatched Miss Lillian away. "You come home, you hear me. You're a young lady and you get-ting too big to play with niggers." And Miss Lillian, broken with tears and misery, allowed herself to be dragged along.[49]

The book's storyline is complicated, and Big Missy's intervention could have sprung from several wellsprings of frustration and anger, yet her action violated the bonds that were forming between the children of different races. If left alone to play, they would play. Big Missy's insult also implies that Black children are more childish than Miss Lillian, an attitude that reinforces the minstrelsy image of the lazy, immature, enslaved person. The saddening, effective scene demonstrates how Big Missy's intervention might have demoralized the young children, Black and white.

A toothless dark-skinned Black woman arrives in what might be the north-ern town of Cleveland. She has traveled toward Mr. Ryder from slavery days and will compel him to make a moral decision. Her name: 'Liza Jane. An interracial pair are out on a date in another northern town, Chicago when a nightclub performer sings "Little Liza Jane." This spurs the character Paul to imagine a negress singing a lullaby on a southern plantation, presumably from another era. In antebellum Georgia, the daughter of the enslaver steals away from the Big House to the Quarters, where the enslaved children live. They welcome her. They make her the pretty maiden, but not before playing "Steal Miz Liza, Steal Liza Jane."

If nothing more, these three seminal works of fiction preserve the "Liza Jane" family as well as the character who populates the songs. Yet these three authors seem to know much more, and their inclusion of the character or the lyrics would look to emanate from a place of considerable perception. Liza Jane, the character, and lyrics from the "Liza Jane" family find their way into other literary works. Admittedly, this portion of the examination is incomplete. Afterall, it is but an intermission. "Steal Miss Liza"—more on this variant will be forthcoming. "Little Liza Jane"—this variant will conquer the entire twen-tieth century. As for Chesnutt's character, 'Liza Jane, her loyalty calls to mind the young woman, Liza Jane, from the mangled South of 1864, who wrote the halting letter to her boyfriend, the Confederate soldier Sol, lost in the War of the Rebellion . . .

YOU WENT A-DRIVING WITH MISTER BROWN

The Tin Pan Alley Publishing Bonanza

1896 TO 1904 / 1930 / 1948

Despite some musicians like George W. Johnson thriving throughout the 1890s, the United States endured an economic depression in the middle years of the decade, beginning with "The Panic of 1893." As the crisis ebbed a few years later, the country would witness the arrival of new music in the form of ragtime, and a dance, the cakewalk, that originated on southern plantations before minstrelsy repackaged its steps. In his book *They All Played Ragtime*, jazz critic Rudi Blesh links the new musical genre and the emerging dance: "Ragtime ascended with the cakewalk rocket and by 1897 was a hit in its own right."[1] The cakewalk evolved from a "prize dance," in which the winner of a competition would be awarded a cake, would "take the cake," as the saying goes, and the economically-battered country may have hungered for a carefree movement of the body, whatever its evolution. Amiri Baraka / LeRoi Jones reflects on the origins and significance of the cakewalk in *Blues People*, stating:

> [It] was one of the most famous dance steps to come out of minstrelsy; it has been described as "a takeoff on the high manners of the white folks in the 'big house.'" If the cakewalk is a Negro dance caricaturing certain white customs, what is that dance when, say, a white theater company attempts to satirize it as a Negro dance? I find the idea of white minstrels in blackface satirizing a dance satirizing themselves a remarkable kind of irony.[2]

By the turn of the century, the popularity of minstrel troupes had begun to wane, but the relentless mockery aimed at African Americans (a mockery that chose not to fathom its inherent layers of contradictions) had not abated. Following the bloodshed of the Civil War, reconciliation between the races may have seemed possible, but the eventual proliferation of Jim Crow laws—themselves named for the caricature portrayed by the minstrel T. D. Rice—doomed the country to decades of reinstitutionalized oppression and segregation. Fortunately for America and the world, the new century would find a youngster named Louis Armstrong growing up in the Storyville neighborhood of New Orleans, a vibrant area that needed, according to biographer James Collier, "a lot of music."[3] As a youngster, Armstrong may have even heard legendary cornet player Buddy Bolden at Union Sons Hall, also known as Funky Butt Hall.[4] Jazz was astir.

As soon as the term "ragtime" had graced the columns of newspapers (as a mainstream term) in 1897, publishing houses competed, as Blesh describes, to commit the first ragtime songs to sheet music.[5] Just before the turn of the century, an exciting Black composer, Scott Joplin, would publish the most popular piece, "Maple Leaf Rag." Known as the King of Ragtime, Joplin would benefit financially from this publication for the rest of his life. Where the bandleader Eddie Fox may have published the first piece of "Liza Jane" sheet music in 1871, the copyright laws during his era may not have fully protected his interests, allowing, for example, the publisher Henry De Marsan and the performer Frank Lum to publish lyrics a few years later boasting several similarities. The laws had been changing, however, presenting an opportunity for songwriters to earn a lasting income should one of their compositions prosper. If a composition succeeded, it would enjoy copyright protection. This environment may have resembled the gold rush at first, with several "Liza Jane" songs appearing as sheet music during the flickering embers of the nineteenth century. The compositions and/or their cover art smacked of minstrelsy and Jim Crow, though eventually, one slightly less distasteful version of "Goodbye Liza Jane" would achieve popular adoption. Around the same time, the "publishing neighborhood" Tin Pan Alley cemented its reputation as the songwriting center of the country.

A year before penning his best-known piece, the 1897 sensation "On the Banks of the Wabash, Far Away," Vaudeville figure Paul Dresser published sheet music for a "Liza Jane" song. Perhaps he sought to capitalize on the enduring popularity of the "Liza Jane" family, which had been performed widely and printed in a variety of popular songbooks, including those brought out by Ditson (1882) and Delaney (1896). The Indiana native revealed in an 1898 interview that he "had traveled with all sorts of bum troupes out of Terre Haute until [he] became ambitious and went to New York."[6] Dresser's biographer Clayton Henderson prints this observation in his book *On the Banks of the Wabash*. Once in New York, Dresser would enhance his growing reputation by venturing into song publishing. Three years after joining Howley, Haviland & Co. as a silent partner and front man,[7] the firm published Dresser's sheet music for "I'se Your Nigger If You Wants Me Liza Jane."[8] The 1896 song is also billed as "A Coon Serenade," and the cover contains distorted images of a Black couple dressed in plantation clothing, with a banjo-strumming male figure singing to a woman who swoons over this attention. The cover also depicts a performer identified as Miss Vernona Jarbeau, who evidently sang the piece with "great success." In addition to the obvious slur in the title, the lyrics promote the singer's tiresome preferences for watermelon, chickens, knife fighting, and gunplay. Clearly influenced by minstrelsy, the song nevertheless continues in the tradition of other "Liza Jane" courtship pieces, with the singer professing admiration ("I loves ye") to the object of his attention ("mah little Liza Jane") even as each chorus ends with the registration of doubt: "if ye wants me." While it did not achieve "hit" status, the Dresser piece does emphasize the growing influence of Music Row, the predecessor appellation to Tin Pan Alley,[9] and the willingness of publishing companies to pursue new renditions of "Liza Jane." By the time Hollywood commemorated Dresser's life with the 1942 film *My Gal Sal*, the song's title had been judiciously amended to "I'se Your Honey If You Wants Me, Liza Jane."[10]

"Git Up Dar!" appeared in 1897, billed as "Great Ethiopian Song, With Chorus." Words and music are attributed to G.M. Blandford, with the publication by Hamilton S. Gordon in New York.[11] The cover depicts two Black men engaging in an equine competition, with one riding a donkey and the other a mule, in order to win Liza Jane's admiration; she waves to the front-runner from an open window. All three characters present with overemphasized features, which follow from exaggerations typical of minstrelsy. Toward the bottom right, the chorus appears: "Git up, you lazy bones now git up I say! / Doan you know we'se racing fo my lady's heart today? / Git up, Augustus, fo dere's Miss Liza Jane, / Waiting and watching fo us two down in the lane." Elements of the chorus, as well as the name "Miss Liza Jane," loosely connect to another variant in the "Liza Jane" extended family, "Whoa Mule." An early rendition of the "Whoa Mule" chorus was printed in the *Montpelier Daily Record* (Vermont) on February 24, 1898, as part of an advertisement for the first appearance of the Montpelier Mandolin Club.

Whoa Mule

Whoa ! whoa ! I tell you
Whoa ! whoa ! I say ;
Oh, keep your seat Miss Liza Jane
And hang on to the sleigh.[12]

Here, the young woman intrudes into yet another equine song, this one associated singly with an unruly mule. In addition to the situations, cadences, and presence of "Miss Liza Jane," the lyrical similarities between "Git Up Dar!" and "Whoa Mule" can be seen in the urging of the animals: "git up I say" and "whoa ! I say," respectively. Two noteworthy musicians recorded songs that reflect elements of the sheet music and newspaper lyrics. Silas Leachman's 1901 recording of "Whoa Dar Mule" includes the line "Eliza, get your bonnet" as well as a reference to "Miss Liza Jane." It is one of the earliest known recorded references to the Liza Jane character, following George W. Johnson's "The Laughing Coon" by about three years.[13] In 1924, Roba Stanley became one of the first women to record old-time country music, including a rendition of "Whoa Mule" in a trio format.[14] The lyrics were already moving toward her, from traditional sources as well as Music Row. For its part, "Git Up Dar!" did not achieve widespread popularity.

Two years before a Tin Pan Alley "Liza Jane" song would demonstrate success, "I Needs You Very Badly, Liza Jane" rolled off the press.[15] Subtitled "Southern Love Plaint," this 1901 publication took obvious pains to connect the twentieth century, despite its blossoming new musical genres, to melancholy longings for the nineteenth-century South. The lyricist Charles Horwitz douses the proceedings in floral, ethereal love language. Even as the singer croons in offensive showbusiness dialect—"de spring-time, it am comin'" for example—the song defaults to a flaccid separation tale, with limited adoption in the performance world of its day. A portrait of Spenser Kelly, presumably a ballad singer, features on the cover; otherwise, the cover displays a moonlit rural scene with a lonely male figure adrift. The music had been written by Frederick Bowers, and the significance of this publication may have evaporated entirely were it not published by the firm of Shapiro, Bernstein & Von Tilzer in New York. Perhaps it was Von Tilzer who had shepherded this song into existence. A couple of years later, he would publish his own "Liza Jane" composition at the head of his own publishing company. And that song would succeed.

There may be no greater embodiment of Tin Pan Alley than Harry Von Tilzer, who is said to be involved in the naming of the iconic publishing area. In his book *Automats, Taxi Dances, and Vaudeville*, historian David Freeland explores the widely known and moderately doubted naming myth. As he points out, publishers had situated themselves in the Tenderloin section of New York well before it had acquired the name Tin Pan Alley, but in 1902, a sportsman-newspaperman Monroe Rosenfeld was visiting Von Tilzer's office on West 28th Street, when the "Eureka!" moment may have transpired. "Rosie," as Rosenfeld was known, had been listening to the unusual sound of Von Tilzer playing piano. To simulate guitar and banjo and to "help create the kind of jingling effect that aided him in composition," Von Tilzer had woven paper strips between the strings and keys of his upright piano and pointed this out to the inquiring Rosie. Upon hearing the unusual music, Rosie linked Von Tilzer's tin-pan piano sound to the area of Manhattan's songwriting companies, thereby dubbing it Tin Pan Alley. Allegedly, Rosie published an article entitled "Down in Tin Pan Alley" in a New York newspaper, perhaps the *Herald*, thereby solidifying the coinage.[16]

By this point, Von Tilzer had left Shapiro and Bernstein to found the Harry Von Tilzer Music Publishing Company. In this capacity, he issued a 1902 love song, "Won't You Roll Dem Eyes Eliza," which refers to the female character as "Liza," "Lize," "Eliza," and "Miss Liza," but does not include "Jane."[17] Perhaps that publication "warmed things up" for his 1903 reinvention of "Goodbye Liza Jane." Von Tilzer's rendition would be titled "Good Bye Eliza Jane," with music credited to him and words credited to Andrew B. Sterling. A picture of Von Tilzer occupies the upper left-hand portion of the cover, whereas a variety of performers, depending upon the edition, grace the lower right-hand corner, including the Connolly Sisters (May, Dolly, and Belle), Empire Comedy Four, Madge Fox, (Ms.) Artie Hall, Harold Kennedy, Arthur Klein, Zoa Matthews, Joe Maxwell, and Cecil Spooner.[18] Otherwise, the red, white, and blue cover presents distasteful caricatures of two African American faces. The lyrics, in their entirety, read as follows:

Good Bye Eliza Jane
Von Tilzer and Sterling

Look a' here, Liza, listen to me;
You ain't the gal you promised to be;
Didn't you say you always would be true, oo, oo, oo, oo?
You went a-driving with Mister Brown;
Now I'm the laughing stock of the town;
Folks say that I was crazy to trust you, oo, oo, oo, oo.
Throw up my hands, babe, I'se gwine to go;
Can't stand the blow; I loved you so;
I was the good thing while I had the "dough,"
Now I must whisper low:

Chorus:
Good-bye, Eliza Jane, I'm gwine a' for to leave you!
Well, you'll know, when I go
That I was the fellow with the "dough, dough, dough";
So I'm gwine for to sing a little song;
And travel along; just travel along;

Wish you good-day, babe; I'm on my way;
Good-bye, Eliza Jane.

Look a' here, Liza, take off those rings;
Dig in that trunk, gal; hand me those things;
I'm gwine to take the clothes I paid for, too, oo, oo, oo, oo!
Cough up that old gold watch, and de chain;
Wants that umbrella, cause it might rain;
Ask Mister Brown to fix you up all new, oo, oo, oo, oo.
Rent time is here, babe; landlord today;
I'll be away; who's gwine to pay?
P'r'aps Mister Brown will, if he's a jay,
Once more to you I say:

[Chorus twice]

It might be appropriate to consider Von Tilzer a third-generation "Liza Jane" composer since this piece depends upon previous works by Eddie Fox and Frank Lum if not others. Gone are the chickens sneezing, monkeys growing on grapevines, the singer going down to Lynchburg town, plantation scenery, and the image of the lazy, childlike enslaved person, but some of the conventions from those nineteenth-century publications persist. Predecessor composers-arrangers Fox and Lum address the girl through the phrase "hear me now," and Von Tilzer would retain this construct through "listen to me," "now I must whisper low," and "once more to you I say." The phrase "now I must whisper low" is especially suspicious since the word "low" corresponds to the progression "Walk dad Lew" (Fox), "Walk that loo" (Lum), and "Always low" (George W. Johnson). Approximations of African American dialect—"I'se gwine to go" and "I'm gwine a' for to leave you"—do not necessarily refer to Fox or Lum, but instead to minstrelsy catchphrase, although the soldiers in the Forty-Third United States Colored Troops Regiment were reported to have sung in this manner and George W. Johnson did begin the refrain of "The Laughing Coon" with portions of this language.

Despite the insulting imagery on the cover and the song's orientation as a "coon song," the lyrics do not convey overt racist slurs. This updated version of "Goodbye Liza Jane" focuses more on a lover's rift and its consequences. Eliza Jane may have betrayed the singer by going out with Mister Brown, a development that causes the singer to face ridicule from all the townspeople. While the song cannot be definitively situated in a metropolis, the mention of modernizations and woes—such as going for a drive and the necessity to produce the rent—do recommend a more concentrated setting. Someone living on a plantation, moreover, might not seek shelter underneath an umbrella. Still, any suitor anywhere might ply his gal with rings, clothes, a gold watch, and its chain, then expect those items to be returned upon the demise of the relationship. Despite this lover's rift, the tone is bouncy and affable. The singer bids Eliza Jane a "good-day," and his singing often trails off "oo-oo-oo-oo" despite his apparent heartbreak. He also proposes an answer to Eliza Jane's biggest problem—the rent due—by suggesting Mister Brown can handle it "if he's a jay." Thus, the song "travels along" without too many worries. The Liza Jane character may have rejected another in a long line of suitors, proving her elusiveness, but the song's otherwise moderate tone does not predict too much inconvenience. In fact, a case could be built that the suitor will return and try again. "I'll be away," he croons. There is no mention of being away forever, in any case. At the end of the day, singers may have approached their "Good Bye Eliza Jane" performances in the long tradition of comic ditties.

Unlike the other "Liza Jane" songs that emanated from the turn-of-the-century Music Row / Tin Pan Alley publishing bonanza, Von Tilzer's "Good Bye Eliza Jane" did succeed as a popular song. The numerous cover pages featuring the photographs of different singers—at least nine acts and fourteen men and women—attest to widespread adoption, but there were also opportunities to make recordings. The Discography of American Historical Recordings website (DAHR) at the University of California, Santa Barbara Library indicates that Billy Murray recorded "Goodbye, Eliza Jane" on January 7, 1904, in Philadelphia.[19] This recording has not been heard, and it is not known if it ever reached large audiences. On the other hand, a recording of "Good Bye Eliza Jane" by Bob Roberts, also known as "Ragtime" Bob Roberts, can be heard at the Library of Congress website.[20] Roberts recorded the song several times in 1904–1905 on at least three different labels.[21] It is unknown if these recordings reached large audiences.

At least one recorded version of the Von Tilzer composition may have achieved "hit" status. The DAHR website notes that Arthur Collins recorded "Good-Bye, Eliza Jane" on October 26, 1903, in Philadelphia.[22] According to *Joel Whitburn's Pop Memories*, a book that can provide estimates of charting information for records released during the early days of the recording era, the Arthur Collins 1903 version of "Good-Bye, Eliza Jane" would have reached the charts on October 31, 1903, stayed on the charts for seven weeks, and for four of those seven weeks, peaked at number one.[23] To arrive at this estimate, Whitburn takes into account sales of sheet music (among other factors), which would have been strong in this case.[24] Beyond the many variations in covers described above, additional evidence of strong sales can be seen on the cover of a separate 1904 publication by the Von Tilzer Company for "Hannah Won't You Open the Door." Underneath the title, additional text proclaims "by the authors of the famous 'Good Bye Eliza Jane.'"[25] Confident of his hit, Von Tilzer employed its celebrity status to influence sales of other compositions.

Estimated or otherwise, the Collins recording would become the first "number one hit"—and the *only* number one hit—in the extensive history of the "Liza Jane" family. Music historian Tim Gracyk, in his book *Popular American Recording Pioneers*, situates Collins amidst the most productive recording stars of his era, writing:

> The baritone Arthur Collins was among the half dozen most prolific recording artists during the acoustic era, with nearly every American company employing him as a solo artist, as a member of the duo Collins and Harlan, and as a member of quartets and minstrel companies.[26]

The duo Collins and Harlan would record "(I'm Waiting for You) Liza Jane" roughly fifteen years later, in 1918, making Collins one of the few singing stars to record more than one variant in the "Liza Jane" family. Developed by the lyricist-composer team of Henry Creamer and Turner Layton, the sheet music was published in New York by Broadway Music Corporation, with Harry Von Tilzer's brother, Will, serving as president.[27] In the end, the Von Tilzer family had produced sheet music for three different "Liza Jane" songs across three different Tin Pan Alley publishing firms, and the star baritone vocalist Arthur Collins had recorded one of them solo and another as part of a duet.

The Harry Von Tilzer composition "Good Bye Eliza Jane" would be resurrected by old-time country singer and banjoist Charlie Poole along with his band, the North Carolina Ramblers, in 1930.[28] Noting that "Poole worked most of his life in textile mills," Richard Carlin's *Folk* describes Poole's first recording session with the North Carolina Ramblers for Columbia Records in 1925, calling the output "immediately successful."[29] If he did not write much original material, Poole apparently had facility as an arranger. Specifically, as Patrick Huber points out in his book *Linthead Stomp*, "[Poole's] unusual ability to arrange old Tin Pan Alley standards marked another of his musical innovations that contributed to the North Carolina Ramblers' commercial success."[30] Poole's distinctive adoption of the Von Tilzer composition for string band trio contains a forty-second instrumental introduction and emphasizes the curvaceous drawl of the fiddle; the original lyrics are mostly preserved with slight modification to the title, "Good-bye Sweet Liza Jane." At the time, not many people would hear the sides from the 1930 recording date at Columbia Records, which would turn out to be the group's final session. "As the Great Depression worsened," Huber indicates, "sales of their records continued to slump."[31] Poole himself would be dead less than a year later, with the death certificate designating the likely cause of death: "intoxication 13 weeks."[32] As a transformational arranger of tunes, Poole's influence on other musicians would not depend upon his "Liza Jane" recording, but its fluency in translation from Tin Pan Alley to Piedmont phrasing would reemphasize the ability of the "Liza Jane" family to transcend boundaries. The Von Tilzer composition would, however, cross the aisle at least one more time, reaching an icon of twentieth-century folk blues.

Lead Belly's 1948 recitation of the song in the home of musicologist Frederic Ramsey Jr. begins as a spoken introduction to the song's essential situation, the betrayal, before it settles on an affectionate performance without instrumental accompaniment. The song would be titled "Liza Jane" or "Miss Liza Jane" and was released by Smithsonian Folkways with dozens of other songs recorded by Ramsey, first on vinyl in 1953, and later, expanded, on compact disc.[33] Lead Belly would pass away in 1949, but his "Last Sessions" fortuitously demonstrated his absorption of the piece. It is neither a masterpiece nor an influential rendition, but its existence in his repertoire requires excavation. In his voice, after all, might exist percentages of the voices of enslaved people, African American soldiers, minstrelsy composers and performers, the first African American recording star, a Tin Pan Alley composer, and perhaps a singer such as Arthur Collins, since his version did enjoy widespread sales and may have prolonged awareness of the composition. On the one hand, the circumstances lack the kind of thudding irony that Baraka/Jones identified in the history of the cakewalk dance, but the same principle—the need to accurately situate a reacquired folk song that had been altered by blackface minstrelsy and the "coon song" environment—does indeed apply. By 1948, "Goodbye Liza Jane" had traded hands between Blacks and whites for nearly nine decades, with many individuals influencing its form. Lead Belly's rendition applies a regal stamp.

At this point, Von Tilzer's variant, though financially successful in terms of record and sheet music sales, largely fades. It may have been linked to a vanishing preference for bigoted plantation material, however updated the composition attempted to be. It was not, moreover, the only "Goodbye Liza Jane" variant to appear in the twentieth century. Arguably, more important variants would connect—perhaps with greater legitimacy—to "play party" traditions as well as other styles, such as western swing. The "Goodbye Liza Jane" branch of the family may have been sturdiest at the start of the new century, but the family dynamics would shift. One can croon about loving Liza Jane and how it feels to be rejected by her and even declare "goodbye" in response to this ticklish disarray, but did the song ultimately possess a structure for long-term popular adoption?

Hampton Institute students and Lend a Hand students were not singing the refrain of "Goodbye Liza Jane" *ad infinitum*. They were clapping, shouting, and stealing dance partners, all in the name of "Little Liza Jane." Their devotion was necessary. Without it, the entire "Liza Jane" family may have faded. Yet before this study considers a countess and an aviatrix, it will first consider a branch of songs so populated with versions Carl Sandburg would declare, "There are as many Liza songs in the Appalachian Mountains as there are species of trees on the slopes of that range."[34]

POOR GAL

1897 / EARLY TWENTIETH CENTURY

Four years after folk music collector Lila Edmands offered a peek into the musical traditions of North Carolina mountaintop dwellers, newspapers around the country carried a syndicated piece entitled "North Carolina Mountain Songs," crediting "Rev. Hanford A. Edson, in the Independent." Published on December 5, 1897, in the *Indianapolis Journal*, among other newspapers, the article emphasizes the "British ancestry" of the mountaineers, as well as their proximity to "the negro and [. . .] negro slavery."[1] While establishing the importance of this influence, Edson quickly goes on to reassure jittery readers that the mountaineers do not equate themselves with Blacks who live nearby: "The African element in the mountain songs is evident and often predominant. Not the slightest suggestion of social equality with the colored people is ever allowed, even at corn-shuckings or funerals, but the patient, cheerful, music-loving darkey has, notwithstanding, sung his love and his religion into the air." After establishing this biased rapport with the reader, Edson prints lyrics for songs with British origins and Black origins alike, such as "Barbara Allen" and "Fair Annie of Lochroyan" (British), and "Apple Jack" and "Goin' Down-town" (Black).

He describes the instrument of choice, the "banjer," which would cost a mountaineer "sixty dollars down in the settlement," and discusses the homemade quality of the fiddles up in the mountains. "The theme," Edson writes, "seldom gets far from thoughts of love. Minor strains prevail, like:

> O little Liza, pore gal,
> O little Liza Jane;
> O little Liza, pore gal,
> She died on the train."

Unlike Angus S. Hibbard's likely misapprehension of Black dialect ("Oh, Hoopo Liza, poor gal") in his 1883 operetta, *Chic*, Edson, on the other hand, reports this refrain directly from white musicians, who probably absorbed some portion of it, or all of it, during communal corn-shuckings with their African American neighbors. Importantly, the phrase "little Liza Jane" manifests itself in a relatively isolated Appalachian setting in North Carolina. It is impossible to ascertain just how much Black tradition influences the quatrain, but the presence of the phrase "little Liza Jane" within a nineteenth-century mountaintop version speaks to its uncanny transcendence—from WPA respondents and Hampton Institute students to the Appalachian Mountains. Importantly, this "pore gal" dies on the train, just as Hibbard relates in his operetta.

Though reporting ostensibly on North Carolina tradition, Edson likely encountered regional song, including, as in the case of Edmands, Tennessee influence as well. Edson concludes his article by mentioning a chimney builder and fiddler, Webb Cable, who danced, fiddled, and sang. "Encores are likely to be most boisterous," writes Edson, "for 'Cindy,' 'Liza Jane,' and 'Daisy.'"

Several folklorists who published articles in the *Journal of American Folklore* documented this variant in the early decades of the twentieth century. To begin, E. C. Perrow depicts a nearly identical refrain, down to the spelling of "pore." He attributes the song to "East Tennessee; mountain whites; 1905."[2] Perrow presents this quatrain alone, without any accompanying stanzas, as example "A" of eight variants in the "Liza Jane" family:

> Pore little Liza, pore little gal!
> Pore little Liza Jane!
> Pore little Liza, pore little gal!
> She died on the train.[3]

His 1915 article "Songs and Rhymes from the South," resembles a book-length collection, offering examples of eighty-four songs widely scattered throughout the South.

Meanwhile, Florence Truitt's 1923 article "Songs from Kentucky" offers a well-organized, untitled song containing nine verses plus the following refrain:

> Hop along, old Miss Lizy!
> Hop along, Liza Jane!
> Hop along, Lizy, poor gal!
> And she died on the train.[4]

Truitt ascribes the song to one Mrs. Duckworth in Batto County, roughly thirty years before the article's publication, thereby establishing the variant in the 1890s. The remainder of the song may present a series of "floating" verses, which include common fare, such as the hijinks of raccoons and possums. Yet another report out of Kentucky, "Some Negro Song Variants from Louisville," came from K. J. Holzknecht in 1928. His untitled song contains the following stanza, which possesses refrain qualities: "So long, Liza, poor girl, / So long, Liza Jane, / So long, Liza, poor girl, / She died on the train."[5]

These four folk reports—by Edson in the newspaper and by Perrow, Truitt, and Holzknecht in the *Journal of American Folklore*—hail from North Carolina, Tennessee, and Kentucky. Collectively, they describe the Liza Jane character as a "poor gal" or "poor girl." Two of the four refrains contain the word "little," which may hybridize the variants and simultaneously depict the young woman as precious or fragile. The phrases "So long, Liza" and "Hop along, Liza" may be distant references to "Goodbye, Liza" and "Oh poor, Liza," respectively. All four collected variants conclude with "She died on the train." While many "Liza Jane" songs were offered as comic ditties, this line does not suggest levity, at least not on its surface.

Carl Sandburg includes two related songs in his landmark 1927 folk music collection, *The American Songbag*. He writes of isolated ranchers in the Appalachian Mountains as part of introducing the first piece, "Liza Jane," a song whose refrain approximates those given above.

> O po' Liza po' gal,
> O po' Liza Jane,
> O po' Liza po' gal,
> She died on the train.[6]

A second entry, "Liza in the Summertime (She Died on the Train)," may offer more insight into the origins, intended tone, and performance rituals surrounding these variants. In his preface to the song, Sandburg writes:

> Lines from old British ballads mingle with mountaineer lingo as in the word "mountings"; negro influence is not absent. This may be an instance of the song that starts among people who have a tune, who want to sing, who join together on an improvisation, reaching out for any kind of verses, inventing, repeating, marrying Scotch lyrics with black-face minstrel ditties; in the end comes a song that pleases them for their purposes. Its mood varies here from the lugubrious to the light-hearted. The way to sing it is "as you like it."[7]

Sandburg corroborates the cross-cultural findings of the other collectors by confirming a multitude of influences: British and Black, mountaineer and "Scotch." The refrain for "Liza in the Summertime" contains lengthier lines:

> Po' li'l' Liza, po' gal, po' li'l' Liza Jane,
> Po' li'l' Liza, po' li'l' gal, she died on the train,
> She died on the train, she died on the train.[8]

In both "Liza Jane" and "Liza in the Summertime," Sandburg writes "po" for "poor" and does not tread into the terrain of "hoopo" or "hop along." He, too, stations the phrase "li'l Liza Jane" in a country or mountain song context. As to the song's tone when sung aloud, here, the singer could veer toward elegy or humor, or both; it would depend upon the context of the performance. Any number of important musicians would record renditions from the "poor gal" branch of the "Liza Jane" family, especially in the 1920s, employing the same or similar melody and refrain. The verses, however, can differ widely. The tones range from overt comedy to those more difficult to penetrate; some versions recommend themselves to dance, while in other instances, a touch of the ballad and a touch of the dirge prevail.

Pete Seeger recorded "Oh! Liza, Poor Gal" in 1955 as part of his studio album *Goofing Off Suite*, which appeared on the Folkways label.[9] Seeger plays banjo, begins by singing the refrain, and includes two verses. The refrain closely follows the variants provided by the *Journal of American Folklore* collectors and Sandburg, capped by the Liza Jane character dying on the train. Seeger's traditional country lyrics narrate two standard voyages. In the first verse, the singer ventures up on the mountain, where he will plant cane, make molasses, and eventually "sweeten" the poor gal who may be resisting courtship:

> I'm going up on the mountain top
> To plant me a patch of cane
> I'm gonna make molasses
> To sweeten Liza Jane

In the second verse, Seeger adopts the formula of one person going down "the road" and the other going down "the lane." He indicates that the other person can hug a fence post, whereas Liza Jane will provide him with more comfort as a hugging partner. On paper, some of these lines supply a comedic bend, but in delivery, Seeger would seem to honor the girl's death. His dirge-like banjo picking may shade the tone toward elegy, but that is not obvious, either. It is possible that Seeger played the song "down the middle" without committing to an obvious emotional center.

In contrast, the Tenneva Ramblers recorded "Miss 'Liza, Poor Gal" as an overtly comic piece. The band participated in the famous "Bristol Sessions" led by producer Ralph Peer, then employed by the Victor label. Conducted in Bristol, Tennessee, these summer 1927 sessions would include the debut recordings by

Jimmie Rodgers and the Carter Family. In his book *Tennessee Strings*, musicologist Charles K. Wolfe describes how fiddling and string band music dominated
the music scene in the Johnson City-Bristol area in the 1920s, and "there was
also considerable interchange with musicians from nearby southwest Virginia
and western North Carolina."[10] According to Wolfe, the Tenneva Ramblers were
named for the Tennessee-Virginia border area, thereby underscoring the cross-
boundary nature of the group's makeup, as well as overlapping musical traditions.
Originally, the group had been the backing band for Jimmie Rodgers and, at the
Bristol Sessions, cut as many as nine sides.[11] "Miss Liza, Poor Gal" was recorded on
August 4, 1927.[12] It begins with the refrain, which is repeated four times throughout the song, while the lone verse is repeated three times.

Miss 'Liza, Poor Gal
Tenneva Ramblers

[Chorus:]
Oh, Miss Liza, poor gal
Oh, Miss Liza Jane
Oh, Miss Liza, poor gal
Too late to catch the train

I went to see Miss Liza
Miss Liza wasn't at home
Her old man took the broomstick
And dragged it o'er my bones

The Tenneva Ramblers—likely comprised of fiddle, mandolin, banjo, and guitar—play the song hot, as a dance number, with obvious comedy centering on
the suitor, who has been cracked "o'er the bones" by the broomstick-wielding
father of Liza Jane. Curiously, someone has missed the train. This could be
the suitor, delayed by the old man and the broomstick, or perhaps owing to
some dark humor, the Liza Jane character herself, who may have perished in
advance of riding the train. African American influence may manifest itself
in the phrase "Miss Liza Jane," which was reported in several WPA narratives.
    Another comic, up-tempo version arrived a year earlier on the Vocalion
label. The Hill Billies, a pioneering country group that wound up lending its
name to an entire genre of music, recorded "Mountaineer's Love Song" in 1926,
in New York.[13] According to folklorist Norm Cohen, the band was named
somewhat accidentally at an earlier recording session. When asked by Ralph
Peer, then working at OKeh Records, what they called themselves, the leader of
the group, Al Hopkins, replied, "We're nothing but a bunch of hillbillies from

North Carolina and Virginia. Call us anything."[14] And Peer did just that. Writing in *The Encyclopedia of Country Music*, Cohen notes that Hopkins's piano playing helped the group flesh out an original sound, which they delivered in numerous shows and radio appearances.[15] Following a forty-five-second musical introduction—which may include piano, guitar, harmonica, banjo, fiddle, and ukulele—the group begins with the first verse, as opposed to the chorus.

Mountaineer's Love Song
The Hill Billies

I went up on the mountain
I gave my horn a blow
I thought I heard my Liza say
"Yander comes my beau"

[Chorus:]
Oh Miss Liza po' gal
Oh Miss Liza Jane
Oh Miss Liza po' gal
A-ridin' on that train

I took old Dick and Dinah
I hooked 'em to a train
To get a barrel of molasses
To sweeten my Liza Jane

[Chorus]

I asked her pa to marry me
She says "ain't you ashamed?"
I stuck my head through a crack in the fence
To get my Liza Jane

[Chorus]

I traveled on a steamboat
I traveled on a train
But when I get married
I'll marry Liza Jane

[Chorus]

The song immediately connects to the writings of Lafcadio Hearn from 1870s New Orleans. Back then, the Black roustabouts sang about climbing on top of a house, giving one's horn a blow, and thinking that yet another character, Miss Dinah, might have mentioned the approach of a beau. Black influence can also be seen in how the Hill Billies shorten "poor" to "po'" in the refrain, as well as in the adoption of "Miss Liza Jane" as a phrase. This rendition also mentions sweetening "Liza Jane" through a barrel of molasses; to do this, the singer improbably hitches his team to a train. "Mountaineer's Love Song" never really completes the singer's courtship adventure. He must grab Liza Jane through a crack in the fence after she suggests he should be ashamed of himself, and by the end of the song, the singer establishes marriage as a distant prospect, although Liza Jane will be the "po' gal" he marries. The proceedings may imply a brand of happy-go-lucky doubt. Throughout the song, the Liza Jane character is said to be "a-ridin' on that train." Indeed, she may be traveling via railroad, but another possible reading could be lightly elegiac, with the chorus, instead, honoring her memory as someone who will always be "a-ridin' on that train" after perishing in one of its cars.

One of the most virtuosic renditions among all songs in all branches of the "Liza Jane" family would belong to the Kessinger Brothers, Clark and Luches, who were not, in fact, brothers but uncle and nephew, respectively. Recorded for Brunswick in 1929, their instrumental piece entitled "Liza Jane" follows the melodic structure of other "Liza, Poor Gal" country songs, and while lyrics are absent, the listener would know exactly when the refrain—"She died on the train" or "A-ridin' on that train"—could be superimposed.[16] Writing in his essay "Clark Kessinger: Pure Fiddling," Charles K. Wolfe describes Kessinger's playing as, indeed:

> pure fiddling, with no real concessions to popular taste. In the 70-plus sides he recorded for the old Brunswick company between 1928 and 1930, and the five LPs he made during his comeback in the 1960s, he had no novelty numbers, no funny vocals, no cute trick playing, no harmony singing. Except for a few square dance calls on his first records, it was all pure Kessinger; if you didn't like fiddling, it wasn't your music.[17]

Following this insight, "Liza Jane," in the hands of the Kessinger Brothers, takes the business of swinging very seriously. It may quote other fiddle songs, and it may possess some percentage of a waltz, which "Kessinger loved anyway."[18] According to Wolfe, whose essay appeared in the book *Mountains of Music*, the Charleston, West Virginia native [Clark] Kessinger opined that the "three-minute length of the 78 rpm records caused him to repeat a tune more times than he thought necessary. But often when he did this, he managed to infuse the different choruses with subtle variations."[19] One could say subtle variations of intensity and beauty. Above all else, Clark Kessinger's fiddle and Luches Kessinger's guitar project an industrious dignity, a resolve to court "Liza Jane" with boundless energy, even as the dance itself may be a solemn memory, the poor gal—the object of affection—having died on the train. "Liza Jane" soars in the treatment given by the duo and recommends itself to numerous listens.

As demonstrated, the line "She died on the train" could be exchanged for "A-ridin' on that train" without disrupting the metrical harmony of the refrain, but the phrase "Goodbye Liza Jane" could be substituted as well. This can be seen in the work of Fiddlin' John Carson, who recorded "Good-bye Liza Jane" in 1926.[20] While the title might suggest a kinship with the branch of "Liza Jane" songs that evolved through minstrelsy and Tin Pan Alley, in fact, the Carson version resembles the melody of the "Liza, poor gal" songs. It connects to virtually all the songs given in this context —those by the Tenneva Ramblers and the Kessinger Brothers, for instance—but not to Harry Von Tilzer or Eddie Fox, except in the title. It may even associate with the Holzknecht report of "So long, Liza, poor girl." Carson begins with the refrain and includes three verses.

Good-bye Liza Jane
Fiddlin' John Carson

[Chorus:]
Oh little Liza poor girl
Oh little Liza Jane
Oh little Liza poor girl
Good-bye Liza Jane

[The cattle's bucking coming
Always in a strain
Give my soul inviting
Feel little Liza Jane]*

[Chorus]

Liza's like a cherry
Cherry's like a rose
How I knew little Liza
Goodness only knows

[Chorus]

Some folks say the devil's dead
Buried him in a pumpkin
Old folks say the devil (and) Liza
Are going to hell a-jumpin'

[Chorus]

*The bracketed verse represents approximate lyrics

Featuring a "deep country sound," Fiddlin' John Carson & His Virginia Reelers produced one of the most unusual, hybridized "Liza Jane" recordings in the family. At its heart an old-time country tune in the "poor gal" tradition, it nevertheless refers to both "Goodbye Liza Jane" and "Little Liza Jane" through its chorus. As previously noted during the first "intermission," the cherry and rose comparison may connect to the Scottish poet Robert Burns. The other verses come off gritty, unexpected, and somewhat evil, with bucking cattle approaching in the first verse and the devil and Liza going to hell "a-jumpin'" in the third verse. Carson's vocals and fiddle, when combined with the guitar, banjo, and potentially a second fiddle of his band, do not arouse giddy comedy in the mind of the listener. The tone may capture resignation, instead, or the possibility of dark humor, but either way, the recording leans toward the edgier side of the spectrum. The song does establish enough pace to succeed as a dance number, so any "evil humor" from Carson would prosper amid a setting well-lubricated by moonshine.

Speaking of those liquid refreshments, Ernest Rogers, an employee of Atlanta radio station WSB during Carson's era, recalls in his memoir, *Peachtree Parade*, the fondness Carson demonstrated for corn liquor. In a story that takes place in the "gents room" at the station, an unknown person produces a flagon of "corn squeezings" and offers it to anyone who wants some. When Carson, a regular performer at WSB, produces a water glass, the unknown man begins pouring and tells Carson to "say when." Carson does not reply. So the man keeps pouring the whiskey into Carson's glass but, growing nervous, urges Carson to "say when." To which Carson finally replies: "I reckon you can tell when hit's a-runnin' over, cain't you?"[21] The story expresses Carson's earthy humor as well as his habits in preparation for performances.

According to Wayne W. Daniel, author of *Pickin' on Peachtree*, Carson made his first appearance on WSB as early as 1922, not long after the station opened.[22] He began his recording career in historic fashion on the OKeh label, which immediately led to national celebrity. As Daniel indicates, it was Carson, on WSB, who first introduced country music to the airways, and it was Carson who recorded "the first real country music record."[23] Ralph Peer, who would later record the Hill Billies and who eventually presided over the Bristol Sessions, produced Carson's historic 1923 session in Atlanta, capturing versions of "The Little Old Log Cabin in the Lane" and "The Old Hen Cackled and the Rooster's Going to Crow."[24] At first, describing Carson's singing voice as "pluperfect awful," Peer limited the initial production run to five hundred records, but as orders grew far beyond that number, Peer conceded that he had miscalculated Carson's appeal and brought the fiddler to OKeh's New York studio for additional sessions.[25] Carson enjoyed a recording career that lasted more than ten years, mostly with OKeh, but also with Edison, Columbia, and Brunswick.[26] According to *The Book of Golden Discs*, two of Carson's early records sold especially well: "You Will Never Miss Your Mother Until She Is Gone" and "Old Joe Clark."[27]

Born in rural Fannin County, Georgia, in 1868, Fiddlin' John Carson grew up playing a Stradivarius-copy fiddle "brought from Ireland in a potato sack many years before."[28] Daniel describes Carson's early vocational experiences as a colorful mixture of blue-collar jobs, including farm and railroad work, jockeying horses, painting houses, and toiling in a cotton mill. Owing to some moonshining activity, Carson briefly landed in an Atlanta jail.[29] Carson's colorful life might call to mind another "Liza Jane" performer, Johnny Tuers, who went as far as to murderously wield a pistol. Carson, for his part, attended the 1915 lynching (in Marietta, Georgia) of Leo Frank, a man who had been convicted of murdering Mary Phagan, a teenage girl who labored in a nearby pencil factory. Daniel incorporates an excerpt from the *Atlanta Constitution*, which describes how "The hundreds of morbidly curious (following the removal of the corpse) congregated around Fiddlin' John Carson, who [. . .] fiddled a symphonic jubilee."[30] The Leo Frank case attracted national attention, and Frank's conviction may have been a miscarriage of justice. Nonfiction author Steve Oney explores the Frank case in his book *And the Dead Shall Rise*, including how Carson penned "The Ballad of Mary Phagan" and, through his fiddling, attempted to capitalize on Frank's death.[31]

Historian James C. Cobb devotes a chapter to "Country Music and the 'Southernization' of America" in his book *Redefining Southern Culture*. In the early parts of the chapter, he describes how the commercial market for country music grew following Carson's first recordings, characterizing the 1920s South as one resisting postwar modernism in favor of antiblack repression, religious fundamentalism, and a spirited defense of traditionalism.[32] While acknowledging "Much of the original material performed by Carson and his contemporaries consisted of folk tunes and hymns," Cobb shows that fresh recording opportunities also created openings for a new slate of songwriters.[33] He writes:

the first commercial compositions [of country music] expressed the values and prejudices of the rural south. Fiddlin' John Carson was a regular at Ku Klux Klan rallies, and his "Ballad of Little Mary Phagan" helped to exacerbate the anti-Semitism that was a major factor in the lynching of Mary's alleged murderer, Leo Frank. Fiddlin' John made light of the evolution controversy in "There Ain't No Bugs on Me" when he asserted "there may be monkey in some of you guys, but there ain't no monkey in me."[34]

These details are not meant to tarnish the accomplishment of Carson's "Goodbye Liza Jane" but to acknowledge the man's worldview, which, despite his widely praised fiddling skills, allies him with the institutionalized torment faced by the original singers of the "Liza Jane" family. And yet, this is the story of the "Liza Jane" songs. The many variants traveled back and forth between Blacks and whites, even into the hands of a gifted, bigoted fiddler, who possibly devised a masterpiece old-time version. Many of this book's historical figures—including minstrel singer Frank Lum, mountaintop reporter Rev. Hanford A. Edson, and Tin Pan Alley composer Harry Von Tilzer, for example—demonstrated a form of bias; some worse than others. Both despite this and because of this, the "Liza Jane" family continued to expand.

Two of Carson's immediate contemporaries would include fellow Georgians Gid Tanner and Riley Puckett, who recorded "Liza Jane" in 1924.[35] According to Daniel's scholarship, Columbia Records saw an opportunity to match sales of Carson's records and invited the fiddler Tanner to visit their studio in New York. In turn, "Tanner invited fellow musician Riley Puckett to go with him."[36] A long-time associate of Tanner, guitarist and banjoist Riley Puckett was blinded as a child, studied piano at the Georgia Academy for the Blind, and taught himself banjo."[37] The duo of Tanner and Puckett—on fiddle and banjo, respectively, with Puckett singing—leads with the chorus:

Git along Liza, poor gal
Git along Liza Jane
Git along Liza, poor gal
She died on the train.

The song contains four verses, which can be difficult to decipher, but some of the lyrics recall the trip to the mountaintop, for instance, to give one's horn a blow. Tanner's fiddling resembles Carson's, or vice versa, and the two were said to be rivals. Perhaps when comparing their recordings side by side, the two fiddlers demonstrate a shared Georgia idiom; their versions of "Liza Jane" may strike a balance between the worthiness of playing for a roomful of dancers and the gratings of a wondrous, if precarious, life. Despite Tanner receiving the invitation to Columbia's studios, Puckett is credited as leader of this record. Together, he and Tanner embrace the outcome in which Liza Jane dies on the train. They also incorporate the "git along" phrase that dates back at least to the mid-1860s. Seeing as how "git along" may have had origins as a dance instruction, the duo could have intended mostly lighthearted possibilities.

In 1929, Kentucky folk singer and guitarist Bradley Kincaid recorded a solo rendition of "Liza Up in the 'Simmon Tree" on the Gennett, Champion, and Supertone labels.[38] Known as "The Kentucky Mountain Boy," Kincaid became a national figure through his four-year stint as host of the *National Barn Dance* on WLS radio station in Chicago. There, according to musicologist Charles K. Wolfe, Kincaid reputedly sang the English folk tune "Barbara Allen" every night for all four years.[39] Writing in his book *Kentucky Country*, Wolfe indicates how, during personal appearances, Kincaid liked to stir-up audiences through comic material, such as "Liza Up in a 'Simmon Tree," which became an audience favorite.[40] Despite an unusual title and an unconventional stanza structure, the song aligns with other "Liza, poor gal" melodies and lyrics.

Liza Up in the 'Simmon Tree
Bradley Kincaid

Lizy up in the 'simmon tree
And the possum on the ground
Possum said, "You son-of-a-gun,
Shake them 'simmons down"

[Chorus:]
Hooty Liza, pretty little girl
A-hoopty Liza Jane
Hooty Liza, pretty little girl
She died on the train
Cheeks is like the cherry
The cherry's like a rose
How I like that pretty little girl
Goodness gracious knows

Well, the old folks down in the mountains,
A-grinding sugar cane
Making barrels of molasses
For to sweeten old Lizy Jane

Whiskey by the gallon
And sugar by the pound
Great big bowl to put it in
And Liza to stir it 'round

[Chorus]

I went to see my Liza Jane
She was standing in the door
Shoes and stockings in her hand
And her feet all over the floor

Her head is like a coffee pot
Her nose is like the spout
Her mouth is like an old fireplace
With the ashes all raked out

[Chorus]

Well, I wouldn't marry a poor girl,
I'll tell you the reason why
Have so many poor kinfolks
She'd make my biscuits fly

[Chorus]

The entry point of Kincaid's song—highlighting a hungry, articulate possum—signals the piece's lighthearted nature, although as a recording, "Liza Up in the 'Simmon Tree" does not project a slapstick brand of humor. The song, indeed comic, nevertheless maintains a quietness, and since the girl does perish on the train, Kincaid delivers the line with slight falling action in acknowledgment of the song's vocabulary. While the possum character does not often "intrude" into the "Liza Jane" family, it does represent a standard figure in other folk matter, often accompanied by the antics of a raccoon. As shall be seen below, the 1922 folksong collection compiled by Thomas Talley recalls a similar scene between the possum and raccoon, with the raccoon taking the place of "Liza Jane."

A few decades before Talley published his collection, however, a syndicated dialect poem, "The Old Persimmon Tree," circulated widely, crediting the *Detroit Free Press*, yet appearing in several newspapers, including the *Florida Times-Union*, on November 25, 1883. Once more the "intruder," Liza Jane stands

to the side or is invoked, almost God-like, as the speaker of the poem pursues
a possum dinner.

The Old Persimmon Tree.

De 'possum know de paff troo de tall broom sage,
    Sing along, my 'Liza Jane!
An' he know whar de 'simmon tree stan' on de aige,
    Sing along, my 'Liza Jane!
An' he scrooches on de lim', chock full to de brim,
De 'simmon juice spatter to his knee;
Wid a tough light'ud chunk, I hits a-kerplunk,
He falls out de ole 'simmon tree!

When I puts dat 'possum in de ashes fer to roas',
    Sing along, my 'Liza Jane!
I feels like a gittin' in alongside him mos',
    Sing along, my 'Liza Jane!
For he look so neat, an' he smell so very sweet.
Dar's jess 'nuff fer two—him an' me.
As I lays down in de sun, wid de 'possum all done,
I blesses de ole 'simmon tree![41]

Since the authorship and intentions of this poem are unknown, nothing definite
can be deduced about it, except to note its broad circulation; its date, roughly
forty-five years before Kincaid recorded his song; and its unusual collection
of characters: a persimmon tree, a narrator, the narrator's girl 'Liza Jane, and a
possum. After the man fells and roasts the possum, he envies its tidy and suc-
culent presentation, oddly proposing to join him in the ashes. Kincaid's song,
in fact, presents the same cast, albeit with the roles and outcomes strewn-about
quite differently. If nothing else, the poem may be evidence of widespread folk
tradition perpetuated by Kincaid as part of his song.

Beyond its floating verses, "Liza Up in the 'Simmon Tree" traces to a few
important sources. Its oscillation between "Lizy" and "Liza" may track to African
American influence; the WPA narrative by Hannah Jameson gave the character's name as "Lizy Jane." The phrasing "For to sweeten old Lizy Jane" calls to
mind Black vernacular as well. And while the same vernacular would not likely
generate a nonsense word like "hoopty," it nevertheless might be the ultimate
source of the word—"o, po'" or "oh poor"—as mistranslated, embellished, or
parodied by whites: whoop, hoop, hoopo, hoopty. The cheek, cherry, and rose
comparison may conjure the Scottish bard, Robert Burns, as noted in the first

intermission. Otherwise, Liza Jane needs sweetening. She is both a "pretty little girl" and unflattering upon the eye: "Her mouth is like an old fireplace / With the ashes all raked out." She is "old." She is "old Lizy Jane" despite being an obstinate young woman of courtship age.

After Fiddlin' John Carson's records began to sell in large quantities, and other record companies sought to capture traditional country musicians on wax, the Vocalion label discovered Tennessee native Uncle Am Stuart or Ambrose Gaines Stuart. His 1924 recording of "Old Liza Jane" represents the earliest recording of "Liza, poor gal" lyrics. In fact, it is likely that Stuart was the earliest-born white musician to record a "Liza Jane" song. (George W. Johnson was likely the earliest-born singer of any background to record one.) Dating Stuart's birth to 1856 or 1857, Charles K. Wolfe suggests that Stuart's recordings "represent probably the oldest fiddling styles preserved on wax, and they made him the country's most popular old-time fiddler after [Fiddlin'] John Carson."[42] Writing in *Tennessee Strings*, Wolfe touches on why Stuart's age is important, namely, because it connected him and his music to the Civil War era. Stuart himself claimed to have "played old southern tunes he had heard [. . .] at southern dances 'befo' th' wah.'"[43] More significantly, perhaps, Wolfe relates (via a *New York Herald-Tribune* article) the fiddler's formative moments in learning to play his instrument through his own words: "Ah used to fiddle around th' kitchen til mah mother she'd chase me out of theah; and I'se go down and fiddle aroun' th' niggah camps til they'd chase me out of theah. Then I's go into th' barn all alone and fiddle theah."[44] It is unknown where Uncle Am Stuart learned "Old Liza Jane," but African American traditions may have influenced this rendition as well as his playing style.

A second source dates Stuart's birth to 1851. In his book *Fiddlin' Charlie Bowman*, Bob L. Cox identifies a "Mr. Hess" from Aeolian Vocalion Company, who had hoped to sign Bowman in mid-1924, but after Bowman rejected his offer, wound up signing the veteran Stuart at the ripe age of seventy-three years old.[45] By subtracting seventy-three from the year 1924, one arrives on 1851 as Stuart's potential birth year. Cox describes Stuart as a fiddler who played by ear since he could not read music. He further indicates that Stuart toured with the Hill Billies, who also recorded a "Liza Jane" song in the same vein. Moreover, "Having been born before the Civil War and knowing all the fiddle tunes from that era, the veteran fiddler was well known all over the area for playing his music at local dances." Newspapers and magazines were garrulously describing the septuagenarian as one who "smokes cigarettes, drinks corn 'likker,' likes the girls and plays a wicked fiddle."[46]

In that frame of mind, Uncle Am Stuart journeyed to New York in June 1924, where he recorded "Old Liza Jane" along with Gene Austin, who sang and may have played piano.[47] A young man at the time, Austin was breaking into the record business as a crooner and would become famous for his hit recording of "My Blue Heaven" a short while later, in 1927.[48] After a brief musical introduction by Stuart and the pianist, Austin's vocals begin with a verse.

Old Liza Jane
Uncle Am Stuart and Gene Austin

I took old Dixie and Dinah
And hitched them to a train
To get a barrel of molasses
To sweeten Liza Jane

Oh miss Liza poor gal
Oh miss Liza Jane
Oh miss Liza poor gal
Riding on that train

I asked that gal to have me
She told me wasn't I ashamed
I took my head to the crack of a fence
And tricked old Liza Jane

Again I asked her to have me
She told me wasn't I ashamed
I turned my back upon her
So get along Liza Jane

Wagon hay is loaded
Coming down the lane
Dark clouds a-rising
Sure sign of rain

I went up on the mountain
To get my sugar cane
Every stalk of cane I cut
Looked like Liza Jane

If you see that gal of mine
Tell her if you please
When she goes to make her bread
Roll up her dirty sleeve

I went up on the mountain
I give my horn a blow
I thought I heard my Liza say
Yonder comes my beau

I've travelled on the steamboat
I've travelled on a train
When I get married
I'll marry Liza Jane

Oh miss Liza poor gal
Oh miss Liza Jane
Oh miss Liza poor gal
Riding on that train.

"Old Liza Jane" effects a more leisurely pace than the other "poor gal" renditions, making it suitable as a "slow dance" number. Notably, it does not operate as a verse-chorus-verse arrangement, with the chorus materializing once after the first verse and again at the very conclusion of the song. Through its melody, "Old Liza Jane" connects with every "Liza, poor gal" song described above, and in terms of lyrics, may resemble "Mountaineer's Love Song" the closest. Stuart may have inherited some of these lyrics from the roustabout song documented by Lafcadio Hearn in New Orleans but perhaps discovered them earlier than Hearn did.

Through the anecdote of fiddling in African American encampments, Stuart may have been referring to wartime "contraband" camps or postwar camps filled with displaced Blacks. His connection to the Civil War era may have been essential in developing his repertoire. In her WPA narrative, Alice Hutcheson mentioned "Old Liza Jane" as a song she recalled, and postbellum "Liza Jane" minstrel numbers often contained the word "old" in the title or refrain. For example, Johnny Tuers performed "My Little Ole Liza Jane" in 1865, when Stuart may have been a teenager. Uncle Am's story concerning his interactions with African Americans in their camps recalls the fictional story of Miss Lillian in Margaret Walker's novel, *Jubilee*, in which the young girl sought companionship in the slave Quarters. In his case, Stuart sought musical fellowship among recently liberated Blacks. It is quite amusing to picture him being "chased out of theah," presumably because he had not yet learned to fiddle in a way that might be agreeable to the ear.

Uncle Am made "quite a hit" in New York, not only through his recordings but radio appearances as well. Writing in *Tennessee Strings*, Wolfe describes how, "Between recording sessions, [Stuart] broadcast over station WJY near

Times Square—probably the first mountain fiddler to be heard over radio in the northeast."[49] Stuart's affable, agreeable nature prompted him to make charitable financial gestures. Cox cites one such example in *Fiddlin' Charlie Bowman*. At the end of a show, Stuart would ask the crowd if anyone who enjoyed old-time music had been too sick or too poor to attend. "If anyone identified such a person, Uncle Am would hand over all the money he earned that night to give to that person."[50] As with Fiddlin' John Carson, however, Stuart also identified with racist institutions.

Historian Felix Harcourt ascribes sponsorship of the 1925 Mountain City Fiddlers Convention to the Ku Klux Klan, attracting virtually every old-time musician of relevance during the period; apparently, the array of talent even outweighed the legendary fiddler contests sponsored by Henry Ford.[51] Writing in his book *Ku Klux Kulture*, Harcourt lists Uncle Am Stuart, Fiddlin' John Carson, and the Hill Billies as attendees. Harcourt especially singles out the Hill Billies, who, having recorded for Peer and OKeh earlier in the year, "made their initial reputation" at the Mountain City convention. This led to enhanced radio and touring opportunities. "By 1927, The Hill Billies were playing at the White House Correspondents' Dinner in front of President Calvin Coolidge. The Ku Klux Klan had launched a phenomenon."[52] Mechanisms that popularized music in the early twentieth century often "sold" or espoused racism, even as a song like "Old Liza Jane" did not contain racist content and, in fact, may owe its existence to Black musical traditions.

The titles in this "Liza Jane" group of recordings range widely, from the more common "Liza Jane" and "Old Liza Jane" to "Liza Up in the 'Simmon Tree" and "Miss Liza, Poor Gal." By virtue of titling their piece "Mountaineer's Love Song," the Hill Billies establish the Liza Jane character as the ubiquitous Appalachian love interest. Many of the songs were recorded in New York or other large cities but represented the musically fertile country areas of Virginia, Kentucky, North Carolina, Tennessee, and Georgia, among other southern locales. Uncle Am Stuart's song was also billed as a "hoe-down." These were dance pieces. Their melodies connect with one another, even as their lyrics vary. Nevertheless, many renditions contained a common word hoard, with emphasis on sweetening, rural features, idyllic or precious beauty, comical unattractiveness, country ritual, and kinfolk.

Owing to their depictions of courtship mishaps, many of the songs commented on the lighter side of relationships, while the tones of still other versions were harder to fathom. Fiddlin' John Carson, the only performer to name his song "Good-bye Liza Jane," may have intended evil humor at the end of his piece. Virtually all the songs referred to Liza Jane as a "poor gal" and situated her, or someone else, on the train. Sometimes Liza Jane dies on the train, misses the train, or simply rides it, but either way, the railroad—a powerful symbol of speed, progress, and brawn—figures into the "Liza Jane" family of songs.

Carl Sandburg prints four complete "Liza Jane" songs in *The American Song-bag*. Included among his lyrics is the classic scenario involving the making of molasses "For to sweeten little Liza Jane."[53] This line, though not unusual, nevertheless calls to mind Black influence. A song group mostly associated with southern white performers also includes recordings by African American musicians, such as Mississippi John Hurt and Henry "Ragtime" Thomas, and demonstrates likenesses with a Black roustabout song collected in New Orleans by Lafcadio Hearn. The Hearn article dates to 1876, yet a young Ambrose Gaines "Uncle Am" Stuart may have encountered some of this material even earlier, given his apparent interactions with encamped African Americans during the Civil War years or shortly thereafter.

A vital folklore collection—*Negro Folk Rhymes, Wise and Otherwise*, published in 1922 by Fisk University Professor Thomas Talley—sheds light on the "poor gal" tradition, as well as other lyrics in the "Liza Jane" family. Music historian Samuel A. Floyd Jr. describes Talley's work as "the first comprehensive and substantive collection of African American secular song."[54] Writing in *The Power of Black Music*, Floyd Jr. notes that Talley's book was "hailed at the time of its publication as a masterpiece in its field" and that its songs, "collected in Tennessee and other locations in the South, were survivals of nineteenth-century folk practices."[55] Talley was not a folklorist by career, according to Lucinda Poole Cockrell, but taught chemistry and biology at Fisk University for many years, where he also served as Chair of the Chemistry Department. He was born in 1870, in Tennessee, to former Mississippi enslaved people. Talley sang bass and eventually toured with the New Fisk Jubilee Singers. Toward the end of World War I, he began to collect African American folksong. According to Cockrell's article in the *Tennessee Encyclopedia*, Talley "sought texts from the Middle Tennessee countryside and elsewhere, through an active network of friends, family, students, and colleagues, and recalled songs from memory or his own travels."[56]

Talley's inclusion of "'Possum up the Gum Stump" initially establishes the shenanigans of the possum and raccoon characters, yet the story of the possum does not end there.[57] Another song, "An Opossum Hunt," describes an occasion where the speaker's dog has treed a possum. The speaker reaches up and catches the critter before taking it home and eventually cooking it. He concludes the piece by noting, "I put sweet taters in de pan, / 'Twus de bigges' eatin' in de lan.'"[58] Even a third piece—"Raccoon and Opossum Fight"—finds the two companions biting and scratching each other, amusing a nearby rabbit.[59] Many possums and many raccoons (among other animals) populate Talley's book. These select rhymes may generally call to mind the Bradley Kincaid song,

"Liza Up in the 'Simmon Tree," as well as the mysterious nineteenth-century syndicated poem "Old Persimmon Tree," but one inclusion really speaks toward this subject matter. "Shake the Persimmons Down" conjures the basic situation of Kincaid's song, with the raccoon taking "Lizy's" place:

> De raccoon up in de 'simmon tree.
> De 'possum on de groun'.
> De 'possum say to de raccoon: "Suh!
> Please shake dem 'simmons down."
>
> De raccoon say to de 'possum: "Suh!"
> (As he grin from down below),
> "If you wants dese good 'simmons, man,
> Jes clam up whar dey grow!"[60]

This humorous interaction proceeds four lines further than Kincaid's introductory verse, and in Kincaid's version, the possum refers to "Lizy" somewhat roughly as a "son-of-a-gun." Here, the two critters converse with enviable politeness, although the raccoon can discern that the possum, by smiling, seeks to obtain a meal without working. To which, the raccoon implores the possum—no longer calling him "Suh!" but the folksy "man"—to exert himself, as he has done, to climb up among the ripening fruit. It is possible the 1872 minstrel song "Oh! Sam" influenced the development of "Liza Jane" songs that include possums and other animals. Written by lyricist Will S. Hays, "Oh! Sam" presents the Liza Jane character as well as a raccoon and a possum; both critters are sitting on a tree limb. "Oh! Sam" is one of the earliest pieces of sheet music to reference the Liza Jane character, appearing only one year after Eddie Fox published "Good Bye Liza Jane."[61]

Two additional rhymes given by Talley are associated with "Liza Up in the 'Simmon Tree." Both excerpts below establish a formula surrounding why the speaker will not marry a person from a given background. First, the assertion is initiated ("I wouldn't marry a poor girl"), and then the reason follows ("I will tell you why.") Kincaid adopts this formula (of not marrying a poor gal) to establish the fear over losing all the biscuits. The second of Talley's excerpts offers some perspective on an additional Kincaid couplet—"Head is like a coffee pot / Nose is like a spout"—with Talley's lyrics concentrating on the girl's nose.

from **"I Would Not Marry a Black Girl"**

> I wouldn' marry a black gal,
> I'll tell you de reason why:

When she goes to comb dat head
De naps'll 'gin to fly.[62]

from **"I Wouldn't Marry a Yellow or a White Negro Girl"**

I wouldn' marry dat White Nigger gal,
(Fer gracious sakes!) dis is why:
Her nose look lak a kittle spout;
An' her skin, it hain't never dry.[63]

Charles K. Wolfe, writing in the expanded edition of the Talley collection, suggests this material may have origins in 1850s minstrelsy songsters, where a family of such songs apparently developed.[64]

Talley himself comments on these two rhymes in his essay—"A Study in Negro Folk Rhymes"—at the back of his book. There, he ruminates on how Blacks:

> under hard, trying, bitter slave conditions [. . .] may have wished for the exalted station of the rich Southern white man and possibly would have willingly had a white color as a passport to position, [but] there never was a time when the Negro masses desired to be white for the sake of being white. Of course there is the Negro rhyme, "I Wouldn't Marry a Black Girl," but along with it is another Negro rhyme, "I Wouldn't Marry a White or a Yellow Negro Girl." The two rhymes simply point out together a division of Negro opinion as to the ideal standard of beauty in personal complexion. One part of the Negroes thought white or yellow the more beautiful standard and the other part of the Negroes thought black the more beautiful standard.[65]

The rhymes themselves, in their own hardscrabble way, deal with the "ideal standard of beauty" in degrees of earthy humor. It would be an open question whether these rhymes predated the songsters Wolfe refers to in his notes.

Talley goes on to vividly demonstrate how the Liza Jane character "intrudes" into a variety of songs, including one named for another girl.

from **"Bedbug"**

W'en dat Bedbug come down to my house,
I wants my walkin' cane.
Go git a pot an' scald 'im hot!
Good-by, Miss Lize Jane![66]

from **"A Wind-Bag"**

A Nigger come a-struttin' up to me las' night;
In his han' wus a walkin' cane,
He tipped his hat an' give a low bow;
"Howdy-doo! Miss Lize Jane!"[67]

from **"Pretty Polly Ann"**

I'll drop Polly Ann, a-lookin lak a crane;
I 'spec's I'll marry Miss Lize Jane.[68]

In the first example, "Bedbug," the "Good-by, Miss Liza Jane" phrase may not be intended for the girl herself but instead may emphasize the notion of moving along from an unpleasant situation, such as having a bedbug in one's house. It is humorous to imagine the person who sought a walking cane in the "Bed-bug" rhyme as the man (with "walkin' cane") who approaches the speaker in "A Wind-Bag." Taken one way, the speaker of the second poem may be Liza Jane herself unless the man refers to all amorous prospects as Liza Jane. While speakers sometimes quote Liza Jane, she rarely appears as the speaker or singer, making this rhyme unusual. Finally, in "Pretty Polly Ann," the narrator deems his second choice, "Miss Lize Jane," as the girl he will marry, given that "Polly Ann" resembles a long-necked wading bird. Liza Jane, the backup option, may not be a sure thing since the narrator only "expects" he will marry her. This injection of doubt, however slight, reinforces the long tradition of Liza Jane's unattainability or obstinacy as a romantic partner.

The book fleshes-out this unattainability through the fully realized wise rhyme, "Rejected by Eliza Jane." In his accompanying essay, "A Study in Negro Folk Rhymes," Talley describes "Verse Crowns"—in this case, the words "So," "An'," and "Well"—as "curtains" that "separate the little Acts of the Rhymes into scenes."[69]

Rejected by Eliza Jane

W'en I went 'cross de cotton patch
I give my ho'n a blow.
I thought I heared pretty Lizie say:
"Oh, yon'er come my beau!"

So: I axed pretty Lizie to marry me,
        An' what d'you reckon she said?

> She said she wouldn' marry me,
> If ev'ybody else wus dead.

An':   As I went up de new cut road,
         An' she go down de lane;
         Den I thought I heared somebody say:
         "Good-bye, ole Lize Jane!"

Well: Jes git 'long, Lizie, my true love.
         Git 'long, Miss Lizie Jane.
         Perhaps you'll sack* "Ole Sour Bill"
         An' git choked on "Sugar Cain."

*Sack = To reject as a lover.[70]

Talley defines the word "sack" in the original 1922 version of the book. This line, referring to the character "Ole Sour Bill," would seem to be the one outlier in a rhyme that otherwise connects to the WPA narratives, several folklore collections, and the suite of "Liza, poor gal" songs recorded in the twentieth century.

Instead of going up on the mountain, the narrator gives his horn a blow in the cotton patch, which may convey more relevance to the nineteenth-century African American experience. Act I concludes with the Liza Jane character appearing to recognize the horn-blowing singer as her beau. This passage connects to recordings made by Uncle Am Stuart, the Hill Billies, and Pete Seeger. It also links to songs collected by Lafcadio Hearn, the De Marsan song-book, and Carl Sandburg, who offers the following couplet—"When I go up on the mountings and give my horn a blow, / I think I hear my true love say, 'Yonder comes my beau'"—as part of "Liza in the Summertime (She Died on the Train)."[71]

Given pretty Lizie's apparent recognition of the horn, the emboldened singer asks for her hand in marriage, after which the Liza Jane character venomously rejects him. Even if he represented the only choice—with every other suitor dead—she would not consent. Act II, therefore, concludes on a sober note, but not perhaps without some hint of comedy. While this stanza may distantly relate to the formulaic "I will not marry so-and-so, and I'll tell you the reason why," it clearly recalls the WPA narrative given by Dosia Harris, who reports nearly identical lyrics.

Similarly, the material in Act III of "Rejected by Eliza Jane" links to WPA narratives by Bryant Huff and Anda Woods, who report the division of the "new cut road" and "the lane." This fork in the road usually serves to separate the two characters and travel them in opposite directions. Talley's version splits the characters accordingly. In addition to WPA material, this passage connects to the quatrain published in the *Weekly Review* of Crawfordsville, Indiana, from November 1865, among numerous other sources. Pete Seeger's "Oh! Liza, Poor Gal" includes the two pathways, and several folksong collectors—such as Perrow and Edmands—report similar lyrics.[72] Surprisingly, the third verse given by Talley concludes with "Good-bye, ole Liza Jane." This signifies the first inclusion of phrasing typically associated with a widely popular refrain.

As the curtain rises on the fourth and final Act of the rhyme, the speaker acknowledges Lizie Jane as his true love but seems to shout after her to "git along," which installs some additional refrain language. When telling her to "git along," the narrator may very well be all by himself, forlorn, on the new cut road. The singer further hopes the Liza Jane character will be unhappy with his rival, Ole Sour Bill, and that she will choke when indulging in sweets. This bitter, witty, and lonely wish closes the piece. "Git along" and all its alternatives—"Go along," "Go on," "Get along," and "G'lang"—are well documented in newspapers, regimental histories, recordings, and folklore collections. Wolfe notes that the Hill Billies and Tenneva Ramblers popularized related songs in white country music.[73]

"Rejected by Eliza Jane" has the feel of a fully organized song whose component pieces can trace their origins to "snotches" or one-verse songs. Consider the sheer number of names given in the rhyme: Eliza Jane, Lizie, Lize Jane, and Miss Lizie Jane. These name choices trace to yet additional WPA narratives, including Lina Hunter and Hannah Jameson, who referred to "Miss Liza Jane" and "Lizy Jane," respectively. As discussed above, Talley's rhyme incorporates refrain elements from "Goodbye Liza Jane" and "Get along Liza Jane" yet also combines classic "Liza Jane" scenarios: give my horn a blow, asked her to marry me, and go down the lane. Taken together, they powerfully narrate the most common "Liza Jane" outcome, namely, how the girl rejects the suitor, who often refers to her in unflattering terms. This fundamental comic orientation, published in 1922, may reflect African American folklore as handed down from one generation to the next, or it may incorporate elements of minstrel songs. It did, however, precede the earliest "poor gal" recording, thought to be made by Uncle Am Stuart in 1924 and may offer a pure picture before commercial interests took hold. Talley's organization of this wise rhyme and his subsequent commentary on "Verse Crowns" are masterful. His book is a gem.

Many other folklore collectors address this branch of the "Liza Jane" family, including Newman Ivey White, whose 1928 work *American Negro Folk Songs* incorporates several variants, and Dorothy Scarborough, whose 1925 collection *On the Trail of Negro Folk Songs* has been mentioned above. Scarborough offers a related variant, which she terms "I Went up on the Mountain Top." There is no information presented on its source, only that it bears the date-stamp of her copyright and her professed interest in collecting, in her words, "proper darky folk songs."[74] Notated music accompanies the lyrics.

I Went up on the Mountain Top

I went up on the mountain top
    To give my horn a blow;
An' I thought I heard Miss Lizy say,
    "Yonder comes my beau."

[Chorus:]
Po' little Lizy, po' little gal,
    Po' little Lizy Jane!
Po' little Lizy, po' little gal,
    She died on the train.

I went into the acre-fiel'
    To plant some 'lasses-cane,
To make a jug of molasses,
    For to sweeten Lizy Jane.

[Chorus]

She went up the valley road,
    An' I went down the lane,
A-whippin' of my ol' grey mule,
    An' it's good bye, Lizy Jane.

[Chorus][75]

If nothing more, Scarborough's version connects liberally to the many historical sources, folklore colleagues of her era, and the 1920s recordings that responded to the widespread demand for old-time country music.

Yet her efforts represent a powerful example of how white folklorists may have understood, and may not have understood, Black folk music. By comparing her first verse with the first verse given by Talley, important differences can be noted within a similar narration of events.

I went up on the mountain top
    To give my horn a blow;

An' I thought I heard Miss Lizy say,
   "Yonder comes my beau."

                                        —Scarborough

W'en I went 'cross de cotton patch
   I give my ho'n a blow.
I thought I heared pretty Lizie say:
   "Oh, yon'er come my beau!"

                                        —Talley

Imagine any contemporary white television news anchor reading the Scarborough verse and then picture a contemporary African American rapper reading
the Talley verse. Both stanzas purport to represent Black singing. Scarborough
clips one word by reducing "and" to "an'" while Talley faithfully reports actual
speech, with numerous words clipped, and, for the sake of accuracy as well
as with an inherent sense of poetry, presents words in improper forms. For
instance, where Scarborough writes "heard," Talley will give the more authentic
"heared." Scarborough may have witnessed an African American folk musician
singing the song, but in reproducing the lyrics, she did so in her unaccented
white voice, an action which contrasts with her blinkered comment about
collecting "proper darky folk songs."

Scarborough should not be faulted for attempting to reproduce Black folksong, but the example of her material adds to the already profound sludge
that accompanies the story of the "Liza Jane" family. Her book, which followed Talley's by about three years, is emblematic of how people acquire and
retransmit cultural information. In its own way, Talley's book probably does
the same. Wolfe notes, for example, the minstrelsy origins of certain rhymes
Talley presents, and Eileen Southern writes about Black musicians reacquiring
Black folksongs from minstrels and repurposing them.

The "Liza, poor gal" songs likely contained both Black and white influences.
They presented a Liza Jane character who perished on the train or hailed from
poverty. They were an integral part of America experiencing the first wave of
popular country music, from Uncle Am Stuart broadcasting between recording sessions at a Times Square radio station to the Tenneva Ramblers waxing
"Miss Liza, Poor Gal" at the legendary Bristol Sessions to Bradley Kincaid
riling up audiences with "Liza Up in the 'Simmon Tree." At the same time,
the plight of this branch would come to resemble the plight of "Goodbye Liza
Jane." The heart of the new century would ultimately require a different song
structure, one that could adapt to the boisterous strains of bebop, rhythm and
blues, and rock.

I'SE GOT A GAL AND YOU GOT NONE

A Countess-Composer and an Actress-Aviatrix
Popularize "Li'l Liza Jane"

1893 / 1904 TO 1916 / WORLD WAR I ERA

More than fifty years before Dizzy Gillespie chanted "I'll never go back to Georgia" as part of the Afro-Cuban jazz song "Manteca," a melancholy article credited to the *Atlanta Constitution* lamented the loss of the "dear old days" along the banks of the Savannah River, when enslaved people marched through the fertile fields amidst merry mockingbird songs. Published on February 22, 1893, in the *Lexington Dispatch* (South Carolina), the author goes on to address culture, faulting minstrels for their "pretty enough verses" that nonetheless lack the simplicity of songs at the traditional "cabin dances." Bandmembers at such a dance are recalled: one who plays a two-dollar fiddle; one who beats straws; two or three to pat-out percussion; and one to call the (dance) figures. Examples of lyrics are given. The recollected set would end with the dancers summoned: "pardners on de flo.'" A singer thus comes forward with the instructions for the final song,

> Steal my pardner, I steal yourn,
> Little Liza Jane;
> Steal all 'er roun', don' slight none,
> Little Liza Jane.[1]

This article draws a distinction between an authentic cabin dance song and minstrel pieces of the era, which, according to the writer, lack true plantation authenticity. It surfaces in mainstream newspapers about six to seven years after General Armstrong noted the presence of "Little Liza Jane" at the Hampton Institute.

Despite its painful treatment of African Americans, the article does offer valuable insights into the "Little Liza Jane" variant. The writer does not associate the song with any popular troupes but instead situates it within the folk tradition. Its orientation as a stealing partners dance song is highlighted. Instruments and performance rituals are noted, with emphasis on fiddle, percussion, and square dance calls. The lyrics themselves present as a snatch of folk material, with two lines affixed to the girl's name. Both Marshall Butler and Lucy Thurston referred to "Little Liza Jane" in their WPA interviews, but Lina Hunter also associated the phrase "don't slight none" with a "Liza Jane" dance song. Butler, Hunter, and three other WPA respondents had been enslaved in Georgia. As opposed to a song that initiates the cabin dance or one performed in the middle of the festivities, "Little Liza Jane" closes the celebration, saving, perhaps, the best for last. And when the chorus arrives, "all join in the shout, and the dance assumes all the life of a perfect south Georgia cyclone."

Skepticism about minstrelsy probably cut different ways as the twentieth century approached. On the one hand, some critics may have longed for a return to the prewar plantation system, and therefore, bright minstrel walkarounds were probably too shiny and theatrical. On the other hand, the increasingly urban theatergoing public probably hungered for something less country and more "uptown." By the turn of the century, alternatives to minstrelsy had arrived in the shapes of "talking machines" or recordings, Tin Pan Alley's somewhat gentrified "race fare," and new musical styles such as the syncopated rhythm of ragtime. While these fledgling technologies and arts found their voices, the "Goodbye Liza Jane" and the "Liza, poor gal" variants had flourished. Another "Liza Jane" variant, however, would prove more adaptable to the lively music—jazz, rhythm and blues, and rock 'n' roll—that would develop as the century progressed. The *Atlanta Constitution/Lexington Dispatch* article demonstrates how a song could have "leaked out" from folk culture without a hit forming in minstrelsy or Music Row. Instead, the song simply steeped, like the coals of a distant fire, while other tunes, dances, performers, and styles jumped onstage.

In 1904, the dialect poet and folklorist Anne Virginia Culbertson published a book of stories, *At the Big House: Where Aunt Nancy and Aunt 'Phrony Held Forth on the Animal Folks.* As part of her introduction, Culbertson writes, "the stories presented in this volume were found chiefly among the negroes of southeastern Virginia and the Cherokee Indians of North Carolina."[2] She notes the source of each story in the table of contents—either "negro" or Indian—and explains that the stories of Indian origin are "told by an elderly negress, Aunt 'Phrony, who is supposed to be Indian on the father's side and negro on the mother's."[3] The author populates the book with all sorts of animal-related folklore and situates the storytelling on a Virginia plantation shortly after the Civil War.[4] One of the chapters, "Mr. Hare and Mr. Flint Rock," relates to the "Liza Jane" family.

The through-action of the book involves a woman visiting her birthplace in Virginia and bringing her children along. As part of the visit, the children regularly interact with the African American people, including the storytellers, who live on the plantation. In "Mr. Hare and Mr. Flint Rock," the children rush over toward the cookhouse after hearing a banjo. There, they discover "Tim, the plow-boy, playing and singing for the benefit of the assembled company, among whom was Aunt Nancy's granddaughter, Cassy."[5] In fact, Tim keeps his eyes focused on Cassy, who had returned from the market in a bright dress, while he sings.

Li'l 'Liza Jane

I got a house in Baltimo',
Li'l 'Liza Jane;
Po'ch behime an' po'ch befo',
Li'l 'Liza Jane.

I got a buggy an' a hoss,
Li'l 'Liza Jane;
Come 'long, honey, an' be der boss,
Li'l 'Liza Jane.

I got a house an' a track er lan',
Li'l 'Liza Jane;
Shake yo' foot an' clap yo' han',
Li'l 'Liza Jane.

Come, my love, an' go wid me,
Li'l 'Liza Jane;
An-a we will go ter Tennessee,
Li'l 'Liza Jane.[6]

The lyrics Culbertson assigns to Tim reflect a modernizing courtship song. Not present are the mountain top horn-blows, the new cut road and the lane, planting a patch of cane, and the cheerful insults that invariably follow the suitor's rejection. "Li'l 'Liza Jane" is not even performed as a "stealing partners" plantation dance. In this newfangled approach, the singer directly addresses the girl. He promises her a house and a tract of land, and not just any old house, but a spacious one sporting two porches. If Liza Jane would only follow him to Baltimore, the couple could take fashionable horse and buggy rides, and she could take charge of the situation. It is perplexing why the singer would later promise to take Liza Jane with him to Tennessee at the end of the song when the allure of a bustling port city would likely outweigh a landlocked country destination, but the importance of rhyme—Tennessee / me—may outweigh a final determination of meaning. The lyrics do not clarify whether the promises of a new life will ultimately sway Liza Jane. Doubt still prevails.

A return to the story finds the singer and his girl—Tim and Cassy—not an openly acknowledged courting couple, "and it was therefore, not etiquette for [Cassy] to encourage him too obviously, so she tossed her head and said that she had not come there to hear any 'ol' co'tin'-songs' but in the hope of listening to some stories."[7] The invocation having been given, Aunt 'Phrony begins the tale about the mischievous hare who meets a very large grey-haired old man, Flint Rock. After the old man relates his woes to the rabbit character, the two agree to build a fire, as the weather has been turning cold. Eventually, the hare strikes the slumbering Flint Rock with a piece of wood, fracturing the man into hundreds of pieces that start to rain down; before long, a stone strikes the hare and bends his nose permanently. The story concludes with Aunt 'Phrony indicating the hare "was a ol' bachelder" with no wife to keep him out of mischief.[8]

Gifted at portraying dialect and referred to frequently as a "dialect poet" in the newspapers of her day, Culbertson's representation of African American speech rivals that by Daniel Webster Davis and Thomas Talley; her efforts easily exceed those, say, of Dorothy Scarborough. For instance, the *Evening Star*, Washington, DC, wrote that, on March 25, 1898:

> Miss Anne Virginia Culbertson will meet the ladies of the Washington Club, socially, this evening at their club rooms and entertain them with her original verses. She knows what the negro dialect and peculiarities are and has a happy way of personating them.[9]

While not written in her own words, the article does describe her entertainment as minstrelsy of a kind. The *Evening Star* took a shine to Culbertson and published the story "Mr. Hare and Mr. Flint Rock" precisely seven years later on March 25, 1905, including the lyrics for "Li'l 'Liza Jane."[10] Mostly a book of folklore, *At the Big House* nonetheless includes snippets of song, as well as some fully-organized pieces, such as "Li'l Liza Jane" and "Cindy, Cindy."[11] The book, therefore, can be regarded as a work of folk *music* as well as a work of folk*lore*. It is a wonder that Culbertson herself did not compose and publish sheet music for "Li'l Liza Jane" or another song. Her version, though placed in the middle of a book devoted to animal tales, nevertheless may represent the first fully organized rendition of "Li'l Liza Jane."

A title such as *At the Big House* unmistakably associates the book with the looming presence of an enslaver's dwellings, and through her storytelling,

Culbertson links "Li'l Liza Jane" to the slavery experience, even if the human characters in "Mr. Hare and Mr. Flint Rock"—Tim, Cassy, and Aunt 'Phrony— had been liberated. Culbertson's reference to southeastern Virginia as an area of the source material will naturally invoke Hampton Institute, where the song's performance rituals were described by its founder, General Armstrong, as well as contributors to the school's publications. Eventually, the musicologist Natalie Curtis Burlin documented the song as part of her *Hampton Series*, but a few years before she did so, another article materialized in the school's flagship publication which would reinforce the presence of "Little Liza Jane" among enslaved people before the end of the Civil War.

Described as a Hampton graduate and the cashier of Hampton Institute, Harris Barrett contributed the article "Negro Folk Songs" to the April 1912 edition of the *Southern Workman*.[12] By means of introduction, Barrett writes:

> After the lapse of fifty years, interest in the folk songs of the Negro still remains unabated, though, as the old slaves pass away, there is danger that many of these melodies may be entirely lost.[13]

He conjures word-of-mouth tradition in the transmission of plantation songs, as well as the beloved status of folk music at Hampton. In noting that freed Blacks sometimes despise "these songs of bondage," Barrett does not fault them when considering "the numberless caricatures put upon the American stage known as 'coon songs' or 'ragtime,' and which form no part of true Negro folk music."[14]

While he does not identify himself as a scholar or researcher, Barrett adds considerable context and performance rituals to his seven-page study. In citing the importance of song to "the Negro race in slavery days," he begins:

> Whether at church under the eyes of "de white folks," or at his own prayer meetings off in the woods; at "de big house" or in his humble cabin; at work "shucking" corn in the fields of Old Kentucky, or pick- ing cotton under the tropical sun of Alabama; handling hogsheads of tobacco on the Ohio River steamboats or piling cotton on the levees of New Orleans—at all times and in all places his voice could be heard in harmonic cadence.[15]

This excerpt calls to mind a compendium of sources situating the "Liza Jane" family in numerous locales and eras, including its presence in Culbertson's book *At the Big House*, although a clear difference can be seen in how Barrett presents the same term. By placing it in quotes, "at de big house," with the slightest bit of dialect, he draws a line between that symbol of power (as well as "de white folks" who wielded that power) and the oasis of song. He acknowledges the deferential language forced upon African Americans in slavery days, whereas Culbertson enjoyed the privilege of naming her book of stories for the enslaver's dwelling.

In describing the moments when songs formed, Barrett emphasizes improvisational qualities as well as performative routines that might, in the case of the "Liza Jane" family, lead to many versions of the same song.

> These songs were usually the outgrowth of some emotion of the moment and were entirely extemporaneous. For this reason, a large number were sung as solos, sometimes as mere recitatives, but almost always with a chorus in which the rest of the people joined, no matter what the gathering or occasion might be. These facts account for the variety of words often sung to the same tune.[16]

Perhaps a tune sung during a "corn shucking" could also be relied upon during a frolic, and while the chorus might be the same during every repetition of the song, the individual lines or verses—snatches of folk melody—may have varied from day to day. Barrett may also imply that a stable chorus would ultimately provide a discernible guidepost from one recitation to the next.

He places these plantation songs into five categories: Spirituals, Cradle songs, Labor songs, Dance and game songs, and Songs of freedom.[17] A definition of each category and at least one example song for each category are presented, some of which are utterly heartbreaking. Examples of the most numerous songs, Spirituals, include the following four-line chorus, which refers to the biblical story of Daniel in the lion's den, and a separate two-voice song that involves a particular form of hardship specific to the African American slave experience:

> My lord delibered Daniel,
> My lord delibered Daniel,
> My lord delibered Daniel,
> Why can't he deliber me?[18]

> Mother, is Massa gwine to sell us to-morrow?
>   Yes, yes, yes!
> Farewell, mother, I must lebe you.
>   Yes, yes, yes!
> Mother, I'll meet you in heaven.
>   Yes, my child.[19]

Examples in three of the four remaining categories—Cradle songs, Labor songs, and Songs of freedom—describe lullabies, tunes that accompanied corn-shucking events, and even a reference to the Ninth United States Colored Troops Regiment led by General Armstrong.

Upon introducing Dance and game songs, Barrett writes, "I believe there was never a people in all history who had more of sorrow and yet found more joy than did the Negroes of the South during slavery days."[20] He indicates that dances might have taken place in nearby cabins or may have required a ten-mile walk. Participants dressed as well as they could, although, in some cases, mistresses dressed their maids properly, fearing their servants might not look as presentable as those from other plantations.[21] The cashier-musicologist refers to ring games, jigs, fancy figures, and cake walks, and in terms of the latter, foreshadows what Amiri Baraka/LeRoi Jones would conclude many decades later, by observing, "many of the movements in the cake walk seen on the stage to-day were entirely unknown to the Negro slaves."[22] In short, popular culture ended up caricaturing a caricature in such a way as to render the end product unrecognizable.

Barrett offers but one example of a Dance and game song, and given its long history at the Hampton Institute, it will come as no surprise.

> Come, my love, an' go wid me,
> Little Liza Jane
> Oh, Eliza, little Liza Jane
> Little Liza Jane.[23]

In order to create the proper atmosphere for this dance song, the participants would sing, clap their hands, and stamp their feet. Occasionally, a crude banjo would appear, fashioned from ordinary wood and an old skin "stretched across its drum." Likewise, two bones might be rubbed together to create additional music.[24] In this way, the celebrants transcended their circumstances, banishing the endlessness of their entrapment.

Barrett does not cite any sources in the presentation of this material except to note the generational transmission of cultural information. According to a brief obituary for him that appeared in the November 1915 issue of *The Crisis*, a publication produced by the National Association for the Advancement of Colored People (NAACP), Barrett was born in Henderson, Kentucky, in 1865. He graduated from Hampton Institute in 1885. During his time as a student, he worked in the treasurer's office and, later, after graduating, he toiled as a cashier for six years. Described as a "quiet, accurate man," he was also said to have selflessly founded an organization that contributed "half a million dollars to colored people to assist in the buying of homes."[25] In all likelihood, the basic outline of his life connects him to immediate family members and family friends who had been enslaved. Similar circumstances probably applied to his wife, who was, according to the same issue of *The Crisis*, "one of Virginia's prominent colored women, [and had] been made superintendent of the school for wayward colored girls in Hanover County."[26] In addition to knowing stories and songs from slavery times, Barrett and his wife no doubt knew many formerly enslaved people.

Barrett's article "Negro Folk Songs" precedes the WPA interviews by twenty-five years. Readers would have little reason to doubt any part of Barrett's narrative, including his description of song lyrics, performance rituals, and celebration details. In any event, he was not speaking to a government interviewer but writing his own article for publication at his alma mater and place of employment and doing so as a confident and "accurate man." The information included in "Negro Folk Songs" echoed General Armstrong's recollections, as well as other Hampton people who wrote pieces for the school's publications. Perhaps more tellingly, Barrett offers details on experiences that would be mirrored through the publication of the *Slave Narrative Collection*. With its 1912 date stamp, Barrett's article was ahead of its time.

Barrett's rendering of "Little Liza Jane" and his detailed description of song formation reinforces W. C. Handy's experiences with "snatches of song," and at the same time, may explain the filled-out Anne Virginia Culbertson rendition. In terms of the former, the song's one-line plea—"Come, my love, an' go wid me"—gets attached to repetitions of the girl's name. There seems to be little difference between it and the W.C. Handy example of the Negro plowman: "I wouldn't live in Cairo-oo / A—O—OO—A—O—OO." Culbertson's version, on the other hand, would seem to add together, in Barrett's estimation, "the variety of words often sung to the same tune." That is, Culbertson may have collected several different "Li'l Liza Jane" snotches and fit them together as part of the same song. Alternatively, she may have encountered a single source who had, essentially, compiled four unrelated or lightly related snotches. Barrett, Handy, and Culbertson roughly hailed from the same generation. All three were alive, as adults, when Culbertson published *At the Big House*, and all three likely had contact with formerly enslaved people who knew "Li'l Liza Jane." All three studied Black folksong and represented Black speech in their works.

Remembering that Culbertson's version of "Li'l Liza Jane" appeared in the *Evening Star* newspaper as well as in book form, it was "out there" in the world, capable of being discovered. Notated music, however, did not accompany Tim's singing for the benefit of his girlfriend, Cassy, in "Mr. Hare and Mr. Flint Rock." Anybody reading Culbertson's story or Barrett's article, who did not otherwise know the tune, would have had to imagine a melody. "Little Liza Jane" was alive and well at the Hampton Institute, alongside the banks of the Savannah River, and in the pages of *At the Big House*. To be fair, the song's verses could have been *anywhere* in the years leading up to the 1916 sheet music publication that would change the trajectory of the "Liza Jane" family for the remainder of the twentieth century and beyond. The materialization of the song's score was not per se mysterious, but the woman who published it, Countess Ada de Lachau, was enigmatic. Did actual royalty participate in the popularization of the song?

If not for her connection to the dancer Ruth St. Denis, even less would be known about the elusive Countess, who turns up in 1905 in New York as St. Denis was attempting to finance her groundbreaking "temple dance." According to St. Denis biographer Suzanne Shelton, numerous acquaintances supported the cause, including a family friend, "the impoverished but stagestruck Countess Ada de Lachau, [who] dramatically donated her last twenty dollars."[27] In her autobiography, *An Unfinished Life*, St. Denis herself recalls a note from the Countess accompanying the donation. It read: "Hold on to your faith. Do not give up. Go straight ahead."[28]

De Lachau turns up again in 1916 when Ruth St. Denis and her students at the dance academy she cofounded—the Denishawn School of Dancing—were invited to stage a show at the University of California, Berkeley. A grand spectacle was choreographed, which would employ "the entire school in producing a dance pageant of Egypt, Greece, and India."[29] In describing the pageant as it unfolded, Shelton conjures the musical accompaniment, where:

> In the orchestra pit, Louis Horst conducted the San Francisco Symphony in a patchwork score of pieces by Walter Meyrowitz, Arthur Nevin, and the Comtesse Ada de Lachau, an old friend of Ruth's mother and one of the earliest backers of *Radha* who wrote the music for the pageant's Greek duet.[30]

By virtue of these details, the Countess, or *Comtesse*, maintained connections to the creative arts world on both coasts. She also demonstrated facility with musical composition, contributing to the success of an American dance pioneer. As it turns out, Countess Ada de Lachau played piano on a transcontinental voyage. While sailing to England in 1925, the American politician Henry Shattuck encountered the Countess while aboard the SS *Cedric*. Shattuck noted, in the diary he kept, "Mrs. Delauchau [*sic*] played the song 'Little Liza Jane.'"[31]

Later in life, Countess Ada de Lachau lived in New Rochelle, New York.[32] Writing in *An Unfinished Life*, St. Denis depicts how the Countess would come down from her home and meet St. Denis in the studio, where "she would sit down at the piano and tempt me with the first strains of her music."[33] Describing sensations at the time of "confusion and drudgery," St. Denis portrays these moments with the Countess as "rare hours of sheer beauty" in which St. Denis would "sing blithely" along to the piano accompaniment. According to St. Denis, the Countess would also "play with concentrated intensity the almost

Wagnerian measures of a beautiful ballet called *The Tigress*, which she had composed for me years ago to a theme of Balzac and which to her and to my infinite regret I have never produced."[34]

St. Denis further characterizes the Countess as "my beloved Ada" who lent "great distinction" to parties, a woman who "interpenetrated my whole spiritual and artistic life," and "a woman of extraordinary sensitivity, and beauty of spirit."[35] Both Shelton and St. Denis describe Countess Ada de Lachau as someone who periodically lacked resources. In particular, St. Denis refers to the Countess and her husband, Fabian, an engineer, as a family who "had fallen upon somewhat evil days," and as a result, "their little daughter, Marie, was singing French songs, sometimes in vaudeville, and more often in people's homes when an evening of entertainment was offered."[36] The detail about de Lachau's daughter, Marie, singing in French may yield some indication of the family's origins. On October 22, 1917, Marie de Lachau acted the role of "Maid to the Clatterbys" in *Anthony in Wonderland*, a comedy in three acts written by Monckton Hoffe. According to *Theatre Magazine*, the production "*Anthony in Wonderland* found New York too prosaic-minded to appreciate its fantastic and romantic satire, and tarried but a week at the Criterion [Theater]."[37] And on this note, scant additional details are known, biographically, of the Countess Ada de Lachau, her husband Fabian, and their "little" daughter Marie.

Yet, in 1916, with the Countess potentially living in California, the actress Ruth Chatterton stepped into the role of Olivia in the comedy *Come Out of the Kitchen* and thus "played to the biggest receipts of her career."[38] Writing in his biographical work, *Ruth Chatterton, Actress, Aviator, Author*, Scott O'Brien notes that the play debuted at the Columbia Theatre on August 14, 1916, in San Francisco, where one critic described Chatterton's character as a "vivacious, coaxing, insinuating little puss" and another praised Chatterton as one of the few who have "the capacity to make a character live and move."[39] Adapted to the stage from Alice Duer Miller's serial story and 1916 novel of the same title, the comedy follows the plight of a Southern clan who have lost their money but attempt to keep afloat by renting their sizeable house to a wealthy northerner, one Burton Crane.[40] As part of the proceedings, the family members adopt aliases and pretend, hence the comedy, to impersonate servants. Thus, Chatterton assumed the dual role of Olivia Dangerfield and Jane Ellen, the Irish cook, who manages the twin stresses of fending off suitors and whipping up imperfect repasts for everyone.[41] Eventually, Olivia must call upon the services of her "Black Mammy," Mandy, to help her succeed while shuffling her out of sight into the cupboard.[42] In the end, Crane discovers the ruse and recognizes Olivia for who she is, just as the two fall into each other's arms at the final curtain. The industriousness of Olivia / Jane Ellen, therefore, saves the plantation.[43] Having achieved critical success in San Francisco, the play moved to Broadway later that year, where, according to O'Brien, it received uneven reviews. The *New York Times*, for instance, praised Chatterton but not the storyline.[44] According to *The Concise Oxford Companion to American Theatre*, the comedy *Come Out of the Kitchen* nevertheless ran for 224 performances at the Cohan Theatre.[45]

At one point during Act II, the script calls for Olivia's brother, Charlie, to whistle "Liza Jane" before Olivia, pretending to be Jane Ellen, sings it outright as she engages in cookery.[46] While the script identifies the song as "Liza Jane," the music for "Li'l Liza Jane" had been simultaneously published by Sherman, Clay & Co. in San Francisco, in 1916, as part of an effort to associate the song with the stage production.[47] The cover page presents a picture of Chatterton sitting atop a stool, clutching a broom. Beneath her, text reads, "Ruth Chatterton as Jane Ellen in Come Out of the Kitchen." In larger print at the top of the cover, additional text reads, "Composed by Countess Ada de Lachau and used as Incidental Music in the Three Act Comedy Come Out of the Kitchen." The lyrics, in their entirety, follow.

Li'l Liza Jane

Southern Dialect Song, Composed by Countess Ada de Lachau

I'se got a gal an' you got none,
Li'l Liza Jane.
I'se got a gal an' you got none,
Li'l Liza Jane.

[Refrain:]
Oh Eliza, Li'l Liza Jane,
Oh Eliza, Li'l Liza Jane.

Liza Jane done cumter me,
Li'l Liza Jane.
Bof as happy as can be,
Li'l Liza Jane.

[Refrain]

Come my love an' live with me,
Li'l Liza Jane.
I will take good care uv thee,
Li'l Liza Jane.

[Refrain]

House an' lot in Baltimo',
Li'l Liza Jane.
Lots of chilluns roun' de do',
Li'l Liza Jane.

[Refrain]

The similarities between this publication and Eddie Fox's sheet music publication of "Good Bye Liza Jane" are striking. Each would represent the first known published piece of sheet music for its branch of the "Liza Jane" family, and at that, the two most popular branches. As opposed to crediting words and music to one or more individuals, the publication of "Good Bye Liza Jane" simply reads, on the cover, "By Eddie Fox," and on the first page of music, "Arranged by Eddie Fox." In the case of "Li'l Liza Jane," there, too, the sheet music does not separately credit words to anyone but instead reads "Composed by Countess Ada de Lachau." Both Fox and the Countess were certainly aware of related songs already in circulation, hence why neither attempted to claim full credit for the lyrics. While the Countess probably overstepped the boundaries of propriety in claiming compositional credit, there was no previous composer, no prior piece of sheet music to prove otherwise. While the song had been in circulation for many decades, and a related set of lyrics had been published by Anne Virginia Culbertson in book form as well as a broadly circulated newspaper, nevertheless, a notated score did not exist before 1916.

To be fair, the de Lachau publication is far from a forgery. It channels a variety of lyrics, making it a complex assemblage. The Culbertson version is the nearest relative, given its status as the only known organized version to precede the de Lachau publication. In this case, the obvious relationship between the two pieces would be the claim of the singer to own a house and land in Baltimore. Singers of both versions would also appeal to "Come my love an' live with me" (de Lachau) or "Come, my love, an' go wid me" (Culbertson), but these are variations on stock lines that surfaced, as noted, in a variety of nineteenth-century contexts, including a Confederate songster and the 1845 minstrel song "Going Ober de Mountain." Where the two versions obviously differ is in the refrain, or more specifically, where Culbertson lacks a refrain. De Lachau's chorus captures the essence of the Hampton Institute reports. From General Armstrong through to Harris Barrett, the simple "snotch" would be represented as either "Oh, little Liza, Little Liza Jane" (Armstrong) or "Oh, Eliza, little Liza Jane" (Barrett). It is the heart of the song, and as Barrett indicates, likely survives from slavery times. However she may have come to overhear it, the Countess installed this refrain in her printed version, whereas Culbertson did not.

The line "I'se got a gal an' you got none" may sound familiar, owing to popular recordings—those by Bob Wills and Nina Simone, for instance—which adopt its slightly cruel braggadocio. Its language derives from a stealing partners dance game, yet the de Lachau sheet music establishes "Li'l Liza Jane" as a popular song, suitable for solo recitation by the fictional Jane Ellen as she whips up a meal. In some ways, this action disassociated "Li'l Liza Jane" from its typical performative routines and, in doing so, launched it into a changed cultural landscape, which had begun to shed its dependence on blackface minstrelsy. While the play *Come Out of the Kitchen* may have reinforced the racial divisions of its day, in the end, its performers were not white men masquerading as Black men and women. The play was produced singularly for the stage, not as part of a burlesque variety show.

Along with the second verse, which is less exceptional, the first half of the de Lachau song establishes a cozy love relationship, although there may be lingering "directions" within the verses regarding dance traditions. The second half of the song does not follow. Seeing as the singer and Liza Jane are "Bof as happy as can be," why would he need to convince her to come and live with him and promise to take good care of her? To further sway Liza Jane, the singer mentions his possessions in Baltimore and implies that the two of them, together, will produce "lots of chilluns." A popular song does not have to "add up," however, and these verses may be of secondary relevance to the highly infectious refrain. If the Countess does scramble the song's storyline, she does preserve the ultimate outcome in many "Liza Jane" songs, namely, the uncertainty of the courtship. Even though the singer has a gal, even though the gal has come to him, even though the two lovers are happy, the singer must still convince her to live with him; he promises her a home and children in Baltimore. Everything is promises. Doubt prevails. Doubt reminds the listener of Liza Jane's elusiveness.

Noting that the sheet music publication coincided with the staging of *Come Out of the Kitchen*, a drama set at the "Dangerfield mansion in Virginia," it obviously suited de Lachau to associate "Li'l Liza Jane" with the South.[48] Unlike certain "Liza Jane" variants, such as the nineteenth-century Frank Lum rendition, no racial epithets can be found among the lyrics. The cover page of the sheet music—unlike, say, the Harry Von Tilzer version, which caricatures two Black faces—presents the portrait of a white actress. Nonetheless, de Lachau terms the piece a "Southern Dialect Song" and fulfills that expectation, for example, with verses like "Liza Jane done cumter me, / Li'l Liza Jane. / Bof as happy as can be, / Li'l Liza Jane." Beyond the question of where she may have overtaken these lyrics, there might also be the question of why she chose to publish a dialect song as opposed to, say, any other kind of song. The short answer may be, in 1916, race-tinged fare continued to appeal, and another example of it would not be unusual; indeed, it might lend atmospheric or historic believability to the story of Olivia and her family members. Otherwise, the brightness of the song hardly clashes with the comedic intentions of the play, which emphasize Olivia Dangerfield's eligibility for marriage. One imagines the Countess, through her connection to Ruth St. Denis, meeting the playwright, Albert Ellsworth Thomas, and spontaneously humming a song she had learned. At this same imaginary Bay Area meeting, Thomas recognizes the bouncy song as the crowning ingredient for his blockbuster southern play and encourages the Countess to seek copyright protection posthaste. But this is all vapor of the mind, not unlike the quintessential San Francisco fog that rolls into town, obscuring otherwise identifiable shapes. In another word: sludge.

The Countess Ada de Lachau does not seem to be a *nom de plume* but an actual person who may have been an actual Countess or *Comtesse*. She had married an engineer named Fabian, and their daughter, Marie, sang professionally in French, perhaps offering clues as to the family's nationality. A dear friend to the celebrated dancer Ruth St. Denis, the Countess composed a piece of music for a 1916 dance exhibition by St. Denis at the University of California, Berkeley. A stone's throw from there, in San Francisco, the vehicle that would present actress Ruth Chatterton with her greatest receipts—*Come Out of the Kitchen*—featured "Li'l Liza Jane" as incidental music. The year: also 1916. Seeing as how the script calls for Chatterton's character, Olivia, to sing verses of the song, the actress may have been the first performer to sing this "Liza Jane" variant professionally. Notably, the script calls for Olivia's brother, Charlie, to whistle the song just before Olivia inhabits it, thereby making the actor Robert Ames the first performer to handle the de Lachau melody professionally.[49] "Li'l Liza Jane" could have vanished after this whistling and incidental singing but did not. *Come Out of the Kitchen* lasted several months in a flagship New York theatre, and during that time, doubtlessly popularized the lyrics and melody.

Duke Ellington and his sage words reappear. The powerful engine of the refrain is bouncy, irresistible, and agreeable to the ear. "Oh, Eliza, li'l Liza Jane" offers regular meter, whereas some of the "Goodbye Liza Jane" lyrics sprawled (syllabically) all the way down to Lynchburg Town. The Culbertson, de Lachau, and Curtis Burlin versions all reference Baltimore, which updates the "Liza Jane" family from a "country hick" environment to one that can imagine the big city. Liza Jane herself could enjoy an enthralling urban life if she would only choose to follow the suitor. Save for her name credited repeatedly on record labels and presumably on royalty checks, the Countess Ada de Lachau would otherwise vanish, departing in the same mysterious fashion as how she arrived in the first place. True, she would play piano for an older Ruth St. Denis, assisting the dancer in overcoming her drudgeries, but she would never publish another composition as Countess Ada de Lachau, not even her unrealized ballet

The Tigress. As for Ruth Chatterton, her career would climb and drop, climb and drop, and so would she. In May 1935, she piloted a Stinson airplane across the United States, beginning in New York and stopping in St. Louis, Tulsa, and El Paso, before landing safely in Los Angeles. She was, therefore, both an actress and an aviatrix.[50] Chatterton projected some healthy mischief and maintained professional connections to both coasts.

It would not take long for the East Coast production of *Come Out of the Kitchen* to generate a "hit"—that is, for "Li'l Liza Jane." On September 10, 1917, Earl Fuller's Famous Jazz Band recorded "Li'l Liza Jane—One-Step" at Victor studios in New York, crediting de Lachau as composer.[51] The subtitle "One-Step" would emphasize dancing. Terming it a "hurriedly assembled band," historian Samuel Charters suggests that Earl Fuller's Famous Jazz Band sought to emulate the success of the "Original Dixieland Jass Band," which had been recorded earlier in 1917.[52] Writing in *A Trumpet Around the Corner*, Charters credits Fuller's group with a lively recording of "Li'l Liza Jane":

> [Having] all the trademarks of a ragtime band's stage novelty. They played a unison melody by the trumpet and clarinet, with trombone fills, the ragtime style that was probably common everywhere, then the band put down the instruments for alternate choruses to sing the words in the classic minstrel show "walk around" manner.[53]

Indeed, Earl Fuller's Famous Jazz Band did not adopt the verses of "Li'l Liza Jane" but shouted the refrain. They did adopt the melody and played it, as Charters notes, in the style of the day, one that emphasized ragtime but also minstrelsy effects. Other "Liza Jane" variants debuted in minstrelsy fifty years earlier, precisely in Part Third of the minstrel show, where they were performed as "screaming walk-arounds." As if to emphasize its connection to that material, "Li'l Liza Jane" was marketed as the A-side to another dance number, "Coon Band Contest—Fox Trot." A December 1917 Victor promotional catalog presents the release under "Dance Records" and adds, "'Li'l Liza Jane' is one of those lively ones who won't keep still. She even makes the players of the Jazz band sing. In spite of the Jazzing, a cornet keeps the melody going, so you can recognize it."[54] Perhaps fearing consumer reactions to this new music, Jazz, the Victor advertisement reassures customers that they will not lose their way while listening. Another popular recording by banjoist Harry C. Browne would follow in 1918.[55]

Together, the Fuller and Browne recordings pushed "Li'l Liza Jane" further into the public consciousness, where the song resonated with an unforeseen group: American soldiers headed to the theater of war. An advertisement from Sherman, Clay & Co. in *Jacobs' Orchestra Monthly*, from September 1918, establishes

"Li'l Liza Jane" in large print, followed by, "The Song the Soldiers are Singing."[56] This was not an exaggeration on the part of the music publishing company. In 1917, the Commissions on Training Camp Activities of the Army and Navy Departments issued a sixty-nine-song, pocket-sized collection, *Songs of the Soldiers and Sailors, U.S.* Patriotic songs, minstrelsy pieces, and Stephen Foster Collins numbers comprise the table of contents, along with ditties about gals, such as "Li'l Liza Jane."[57] Appearing on page twenty-six, with permission from Sherman, Clay & Co., the book follows the de Lachau lyrics, even if one edition bungles the printing of the refrain. Just as some former African American soldiers returned to the Tidewater area of Virginia, where they interacted with Natalie Curtis Burlin, many other soldiers must have returned home to communities across the country, singing "Li'l Liza Jane." According to one source, soldiers sang the variant "as a camp and tramping song and it was almost as popular as 'Over There.'"[58]

To capitalize on this popularity, Sherman, Clay & Co. rereleased "Li'l Liza Jane" sheet music, credited to de Lachau, with cover art featuring three white soldiers sitting on a bench playing harmonica, banjo, and possibly mandolin. Though the copyright stamp reads 1916, this second version lacked any reference to the play *Come Out of the Kitchen* and cannot be conclusively dated. Seeing as the US military included the song's original format in its 1917 songbook, the expanded lyrics may have appeared slightly later, in 1917 or 1918, with the following additional verses:

> Jimmy john is layin' low, Li'l Liza Jane.
> Honey take me for your beau, Li'l Liza Jane.
>
> Gwineter th'ow the dice away, Li'l Liza Jane.
> When yo' name the happy day, Li'l Liza Jane.
>
> Bumble bee he out fer sips, Li'l Liza Jane.
> Takes mah sweet-meats from yo' lips, Li'l Liza Jane.
>
> Ev'y mawnin' when I wakes, Li'l Liza Jane.
> Smell de ham an buckwheat cakes, Li'l Liza Jane.
>
> Never mo' from you I'll roam, Li'l Liza Jane.
> Bestest place is home sweet home, Li'l Liza Jane.[59]

Notably, western swing bandleader Bob Wills would adopt some of these expanded lyrics when he and His Texas Playboys recorded "Lil Liza Jane" in 1941.[60] Another attempt to link the "Liza Jane" family with overseas service in

World War I arrived in the shape of "Good-Bye Lil' Liza Jane (Hello, Alsace Lorraine)," but this 1918 sheet music publication did not gain traction, and its minstrelsy-inspired cover and lyrics seem especially unfortunate, given the heroism of many African American soldiers during World War I.[61]

The newspaper of the Base Hospital at Camp Green, North Carolina, rendered a gripping picture of how soldiers engaged with "Lil Liza Jane" during the World War I era. In its November 30, 1918 issue, *The Caduceus* refers to a "powerful harmony" the camp's Black soldiers "use a good deal."[62] The article describes the leader shrieking, "Ise got a gal and you got none," to which the chorus roars back, "Lil Liza Jane." As the call and response continues, the men become more spirited and conclude the entire routine with an improvised chorus, "O, Liza! / O, Liza! / Lil Liza Jane." The article relates the full slate of lyrics adopted by the soldiers:

> I'se got a gal and you got none—
> Lil Liza Jane.
> House and lot in Baltimore—
> Lil Liza Jane.
> Lots o' chillen round mah door—
> Lil Liza Jane.
> Th' bumblebee out for sip—
> Lil Liza Jane.
> Takes th' sweetnin from yo lips—
> Lil Liza Jane.
> Come mah love an' live with me—
> Lil Liza Jane.
> And I'll take good care o' thee—
> Lil Liza Jane.

Boasting a circulation of nearly ten thousand copies, *The Caduceus* did its part in the popularization of "Li'l Liza Jane," not just circulating Countess Ada de Lachau's (expanded) words, but describing the performance rituals of the base's African American soldiers, who knowingly, or unknowingly, were reacquiring a Black folk song and repurposing it for their own needs: cadence, camaraderie, and perhaps, just perhaps, thinking of their own "li'l" gals back home.

INTERMISSION NUMBER THREE

Effie Lee Newsome's "Charcoal, Leddy, Charcoal" and Betty Vincent's "Problems of the Heart"

1921 TO 1922

With hostilities in most of Europe settled (for the time being) and with the Spanish Flu pandemic having receded, many parts of the Western world entered the so-called "Roaring Twenties." If the cakewalk dance inspired levity in the aftermath of the Panic of 1893, then an eccentric dance like the Charleston, and a magnetic dancer like Josephine Baker, represented this powerful decade, when radio broadcast, air travel, automobiles, and sound movies would become more and more commonplace. "Liza Jane" songs would continue to appear. In 1921, the blues singer Edith Wilson recorded "Vampin' Liza Jane" in New York with Johnny Dunn's Original Jazz Hounds.[1] As music historians Lynn Abbott and Doug Seroff indicate, the song originated as part of Irving Miller's unsuccessful Broadway musical, *Put and Take*.[2] Writing in their book *The Original Blues*, Abbott and Seroff describe "Wilson's 1921–22 Columbia recordings [as] jazzy interpretations of blues, representing the style that suited the market in New York City."[3] The somewhat sultry piece—a cousin to its "Liza Jane" family members—might inspire slow or midtempo dancing as Wilson croons about Liza Jane: "The funniest thing I ever seen / She vamped last week on Deacon Green."[4] Like many performers of her generation, Wilson executed the "black bottom" dance onstage,[5] one that "became a craze, second only to the Charleston."[6]

In a more reflective moment, writer Effie Lee Newsome published a short nonfiction memory piece, "Charcoal, Leddy, Charcoal: An Idyl of the South," as part of her affiliation with *The Crisis*, a publication of the NAACP. Appearing in the August 1922 edition, Newsome's article begins by describing "the primitive wholesomeness in the smell of burning charcoal" and how it connects her to "plantations far removed by time and distance."[7] She asks the reader to "gaze into the little red furnace," and if she or he will do so, Newsome promises that "you will feel this with me." As the fire is built and the coals begin to glow, Newsome establishes its rising "somniferous incense, as [being] rife with messages from nature as is the odor of wet soil in spring."[8] This incantation allows Newsome to fully unleash her multiple powers as a writer, transporting herself and the reader to a representative cabin of the South, where she introduces the mesmerizing character, Mayetta.

A photograph of the radiant twelve-year-old girl appears amidst the text. She is smiling outdoors, clearly in a plantation setting, wearing a white dress. Newsome establishes her role in the cabin—that of ironing clothes—as one that requires charcoal. "She is a wise young woman," Newsome writes, before quipping, "though not an excellent ironer." Mayetta is not "meagerly versed in matters pertaining to the elements and occultism." To the contrary, she informs the author about "the stars, and has a knowledge of (medicinal) simples and information concerning ghosts."[9] The girl, whose "slender legs and rusty feet" are often engaged in "mischievous antics," including song and dance, puts aside her ironing work to demonstrate a children's game to Newsome. In it, "the players are supposed to stand in facing rows, clapping their hands together and singing while one of their number skips forward to 'steal,' as described in the game."[10] At this point, Newsome reveals the game's lyrics:

> Ain't gonna tell nobody, good-bye!
> King George has stole my heart an' gone.
> Good-bye, good-bye, Liza Jane!"[11]

These words recall the plantation songs described by Margaret Walker in her 1966 novel, *Jubilee*. Walker portrays a rendition of "Steal Miss Liza" but also mentions the favorite game of young Missy: the "gentleman just from Spain." Newsome's example might seem like a "mash-up" of two different threads, but either way, the character Liza Jane shows up in Mayetta's game song. Newsome's article does not purport to represent a historical voyage back to slavery times or even the Reconstruction era, but perhaps just a couple of years earlier from the date of publication. Yet the similarity of the game and its rituals—singing, clapping, "stealing" a partner—may conjure Lydia Jefferson's WPA response, which referred to the ring game "Catch Liza Jane." The story also connects "Goodbye Liza Jane" to an old plantation game without any obvious reference to the lyrics that minstrelsy attached to the song. Just how old this connection may be, nobody can say.

Newsome's remarkable descriptions move on to "bandanna capped folk who peer inquiringly into the indigo skies to learn of the moon concerning the time to boil lye soap."[12] Numerous other rites follow. The author describes a pinch of salt on the forehead to cure a headache, thrashing the okra rows with a switch in order to promote the plant's productivity, rubbing a piece of broken mirror on the back to "forestall evil results," and hanging a horseshoe from a peach tree in order to ward off blight.[13] In town, men would sell the purifier, the charcoal, from their "rattling carts." They would call "charcoal, leddy, charcoal," with the word "leddy" probably translating to "lady," who would have been in town for provisions. "O black woman of the 'land of cotton,'" Newsome concludes, "'Oh, charcoal, leddy, charcoal.'"[14]

During a decade that would feature the Charleston and the black bottom dance crazes, Newsome's article would be a reminder of rituals and roots, including a dance game that quoted "good-bye, Liza Jane." According to *Double-take: A Revisionist Harlem Renaissance Anthology*, Newsome was born Mary Effie Lee in Philadelphia and grew up in Texas and Ohio. She was an illustrator of children's books, a storyteller, and a poet, writing for youngsters as well as adults. She published more than one hundred poems in *The Crisis* and edited "The Little Page" in the same publication for more than fifteen years. After marrying Reverend Henry Nesby Newsome, she lived in Alabama before returning to Ohio.[15] One stanza of her poetry, which appeared in *The Crisis* in 1925, displays her complicated relationship with the South:

from **"Exodus"**

The dahoon berry weeps in blood,
I know,
Watched by the crow—
I've seen both grow
In those weird wastes of Dixie![16]

Blood, in this case, may refer to the red drupe fruit of the dahoon holly, or it may refer to the bloody hardships that "Dixie" has visited upon Blacks. Likewise, the "weird wastes" may signify a geographical feature or a sense of loss. The word "evocative" falls short when it comes to an appreciation of Effie Lee Newsome's poetry and prose. Her faith in tradition and devotion to ceremony forge a surprising and powerful connection to the "Liza Jane" family of songs. One can imagine the strong personality of Mayetta frustrating a few suitors as she grew older and experienced her own "Liza Jane" complexities.

Meanwhile, in another corner of North America during the very same year, 1922, a young woman in Winnipeg, Manitoba, Canada, sought help from Betty Vincent, whose "Problems of the Heart" column ran in the *Winnipeg Evening Tribune*. As opposed to syndicated advice columnists of that era, such as Dorothy Dix and Beatrice Fairfax, whose columns turned up in newspapers all over

North America, Winnipeg had its own expert on relationships. In the 1920s, "almost all homes in Canada received a daily paper," writes Winnipeg historian Jim Blanchard, "and papers had a vast readership."[17] Blanchard's book *A Diminished Roar* specifies that, in Winnipeg, "the *Tribune* carried Betty Vincent and her daily column 'Problems of the Heart' during the 1920s." When first introducing Vincent's column to its readership in 1921, "the paper said that Vincent would answer questions about love, etiquette, and home problems."[18]

The young woman's letter, dated Tuesday, February 14, 1922, reads as follows in its entirety.

> Dear Betty Vincent:
>
> I am a girl 16 years old, and, like many other girls, I am coming to you for advice. Now, Miss Vincent, about four months ago, I went to a public dance, chaperoned by my father. While at this dance I did a thing that was, I admit, extremely improper. I had every dance, except four, with one boy. He seemed a very nice boy indeed and I liked him very much. My father was angry at this, as neither my mother nor he approve of a girl having a boy friend or even a few boy friends. Well, he would not let me go to a dance after that until two months after, when I went again with my girl friend and her mother. I saw this boy again and, being naturally timid, I could not find the courage to smile at him, and I left the dance that night without speaking to him. Well, Miss Vincent, I have been to another dance since then and I saw him again with the same results, and I am afraid he will think me a snob and I don't want him to think that, as I like him very much indeed. Now, Miss Vincent, what shall I do? If I ever see him again, shall I not recognize him? Please advise me. Thanking you in advance, and hoping this letter will not take up too much room in your valuable column, I am,
>
> LI'L 'LIZA JANE.[19]

Other people who had contacted Betty Vincent and received responses the same day included "Bertie" and "Troubled." Thus, the young woman could have supplied a partial name or an abstract word in place of her name but instead aligned herself with the "Liza Jane" family. It is also possible Vincent herself installed the song title upon the girl's closing, but either way, the narrative in the girl's letter supports this connection to "Liza Jane." She danced with one boy more than any of the other boys, upsetting her father, who might have liked to drag a broomstick "o'er his bones." Knowing that her actions ran contrary to the proprietary rules of the day, she pursued them anyway. Finally allowed to attend another dance, she encountered the same boy again but not only failed to encourage him with a smile, she also departed without uttering a single word to him. Even a third dance came and went, with the results mirroring the second dance: no smile, no talk. Doubt prevailed.

If this young man had been a singer in the "Liza Jane" tradition, such as Bradley Kincaid, he might have already turned to insult: "If you see that gal of mine / Tell her if you please / When she goes to make her bread / Roll up her dirty sleeve." The "Roaring Twenties" would eventually witness the rise of the "Flapper," a woman who would spark the "traditionalist" to anticipate "the end of American civilization as he had known it."[20] Writing in her book *The Damned and the Beautiful*, historian Paula Fass defines traditional American civilization as "best symbolized by the stable mother secure in her morality and content in her home," which was then being threatened by "the giddy flapper, rouged and clipped, careening in a drunken stupor to the lewd strains of a jazz quartet."[21] Surely, this very dynamic may have emerged to the north, and perhaps the father feared for the traditional values he had instilled in his daughter. Either way, the dances with the boy had unleashed powerful feelings in the young woman, and she struggled to acclimate herself. Thus, she sought the advice of the only person—Betty Vincent—who could enlighten her. One imagines the young woman carrying a handwritten letter to the post office one dreary, blustery, snowy afternoon, and before she dropped it into the mailbox, she took one look around to be sure nobody had been watching her.

Betty Vincent probably responded to a small percentage of the letters she received, but she did not turn away "Li'l Liza Jane." She formulated a succinct reply, aligning herself, at first, but not entirely, with the young woman's parents. Vincent responds:

> You acted very wisely in not being too friendly to the young man in question, upon your second meeting, especially as your parents disapproved of your knowing him. There is no reason for your apologizing to him, although since four months have gone by, it could do no harm to recognize and dance with him again, should you both desire it.[22]

In the end, Betty Vincent recognized true love, even in the snowdrifts of Winnipeg. Her rules were: do not be too friendly, do not apologize for anything, but dance with him again, should it be desirable to do so. If nothing more, the query, and its response, demonstrated that the song had traveled across the border from Minnesota and North Dakota and had influenced a young woman in such a way as she fancied herself being the girl in the song. (Or if not, then Betty Vincent herself fancied the letter-writer as the character Liza Jane.)

A young woman in Winnipeg describing her lovesick travails at the dances. Effie Lee Newsome recounting a southern dance game with clapping, singing, skipping. Both in 1922. And just a year earlier, Edith Wilson crooning, "Liza

Jane had gained her fame / Vampin' all the boys was her game." Indeed, they all reference the "Liza Jane" family of songs. The Roaring Twenties. (Or the "diminished roar" in Winnipeg.) Plantation cabins. The character Mayetta, who has information concerning ghosts. "Dance with him again," says Betty Vincent, "should you both desire it." Edith Wilson performing at a club filled with "rouged, clipped" flappers. Dancing the "black bottom" as the curtain, on this final intermission, slowly drops . . . and the lights fade.

"LIZA JANE" MEETS THE MEDIA

Film, Animation, Radio, Television

LATE NINETEENTH CENTURY / 1929 TO 1961

"Liza Jane" songs would be sung on the big screen as soon as the movies adopted synchronized sound. Billed as a "100 percent talking picture" in advertisement posters, the 1929 Southern drama *Coquette* begins with a guitarist singing "Li'l Liza Jane" while the camera centers on the nameplate for a large house owned by Dr. J. M. Besant. Sitting on stairs outdoors, the uncredited guitar player follows the lyrics established by the Countess.

> Oh Eliza, Li'l Liza Jane
> Oh Eliza, Li'l Liza Jane
> I'se got a gal and you got none
> Li'l Liza Jane
> I'se got a gal and you got none
> Li'l Liza Jane
> Oh Eliza, Li'l Liza Jane
> Oh Eliza, Li'l Liza Jane[1]

The scene then shifts indoors, where the family servant, Julia, hums along to the guitarist's rendition of "Li'l Liza Jane" as she fixes coffee in the kitchen. Played by Louise Beavers, Julia is then accosted by young whippersnapper Jimmy Besant, played by William Janney, who urges Julia to "shake a leg." He turns out to be the brother of Norma Besant, depicted by the lead actress Mary Pickford, who, according to writer Peggy Dymond Leavey, would become the first major star of the silent films to make a "talkie."[2] Meanwhile, Julia rebuffs Jimmy's impatience with measured grace. This early role as Julia would help Beavers establish a career path as an actress.

While citing "a level of unquestionable dignity" Beavers brought to her performances, film historian Charlene B. Regester acknowledges a demoralizing
side to the appearance of Black actresses in a string of subservient roles.[3] In
her book *African American Actresses*, Regester writes:

> Unfortunately, African American spectators witnessed with dismay a
> virtually endless parade of such representations on screen, particularly
> mammies, maids, and matriarchal figures, and Beavers's role as Julia in
> *Coquette* was a harbinger of what was to come for her and for many
> other black actresses in Hollywood.[4]

Combining Beavers's plight as a performer with the specifics of the script—a
Black actress scrambling for a foothold in a white industry, as well as a role calling for her to hum a Black folksong that had been reinvented by a white composer—makes for several impressive loop-de-loops of sociohistorical dynamics.
She and the mysterious guitar player (who seems to be white) combine to open
the film by reminding moviegoers of the bouncy, infectious, "southern dialect
song." Noticeably, in a comparable fashion, Ruth Chatterton acquired the song
from a whistling Robert Ames in *Come Out of the Kitchen*. The choice of "Li'l
Liza Jane" might not be accidental, given the courtship activities hovering
around Norma Besant throughout the film.

Adapted to the big screen from the stage, *Coquette* nearly did not survive a
blown fuse and other technical difficulties upon its April debut at New York's
Rialto Theater, but once these issues were remedied, the film prospered at
the box office.[5] According to Eileen Whitfield, author of *Pickford*, the film
"grossed $1.4 million," a substantial sum in 1929. Pickford herself went on to
receive the second-ever Academy Award for Best Actress, a prize that may
have been deserved but also may have owed, as Whitfield points out, to Pickford's heavy lobbying of the Academy, an institution she helped to found.[6]
Similar to how "Li'l Liza Jane" offered entr'acte entertainment for every performance of *Come Out of the Kitchen*, the song would permanently begin
every showing of *Coquette*. This enabled a beloved American folk tune to
now reach legions of moviegoers. Not only did the "Liza Jane" family participate in the historic changeover from the silent film era, but a groundbreaking actress such as Louise Beavers would claim space for herself in future
Hollywood endeavors.

"Liza Jane" songs would also materialize in musicals or films that presented
"variety fare." For instance, the all-Black 1929 musical *Hearts in Dixie* contained
a rendition of "Li'l Liza Jane" among its forty numbers.[7] The comedian Stepin
Fetchit would be cast as the lazy field hand Gummy, and as it turns out, Fetchit

was no stranger to the romantic dynamics that involved the Liza Jane character. Through prior experience gained on the "carnival circuit," he had portrayed Skeeter, a "plantation boy" who pined for "Miss Liza Jane."[8] Released in 1942, the Paul Dresser "bio-pic" *My Gal Sal* included, as noted above, "I'se Your Honey If You Wants Me, Liza Jane." The actor Victor Mature played Dresser, with a singing voice-over dubbed by Ben Gage.[9] Perhaps most significantly, the western swing bandleader Bob Wills and his bands would become quite familiar with Hollywood, starring in some full productions as well as being the subject of some "musical shorts." In the case of the 1945 film *Blazing the Western Trail*,[10] Wills and the Texas Playboys were featured in a recurring performative role and, in one of their onscreen numbers, presented their version of "Goodbye Liza Jane." It would vary considerably, in lyrics and melody, from earlier songs of the same title.

The sixty-minute film is, on the one hand, a standard guns-blazing oater of middling quality, yet importantly, the *American Film Institute Catalog* defines its sub-genre as being "with songs," thereby acknowledging it as a sort of variety show.[11] Perhaps the most enjoyable scenes feature the character actress Virginia Sale as Nellie and the character actor Dub Taylor as Cannonball, with "wooing" humorously in the air between them. Eventually, the two share a dance—Nellie executing the steps more gracefully than Cannonball—while Bob Wills, vocalist Tommy Duncan, and the other members of the Texas Playboys strike up "Goodbye Liza Jane" nearby. The lightly choreographed dance scene is a minor gem, with Sale and Taylor displaying their knack for scene-stealing. Not present in the refrain of this "Goodbye Liza Jane" variant would be "walk dad Lew," or the promise, often in dialect, to "go away and leave" the Liza Jane character. Instead, a sense of self-pitying resignation overcomes the speaker, however lighthearted or comical:

> Oh, how I love her
> Ain't that a shame
> Oh, how I love her
> Goodbye Liza Jane[12]

The refrain and two verses continue from the 1942 recording of "Goodbye Liza Jane" by Wills and his band on the Columbia label, with a different singer, Leon McAuliffe, handling the vocals three years earlier.[13] Lyrics from the 1942 recording typify, for example, the frontier imagery found throughout the two performances: "Up the river and around the bend / Goodbye, goodbye / Six shooters on and gone again / Goodbye Liza Jane." Still other verses refer to animal hijinks and dancing. In both renditions, film and record, Wills offers his trademark running commentary, such as "Aw, Liza" or lighthearted introductions of the soloists, in a high-pitched voice. Mostly, the "general nonsense" of the verses contributes to the buoyancy of "Goodbye Liza Jane," as well as its orientation as a swing dance number.

Yet one of the lines sung by Duncan in the film—concerning a hawk catching a chicken and flying upstairs—calls to mind a line from the 1871 sheet music published by Eddie Fox: "A hawk flew down and bit an old goose." It may also echo Fox's reference to the minstrel song "Sich A Gittin Up Stairs." The presence of these comedic minstrel-based lyrics may be no accident. According to Charles Townsend's biographical work, *San Antonio Rose*, the bandleader broke into show business through his participation in medicine shows. In 1929, a young Wills was walking the streets of Fort Worth, Texas, "broke, disgusted, and hungry," without regular employment.[14] Then in his mid-twenties, Wills "took a job as a musician and blackface comic on the medicine show" he had helped to construct when he arrived in town.[15] While Townsend indicates that Wills honed his performative skills in this environment, he did not intend to ridicule Blacks.[16] The very style of interjections he would make during "Goodbye Liza Jane" and other pieces instead derived from his youthful experiences interacting with African Americans. "His work in the minstrel shows gave him the opportunity to express the folkways and folk music of the Negroes he had grown up with in East and West Texas."[17]

Townsend elaborates on Wills's relationship to African American folk music while narrating his early years. In one example, the eight-year-old Wills traveled with his family as they "loaded their possessions into two covered wagons and moved five hundred miles northwest to Hall County, near Memphis, Texas."[18] A long trip to begin with, Wills and his family members required more than two months to reach their destination since they "stopped at farms all along the way and picked cotton."[19] The Wills family was not the only one picking cotton in that part of Texas. They lived in shanties alongside Black families, and Wills, as Townsend describes, encountered music styles and instrumentation he would combine with "frontier fiddles" to form his distinctive western swing sound.[20] According to Townsend, Wills learned swing and blues directly from horn-playing and guitar-playing Black folk musicians and not by listening to records. "[Wills] often told close friends and members of his band, for instance, that he learned a great deal about rhythm from the black cotton pickers. These rhythms became a permanent part of his own music."[21]

At some point, Wills must have encountered a "play-party" version of "Goodbye Liza Jane." In 1911, one Mrs. L. D. Ames published an elaborate article, "The Missouri Play-party," in the *Journal of American Folklore*. Her piece describes rituals from thirty years earlier in which "the players did not dance [. . .] to the music of instruments, but kept time through their own singing."[22] While these Missouri dancers were not gyrating to the forbidden music of the "devil's box" (the fiddle), they may have nevertheless violated the no-dancing ordnance installed by the local church. Thus, they adopted the innocuous title—"play-party"—to camouflage the proceedings safely. It was not the kind of dancing, Ames clarifies, as might be found among the gambling and fighting of the "rough element," but harmless "playing" which might break up, nonetheless, around "three o'clock in the morning."[23] Rural and frontier Americans developed these gatherings in the nineteenth century, according to scholar Alan Spurgeon, with a set of "rules, movements, and expectations [. . .] often borrowed from the square dance, which evolved side by side with the play party."[24] In some cases, the lack of instrumentation resulted from poverty or a dearth of musicians among people settling on the frontier, but mostly this condition responded to religious prohibition.[25] Ultimately, the play-party concept may have traveled to the United States from the British Isles.[26]

Ames writes, "As a little girl, I was permitted to sit up and look on when the parties were held at my father's or my grandfather's home."[27] She offers more than twenty-five examples of play-party songs, along with musical notation. As part of these examples, Ames presents music and lyrics for a play-party song that intersects with the "Liza Jane" family.

Shiloh

> Scrapin' up sand in the bottom of the sea,
>   Shiloh, Shiloh.
> Scrapin' up sand in the bottom of the sea,
>   Shiloh, Liza Jane.
> Oh, how I love her! Oh, ain't that a shame!
> Oh, how I love her! By-by Liza Jane![28]

"Shiloh" may refer to a Civil War battle, a biblical site, a town in Illinois, a local church, or even a hazy dance movement. The melody and refrain intersect with the Bob Wills version of "Goodbye, Liza Jane," thereby dating the Wills song to the late nineteenth century or early twentieth century. Wills, for his part, preserves the "double goodbye" noted in Leander Cogswell's observations of the USCT Forty-Third Regiment, Eddie Fox's sheet music, and George W. Johnson's recording of "The Laughing Coon." Both the Ames and Wills variants display similarities to a singing game, "Going Down to Cairo," described by folklorist David S. McIntosh in his book *Folk Songs and Singing Games of the Illinois Ozarks*. McIntosh reports the refrain as "Goin' down to Cairo, / Good-bye and a good-bye, / Goin' down to Cairo, / Good-bye Liza Jane."[29] Thus, place-names may feature prominently in this material, as well as the lighthearted notion of bidding "good-bye" (or a double goodbye) to the Liza Jane character.

Even as the Wills song shares common ground with the Missouri variant "Shiloh" and the Illinois variant "Going Down to Cairo," Wills likely encountered a related tune from his stomping grounds in Texas or nearby Oklahoma. The team of R. E. Dudley and L. W. Payne (from 1916), as well as folklorist Benjamin A. Botkin (from 1937), situate nearly identical refrains in Texas and Oklahoma, respectively:

> Oh, how I love her,
>   An' ain't it a shame,
> Oh, how I love her,
>   An' it's good-by, Liza Jane.[30]

> Oh, how I love her!
>   Ain't that a shame!
> Oh, how I love her!
>   An' a by-by, Liza Jane.[31]

Moreover, as part of her 1916 book *The Play-Party in Indiana*, folk music collector Leah Jackson Wolford offers notated music as well as lyrics for "Black the Boots," a folk song that stresses the shiny presentation of footwear, presumably required to court Liza Jane or another woman. The refrain all but duplicates the observations made by Ames, Botkin, and others, while the lone verse reads, "Black the boots and make 'em shine, / A goodby, a goodby, / Black the boots and make 'em shine, / A goodby Liza Jane."[32] There, too, in Wolford's play-party variant, the "double goodbye" persists.

Numerous folk music collectors, therefore, document a large group of the late nineteenth century and early twentieth century "Goodbye Liza Jane" play-party variants from Indiana to Oklahoma, from Texas to Missouri. These folk songs may be named for towns such as Shiloh or Cairo or even for the act of polishing one's shoes, yet they clearly showcase the Liza Jane character. The sense of "going down" to a town can be traced to minstrelsy, including Eddie Fox's "Good Bye Liza Jane" sheet music, which installs Lynchburg Town as a destination. Thus, someone may be "going down to Cairo" in order to woo Liza Jane or another woman. Other related variants might substitute a town that is "burning down." The folk singer Judy Henske begins her 1963 single "Charlotte Town" by sweetly crooning, "Charlotte Town is burning down / Goodbye and a bye-bye," before launching much more energetically into "Burning down to the ground / Goodbye Liza Jane!"[33] Similarly, banjoist Nora Brown sings "Scarlet Town is burning down" during her remarkable 2021 recording of "Liza Jane," which may distantly conjure the folk song "Barbara Allen."[34] The concepts of "going down to a town" and "the town burning down" may be interchangeable, given the similar profiles of the words and rhymes. Nevertheless, the conflagration imagery may ultimately derive from a widely-reported July 1866 fire that devastated four city blocks in Charlottetown, Prince Edward Island, Canada.[35] No date-stamped materials have been unearthed to conclusively establish the exact origins of these many "Liza Jane" variants, but in all likelihood, the nineteenth-century "Goodbye Liza Jane" minstrelsy "hit" was transformed within the play-party environment, albeit with certain conventions—such as the "double goodbye" of the refrain or verses—continuing onward.

These "play party" songs were supposed to be enacted in an antiseptic environment, devoid of fiddles and other temptations, yet according to "The Ozark Play-Party," a 1929 article published by folklorist Vance Randolph, the participants often found ways to compensate for these restrictions. Writing in the *Journal of American Folklore*, Randolph portrays wild dances held in the Ozark Mountain region of Missouri and Arkansas, where young men and women gathered from miles around with no orchestra but for their own singing, clapping, and stamping of feet.[36] The men, according to Randolph, would swing their gals inside or outside the house with a jug of whiskey kept where the horses were tied.[37] Randolph also notes the presence of "tom-cattin'" by the dancing partners but concludes, "there is less drunkenness and sexual irregularity than at most college dances."[38]

The lively "Goodbye Liza Jane" performances by Bob Wills and His Texas Playboys conjure the rural environment documented by Randolph. They present a distinctly "frontier" and "pioneer travel" word hoard, including "around the bend," "six-shooters," "wagon," and "chew tobacco." A rhyming couplet in which the singer instructs dancers to swing their ma and swing their pa, as well as that girl from Arkansas, may refer to African American square dance calls, but to be fair, these lines can be found widely in numerous songs which straddle many genres and time periods. A brisk pace and multiple threads of influence make for a garrulous song that inherits much, integrates much, and generates its own mythology. While *Blazing the Western Trail* may not have grossed as much at the box office as *Coquette*, it nevertheless placed another "Liza Jane" family member on the big screen, accompanied in this case by its band.

Collectively, the two films—*Coquette* and *Blazing the Western Trail*—demonstrate the "Liza Jane" family's appeal to early filmmakers. When Bob Wills presented his swinging version of "Goodbye, Liza Jane" in *Blazing the Western Trail* and on record, he performed a rendition incorporating the African American musical traditions he learned firsthand while picking cotton as an eight-old-boy in Texas. Wills affixed these Black traditions to a song that had probably been shaped by the play-party environment in the same geographical region. And yet, before these two movies came the mysterious (and unavailable)

1915 silent film, *The Rejuvenation of 'Liza Jane*, which may have attempted to reproduce the girlfriend character from so many "Liza Jane" songs.[39]

Perhaps seizing on the popularity and soundtrack of *Coquette*, both the Van Beuren and Walt Disney studios included "Li'l Liza Jane" in 1930 animated shorts. Billed as an "Aesop's Sound Fable," the 1930 Van Beuren cartoon *Dixie Days* offers a parody of *Uncle Tom's Cabin* and produces animals in the roles of Uncle Tom, Little Eva, Topsy, Liza and her baby, and Simon Legree. Film historian Henry T. Sampson offers a strong summary of the plot in his book *That's Enough Folks: Black Images in Animated Cartoons*. Among stereotypical scenes of watermelon eating and cotton picking, *Dixie Days* presents a variety of songs, such as "Carry Me Back to Old Virginia" and "Swanee River."[40] Eventually, the Simon Legree character "arrives [at Uncle Tom's cabin] holding a long whip in his hands."[41] Speaking only in trumpet noises, "he is unhappy with Uncle Tom, and before long, Tom and Topsy are marched off to the slave auction."[42]

There, the attendees bellow, "We want Liza!" At which point, Liza is shown doing laundry with her baby at her feet. The viewer can discern offscreen male voices rendering just a few seconds of the standard "Li'l Liza Jane" refrain: "Oh li'l Liza, Li'l Liza Jane." Hearing the shouts of the mob, Liza flees with her baby, and in the madness that ensues, Legree is defeated while sailing over a waterfall. The group is reunited at the cabin and happily sings "Way Down South in Dixie" until a chicken arrives, at which point the group chases it as the screen fades.[43] There does not appear to be a "moral" at the end of this "sound fable," but rather a visual gag of the formulaic "weakness for chicken," an obvious holdover from burnt cork minstrelsy. In his entry for *Dixie Days*, Sampson incorporates four largely positive reviews. Excerpts include those from *Bioscope* ("The scene is laid in the cotton fields of the south, and the subject is a clever burlesque of Uncle Tom's Cabin"); *Billboard* ("The comedy is well done and the animation perfect"); *Motion Picture News* (". . . many highly entertaining gags are pulled by Van Beuren"); and *Variety* ("A number of southern airs, some given a novel freak arrangement.")[44]

Even as "Li'l Liza Jane" assumes the slightest of presences in the cartoon, it accompanies yet another expression of "racial masquerade," to borrow a phrase from scholar Nicholas Sammond. His essay, "Gentlemen, Please Be Seated," from the book *Burnt Cork*, studies "Racial Masquerade and Sadomasochism in 1930s animation."[45] Employing the 1932 Disney animation *Trader Mickey* as an example, Sammond establishes the Mickey Mouse character as a vestigial blackface minstrel who encounters cannibals after a shipwreck; he chooses the word "vestigial" owing to the waning presence of minstrelsy in American popular culture of the early 1930s.[46] Sammond nonetheless likens the physical characteristics of the mouse to those of the standard minstrelsy figure: "Mickey sports the uniform of white gloves, black face, exaggerated mouth, and wide eyes that marked both the popular animated characters of the day and their progenitor, the blackface minstrel."[47] This analysis can be transported to *Dixie Days*, where the entire "animal cast" could be described as minstrels, and the cartoon's activities—singing, dancing, and joking, all the while lampooning Blacks—could be termed a minstrel show. As noted above, *Uncle Tom's Cabin* was a frequent target of nineteenth-century burlesque, with numerous adaptations materializing among minstrel troupes; the Van Beuren animation seems to have embraced those blueprints.

"Li'l Liza Jane" makes a more emphatic appearance during the 1930 Disney animation, *Mickey Mouse Pioneer Days*, which likewise contains animals in lieu of people. Also featuring Minnie Mouse, the action does not tread into the realm of cannibals, but it places the duo of Mickey and Minnie aboard a wagon train which is spotted by stereotypical "movie Indians" who, that night, conduct a war dance in preparation for an attack. Meanwhile, at the pioneer camp, the unsuspecting Mickey and Minnie hold hands while a musical trio plays "Li'l Liza Jane" for a circle of clapping settlers. Represented by a banjoist, a fiddler, and a squeezebox player, the three musicians pause their playing long enough to spit tobacco juice high into the air and emit a canine howl, "Wooooo, Eliza! Li'l Liza Jane!" As opposed to the Van Beuren short, here, the song carries on for thirty seconds and takes center stage. At daybreak, the "movie Indians" attack. Numerous gags ensue, such as an arrow entering a stovepipe before curving around to strike the backside of a harried pioneer. Eventually, Minnie is captured and tied up. When Mickey arrives to liberate her, he must grapple with Minnie's oversized abductor, and during their wrestling match, Minnie liberates herself and places a hot coal in the seat of the Indian's trousers, forcing him to charge off squealing into the distance. That scene concludes one version of the cartoon, while other cuts of the cartoon may present slightly altered finales.[48]

The mockery in *Pioneer Days* carries in various directions. While there are no cannibals as with *Trader Mickey*, the "movie Indians" represent the villains and are portrayed in unflattering terms with savage war dance, sharp teeth, and unprovoked polemic. On the other hand, the settlers are portrayed as typical "hillbillies" with chaws of tobacco, square dance hoedown, and frontier britches. The entire presentation, as with the Van Beuren animation, could be considered a minstrel show unto itself, with song, dance, comedy, and ever-present racial stereotyping. Ultimately, *Pioneer Days* also puts forward the Mickey and Minnie Mouse characters, as Sammond would describe, with black faces, white gloves, large mouths, and bulging eyes.

A "Liza Jane" song would materialize in at least one more animation. Though unavailable, Universal released a 1949 "musical short" *Minstrel Mania*, which features "Little Liza Jane" as rendered by The King's Men, who also play a role, as shall be shown, in the popularization of the song on the radio.[49] These animated shorts would typically screen as part of a multi-film program. On January 9, 1931, for instance, *Nogales International* (Arizona) published an advertisement for the Nogales Theatre, where patrons could catch *Sin Takes a Holiday* featuring Ann Harding. During the same engagement, moviegoers could watch Mickey Mouse in *Pioneer Days* as well as the Fox Movietone News.[50] When considering original screenings, reruns, and online streaming, these cartoons may have had significant viewership, although a precise number cannot be stated.

Yodeling, according to musicologist Timothy E. Wise, "has enjoyed an unbroken tradition" in American popular music, dating to the early nineteenth century and continuing through "minstrelsy, vaudeville, ragtime, [. . .] virtually everything."[51] In his book *Yodeling and Meaning in American Music*, Wise traces the evolution of yodeling well into the twentieth century to include one of its most famous practitioners, Jimmie Rodgers, and the trademark techniques he applied to popular recordings such as "Blue Yodel No. 1." Among Rodgers's fans likely numbered a musical family in Minnesota, the DeZuriks, who would produce one of the most memorable acts in American music history. Known professionally as the DeZurik Sisters or the "Cackle Sisters," this startling duo would eventually sing (and yodel) about a "li'l" gal from Baltimore.

Hailing from the town of Royalton in the middle of Minnesota, "Carolyn (born 1919) and Mary Jane DeZurik (born 1917) were," in the estimation of music writer Paul Tyler, "part of a musical family [. . .] that included a fiddling father, an accordion-playing brother, and five sisters (out of six) who could sing and play the guitar."[52] In his essay, "The Rise of Rural Rhythm," Tyler describes the sister duo as one that converted the natural music of animal noises around them into "elaborate trick yodels and novel harmonies that won them many amateur talent contests in central Minnesota."[53] Eventually, a scout for radio station WLS "caught their act and invited them to Chicago, where they were hired for the *National Barn Dance* in November 1936."[54] Shortly thereafter, the DeZurik sisters "were engaged by Purina Mills in 1937 for a series of transcribed programs called *Checkerboard Time*, to be broadcast in all forty-eight states."[55] Only in their late teens or early twenties, the sisters from a small town in rural America were being heard across the country via popular radio shows.

Carolyn and Mary Jane were known as the DeZurik Sisters on WLS but adopted a different name for other appearances in order to avoid contractual issues. Writing in his book *Rural Rhythm*, music historian Tony Russell notes, "since 1937, the DeZuriks had also been appearing on *Checkerboard Time*, a show sponsored by Ralston Purina. Working for chicken feed—literally, because Purina manufactured foods for farm animals, including Chick Startena—they were known as the Cackle Sisters."[56] Through transcription discs, the DeZuriks, billed as the Cackle Sisters, performed several pieces for *Checkerboard Time*, including "Li'l Liza Jane."

Sparely presenting the song with one guitar and both women singing, the Cackle Sisters follow the melody and some of the lyrics established through the Countess Ada de Lachau sheet music, adding their remarkable animal mimicry. After the host introduces them, they sing:

> Oh, li'l Liza, li'l Liza Jane
> Oh, li'l Liza, li'l Liza Jane
> Now I've got a gal that you don't know
> Li'l Liza Jane
> Away down south in Baltimore
> Li'l Liza Jane
> Oh, li'l Liza, li'l Liza Jane
> Oh, li'l Liza, li'l Liza Jane
>
> [Cackling, trilling, chicken calls, yodeling]
>
> Now when she lived [unclear]
> Li'l Liza Jane
> Chickens round the kitchen door
> Li'l Liza Jane
> Oh, li'l Liza, li'l Liza Jane
> Oh, li'l Liza, li'l Liza Jane
>
> [Cackling, trilling, chicken calls, yodeling]
>
> Oh, li'l Liza, li'l Liza Jane
> Oh, li'l Liza, li'l Liza Jane.[57]

Their substitution of "chickens" for "chillun" must have been a lively inside gag to the sisters. The "cackling, trilling, chicken calls, yodeling" is immediately arresting and remarkable in its virtuosity and timing. Scholar-novelist John Biguenet indicates that the Cackle Sisters "joined the Ralston Purina Company's *Checkerboard Time* radio program as regulars from 1937–1941," thus the "Li'l Liza Jane" transcription disc can probably be dated to those years.[58] In his essay "The DeZurik Sisters: Two Farm Girls Who Yodeled Their Way to the Grand Ole Opry," Biguenet quotes Carolyn DeZurik as saying, "We listened to the birds and tried to sing with the birds and yodel with them, imitate them. And that is how we got into all the bird stuff and animal sounds, and we would include them in our songs. That was quite a joke to us, too."[59]

Many writers have attempted to describe the yodeling and animal noises of the DeZurik Sisters. Tony Russell calls it "[the imitation of] whippoorwills or mandolins, and clucking, chirping, and crowing in harmony like Disney-fied chickens."[60] Writing in his book *Meeting Jimmie Rodgers*, Barry Mazor notes that the DeZuriks "had built their act, and most of their yodeling songs, on pulsing, triple time, harmonized chicken cackles; they even answered announcers' questions in pure, indecipherable Poultryese."[61] In addition to acknowledging their extended repertoire of "chime bells, trumpets, muted trombones, Hawaiian guitars, mandolins, and even musical saws," Biguenet emphasizes the sisters' beautifully matched voices, where one barely shadows the other."[62] Mary Bufwack and Robert Oermann, holding forth in *Finding Her Voice*, describe how the "unique, birdlike style featured complex chirps, whistles, trills, and vocal effects executed with precision timing. The sisters' ability to hear musical possibilities in the sounds of barnyard animals, cuckoo clocks, whippoorwills' songs, and nature's noises, plus their devotion to practice and presentation, made them one of the most original acts in the annals of pop music."[63]

In the mid-1940s, the DeZuriks became regulars at the *Grand Ole Opry*, which made them, according to Bufwack and Oermann, "the only women to have achieved stardom on both of the two most important radio programs in country music history.[64] Between *Checkerboard Time*, the *National Barn Dance*, and the *Grand Ole Opry*, countless radio listeners heard them perform their distinctive version of "Li'l Liza Jane" if they indeed produced the song for the latter two shows. Given that Fiddlin' John Carson and Uncle Am Stuart, among many others, broadcast country music through radio appearances in the 1920s, the Cackle Sisters did not achieve any firsts in this regard, but owing to the presence of many more radios in homes and broadly developed radio infrastruc-ture, they did reach wider audiences, and arguably, achieved greater stardom. Along with their success traveled "Li'l Liza Jane." In keeping with tradition, the DeZurik sisters added their own imprint to the song, forever bestowing upon it their unparalleled clucking and yodeling. They would not be the only musicians, however, to achieve a large "Liza Jane" audience moment over the airwaves. The King's Men vocal quartet would reach millions of listeners on *Fibber McGee and Molly*, a popular husband-and-wife comedy program that also featured music.

Fibber McGee and Molly's audience came to depend upon the boastful exag-gerations by "Fibber" and the straight-arrow balancing by his amiable wife, "Molly," who would often check his questionable assertions by saying, "'Taint funny, McGee." Played by real-life couple Jim and Marian Jordan, the comedy team presided over their fictional address at 79 Wistful Vista where, according to writer Gary Poole, "the formula was simple: The McGees were usually at home while various characters came knocking at their door in what amounted to be two- or three-minute vaudeville routines."[65] Devotees would especially anticipate the "closet gag," which Poole describes as "the one sound effect on radio that became immortal, perhaps rivaled only by Inner Sanctum's squeaking door."[66] Historians William and Nancy Young, in their book *The 1930s*, supply an example scenario—Fibber's absentmindedness—which would unleash the closet's vast powers:

> [He] might not remember where he put something, and then he would recall: In the closet! Fibber McGee's Closet became, in the 1930s and 1940s, a national joke. He would open the closet door, and for the next few seconds all the audience would hear was the crashing of every conceivable object that might be stored there. The sound effects team had the responsibility for the aural chaos, and they always rose to the occasion. Listeners knew the crash was coming; it was just a question of when.[67]

In addition to gags such as the overflowing closet, certain characters repeated and became famous in their own rights. Many powerful forces collide, therefore, when the popular character, Gildersleeve, drops in during the September 30, 1941 episode, one devoted to Fibber's exaggerations regarding a vacation in Alaska.[68] When Gildersleeve and McGee argue about the ownership of a lawn-mower, Fibber begrudgingly tells Gildersleeve he can find it "right in there," whereupon his guest opens the closet, only to be snowed under by all the junk tumbling out. The orchestra adds a flourish, and the announcer introduces the King's Men as "your favorites and ours." At the time, Ken Darby, Rad Robinson, Bud Linn, and John Dodson made up the group.[69]

Easily one of the single largest audience moments in the history of the "Liza Jane" family, the performance would have been heard by tens of millions of listeners across the country.[70] With the darkness of war consuming the world, the quartet would remind the national audience about this bright song. The King's Men follow the Countess Ada de Lachau melody and, to an extent, the lyrics, but in true "Liza Jane" tradition, the singers adapt the piece to their own purposes, relating a comedic romance story that emphasizes the crescendos and tightness of the quartet.

Little Liza Jane
The King's Men

I got a gal and you got none
Little Liza Jane

I got a gal and you got none
Little Liza Jane

[Chorus:]
Oh little Liza
Little Liza Jane
Oh little Liza
Little Liza Jane

Come my love and marry me
Little Liza Jane
How happy we will be
My little Liza Jane

Now go buy a wedding ring
Little Liza Jane
We'll be married in the spring
My Little Liza Jane

[Chorus]

Then one day in the middle of May
Little Liza Jane
Away she ran with a traveling man
Who stole my Liza Jane

Oh little Liza Jane
When I heard the news
Oh-ho little Liza Jane
I got the blues

Liza come back my Liza Liza
Come back my Jane
Liza, Liza, Liza, Liza
Little Liza Jane

[Chorus*]

Had the blues so awful bad
I jumped aboard a train

Made up my mind
I'd try to find my little Liza Jane

Away down south in Tennessee
I got off the train
Who was waiting there for me
But little Liza Jane

[Chorus]

Took my honey by the hand
Got back on the train
Stole her from that traveling man
Sweet sweet Liza

Now we live in Baltimore
Me and Liza Jane
Lots of chillun round the door
Just like Liza

Liza Jane, Liza, Liza, Liza
How I love my Liza Jane

[*The lyrics vary slightly in this rendition of the chorus]

The nearly two-and-a-half-minute rendition is extended by ten seconds of stout applause. It begins, as noted, with lyrics by the Countess and generally sticks to her melody throughout, although the ensemble tumbles and soars, quavers and pounces. During the song, Liza Jane eventually runs off with a "traveling man," that is, a salesman or a sly womanizing scoundrel. In some ways, this calls to mind the Liza Jane character who went "a-driving with Mister Brown" in the Harry Von Tilzer variant from Tin Pan Alley. Once again, a Liza Jane suitor finds himself, however comically, doubting Liza Jane's faithfulness. Given the emotive overemphasis on some of the "oh Liza" passages, the narrative hardly projects more than superficial wounds. "The blues," in this case, would be dripping with the inevitability of a swift reversal.

Sure enough, the quartet depicts an odyssey that takes the fellow "away down south in Tennessee," a line referring to minstrelsy lyrics, such as "away down south where I was born." While it may be accidental, the choice of the word "steal" calls to mind the stealing partners game song variants. The traveling man steals Liza Jane, only for the singer to steal her back, returning with her to Baltimore, where the song reattaches itself to the familiar de Lachau lyrics. What might otherwise pass for a dramatic updating of the song may instead represent a complex assemblage of references to numerous popular traditions: the 1916 sheet music, Tin Pan Alley, minstrelsy, and dance game motifs. Why the group decided to produce a version of "Little Liza Jane" may be a mystery, although recordings of the variant continued to circulate, including those in 1939 by Ollie Shepard & His Kentucky Boys (a Black group)[71] and in 1940 by Louise Massey & the Westerners (a white group);[72] notably, these two upbeat versions incorporated ensemble singing as well as call and response.

White singers comprised the King's Men quartet, which was widely enmeshed in show business, from radio to film engagements. Nothing in the group's history would be more startling, however, than its connection to an iconic 1939 fantasy movie. Writing in *The Making of the Wizard of Oz*, Aljean Harmetz describes how Ken Darby, the vocal arranger for the film and leader of the King's Men, "was given the job of creating voices for the Munchkins and the Winkies."[73] In the end, Darby instructed his colleagues in the King's Men vocal quartet to sing a line such as "Ding . . . Dong . . . the . . . witch . . . is . . . dead" quite slowly. He then sped up the line during playback, which yielded the desired high-pitched results. None of the actors who played the Munchkins did any singing, as none of them, apparently, could carry a tune.[74] A nominee for and winner of several Academy Awards, Darby wrote the book *Hollywood Holyland*, which concerns itself with the 1965 film, *The Greatest Story Ever Told*. In the prologue, film critic Page Cook establishes how the King's Men came to *Fibber McGee and Molly* on a trial basis in 1940, "but the engagement lasted almost fifteen years!"[75]

Back onstage with Fibber and Molly, the "Old Timer" character describes his own trip to Alaska, thereby depriving Fibber of his final chance to triumph through exaggeration. After the two leading stars had bid the nation good night from their Tuesday evening slot on NBC, and the radio sets were turned off, the refrain of "Little Liza Jane" must have been hummed, whistled, or sung in many households. The "Little Liza Jane" rendition produced by the King's Men shared some characteristics with the rendition developed by the Cackle Sisters. In addition to inheriting certain lyrics, both songs required great precision, and both ministered to Depression-weary audiences who feared another global conflict. By escaping into the variety shows and dreamy comedies of radio, audiences encountered a sister duo who emulated the animal noises on their Minnesota farm and yodeled about them. Listeners also encountered a quartet who had inhabited the voices of the "Munchkins" in the over-the-rainbow Land of Oz before helping a suitor steal back his beloved Liza Jane from that meddlesome traveling man, away down south in Tennessee.

The magazine *Ebony* devoted several pages of its April 1961 edition to chronicling the rising fortunes of Gloria Lynne, a jazz singer who had performed five months earlier alongside Harry Belafonte "in his second TV spectacular, *New York 19*, which was seen by over 30 million viewers."[76] Describing Lynne as a "vibrant contralto," the article indicates "she sang four songs, two of them in duos with Belafonte." Prestige, publicity, and a "flood of inquiries" followed.[77] Chiming in just a week after *New York 19* aired, television critic June Bundy praised the entire effort in the November 28, 1960 issue of *Billboard*. Titling her review "Belafonte Bunch in Set-Smasher," she notes that the "talented troupe of racially integrated singers and dancers presented one of the best TV musical shows in the history of the medium."[78] Bundy's review lists the particulars—the show aired on the CBS network from 10:00 to 11:00 p.m. on Sunday, November 20—and highlights "the versatile, jazz-oriented thrush Gloria Lynne" as well as the Modern Jazz Quartet and Contemporary String Quartet. She additionally praises Revlon for sponsoring the show, given its "potentially explosive material."[79] By this, the critic alludes to the integration of white and Black performers.

As chronicled in his autobiography, *My Song: A Memoir of Art, Race, and Defiance*, Harry Belafonte had already produced a successful television special on CBS, *Tonight With Belafonte*. The 1959 special featured the singer Odetta, an all-Black cast, and director Norman Jewison, and resulted in an Emmy Award for Belafonte, the first of its kind awarded to a Black producer.[80] Laudatory reviews had ensued. Thus, CBS and the show's sponsor, Revlon, contracted with Belafonte for five more shows. Belafonte describes the choice and importance of the second show's title by noting:

> A local phone directory gave me the idea for the first of these five hour-long specials. In those days before ZIP codes, the city was divided into larger postal zones. One of them, Zone 19, went from Forty-second to Fifty-ninth streets, and from Riverside Drive over to Fifth Avenue. Within that broad swath, I realized, one could hear, on any given day or night, most of the world's musical styles and cultures, from classical in Carnegie Hall to show tunes on Broadway to bebop on Fifty-second street, but also salsa in Latin bars, jigs in Irish joints, the music of Israel in synagogues and the Yiddish recitals in theaters—the list went on and on. Why not a variety show with a song from each culture and genre within that small, dense district? The show was called *New York 19*.[81]

Belafonte's *New York 19* would be organized as the opposite of a minstrel show. Rather than burlesquing one or more cultures, he would celebrate many different traditions. His television spectacular would not feature white men blacking-up into absurd racist representations of Black men and Black women, but instead, whites would be whites, and Blacks would be Blacks. They would share the same stage, singing and dancing together. Sponsored by Revlon, a company that produced makeup as part of its product line, the situation could not have presented a more thorough reversal from the days of burnt cork minstrelsy. A cosmetics company would be sponsoring a mixed-race cast who, without altering their skin colors, would celebrate all the music and culture found in postal zone 19; certainly, this was an acknowledgment of changing times. On top of that, Belafonte and Lynne would sing "Li'l Liza Jane" as a towering duet.

The number begins with Belafonte and Lynne having a cup of coffee on the set of a small café while members of the Modern Jazz Quartet play behind them.[82] As there are many chairs stacked atop tables, the fictional café would seem to be closed. Belafonte improvises some lyrics before he and Lynne leap into the refrain popularized by the de Lachau sheet music. "Leap" may be an understatement. The two singers powerfully engage the song with enviable joy. Rising to his feet, with Lynne eventually standing as well, Belafonte sings a verse inspired by the de Lachau sheet music, with Lynne joining him in the second and fourth lines:

> I got a gal and you got none
> Li'l Liza Jane
> I got a gal she calls me hon
> Li'l Liza Jane

At this point, Lynne accompanies Belafonte as the two performers stroll arm-in-arm up a staircase and out of the café. The camera follows them through a portal and down into a city neighborhood set, where they are joined by whirling dancers. Belafonte delivers more verses as Lynne eventually dances her way into the ensemble cast around her, who take up the "Li'l Liza Jane" responses as well as the refrains. By this juncture, the orchestra's horns have joined the festivities and the number of dancers has swelled to exceed twenty. Belafonte leads them forward and backward, side to side, up and down, as everyone belts out the chorus. The camera has traveled upwards to capture the entire company dancing. At the conclusion of the two-and-a-half-minute piece, all the singers and dancers bow their heads save Belafonte, who noticeably exhales, unable to suppress a proud, beaming grin. The studio audience applauds vociferously.

Belafonte's glowing dance number embraces the courtship theme prevalent in many variants, and yet, nowhere in his rendition does the girl, Liza Jane, officially say "I do." Though highly choreographed and rehearsed, the dance number did restore some of the original performance practices ascribed to the "Liza Jane" family. Several voices from the WPA *Slave Narrative Collection* referred to dance, including Lina Hunter, who referenced square dance figures, and Hannah Jameson, who named certain dance steps, such as the "pigeon wing" and the "duffle shiffle." Roughly one hundred years later, an outspoken civil rights activist, singer, dancer, producer, and cultural humanist produced the song in front of a sizable percentage of the country's population. In fact, 1960 would be a magical year for the "Liza Jane" family, with Belafonte's version following Nina Simone's stirring rendition at the Newport Jazz Festival. Soul jazz pianist Ramsey Lewis recorded a suave instrumental treatment of "Little Liza Jane" in a trio setting, while drummer Panama Francis recorded a powerful instrumental version featuring a big band jazz ensemble. Numerous renditions from 1960 and earlier were in circulation, and therefore, Belafonte could have drawn upon multiple threads of inspiration as he crafted his own approach. Of course, his relationship to the tune may have dated much farther backward in time to noncommercial folk traditions such as those documented at the Hampton Institute. One of Belafonte's lines, "Come my love and walk with me," (as Lynne takes his hand), ultimately refers to the antebellum South, when its ancestor line "Come, my lub, and go wid me" turned up in the *Bold Soldier Boy's Songbook*, as well as the mid-century minstrel song, "Going Ober de Mountain."

The institutional racism symbolized by the Confederacy would reappear after *New York 19* aired, this time in the form of corporate pressure. As narrated in his autobiography, *My Song*, Belafonte had been preparing for the next television special when the Revlon chief executive officer Charlie Revson summoned him for a lunchtime meeting. Citing complaints from television stations in the South, Revson asked Belafonte to produce future episodes with an all-Black cast, as he did in his earlier 1959 televised special. By his account, Belafonte replied, "when you tell me no whites, you've crossed a line: morally, politically, and socially. I cannot become resegregated."[83] As a result, Revlon canceled the remaining four shows.[84] Would the cosmetics company have been satisfied if the white performers had applied blackface makeup? In the end, Revlon had deemed offensive the same-stage performance of a mixed-race cast who, never once, pretended to be from another race, never mind humiliating that race. If anything, Belafonte had structured *New York 19* to celebrate the works of multiple cultures, and as it turns out, a joyous folk song that had crossed the "race line" throughout its history featured prominently in this television special.

"The show's ratings were high," writes biographer Judith E. Smith in her work, *Becoming Belafonte*, "and there was talk of another Emmy. Then in August 1961, Revlon canceled the remaining specials Belafonte had contracted to produce, ostensibly due to a 'change in advertising policy.'"[85] A powerful opportunity had come about, but rather than opting to support Belafonte, Revlon apparently resorted to doublespeak. Nonetheless, the performance of a folk song such as "Li'l Liza Jane" demonstrated how Blacks and whites could "play together" just as the children had done in Margaret Walker's novel *Jubilee* before Big Missy dragged Miss Lillian home.

A few months later, in a very different postal code, *The Andy Griffith Show* enjoyed strong ratings in its inaugural season, placing fourth in viewership behind only *Gunsmoke, Wagon Train*, and *Have Gun Will Travel*.[86] Millions of households tuned in each week to catch a program set in the American heartland, the small town of Mayberry. "Populated with rural archetypes, [the show] provided the backdrop for Sheriff Taylor to employ traditional folk wisdom to settle local disputes and humorously outwit arrogant 'city slickers.'"[87] The CBS comedy would run for several years, remaining popular throughout its stretch. Songs were not uncommon, owing perhaps to the namesake character's training. According to a *New York Times* obituary, Griffith earned a music degree at the University of North Carolina and "tried teaching music and phonetics in a high school but left after three frustrating years."[88] He recorded music often, and "in 1996, released a gospel album, *I Love to Tell the Story: 25 Timeless Hymns*, which won a Grammy."[89] Therefore, it would not be unusual for a scene to open with Griffith, backed by his costars, engaged in singing.

Drawing inspiration from the play *Cyrano de Bergerac*, the show's twenty-second episode, "Cyrano Andy," aired during the debut season on March 6, 1961. In their book *The Definitive Andy Griffith Show Reference*, Dale Robinson and David Fernandes summarize the episode's plot, a summary of which might read as follows: Barney (played by Don Knotts) tells Sheriff Taylor (played by Andy Griffith) that he likes Thelma Lou (played by Betty Lynn). In turn, Andy visits Thelma Lou and reveals as much directly to her. At this point, Thelma Lou approaches Barney with the misinformation that Andy wants to date her. Barney, therefore, avers to Andy that he can steal Andy's girlfriend, Ellie (played by Elinor Donahue). Owing to these events, Ellie and Andy conspire to woo Barney and Thelma Lou, respectively, which scares the latter two into each other's arms. In their episode notes, Robinson and Fernandes confirm that all four main characters sing "Liza Jane."[90]

The episode's final sequence begins with lights rising on the four characters, Andy, Barney, Thelma Lou, and Ellie, singing the chorus of "Little Liza Jane." Seated beside Ellie, Andy clutches a guitar, while adjacent to them, Barney and Thelma Lou sit side by side. Together, the characters cycle through several repetitions of "Oh Little Liza / Little Liza Jane" until Ellie rises to get some snacks. The scene plays out with the conventional gag of Andy continuing to interrupt Barney as he attempts to kiss Thelma Lou or propose a kiss.[91] Difficulties in the realm of courtship would not be lost on connoisseurs of the "Liza Jane" family, and the song's placement in "Cyrano Andy" would appear to be deliberate. Of course, "Little Liza Jane" continued to demonstrate popularity, especially after Nina Simone and Harry Belafonte had performed gripping

1960 renditions. Millions more Americans were reminded of the song's catchy chorus in March 1961.

The phrase "millions more" could apply since there may not have been too many crossover viewers between *New York 19* and *The Andy Griffith Show*. By pooling the Belafonte and Griffith audiences, it is possible that forty to fifty million American households, give or take, would have caught productions of the song within the space of three-and-a-half months. "Liza Jane" variants would be seen on several other popular television shows—including *Gunsmoke* (1965),[92] *The Ed Sullivan Show* (1967),[93] and *Hee Haw* (1973)[94]—in the years to follow, further expanding audience interaction with the "Liza Jane" family. By the time Harry Belafonte and Andy Griffith presented "Liza Jane" renditions, there were no singers slathered in burnt cork makeup, no racist distortions attached to the lyrics. If anything, the two versions reinforced the song's relationship to dance and lighthearted, upbeat performance.

The arrival of "Little Liza Jane" in the early "talkie" movie, *Coquette* accompanied the menial labor depicted by African American actress Louise Beavers, servant to the Besant household. Early cartoons were even less friendly, as they unveiled animal characters in minstrel costumes, or in the case of the Van Beuren cartoon, being marketed at a slave auction. Even the development of American yodeling may have traveled through blackface medicine shows, although the DeZurik Sisters were not lampooning African Americans but rather barnyard fowl in their cackling version of "Li'l Liza Jane." Single-episode audience tallies of certain performances could number in the tens of millions, with repeat showings of films and reruns of television episodes adding to that tally. Star shows, performers, and characters featured in this context alone—*Coquette*, Bob Wills, Mickey Mouse, the Cackle Sisters, *Fibber McGee and Molly*, Harry Belafonte, *The Andy Griffith Show*—reveal great affection for the "Liza Jane" family at the very upper echelon of American popular culture.

Harry Belafonte repurposed "Li'l Liza Jane" for a television special that sought to celebrate all cultures and demonstrate the racial harmony of its singers and dancers. In doing so, Belafonte projected his formidable vision of American performance, one that showcased unvarnished white faces and African American faces together, without the masks of burnt cork makeup. His sponsor, the Revlon cosmetics company, would cancel the series of shows Belafonte had been developing after failing to pressure him into utilizing a single-race cast. Presented with an ultimatum, Belafonte did not bend. When considering all the incongruity in this moment, the mind does somersaults. For numerous decades, white men had pretended to be Black men and Black women, deliberately acting dumb, lazy, and foolish behind burnt cork makeup. The first Black producer to win an Emmy Award—Belafonte—pretended to be nobody other than himself. The singer Gloria Lynne did not pretend to be anybody but herself. The Black and white whirling dancers, the all-Black Modern Jazz Quartet, and the all-white Contemporary String Quartet did not distort their skin colors. A white body may have stood beside a Black body on national television, and with that great horror in mind, a powerful cosmetics corporation raised an objection. In essence, a company devoted to "beautification" required the ugliness of segregation. Belafonte did not bend. For its part, "Li'l Liza Jane" popped up yet again as if the "musical weed" possessed an organic mechanism that recognized a striking historical moment.

THE LOMAXES

LATE NINETEENTH CENTURY / 1910 TO 1982

While any number of commercial labels such as OKeh, Victor, and Columbia recorded groundbreaking versions of "Liza Jane" songs, the father-son duo of John and Alan Lomax recorded a considerable number of striking renditions themselves, not to mention achieving additional documentation through print and film. Father and son worked together and independently of one another; both Lomaxes collaborated with others. Their body of work, as applied specifically to the "Liza Jane" family, crosses the race line, cultural eras, and geographical boundaries. In many ways, it symbolizes the progression of the "Liza Jane" family itself. In all, the Lomaxes would collect variants across a host of musical genres, including old-time, folk blues, game song, hot jazz, and street band examples.

Born in Missouri in 1867, John Lomax moved with his family two years later to Texas, a restive region that biographer Nolan Porterfield portrays as being just as chaotic as the Civil War itself.[1] Yet nearby this new home, a young John Lomax would eventually encounter cowboy tournaments which concluded with lively dances afterward; these events featured "promenades and jigs accompanied by songs and calls in cowboy vernacular."[2] Perhaps this early infusion of folk culture would convince the future musicologist of a colorful (if "soused to the gills") world beyond the mundane tasks of "frontier agriculture."[3]

The cowboy tournaments described in Porterfield's biography, *Last Cavalier*, may have also propelled John Lomax in some formative way toward the material that would eventually comprise his influential 1910 collection *Cowboy Songs and Other Frontier Ballads*. Famously endorsed by Theodore Roosevelt, an updated edition would eventually include "Bronc Peeler's Song," a piece with a relationship to the "Liza, poor gal" variants described above. Its chorus especially conveys the likenesses:

> Goodbye, Liza, poor gal,
> Goodbye, Liza Jane,

Goodbye, Liza, poor gal,
She died on the plain.[4]

Notably, the word "Goodbye" substitutes for the more traditional "Oh poor." Instead of dying on the train, here, the Liza Jane character perishes on the plain, which would reflect an adaptation to the local scenery.

The "Liza Jane" family would be represented in other John Lomax collections, including *American Ballads and Folksongs*, which he coedited with his son, Alan. First published in 1934 and the subject of numerous reprintings, this book includes a variant, "Liza Jane," which also continues in the "Liza, poor gal" tradition. Cobbled together from numerous sources, such as Carl Sandburg's seminal work, *The American Songbag*, the variant's refrain corresponds to the refrains from "Bronc Peeler's Song" as well as the suite of "Liza, poor gal" songs discussed earlier.

O Law,' Liza, po' gal,
O Law,' Liza Jane,
O Law,' Liza, po' gal,
She died on the train.[5]

With "O Law'" translating to "Oh Lord," this refrain restores the traditional ending, in which the Liza Jane character perishes on the train. The verses include many of those traditionally linked to this branch of the "Liza Jane" family, including "Goin' up the mountain / To raise a patch of cane, / To make a barrel of sorghum / To sweeten up Liza Jane."[6] Independently and jointly, these two collections served to establish John Lomax's towering credentials and inspire a generation of musicologists to come.

In addition to these important texts, John Lomax made a host of essential field recordings, including those documented by Joshua Clegg Caffery in his historical work *Traditional Music in Coastal Louisiana*. Documenting that, together, John and Alan Lomax ventured into Louisiana's southern parishes during the summer of 1934, Caffery devotes space in his chapter on Lafayette Parish to the "somewhat mysterious ensemble" of Wilson "Stavin' Chain" Jones (guitar), Charles Gobert (fiddle), and Octave Amos (banjo), and as it works out, to "Li'l Liza Jane" as well.[7] Caffery's reported lyrics and his associated analysis of the song's history demonstrate rare acuity in connection to the "Liza Jane" family; still, the lyrics given below are thought to be slightly truer to the recording of Jones made by the Lomaxes, and the ensuing discussion may offer some improvements over what Caffery has proposed in terms of historical connections. Caffery's substantial curatorial efforts have brought this song and many others from the 1934 father-son voyage into the spotlight.

Li'l Liza Jane

Wilson "Stavin' Chain" Jones, Charles Gobert, Octave Amos

Don't you hear li'l Liza say, li'l Liza Jane
I said, don't you hear li'l Liza say, li'l Liza Jane

I say, li'l Liza, li'l Liza, li'l Liza Jane
Said, li'l Liza, li'l Liza, li'l Liza Jane

Yes I see li'l Liza walking 'round, li'l Liza Jane
Yes I see li'l Liza walking 'round, li'l Liza Jane

I mean, li'l Liza, li'l Liza, li'l Liza Jane
I mean, li'l Liza, li'l Liza, li'l Liza Jane

Yes, people say that Liza don't steal, li'l Liza Jane
Yes, some people told me Liza won't steal, li'l Liza Jane
And I caught li'l Liza in my cornfield, li'l Liza Jane
Yes, I caught li'l Liza in my cornfield, li'l Liza Jane

I mean, li'l Liza, li'l Liza, li'l Liza Jane
I mean, li'l Liza, li'l Liza, li'l Liza Jane

Yes, li'l Liza dressed in blue, li'l Liza Jane
And I can't see how she know what to do, li'l Liza Jane

I mean, li'l Liza, li'l Liza, li'l Liza Jane
I mean, li'l Liza, li'l Liza, li'l Liza Jane

Now, tomorrow morning purty soon, li'l Liza Jane
Yes, tomorrow morning purty soon, li'l Liza Jane

I mean, li'l Liza, li'l Liza, li'l Liza Jane
I mean, li'l Liza, li'l Liza, li'l Liza Jane

Yeah, got two mules in my cornfield, li'l Liza Jane
Hear yeah, I got two mules in my cornfield, li'l Liza Jane

I say, li'l Liza, li'l Liza, li'l Liza Jane
I say, li'l Liza, li'l Liza, li'l Liza Jane

I'm gwan get my hog but it won't be long, li'l Liza Jane
I'm gwan get my hog but it won't be long, li'l Liza Jane
I'm gwine call my dog for your hog, li'l Liza Jane
I'm gwine call my dog for your hog, li'l Liza Jane

I mean, li'l Liza, li'l Liza, li'l Liza Jane
I mean, li'l Liza, li'l Liza, li'l Liza Jane[8]

This June 1934 rendition may share certain characteristics with the Sam Chatmon version filmed by Alan Lomax. For one, Chatmon and Jones both holler
as if to support field workers or to encourage dancers at a breakdown. Both
songs refer to the color of Liza Jane's clothing—red in Chatmon's case, blue in
the Jones version—and both offer a sense of Liza Jane's whereabouts. In the
Chatmon film, the singer may be issuing dance instructions, whereas Stavin'
Chain can hear Liza Jane, can see her walking around, and catches her, humorously enough, stealing corn in his cornfield. The classic courtship adventures
do not pervade these renditions, with Liza Jane represented as more of a dance
game crony or mischief maker.

Caffery portrays the Wilson Jones recording as "[detailing] a series of unrelated episodes constructed largely out of stock phrases."[9] While the song does
absorb phrases that float from one folk song to another—Caffery puts forward
the cornfield lines as an example—the verses may not be as unrelated as he
proposes. Overarchingly, the setting is agrarian in nature, with cornfields, mules,
hogs, and dogs abounding. The singer, moreover, does have a girl on his mind,
and even as he may wander from thoughts of his mules to thoughts of someone
else's hog, he always returns to her, at the very least, in the chorus. That said,
the song need not "make sense" in a narrative context, especially if it derives
meaning through ear-pleasing repetitions of the girl's name or by facilitating
dance or labor. The refrain differs metrically from the Countess Ada de Lachau
refrain, owing perhaps to decades of tradition in Lafayette Parish.

When proposing origins for Stavin' Chain's version of "Little Liza Jane" and
other renditions, Caffery looks beyond the likely African American roots and
discusses the character Eliza in *Uncle Tom's Cabin*, the notion that "Eliza"
and "Jane" were stock characters in minstrel show repertoire, and the presence
of "loftier" language such as "Come my love and go with me / I will take good
care of thee."[10] As discussed throughout this book, a definitive link to literary
and minstrel sources has not emerged. Also noted above, stock phrasing like
"Come, my lub, and go wid me" traces back, for instance, to an 1845 minstrel
publication and not to wells of loftier English terminology. Caffery points to
Natalie Curtis Burlin's documentation of "children at the Hampton Institute

in Virginia"[11] as evidence of ring game adoption, but Curtis Burlin identifies a group of the singers as returned World War I veterans, and in any event, the lengthy history of the song at Hampton Institute seems to involve both young and older adults. The Institute's long-time cashier, Harris Barrett, chronicled "Little Liza Jane" in 1912 as a song sung by enslaved people, and this account, coupled with ten WPA narratives, plus the recollections of Sam Chatmon, offer powerful evidence that the family of songs originated among enslaved people on southern plantations, preceding regimental and minstrelsy adoption.

This analysis is not meant to visit any harshness on Caffery. On the contrary, his efforts to preserve the history of folk music in Louisiana are remarkable and have visited enhanced attention on the Wilson "Stavin' Chain" Jones recording. Moreover, in identifying the song's history, Caffery does propose the possibility "that an unknown minstrel show number antedates the ring game songs."[12] Indeed, this cannot be conclusively ruled out, although extensive efforts to identify such a number have not uncovered any examples. Instead, there appears to be a precipitous cutoff before the war correspondent Dr. Adonis penned the phrase "good bye, 'Liza Jane'" in February 1864. The months between then and January 1865, when the Kansas newspaper published "the fourth stanza of that new piece," likely saw "Liza Jane" variants emerge from the tradition of enslaved people, with no identified sources pointing toward a broadly adopted minstrelsy piece that might have preceded this activity. Caffery notes the differences between certain "Liza Jane" family members such as "Little Liza Jane" and "Goodbye Liza Jane"—terming them "second cousins once removed"[13]—but the larger of these differences owes to the intervention of postwar minstrelsy and not so much to regional folk customs. While not mirror images, many "Liza Jane" variants demonstrate similarities with one another, and as shown, facets of two or more variants often appear in the same songs. Terming them first cousins or even siblings might be more accurate.

For example, the 1897 article published by Rev. Hanford A. Edson demonstrates that the "Liza, poor gal" and the "Little Liza Jane" traditions can be found together in a North Carolina refrain: "O little Liza, pore gal, / O little Liza Jane; / O little Liza, pore gal, / She died on the train." Edson also notes the influence of African American music in this rough-and-tumble mountainous area, suggesting that Black and white music traditions may have mixed more easily than the groups of people themselves. The 1926 recording of "Goodbye Liza Jane" by Fiddlin' John Carson also includes the phrase "little Liza Jane" amidst an old-time melody aligned with the "poor gal" branch of the family. Numerous other examples, such as Carl Sandburg's folk music collecting, support hybrid relationships among "Liza Jane" branches.

Another such example involves the Lomaxes themselves, who collected an eclectic "Liza Jane" song a month before they recorded Wilson Jones. In

May 1934, they visited guitarist and singer Pete Harris in Richmond, Texas. As discussed above, Harris sang and played a piece, "Square Dance Calls," that contained a good amount of "Liza Jane" content. Among other information, the Library of Congress card catalog entry identifies the first line (or two): "I wouldn't marry a black gal / Tell you the reason why."[14] Reminiscent of Thomas Talley's wise rhymes, this couplet concludes with traditional lyrics from the "Liza, poor gal" branch, alluding to biscuits flying.[15] Yet the song incorporates other "Liza Jane" snotches, including "the new cut road" and "the lane." Harris refers to the girl as both "Liza Jane" and "Little Liza Jane." As the title indicates, the singer issues square dance calls interspersed throughout, and owing to his cowboy culture, yodels as well. Harris's moaning delivery and mournful guitar might establish the piece as a blues, and yet, this recording might signify one of the most diverse blending of styles and lyrics in the entire arc of the "Liza Jane" catalog. Harris may have combined these traditions himself, or he may have inherited the combination through the generational transmission of performance rituals. Either way, the Pete Harris rendition—as collected by the Lomaxes—underscores the closeness of variants, as opposed to their distance from one another.

John Lomax not only published examples from the "Liza, poor gal" branch, recorded a country blues version of "Li'l Liza Jane" by Wilson "Stavin' Chain" Jones, and presented the eclectic square dance rendition by Pete Harris, but he also collected an important version of the children's game "Steal Miss Liza." Recorded at the Florida State Prison, Raiford Penitentiary, in 1939 by Lomax and his wife Ruby, this rendition features the singing and clapping of three young African American women, Johnny Mae Medlock, Gussie Slater, and Ruth Hines.

Steal Miss Liza
Johnny Mae Medlock, Gussie Slater, Ruth Hines

Steal Miss Liza
Steal Liza Jane
Steal Miss Liza
Steal Liza Jane

That old man ain't got no wife
Steal Liza Jane
Can't get a wife to save his life
Steal Liza Jane

Steal Miss Liza
Steal Liza Jane

Steal Miss Liza
Steal Liza Jane

This old man ain't got no wife
Steal Liza Jane
Can't keep a wife to save his life
Steal Liza Jane

Oh, steal Miss Liza
Steal Liza Jane
Steal Miss Liza
Steal Liza Jane[16]

In this piece, the lead singer takes every first and third line, while the entire group responds in the second and fourth lines. The three singers, as noted, provide their own percussion via handclapping, and the lead vocalist displays an especially sweet voice, bordering on angelic. The children's game "Steal Miz Liza" will come to mind, from Margaret Walker's novel, *Jubilee*, as will the game "Catch Liza Jane," as mentioned by WPA respondent Lydia Jefferson. Through his collecting efforts, John Lomax reported several variants of the "Liza Jane" family, from Texas to Louisiana to Florida, among other locales.

Like father, like son. In June 1935, Alan Lomax and two of his colleagues recorded a rendition of "Steal Miss Liza Jane," which, according to the Library of Congress card catalog, was "sung by group of little Negro girls" in Eatonville, Florida.[17] The two colleagues—novelist Zora Neale Hurston and folklorist Mary Elizabeth Barnicle—also accompanied Lomax to Frederica, Georgia, where they recorded the same song, "Steal Miss Liza Jane," in the same month and year, June 1935. The Library of Congress card catalog identifies the singers, in this case, as a "group of Negro girls."[18] From a Florida penitentiary setting to a couple of towns in Florida and Georgia, respectively, the Lomaxes, as well as Hurston and Barnicle, situate "Steal Miss Liza" across three unrelated groups of performers and two states. In each case, the song is produced without instrumentation by girls or young women. These details underscore the likelihood that the game would be played in an impromptu playground fashion, not unlike the enslaved children and Miss Lillian in *Jubilee*.

Alan Lomax would record "Steal Miss Liza" again, many years later, in his New York apartment. Gospel and folk singer Bessie Jones sang the tune on October 6, 1961, precisely in the same manner as the Raiford, Florida version: without instrumentation, save the percussive clapping of her hands. Available at the Association for Cultural Equity website, the singing and clapping cut into the listener immediately. Jones largely follows the song's standard lyrics but adds a unique verse and varies the refrain as she sings.

Steal Miss Liza
Bessie Jones

Steal Miss Liza
Steal Liza Jane
Steal Miss Liza
Steal Liza Jane

That old man ain't got no wife
Steal Liza Jane
Can't get a wife to save his life
Steal Liza Jane

Won't you steal Miss Liza
Steal Liza Jane
[Let's] steal Miss Liza
Steal Liza Jane

I steal yours and you steal mine
Steal Liza Jane
I'm gonna keep these mens [of gwine]
Steal Liza Jane

Won't you steal Miss Liza
Steal Liza Jane
Let's steal Eliza
Steal Liza Jane[19]

Although "Steal Miss Liza" may not be a handclapping game per se, the Raiford Penitentiary and Bessie Jones recordings both contain this characteristic, which may regulate the pace of the action: namely, "stealing" a dance partner. The Lomaxes, however, were not the first to document "Steal Miss Liza." A detailed observation of the song appeared in the June 1927 issue of *The Playground*, a publication devoted to the recreational activities of children, including school-yard games. This account was part of an article, "Negro Folk Games," written by Willie Dean Andrews, who described herself as a "supervisor of physical educa-tion" for schools in Athens, Georgia.[20] Andrews lists nearly identical lyrics to the

Raiford, Florida and Bessie Jones performances: "Steal Miss Liza, steal Liza Jane /
That old man ain' got no wife / Steal Liza Jane / Can't get a wife to save his life /
Steal Liza Jane."[21] In terms of "Directions for playing," Andrews emphasizes a
ring formation populated by dance partners, save "one odd person" left out.
This lone dancer would "steal" a partner from the couples assembled in the
circle, leaving another lone dancer to begin the cycle all over again. "As soon
as singing starts," she writes, "all begin to clap hands and pat feet."[22]

In her 2006 book *The Games Black Girls Play*, musicologist Kyra Gaunt
observes that "African American girls embody the ideals of black music-making
in the games they play; syncopation and rhythmic complexity spark handclapping and foot-stomping."[23] To be sure, the "Steal Miss Liza" game song
presents ample opportunities for singers to accompany and complicate the
rhythm with handclapping. The three young women at Raiford Penitentiary
and Bessie Jones do so, adjusting their percussiveness in a way that might signal
fellow participants—were they on the playground, for example—to slow or
hasten their motions. Gaunt might concur when indicating "the patterns of
clapping gestures that accompany any rhyme or game-song are inseparable
from, and integral to, understanding its musical structure."[24] This reason-
ing admits "Steal Miss Liza" into a broader category in which hand clapping
can accompany any game song, and the handclapping rituals themselves can
serve as an inroad into estimating the song's subtle (or blunt) instructions
to participants.

While clapping might be handled straightforwardly enough by one singer in
Alan Lomax's apartment, what about the three participants in Raiford, Florida?
They could not afford to fall out of step with one another, lest the game perish.
Gaunt recognizes the necessity of harmony by linking it to a sense of pride or duty.

> Girls' handclapping games [. . .] are as much a social and phenomeno-
> logical formula as they are motor-rhythmic formulas that contribute
> to musical events. The games put into motion another ideal of black
> music-making: the art of having rhythm, of being able to be in sync
> with others while dancing and/or singing, without the aid of an external
> conductor or timekeeper.[25]

From the childhood of former enslaved person Lydia Jefferson to the fully
conceived world of Margaret Walker's novel *Jubilee* to field recordings in small
towns and the big city alike where young women and an older gospel singer
dedicated their efforts to recordings, "Steal Miss Liza" (as well as the reported
variant "Catch Liza Jane") could spring to life with no instrumentation, just
the ardent voices and the handclapping of the singers. Alan Lomax, for one,
experienced this "social and motor-rhythmic" phenomenon in at least three

states, separated by twenty-five years, and yet, he dedicated himself to collecting a wide swath of "Liza Jane" variants in several idioms throughout his career. In particular, he recorded and/or filmed numerous renditions from the "Li'l Liza Jane" and the "Liza, poor gal" branches of the "Liza Jane" family.

As mentioned above, Alan Lomax filmed Sam Chatmon's forceful rendition of "Little Liza Jane" in Hollandale, Mississippi, in 1978. A few years later, he filmed another forceful, hollered version, this time with a Mardi Gras connection. Specifically, he captured the White Eagles Mardi Gras Indians performing "Li'l Liza Jane" at a 1982 practice session.[26] Transpiring in a crowded, sweaty New Orleans bar at night, the rehearsal features several members of the White Eagles, who play instruments, sing, and dance. The visible instrumentation includes a variety of percussion devices—bongos, tom toms and drums, drumsticks and plastic buckets, and tambourines—but there may be additional sources of music, such as whistles and noisemakers. The key feature is call-and-response singing, with the leader, the Chief, calling out the verses and the tribal members responding with the chorus. Many of the White Eagles dance with fervor, and some practice confrontational stare-downs, which may anticipate the competitiveness between different Mardi Gras Indian tribes. While the verses can be difficult to understand, the chorus of "Li'l Liza Jane" rings throughout the eight-minute clip. At times, the Chief signals a change by shouting "in the morning!" or another phrase and the big drums fall out momentarily while the tribal members holler the refrain. Lomax, in this instance, captures two cultural marvels: first, the long-standing tradition of the Mardi Gras Indians, and second, the presence of "Li'l Liza Jane" within that extensive history.

The Mardi Gras Indians' tradition of masking and parading "[dates] back at least to the late nineteenth century," according to historian Reid Mitchell, writing in his book *All on a Mardi Gras Day*.[27] "Unfortunately," he explains, "nobody recorded the first appearance of a black tribe on Mardi Gras Day or when other black people began to copy this tribe."[28] A reader unfamiliar with the Mardi Gras Indian tribes might wonder about the identities of these "Indians," and whether this might involve another cultural ritual in which one race ridicules another, and yet, it turns out to be an enduring tribute by Blacks to groups of Native Americans who saved the lives of some of their ancestors. Writing in his 2020 article "The Aesthetic of Asé in the Black Masking Indians of New Orleans" music historian Oliver N. Greene Jr. defines the pageantry and roots of this tradition in more depth, specifying:

> The Black Masking Indians of New Orleans, commonly called the Mardi Gras Indians, are groups of African Americans who have maintained, arguably, the oldest surviving festival arts tradition by

African-descended people in North America. Elaborate handmade suits depicting Native American and African-inspired designs are personified through dance and call-and-response singing on Mardi Gras, St. Joseph's Day, and Super Sundays. This tradition pays homage to Native Americans who provided refuge to escaped African slaves. Masking Indian empowers practitioners by celebrating resistance and the survival of marginalized peoples. Records reveal that enslaved Kongolese, Senegambians, and Yoruba were brought to Louisiana in significant numbers and that these Africans interacted with Native Americans in and surrounding New Orleans.[29]

As opposed to the ridicule of blackface minstrelsy, the practice of "Black Masking Indians" offers a tribute to the Native Americans who attempted to shield escaped enslaved people from enslavers, with origins dating at least to the late nineteenth century. Historical sources cannot establish the precise date this tribute began, nor can they establish the date upon which one or more of the tribes adopted "Little Liza Jane." Owing to Lafcadio Hearn's report from New Orleans in 1876, however, the "Liza Jane" family likely circulated there in advance of the Mardi Gras Indians tradition taking hold. Moreover, numerous jazz musicians and marching bands native to New Orleans would adopt "Li'l Liza Jane." For instance, pianist Sweet Emma Barrett recorded a classic "Big Easy" rendition of the song in 1964 with the Preservation Hall Jazz Band.[30] While her effort did not involve Alan Lomax, the famed musicologist did record Jelly Roll Morton, and in the process, "Li'l Liza Jane" popped up yet again, this time among the repertoire of a New Orleans musical icon who emphasized his "founding father" status in the hot jazz world.

In addition to recording hours of music and reminiscences, the younger Lomax also served as Morton's biographer, publishing *Mister Jelly Roll* in 1950. Lomax recorded Morton in 1938, around the time the pianist had been holding court at the Jungle Inn, located in Washington, DC's Shaw neighborhood. There, Morton's career had been somewhat resurrected, as "hot jazz fans began drifting in [. . .] to watch in reverence 'those two perfect hands.'"[31] Tragically, one of these patrons ended up stabbing Morton after the two had quarreled, with the bloody wounds requiring hospitalization.[32] The incident may have ultimately contributed to the musician's demise. He passed away in 1941, but not before Lomax documented Morton's music and life.

Having left Chicago in 1917 for the west coast, Morton ended up playing at a joint known as the Cadillac Café in Los Angeles. The local musicians could not, according to Morton, play New Orleans jazz, so they entertained patrons by playing what they could scrape together. This would include songs like "The Russian Rag," "Black and White," and "Maple Leaf Rag."[33] In 2005, the entire set of Jelly Roll Morton recordings made by Lomax in 1938 was released as part of a large box set spanning seven compact discs. (An eighth disc contains demonstrations of Morton's music and reminiscences from Morton's contemporaries.) Just toward the end of the seventh and final Morton disc, on a track entitled "At the Cadillac Café, Los Angeles," the pianist recounts a bunch of the songs that he and his fellow musicians played at the venue in 1917.[34] "There was a number we used to sing," Morton adds, while lightly tapping the piano, "in Los Angeles at that time." He begins to hum the chorus from the Countess Ada de Lachau sheet music, searching for a way to identify the tune, which he cannot quite recall. Morton's "two perfect hands" begin to work the piano, spurring his vocals, which become a half-scatted, half-hummed approximation of the "Li'l Liza Jane" refrain, once even substituting "oh baby" for "oh Liza." With obvious enjoyment of the music, Morton proclaims that he cannot remember it, terming it a "little comedy song" and repeating, "we used to sing that little number." The conversation drifts into some other areas.

By the start of the very next track, "Little Liza Jane, Continued / On the West Coast," Morton has recalled the song's title.[35] "Oh, Liza," he sings, "Li'l Liza Jane." Perhaps Lomax had halted the recording and reminded him of the particulars. The pianist's rendering of one verse, imbued with some light scatting, might be transcribed as follows:

> A doot doo doo
> Diddle liddle loo
> Li'l Liza Jane
> A dum dum dum dum
> Dah dah dum
> Li'l Liza Jane

Morton, therefore, engaged with a "snatch of folk material" as he recollected the melody and some of the words. The pianist enforces some enjoyable raggedness on the metrical framework arranged by the Countess Ada de Lachau, and he can be forgiven, mightily, for his "Li'l Liza Jane" memory lapse. On the other hand, perhaps he performed the tune like this, if not with humming and scatting, but with a syncopated rhythm. By 1917, the melody would have traveled from San Francisco to New York, accompanying actress Ruth Chatterton, star of *Come Out of the Kitchen*, and in the same year, Earl Fuller's Famous Jazz Band would have recorded its popular version. Morton had probably not seen the play, but he may have heard the Fuller record, and he may have encountered the sheet music, which was published in San Francisco. Once arriving in California, of course, he may have learned the tune from another musician.

Either way, his copious gifts are evident in the "Diddle liddle loo" of his singing and in the "two perfect hands" floating over the ebonies and ivories. Morton's brief performance offers powerful insights as to how "Li'l Liza Jane" may
have been performed in a ragged rhythm context, as adopted by an influential
jazz practitioner.

Drifting forward to 1959, Alan Lomax's recording of the Virginia-based
Mountain Ramblers displays a mid-century interpretation of "Little Liza Jane" in
an Appalachian string band context, replete with banjo, double bass, guitar, and
mandolin.[36] In a year's time, the Harry Belafonte show *New York 19* would beam
"Li'l Liza Jane" into living rooms all over the country, but the Mountain Ramblers recording demonstrates the continued evolution of folk versions outside
the spotlight. Together, John and Alan Lomax encountered and collected "Little
Liza Jane" variants from Mississippi (Sam Chatmon), coastal Louisiana (Wilson
"Stavin' Chain" Jones), Mardi Gras Indian, Appalachian, and when considering
Jelly Roll Morton, "hot jazz" and/or ragtime traditions. Louisiana renditions
figure prominently in this context, as does the melody published by the Countess, although she certainly did not invent the refrain. In particular, the Chatmon
and "Stavin' Chain" Jones versions would appear to contain higher percentages
of folk tradition and fewer points of reference to popular recordings of the
twentieth century.

As did his father, Alan Lomax collected multiple forms of the "Liza Jane"
family, leading him to document variants from the "Liza, poor gal" branch.
In 1939, he recorded music and commentary from "coal country" folk singer
Aunt Molly Jackson in his New York apartment.[37] During a four-minute clip
entitled "Commentary on Dan Hawk's songs / John Henry / Little Liza Jane,"
Jackson describes Dan Hawk as a "half-colored and half-white" musician from
Clay County, Kentucky, and "one of the best banjo players and singers" she had
ever heard. Her commentary on Hawk is important since she describes him
as a descendant from "the old slaves [...] in slave times" and as someone who
played "Liza Jane," among other tunes in his repertoire. Toward the end of the
track, Lomax can be heard asking Jackson how Dan Hawk sang "Liza Jane."
Jackson obliges him by producing a piercing rendition of Hawk's style, singing
traditional "Liza, poor gal" (but not "Little Liza Jane") lyrics.

> Oh poor Liza poor gal
> Oh poor Liza Jane
> Oh poor Liza poor gal
> She died on the train
>
> Went up on the mountaintop
> Give my horn a blow

Every gal in Georgia
Come running to the door

Oh poor Liza poor gal
Oh poor Liza Jane
Oh poor Liza poor gal
She died on the train

Jackson's "poor gal" rendition continues the traditions of the Liza Jane character perishing on the train as well as the voyage up the mountaintop to give one's horn a blow. The floating couplet "Every gal in Georgia / Come running to the door" adds some levity to a variant that can induce, in Jackson's voice, a carving state of solemnity.

Folklorist Archie Green spent time with Jackson in 1958 at her home in Sacramento, California, and titled his book—*Only a Miner*—for the refrain in her early 1930s composition, "Poor Miner's Farewell."

Only a miner, killed under the ground,
Only a miner but one more is gone.
Only a miner but one more is gone,
Leaving his wife and dear children alone.[38]

Green describes a desperate environment in the Kentucky coal mines around the time of Jackson's emergence as a folk singer and songwriter circa 1931 and how "the terror and pathos of blood on the coal and brother fighting brother in feud-like strikes is preserved in Aunt Molly's songs."[39] Ultimately, the connection of her music to this strife would have interested Alan Lomax in recording her, and she would bring the raspy, piercing rendition of "Liza Jane" to these sessions.

Shelly Romalis, author of *Pistol Packin' Mama*, specifies that Alan Lomax first met Jackson in 1935 through Lomax collaborator Mary Elizabeth Barnicle and recorded seventy-five songs of hers, which were later donated to the Library of Congress without compensation for the singer. This had upset her.[40] Lomax reportedly referred to Aunt Molly Jackson as "the finest traditional singer he met in the United States" as well as an "incredible fictionalizer, hellcat, hard drinker, wonderful, meaner than a nest of rattlesnakes, ten feet tall."[41] The objections of Aunt Molly Jackson—regarding the treatment of her music by Alan Lomax—are important to note, and it is equally important to note in a musician such as Aunt Molly Jackson, a recordist such as Alan Lomax would have had his hands full with a complex personality.

Lomax had some experience, as things went, with hard drinkers from Kentucky. Musician and writer Stephen Wade devotes a chapter in his book *The Beautiful Music All Around Us*, to another Kentucky musician, Luther Strong, whose fiddling, according to Wade, became revered nationally through his Library of Congress discs. On the day Strong would make these recordings, in 1937, he woke up in the Hazard, Kentucky lockup, having been arrested for public drunkenness.[42] When Alan Lomax came looking for Strong at his home, his daughter Faye reluctantly admitted he had been jailed.[43] Not to be deterred, Lomax drove to the jail, bailed out Strong, and even bought the fiddler a pint of whiskey to facilitate the ensuing session.[44] While Wade describes Strong as a practitioner of the "high lonesome sound,"[45] Strong's one-minute version of "Liza Jane" climbs well past the "high lonesome" register with its alarming, bloodshot, greasy electricity. Recorded in the "Liza, poor gal" idiom, the song may recall a swinging rendition performed, as noted above, by the Kessinger Brothers several years earlier, and then again, Strong's rendition could have torn a building down.[46] The Kessinger Brothers and Strong versions depend upon the same melody, but Strong's performance cannot unfasten itself from his chaotic circumstances. One questions whether he would have been effective at all had he awoken completely sober in his own bed. Halfway through the tune, a voice in the background utters what must be an admission of shock. In addition to Strong's family, the fiddler's teacher, Bev Baker, witnessed the session, and he may be the one voicing astonishment in his notoriously "craggy voice."[47] At the very end of the tune, a single sharp clap resonates. It is probably not Strong himself since he would have still been clutching the bow and fiddle. It is the kind of noise someone makes when he or she dismisses everything that has come before.

The Lomaxes were criticized in some quarters for creating edited "composites" from unrelated (or lightly related) folk songs as opposed to presenting the genuine articles.[48] Archivist Matthew Barton acknowledges this complaint, remarking "[the] creation of composite song texts [by the Lomaxes] was controversial with folksong scholars," yet quickly refutes the complaint by observing "the practice was certainly widespread among the folk themselves."[49] Whatever their sins may have been, the Lomaxes did not resemble much of a callous corporate entity. They came to preside over an empire, with their "Liza Jane" collection approximating its own moderate principality. From the imprisoned African American girls to the jailed Luther Strong; from the hot jazz of Jelly Roll Morton to the raspy temper of Aunt Molly Jackson; from the bust-out hollering of Wilson "Stavin' Chain" Jones to the reenactment of a field holler by Sam Chatmon; from the solo handclapping of Bessie Jones to the roomful of percussion at the White Eagles Mardi Gras Indians rehearsal, the Lomaxes assembled a substantial collection of "Liza Jane" material that

crossed from Black to white, female to male, 1930s to 1980s, folk to blues, piano
to fiddle. One can only imagine the novelist Zora Neale Hurston humming
"Steal Miss Liza" after recording it with Alan Lomax, and just perhaps, the
reel-to-reel device caught this bit of her voice. Hopefully, more "total Lomax"
is being digitized, and if so, just how much would this "Liza Jane" principality
expand? One cannot feel gluttonous in these thoughts because hungering for
more "Liza Jane" does not represent greed but dutiful attention to the gal who
Dr. Adonis called a "little rogue." And this is to say nothing of one Rawlingson
Hector, leading a chorus of "Miss Eliza Jane" in Trinidad and Tobago, 1962, as
Alan Lomax hovered over the tape recorder . . .[50]

While Alan Lomax's skill at the helm of the reel-to-reel device cannot be
called into question, his greatest talent possibly rested in his adaptation to local
circumstances, such as those of a jailed fiddler who just needed another pint
of whiskey to get through a recording session. Oh, and bail money, of course.

THE CONSTELLATION THAT CONNECTS LANGSTON HUGHES AND DAVID BOWIE, ANTONÍN DVOŘÁK AND NINA SIMONE

1892 TO 1895 / TWENTIETH CENTURY TO THE 1970S

Even as Alan Lomax may have been the greatest American folk music collector, many other important authors and recordists presented "Liza Jane" variants, including the duo of Langston Hughes and Arna Bontemps. Among other works, the two Harlem Renaissance figures and lifelong friends collaborated on *The Book of Negro Folklore*, which offers a wide range of material, from "Animal Tales" to "Ghost Stories," from "Spirituals" to "Blues."[1] As it turns out, "Liza Jane" songs can be found in several places throughout the 1958 collection.

For instance, Hughes and Bontemps print Lafcadio Hearn's entire 1876 "roustabout" report from New Orleans. Termed "Levee Life," the piece recalls how the "Liza Jane" variant in question "was sung to us in a Broadway saloon" and proclaims the triumphant refrain: "Farewell, 'Liza Jane! / Farewell, 'Liza Jane! / Don't throw yourself away for I / Am coming back again."[2] The duo does not stop there. They incorporate an excerpt from Thomas Talley, namely, the "Bedbug" rhyme in which the speaker threatens to "Go get a pot and scald him hot! / Good-by Miss Liza Jane!"[3] A bit later, in a chapter devoted to "Playsongs and Games," Hughes and Bontemps give two versions of "Little Liza Jane," distinguishing them through variations in titling—"Lil Liza Jane" and "O, Li'l 'Liza Jane"—as well as lyrics. Collectively, the lyrics and dance instructions may have been drawn from various folk and popular traditions: stealing partners game song language, the variant "Steal Miss Liza," the Countess Ada de Lachau sheet music, and Natalie Curtis Burlin's report from the Hampton Institute.[4]

Not quite finished with the "Liza Jane" family, Hughes and Bontemps offer lyrics and performance rituals for a brief, unexpected ring game entitled "Miss Sue Liza Jane." Ultimately, the song would seem to feature the intrusion of the

Liza Jane character into the children's clapping game "Miss Sue from Alabama." Organized in two quatrains, the first is rendered as:

> Somebody's in your cellar, Miss Sue,
> Miss Sue, Miss Sue,
> Somebody's in your cellar,
> Miss Sue—Liza—Jane.[5]

Alan Lomax recorded "Miss Sue from Alabama" in 1942, as sung by Mary Johnson, Etherine Harris, and other unidentified girls in Moon Lake, Mississippi. In place of "cellar," the ensemble sings "parlor" and never mentions "Liza Jane" at all, instead concluding both verses by singing "Miss Sue from Alabama."[6] Hughes and Bontemps present performance instructions for "Miss Sue Liza Jane," which resemble those of many ring games. "Miss Sue" dances in the center of the ring until she chooses someone to take her place.[7] It is unknown why the Liza Jane character materializes in this children's game and when the "intrusion" may have first transpired.

An unusual book published in 1980 by the US Education Department, *In Search of Our Past* establishes this variant as a song sung by enslaved people but credits no source. The Education Department book titles the song "Liza Jane" and largely mirrors the Hughes and Bontemps text, albeit with some minor variations. *In Search of Our Past* relates the second of the two quatrains as:

> Did you ever see a monkey motion
> Miss Sue, Miss Sue?
> Did you ever see a monkey motion
> Miss Sue—Liza Jane?[8]

Here too, the lyrics tend to follow those of "Miss Sue from Alabama," save the appearance of the Liza Jane character. If nothing more, the example of "Miss Sue Liza Jane" demonstrates the borderless fluency of many game songs.

Ultimately, Hughes and Bontemps situate several "Liza Jane" variants among a comprehensive survey of African American folklore, including performance rituals likely dating to "slavery times." Toward the end of the collection, as part of a section entitled "Poetry in the Folk Manner," the editorial duo prints a poem entitled "Li'l Gal" by Paul Laurence Dunbar. Nothing ties this poem overtly to the "Liza Jane" family except for the sense that "Li'l Gal"—which is repeated nine times as both a refrain and a dedication—may conjure some elements of the classic "Liza Jane" setup. The speaker of the poem expresses his "honest heart a-beatin' underneath" the rags of his clothing, but in a vaguely mournful and lonely way, laments his inability to express himself directly to his love interest, which is the reason why, in his words, "I's a-sighin' an' a-singin' now for you, / Li'l Gal."[9]

Throughout the twentieth century, "Liza Jane" folk material drifted into the recording plans of several international pop icons. Little Richard, for example, recorded the song "Steal Miss Liza" in 1975.[10] His thundering record did not achieve "hit" status, but he transformed the ring game material into a rhythm and blues artifact. He begins with the traditional lyrics presented by the Lomaxes, Hughes and Bontemps, and Margaret Walker, among others, before adding his own verses. Little Richard's version of "Steal Miss Liza" would hardly represent the only time famous, important, or virtuosic musicians chose to record a member of the "Liza Jane" family. A voyage down to Louisiana, for instance, will reveal how "Little Liza Jane" intersected with the work of a famous Czech composer.

Mac Rebennack's 1972 album, *Dr. John's Gumbo*, contained, in the artist's words, "both a tribute to and my interpretation of the music I had grown up with in New Orleans in the late 1940s and 1950s."[11] Better known, indeed, as Dr. John, the rhythm and blues musician commented on the recording session in the biographical work, *Under a Hoodoo Moon*. He credits cornet player Melvin Lastie and tenor saxophonist Lee Allen as "two of the horn players who did so much to create the original New Orleans R&B sound" yet singles out Allen for his indispensable playing: "Lee is especially famous for the many, many smoking tenor solos he did on records that came out of New Orleans. I mean, his sound made hits out of a lot of records that might otherwise have been ho-hum."[12] Dr. John and his band record a version of "Little Liza Jane" for *Gumbo*, splashing updated lyrics on the traditional folk melody.[13] With Dr. John serving as lead singer or "caller" of verses, a chorus of women's voices backs him in the "responses" and the refrains. At about the one-minute mark, Lee Allen enters on tenor saxophone, at first quoting Antonín Dvořák's seventh "Humoresque." Dr. John indicates how Allen "put the fine" on the song and joined the other musicians at the end to create a "New Orleans-patented 'ride' chorus" with all the horns jamming.[14] The song pursues a medium burn and may be the inspiration behind a ditty—"Poor Little Liza Jane"—reputed to exist someplace within the fictional universe of the popular video game *Red Dead Redemption II*, released in 2018. Lee Allen, however, had not constructed the "Humoresque" riff uniquely for the *Gumbo* recording session.

He had played the riff many years before, at the onset of a trademark "smoking tenor saxophone solo." In fact, he began his solo at roughly the same point—the one-minute mark—in this earlier piece, which also happened to be a recording of "Little Liza Jane." According to John Wirt, author of *Huey "Piano" Smith and the Rocking Pneumonia Blues*, the namesake rhythm and blues musician also grew up hearing the tune "sung by children in his neighborhood. [. . .]

In the streets."[15] The New Orleans native would eventually record "Little Liza Jane" with his band, the Rhythm Aces, in 1956, bundled with "Everybody Whaling."[16] Both of those songs cooked. Allen's rambunctious saxophone soared. Similar to Dr. John's treatment more than fifteen years later, Huey "Piano" Smith depended upon the classic folk refrain but substituted his own unique verses. Perhaps the most telling of these verses would involve the promise of finery and marriage if only the gal would say "yes."

> Take you downtown buy you everything
> Little Liza Jane
> If you be my girl you can wear my ring
> Little Liza Jane[17]

Lee Allen quotes the seventh "Humoresque" again toward the ending, seeing out the song as it fades. Smith indicates he specifically told Allen to blow the classical piece, "Humoresque," during the "Little Liza Jane" recording session.[18] The record, according to Smith, "[got] a lot of local play around New Orleans, what they call regional sales."[19] Call it upbeat or jubilant, but either way, the song jumps and, while doing so, retains the essential "searching" quality of the "Liza Jane" family. Namely, the suitor keeps plying Liza Jane with questions and promising her that she could be his girl, and yet nowhere in the song does she accept his proposal. These modernized lyrics had traveled quite a way from Lafcadio Hearn's reported New Orleans roustabout version, with nobody getting "up on a house-top" and giving his "horn a blow." (Except, of course, Lee Allen.) On the contrary, the singers promise to take Liza Jane "downtown" for a legendary shopping spree. Even though Smith's rendition of "Little Liza Jane" did not become a national hit, it probably influenced the song's enduring popularity in New Orleans as well as subsequent New Orleans-based recordings, such as the Dr. John version, but also those by Smiley Lewis (1958) and Fats Domino (1959). Smith, for his part, continued to reference the Liza Jane character in other songs, including "Just a Lonely Clown" (1957) and "More Girls" (1961).[20]

The magical homage to Dvořák, who completed his suite of eight "Humoresques" in 1894 while residing in New York, bonds the "Liza Jane" family to the Czech composer.[21] "The seventh humoresque," writes critic David Hurwitz, "is probably the most famous small piano work ever written after Beethoven's *Für Elise*."[22] On the one hand, Huey "Piano" Smith and Lee Allen could have chosen the melody for its agreeableness to the ear, yet African American musicians, on the whole, were well aware of Dvořák's belief in the importance of their music. In 1892, Czech composer Antonín Dvořák became the director of the National Conservatory of Music in New York. During the year, according to musicologist Jean E. Snyder, he would come to know a Black student, Harry Burleigh, "who would be Dvořák's most direct link to the African American music traditions in which he was keenly interested."[23] Writing in her book *Harry T. Burleigh*, Snyder points out that Dvořák's "use of traditional Bohemian songs and dances in his compositions arose partly from his belief in the intrinsic value of the music of ordinary Czech people."[24] Dvořák may have been chosen to lead the conservatory precisely for this focus, "to help American composers [. . .] transcend their reliance on European models and fully embrace the indigenous music of America's 'peasant classes'—Americans of African and Native American descent."[25] To a student like Burleigh, this transformative philosophy would reverberate powerfully and indicate that he, as a grandson of formerly enslaved people, would need to reclaim his own musical heritage and display its inherent artistic value.[26] As much as Dvořák influenced Burleigh, the friendship shared by the two men "had a profound effect on them both, finding eloquent expression through their music."[27]

After the two had met, "Dvořák invited Burleigh to his apartment to sing the songs he had learned from his grandfather and his mother, and Burleigh became a frequent visitor."[28] Snyder relates the essence of a 1941 interview in which Burleigh described the visits to his mentor's home. After supper, Burleigh would sit down at the grand piano, surrounded by the composer and his family, which included at least two of his children. Longing for the pigeons from his native Bohemia, Dvořák kept thrushes in bird cages and opened the cage doors to let the birds fly about and join in Burleigh's singing and piano playing. Dvořák would frequently ask Burleigh about the backgrounds of the songs but also about the people who sang them. Burleigh related that "[Dvořák] asked hundreds of questions about Negro life."[29] Thus, through his friendship with Burleigh, the Czech composer familiarized himself with African American folk music.

According to classical music conductor Maurice Peress, author of *Dvořák to Duke Ellington*, Burleigh learned many of the plantation songs he sang to Dvořák "from the singing of his blind maternal grandfather, Hamilton Waters, who in 1832 bought his freedom from slavery on a Maryland plantation."[30] Despite this hardscrabble life, "Waters put his daughter, Elizabeth, the mother of Harry T. Burleigh, through college."[31] Even as Burleigh lived a different life than his grandfather did, one might imagine the powerful ways in which he conveyed these familial hardships and sacrifices through his singing while the thrushes flew about in Dvořák's New York apartment. Unlucky to be captives, those thrushes, but lucky to hear Burleigh and Dvořák holding forth, and as things go, Burleigh knew the "Liza Jane" family.

Writing in a 1934 essay, "The Negro and His Song," Burleigh refers to "songs [. . .] of play," adding that "none is so gay as 'Lil 'Liza Jane' of the Mississippi levees."[32] He reinforces the observations of W. C. Handy and Howard

Odum by emphasizing simplicity as the main feature "in the most intimate and finest of the Negro's songs."[33] Such a song, Burleigh avers:

> is usually made up of just one idea repeated over and over in the stress of deep fervor in an effort to give some expression to an inner emotion. The Negro takes just a few simple words, and about their rhythm creates a beautiful musical picture. When given the right interpretation, this reiteration does not produce monotony, but seems absolutely inspired, as illustrated in the appealing "De Blin' Man Stood on de Road an' Cried," where a simple phrase is repeated sixteen times.[34]

Burleigh notes how he frequently sang for Dvořák during their two-year association in New York and how the Czech composer steeped himself in African American spirituals and folk songs before composing his own themes.[35] It is not clear when Burleigh learned "Little Liza Jane" or if he ever sang it for Dvořák and his family, but at the very least, he situates the tune on the waterways, which, as noted above, reinforces the report by Lafcadio Hearn and the scholarship of Eileen Southern, among others.

Burleigh's visits to Dvořák's home acted powerfully upon the Czech composer. In May 1893, Dvořák published two articles a week apart from one another in the *New York Herald* as well as its English-language sister publication, Paris *Herald*, in which he praised the importance of Black music, establishing its role as the cornerstone of a new movement.[36] A highlight of the first article, which appeared May 21, reads, "In the Negro melodies of America I discover all that is needed for a great and noble school of music."[37] On May 28, Dvořák pushes a bit further, asserting that the coming American school of music must be based on Negro melodies and prophesying that this development "will be a surprise to the world."[38] Indeed, these declarations made international headlines, with some figureheads voicing support and others proclaiming opposition.[39] Dvořák may have envisioned a purely classical school of music when in fact, jazz musicians in the next century would fuse "Negro melodies" with European instrumentation, creating, arguably, the most important tradition within this "new national school of music." Together, jazz and blues forms, pioneered predominantly by African Americans, would contribute heavily to the formation of another form—rock 'n' roll—which would not have been visible during Burleigh's performances in Dvořák's apartment after suppertime. Or would it? Dvořák could peer into the future, apparently.

In the Huey "Piano" Smith 1956 recording of "Little Liza Jane," the musicians not only reinterpret a Black folk song but attach their international champion, Antonín Dvořák, and his seventh "Humoresque," to the proceedings. The many somersaults of significant events —folk song developed by enslaved people;

esteemed Czech composer endorsing the folk music of African Americans; rhythm and blues saxophonist as part of this "new school" of American music affixing the Czech's melody to a repossession of the folk song—are inherently jubilant. As for his role at the Conservatory, Dvořák lingered partway into the downturn that began with The Panic of 1893 but departed in 1895. Burleigh would become, in Eileen Southern's estimation, "the earliest of the black nationalistic composers." Burleigh was also, according to Southern, "the first Negro to achieve national distinction as a composer, arranger, and concert singer."[40] One can only dream about Burleigh singing "Li'l Liza Jane" to Dvořák and his uncaged thrushes. Yet it may have happened.

Several decades later, Nina Simone generated one of the most emotionally charged versions of "Little Liza Jane" ever produced. Author Nadine Cohodas chronicles Simone's life and career in *Princess Noire*, detailing how she and her trio performed on the opening night of the 1960 Newport Jazz Festival.[41] The festival host, Willis Conover, introduced Simone in the tradition of pianists who sing and singers who play piano, offering a continental interpretation of her name, "Miss Nee-na See-mone!"[42] There would be only one live performance of "Little Liza Jane" given by Simone and her trio, but studio manipulation or overdubbing likely created certain differences which emerged later on records. In the Colpix LP release, Simone asks for her tambourine, then engages humorously with the band and audience while she receives the instrument.[43] At the same time, she says, "This is a folk tune, and it's called 'Little Liza Jane.'" Cohodas, who may have seen complete film footage of the 1960 performance, writes instead that Simone's introduction went, "This is a folk tune—you must have heard it all your life. I did. It's called 'Little Liza Jane.'"[44] For Simone, "all her life" would have begun in 1933, when she was born Eunice Waymon as the sixth of eight children. She grew up in Tryon, North Carolina, a town on the southern slope of the Blue Ridge Mountains. Both of her parents were descendants of enslaved people.[45] It is unknown if Simone learned the song as an inheritance from "slavery times," but African Americans of her generation could have learned a slavery-era song such as "Little Liza Jane" from their parents or grandparents.

One stretch of footage from Newport shows Simone occupying a stool, snapping her fingers and clapping as the band leads her toward the first verse.[46] At various points throughout her performance, the film catches Simone in thoughtful communication with the song, her eyes closed. The intensity climbs as "Little Liza Jane" enters the choruses, at which point Simone grabs the tambourine and delivers a sharp clap to its skin. During the choruses, she can be seen lightly shaking the tambourine to one side of her body before striking it again as part of the refrain's emphasis. At other times, Simone continues to clap her hands and snap her fingers, therefore making use of her own body in a percussive manner. She does not play piano. Towards the song's conclusion, Simone signals the band to drop out as she enters a soulful exploration of the girl's name. Her powerful contralto voice then propels the final syllables upward, "Jane, Jane, Jane," as the band returns for a final flourish. It is hard to imagine more soul, more gospel, more folk than what Nina Simone brought to her rendition of "Little Liza Jane" at Newport in 1960.

Simone flips some of the language in order to reverse the typical male-female courtship narrative. In her version of "Little Liza Jane," the stealing partners dance language involves a "beau" or boyfriend: "I got a beau you ain't got none / Little Liza Jane." As noted above, one of the song's most romantic lines—"Come my love and live with me"—derives from nineteenth-century sources such as an 1845 minstrel piece, "Going Ober de Mountain." As did many musicians before her, Simone adds her own folk verses (as well as a second refrain) to her unique arrangement of "Little Liza Jane." Her couplet "Hambone hammer where you been? / Down by the creek making gin" probably derives from the "Hambone" song and body-slapping game. In Simone's rendition, either the Hambone character or another man takes her to a "great big town" where the couple witnesses the "bestest music in the land." That land would be America, flush in the middle of Dvořák's prophecy.

The years between 1956 and 1963 were a fertile period for the "Liza Jane" family. Select recordings and performances, when considering leader and genre, resemble a "who's-who" and "what's-what" of various American musicians and styles. The following list offers a picture of these years, including one or two near-miss performers, who did not become stars, but whose records score highly.[47]

1956   Huey "Piano" Smith. "Little Liza Jane." R&B.
1957   Merle Travis. "Possum Up A Simmon Tree." Country.[48]
1957   Hank Thompson. "Li'l Lisa Jane." Country.[49]
1957   Don Hager. "Liza Jane Bop." Rockabilly.[50]
1958   Smiley Lewis. "Lil Liza Jane." R&B.[51]
1959   Pete Seeger et al. "Goodbye Liza Jane." Folk.[52]
1959   Dale Hawkins. "Liza Jane." Rockabilly.[53]
1959   Fats Domino. "Lil' Liza Jane." Rock.[54]
1960   Ramsey Lewis. "Li'l Liza Jane." Jazz.[55]
1960   Panama Francis. "Lil' Liza Jane." Jazz.[56]
1960   Nina Simone. "Little Liza Jane." Folk.
1960   Harry Belafonte. "Little Liza Jane." Folk.
1960   Scotty McKay. "Little Liza Jane." Rockabilly.[57]
1961   Slim Harpo. "Little Liza Jane." Swamp Blues.*[58]
1961   Duane Eddy. "Big 'Liza." Pop.[59]

1962 Coleman Hawkins. "Go Lil Liza." Jazz.[60]
1962 Don Reno and Red Smiley. "Goodbye Liza Jane." Bluegrass.[61]
1962 Wayne Cochran. "Liza Jane." Rockabilly.[62]
1963 Mississippi John Hurt. "Liza Jane." Country blues.
1963 New Lost City Ramblers. "Liza Jane." Old-time.[63]

*Recorded 1961; released 1997.

Not all this vinyl would end up crossing the Atlantic Ocean to London, but some of these discs undoubtedly turned up in record stores there, while others may have been played on the radio. In a nation priming itself to reinvade the Colonies, this time with rock 'n' roll musicians, there were, according to music historian Chris O'Leary, twenty thousand beat groups astir within 1963 England and, of whom, twenty auditioned for record labels every week.[64] Just such a group—Davie Jones with the King Bees—materialized at a Decca recording studio in May 1964, armed with a song that Davie Jones and a bandmate, George Underwood, assumed to be "an old Negro spiritual."[65] It is unclear how these British teenagers arrived at this misunderstanding, but they were part of a mechanism that would end up making rock 'n' roll history.

At the time, Davie Jones was still Davie Jones, and not yet David Bowie, although the saxophonist-singer was David Bowie already at heart. He exuded the confidence of a superstar. Writing in his book *Rebel Rebel*, O'Leary contends that the American rock 'n' roll ferment leading to Bowie's selection of the song might have included "Liza Jane" songs by Huey "Piano" Smith, Fats Domino, Dale Hawkins, and Scotty McKay.[66] Of course, those renditions do not resemble spirituals. Bowie may have heard multiple renditions in multiple genres; he may not have fully grasped the word "spiritual." Whatever the case may be, the seventeen-year-old Jones / Bowie recorded "Liza Jane" as his very first single, his very first A-side. It would be bundled with "Louie, Louie Go Home."[67] The recording, though historic, had chronically embarrassed Bowie and may have been, as O'Leary suggests, "a memento of being young, hapless, and obscure."[68]

"Liza Jane" would not become a hit for the future international pop icon. What it may lack in polished musicianship, it decidedly does not lack in raw boisterousness. The song began, O'Leary notes, "with a three-chord riff [. . . but] the track's main hook was Bowie's overdubbed tenor saxophone, which zipped around, wasp-like."[69] Indeed, the saxophone buzzed like a "king bee" and at times came off rather "phat" or juicy. At that moment, the rock 'n' roll scene—gravitating toward what O'Leary calls "a generation of boys with guitars"—may have had enough, sadly, of the jumping saxophone.[70] The chorus would simply be a repetition of "Little Liza Jane," whereas the verses would conclude each line with the phrase "whoa, little Liza." The first couplet of the first verse immediately establishes the courtship dynamics:

> Well, I got a girl that's a-good for me (whoa, little Liza)
> Well, now she ain't more than five foot three (whoa, little Liza)[71]

According to O'Leary, the bandmates Jones and Underwood drew up an arrangement for the song, but their manager, "[Leslie] Conn wound up credited as sole composer."[72] However much the song may have embarrassed Bowie, it possesses scads of forward momentum. Bowie's execution of the lyrics may not have approached the level of, say, "I Saw Her Standing There," a Beatles song that had been circulating for longer than a year. Yet "Liza Jane" did fit a rapidly intensifying genre that prompted teenage girls to scream at band members often sporting shaggy haircuts. O'Leary portrays a singer who "already has the girl, he has too much of her, she's driving him crazy."[73] Indeed, the singer is so sufficiently addled by lust he cannot settle on her true height, although by subtracting an inch later in the song—by then she is "five foot two"—Bowie may depict her as "littler" and therefore more precious.

Had Bowie turned to "Liza Jane" at the height of his popularity, he might have experienced a moment similar to the one enjoyed by Kurt Cobain when he channeled Lead Belly during Nirvana's performance of "In the Pines." This sort of hypothetical really raises the question of who Jones / Bowie sought to emulate in the first place. The three white rockabilly bandleaders listed earlier in this chapter stand out as potential influences, although the singles recorded by Dale Hawkins, Scotty McKay, and Wayne Cochran lead with stealing partners language. Two of the three Black rhythm and blues recording artists—Huey "Piano" Smith and Fats Domino—do not employ "I got a girl" lyrics, but the opening verse of the Smiley Lewis recording does, minus any reference to dance games:

> I got a girl in Irontown, li'l Liza Jane
> She is fine and always around, li'l Liza Jane

Moreover, a tenor saxophonist (thought to be Herb Hardesty) buzzes in and out of the Lewis rendition, accenting the vocals before conferring a classic jump. A case could be made that the Smiley Lewis recording of "Lil Liza Jane" represents the closest model to what Jones/Bowie ended up producing during his 1964 Decca recording session. The Lewis version—which also features New Orleans legend Dave Bartholomew as producer and trumpeter—charges forward breathlessly.[74] On the grounds of breathlessness alone, the two songs amply resemble one another.

One hundred years after the war correspondent Dr. Adonis referenced "Liza Jane" in a Kentucky newspaper, a future pop icon took his first awkward steps as a recording artist and, in a London studio, cut "Liza Jane" as his first attempt to score a hit single. A few years earlier, saxophonist Lee Allen had connected the song to Antonín Dvořák, whose earnest appreciation of African American folk music defied the expectations of the world. The earlier sludge of origins had been replaced by a sludge of connections, travels, and meanings: many hundreds of people, places, and renditions. Above all else, "Little Liza Jane" had come to symbolize the magnificence of human transformation.

XVI.

PORTRAIT OF A YOUNG ENSLAVED WOMAN STANDING STILL IN THE CATHEDRAL SILENCE OF THE DEEP WOODS AFTER A DANCE

To better understand a story, sometimes it makes sense to single out the main character and, simply put, describe what happens to that character. In terms of the "Liza Jane" family, many candidates might vie for the lead role, but in the end, "Little Liza Jane" is the main character. This song variant was likely there from the very beginning when, in all probability, enslaved people first fashioned the "Liza Jane" snotches of folk melody. It survived outside of minstrelsy and, as noted above, conquered the twentieth century by appealing to a host of recording stars, not to mention filmmakers, animators, radio hosts, television producers, newspaper editors, seemingly every resident of New Orleans, and folklorists. Some of these renditions accompanied offensive subject matter, but most did not. The heart of the song, the engine of its "classic refrain," can be examined through these three examples, all documented at the Hampton Institute.

O, little Liza, little Liza Jane
—reported by General Armstrong (1886)

Oh, Eliza, little Liza Jane
—reported by Harris Barrett (1912)

O Eliza, L'il ʼLiza-Jane
—reported by Natalie Curtis Burlin (1919)

In these three examples, there are quibbles to be made regarding "little" versus "li'l" or "Liza" versus "Eliza," but they are, in effect, the same "snotches" of folk material. Each of these refrains may have been a song unto itself, remembering how General Armstrong noted the *ad infinitum* nature of its repetition.

By virtue of the exclamation—"O" or "Oh"—the tune recommends itself for loud delivery. Two of the three forms choose the name Eliza to follow the exclamation. Thus, the woman can be Eliza, Liza, and Liza Jane. As noted earlier, Eliza is more formal, whereas Liza is more folk, and the two forms in the same refrain emphasize both formality and folkways. Many of the other major variants, such as "Steal Miss Liza," also isolate Liza at first, only to reunite the woman with the second half of her name, "steal Liza Jane." Without that reunion, the song would not be able to honor its rhythmic promise or, rather, fulfill its rhythmic need.

The three "Little Liza Jane" choruses presented above differ syllabically from one another, with General Armstrong reporting a five-foot line, Natalie Curtis Burlin reporting a four-foot line, and Harris Barrett reporting a line that fits in between. During a performance, those rhythmic differences would even out, usually through the exuberance of the singers or clipping of sounds, although an unhurried pianist, such as Jelly Roll Morton, sitting at the ebonies and ivories by himself, might sing "diddle liddle loo" as an unusual balancing act for "Li'l Liza Jane." Another pianist-singer, the great Nina Simone, devised a second chorus for her rendition—"Little Liza Jane Jane little Eliza"—that not only repeats Jane but seems to invert the refrain en route to its presentation of an eleventh syllable. Formal English poetry has tended to revolve around a five-foot or ten-syllable line. When an eleventh unstressed syllable occurs at the end of a line, some scansion professionals might classify that syllable as a "feminine ending," which would yield some irony in this case, given that the reason for the extra syllable would be the female name Eliza, sung by a stellar chanteuse.

Other than the women's names Eliza, Liza, and Jane, and combinations thereof, the only words beyond the exclamation ("Oh") would be "little" or "li'l." One of the three Hampton Institute refrains—General Armstrong's mostly iambic line—installs the word "little" twice. It is possible that Armstrong imposed "proper" English upon his report of the refrain, as it can be slightly awkward to pronounce both syllables of "little" when another "L" sound follows. The line reported by Curtis Burlin, which could read spondee / trochee / spondee / iamb, may better approximate the chorus in performance, with li'l and Liza gliding together, joined at the "L." David Bowie notwithstanding, most renditions do not tend to comment overtly on height or body size. More likely, "little" and "li'l" may imply cuteness, sweetness, levity, lightheartedness, or rural origins; it could be a nickname.

Across many dozens of renditions, the suitor and the young woman never quite seem to consummate their interest in one another. The scenario proposed in the Huey "Piano" Smith version—"If you be my girl you can wear my ring"—never quite seems to reach fruition. Liza Jane never quite becomes the singer's girl and never demonstrably wears his ring. Perhaps there is something about little Liza Jane's youthfulness that emboldens her, in the male-dominated courtship environment, to say no, or at least to delay the suitor's advances for the time being. With roots in the stealing partners dance game environment, the song may have been performed, deliberately, with one extra male dancer. There would always have been, therefore, a fellow who did not have a dance partner: "I got a gal and you got none," the others might have sung. It is easy to see how this unbalanced scenario might have carried forward, given that another dancer was always whirling into place, and the girl, under those circumstances, would have no reason to say, in effect, "I do." She might wait around to see if she could improve her situation, either through another dancer arriving or another suitor calling.

Though acknowledged throughout this study, it should be reemphasized that the alliterative phrase "li'l Liza" or "little Liza" is agreeable to the ear. Some of the "Liza, poor gal" singers realized this too, including the controversial figure Fiddlin' John Carson, whose eclectic chorus simultaneously refers to the three most popular branches in the "Liza Jane" family.

> Oh little Liza poor girl
> Oh little Liza Jane
> Oh little Liza poor girl
> Good-bye Liza Jane

In addition to its cross-variant references, the refrain features intricate sound work. The "O" sounds in "oh" and "poor" (and even "good") connect, as do the "L" sounds in "little," "Liza," and "girl." Carson could simply repeat lines two and four, just as he repeats lines one and three, but instead, the substitution of "Good-bye" for "Oh little" unspools the emphatic recognition of the rift, however serious or lighthearted, between the singer and Liza Jane. Unlike some of its "Liza, poor gal" kinfolk, Carson's rendition does veer towards the darker side of the spectrum.

He would not be alone in presenting an edgier interpretation of a "Liza Jane" song. As noted above, the Kessinger Brothers recorded a madly swinging instrumental. Luther Strong, perhaps under the influence of liquid refreshments (i.e., corn liquor), fiddled a soaring, grinding, electric version that may have caused his own fiddle teacher to cry out in admiration. Aunt Molly Jackson's raspy voice brought a bittersweet tone to her "Liza Jane" recording. Jackson and many other musicians who performed the "Liza, poor gal" songs refer to the Liza Jane character perishing on the train; this would include the song "Run, Mollie, Run" by the under-celebrated Henry "Ragtime" Thomas, into whose lyrics the Liza Jane character intrudes. No matter how jokingly a song might be presented, the concept of a woman dying on the train requires some acknowledgment of—the mortality of all things—by singer and listener alike. After all, the singer could have chosen to croon "riding on that train" instead, a variation that appears in a fair number of "Liza, poor gal" renditions.

Aficionados of dark humor might appreciate the old-time country version of "Liza Jane" by Carter Brothers and Son. Recorded in 1928 on the OKeh label, the tune romps through its lyrics and arrangement at too great a clip for it to be a purely benevolent piece.[1] While some of the lyrics are difficult to make out, the singer does repeat the notion of sending his scolding wife down to New Orleans and trading her off for corn. This is clearly adapted from the nineteenth-century minstrel song "Lucy Long," which otherwise gives "Georgia" as the destination for the scolding wife.[2] A related song or "cover" version appeared from New Lost City Ramblers in 1963, as part of their album *Gone to the Country*, with lyrics in estimation of a murder ballad. A sample verse— "Now if I had a scolding wife / I sure would whip her some / I'd run my finger down her throat / And gag her with my thumb"—walks the line between dark humor and matter-of-fact abusiveness.[3] Undoubtedly, some folk songs can center on "a bad man" (for example, "cruel Stagolee"), and the extended "Liza Jane" family follows suit. Some "Liza Jane" branches stretched out in ways the main character, "Little Liza Jane," did not, even as the unfulfilled male-female dynamic may have flourished virtually everywhere. Recordings such as those by Carter Brothers and Son and New Lost City Ramblers might call to mind the harsh climatology of Appalachian mountaintops and could veer from tragi-comic to worse. While Nina Simone's rendition of "Little Liza Jane" projects copious emotional content, it does not stir anything obviously elegiac. The White Eagles Mardi Gras Indians strike some confrontational poses since they compete with other tribes on certain New Orleans holidays, but their version of "Little Liza Jane" does not otherwise tread into the realm of physical conflict.

If the "Little Liza Jane" branch lacks any "wickedness," it compensates with instrumental and vocal exuberance as well as with its materialization in virtually every genre of popular music. A sampling of twenty-five musicians or groups—unmentioned until now—who have recorded or performed "Little Liza Jane" would include:

> AKA, Sam Butera and Louis Prima, Robert Cage, The Carlisles, Oscar "Papa" Celestin, Bing Crosby, Tommy Dorsey, Scott Dunbar, Grandpa Jones, Kaia Kater, Rahsaan Roland Kirk, George Lewis, Levon and the Hawks (also known as The Band), Taj Mahal, Wynton Marsalis, John and Emery McClung, Elizabeth Mitchell, Bill Monroe, Art Neville, Trombone Shorty, George Strait and the Ace in the Hole Band, Otis Taylor, Conny van Bergen, Doc Watson, and Chubby Wise.

Some of these names will be instantly recognizable; others are rare; the list is hardly exhaustive. Genres and styles among this group of musicians might include punk, folk, rhythm and blues, electric blues, novelty, pop, jazz, country blues, country, rock, old-time country, children's songs, and bluegrass, among others. A fair number of these musicians have recorded or performed renditions of "Little Liza Jane" in the twenty-first century. All the renditions are available through records, digital streaming, YouTube, or other sources, with one exception.

Music critic Michael Bourne published an October 1970 interview with the multi-instrumental jazz musician Rahsaan Roland Kirk in *Downbeat* magazine, and as part of the article, referred to Kirk's "riotous clarinet march through the crowd on 'Little Liza Jane.'"[4] The jazz discography website "JazzDisco" confirms that Rahsaan Roland Kirk & the Vibration Society recorded "Little Liza Jane" live a few months earlier at the Village Vanguard in New York as part of a second set on May 15, 1970.[5] The site categorizes "Little Liza Jane" and many other tunes from the musician's Village Vanguard sets as "Atlantic unissued." One of the most wildly original figures in jazz history, Kirk often played three instruments at once, practiced his art in different jazz idioms, and professed a love for the classical Black music of New Orleans.[6] He also traveled frequently enough to Maine, as it turns out.

On April 9, 1971, a student named David Washington published a short piece in the *Colby Echo*, a student publication at Colby College, in promotion of a performance for the following day. The student refers to a Rahsaan Roland Kirk concert he attended at Bates College (also in Maine) the prior fall and notes that "yes, he does blow three horns at once; yes, he does blow a flute through his nose; yes, he does beat a Chinese gong; yes, he does blow two melodies simultaneously on two horns; yes, he does make use of a coach's whistle; yes, he is blind."[7] College campuses, during the Vietnam War years, might have been very receptive to an anti-establishment figure like Roland Kirk, but if that were not enough of a reason to go see him, the student also notes that part of Kirk's routine is "singing Liza Jane."[8]

A review of Kirk's performance at Colby College appeared in the *New York Times* on May 30, 1971. The reviewer, Ty Davis, describes a crowd both enthusiastic and somewhat uncertain of what to expect as it filed into the school's gymnasium. Davis leads the reader through the sets by Kirk and his band, describing many of the songs, such as "Blacknuss," which the band's pianist plays only on the black keys of the piano, and the increasingly rapturous reception by the college students. After a long, extended blues:

> Rahsaan slows things down (the audience grudgingly sits again) with an introduction to "Liza Jane," one of America's best loved gospel folk

songs about New Orleans' most famous black madam (who always took care of the musicians for free on Sunday—"Musician's Day"). There is a dramatic pause as the drums set up a solemn rhythm. Then Rahsaan bursts into it with a strong verse, speeding up the tempo to the correct, fast speed. The audience is up again.[9]

Perhaps Kirk advanced the "black madam" story as part of a colorful onstage rap, although the reviewer may have added (or embellished) the tale himself. Either way, Rahsaan Roland Kirk & the Vibration Society performed a rousing version of "Liza Jane," contributing to the mounting frenzy of the audience. By the end of the show, Davis writes, "The crowd is dancing onstage and on the floor." The critic portrays a stage so crowded that Kirk can hardly maneuver, even as he launches into "Serenade to a Cuckoo."

Through the reports of a *Downbeat* critic, a Colby College student, and a *New York Times* reviewer, Kirk had been singing "Little Liza Jane" in addition to leading a "riotous clarinet march" of the song. Sadly, the Village Vanguard recording has not been made available if it still exists and has not been misplaced or destroyed. There, at the Vanguard, Kirk apparently took the tune directly into the audience, but at Colby, the enraptured college students rushed toward Kirk. Even if they did so after he concluded "Liza Jane," the tune nevertheless prompted another "bright moment" in a history that has crossed three centuries, a history which includes a blind, multi-instrumental iconoclast who was, himself, famous for the phrase (and song) "bright moments."

Rahsaan Roland Kirk may have invented a "spicy" story to captivate the audience, in this case, college students at quite a remove from New Orleans. Many musicians did toil, however, in the notorious brothels of Storyville, "[revolutionizing] American music" in the process.[10] The "hot jazz" pianist Jelly Roll Morton was one such musician, and his travels to Chicago and the West Coast, as discussed earlier, resulted from the Storyville neighborhood being shut down by the government in 1917.[11] Nevertheless, the "black madam" tale does raise the question, inadvertently, of who the original Liza Jane may have been and who she came to represent after generations of performances. She can be characterized, as noted above, by the many nuances of the words "little" or "li'l." Given the song's likely origins among enslaved people, one would imagine that the first "Liza Jane" of the song was African American.

The historian Joel R. Williamson addresses naming conventions associated with enslaved people as part of his essay, "Black Self-Assertion Before and After Emancipation." In addition to commenting on how "the great mass of black people" were assigned only one name throughout slavery, Williamson also describes the necessity for differentiation on large plantations where two enslaved people might have had the same name.[12] In some cases, descriptive adjectives were added to names, while in other instances, family connections were emphasized.[13] Quite surprisingly for the purposes of this book, Williamson proposes how the phrase "Little Liza Jane" may have developed.

> Children of the same name were commonly distinguished by reference to a parent. Thus daughter Jane might become Liza's Jane. Perhaps over the years, and particularly after Liza died, slurred pronunciation might yield a Liza Jane. Also often a child was given the name of the parent with the prefix "Little" added. Liza Jane's first daughter might thus be called Little Liza Jane.[14]

Published in *Key Issues in the Afro-American Experience* during the same year, 1971, when Rahsaan Roland Kirk played to a gymnasium full of Colby College students, Williamson's article establishes a mechanism that might have led to the song's namesake young woman. This is at least as plausible as ascribing a title, for instance, to a combination of Robert Burns's "Farewell to Eliza" and the minstrel tune "Susan Jane." While it may be difficult to overlook the affront caused by slavery-era naming conventions, it is possible, according to Williamson's example, that an actual woman existed who fellow enslaved people referred to as Little Liza Jane. She may have inspired the earliest "bright moment" associated with the "Liza Jane" family of songs more than 150 years ago.

White audiences began to encounter the classic "Little Liza Jane" refrain during the World War I years, and undoubtedly, they may have imagined a white woman as the girlfriend character. That said, most renditions do not focus on the girl's skin color but instead on her desirability (and reticence) as a love interest. Only a country obsessed with the segregation of whites and Blacks would have recoiled at the image of Harry Belafonte's mixed-race cast singing "Little Liza Jane" together in 1960. During the *New York 19* production, the performers may have been thinking of all skin colors or no skin colors at all. Liza Jane may have become the young woman from all backgrounds who does not want to wear the guy's ring and be his girl—or at least not yet. The "every-woman" still making up her mind.

Actress-aviatrix Ruth Chatterton became the first performer to sing the Countess Ada de Lachau lyrics during the 1916 stage comedy *Come Out of the Kitchen*. Louise Beavers became one of the first performers with a specified role to offer the melody—via humming—on the big screen in the opening sequence of the 1929 film *Coquette*. A song typically presented by men, the "Li'l Liza Jane" twentieth-century boom depended upon the composition and appearances of three women, white and Black. Eventually, the variant's most emotionally charged moments may have transpired at the 1960 Newport Jazz Festival. The film footage from Nina Simone's performance captures the singer in a deep trance-like conversation with the song as if she were imagining a young enslaved Black woman, the original Little Liza Jane. Indisputably, women and men from many different backgrounds have influenced "Little Liza Jane," a bright, irresistible "snotch" of folk material that lends itself to boisterous, repetitive choruses. A case could be made that the trajectory of the tune, especially when situated alongside the other members of the "Liza Jane" family, cannot be matched by the voyages of other American folk songs.

I spoke directly to you, Dear Reader, during the front matter of this book, and I am returning now, briefly, in the "first person" voice, at its very conclusion. It is I who endorse the minimalist approach—defining the main character; listing what happens—in determining the cultural meanings of the "Liza Jane" family. In the end, this strategy may orient us, helpfully, to what can be an unruly lot.

All the biggest variants survive to this day, yet "Little Liza Jane" possesses by far the most recognizable melody. I believe that all the "Liza Jane" songs were treasured when first sung by enslaved people. This belief derives from the ten WPA narratives but also from the testimony of Sam Chatmon and the quiet heroism of Harris Barrett. When large numbers of enslaved people began gravitating towards contraband camps or other destinations during the Civil War years, the variants probably "leaked out" into white society if they had not done so already. The war correspondent "Dr. Adonis" may have applied the earliest date-stamp to "Goodbye Liza Jane," but in the end, a related "snotch" of folk melody—"Oh, Eliza, li'l Liza Jane"—would predominate.

There are too many noteworthy moments in the entirety of the "Liza Jane" constellation, some painful, some beautiful, to revisit here, at the book's conclusion, so perhaps we should trust our imaginations to envision a scene that few, if any, of us, can comprehend. How about a young enslaved woman walking home after a Saturday night frolic during which she traded dance partners to the tune of "Little Liza Jane." If she, during the dance, ever feigned reluctance to accept the arm of a particular dancer, perhaps the other singers and dancers immediately adopted this performative ritual. What if she stood still in the cathedral solitude of the deep woods after the frolic had ended, her heart beating rapidly with the excitement of dancing to "Little Liza Jane." She might have been considering the charms of a particular admirer at that moment, or the specifics of a dance step, or simply put, the expansive word "Freedom."

APPENDIX 1: LOOSE ENDS

WPA narratives reporting songs related to the "Liza Jane" family. Three narratives from the WPA *Slave Narrative Collection* report related titles and lyrics. [1] The narrative of Missouri respondent Eliza Overton reports details concerning a song "Swing Ole Liza Single" that may have a distant relationship to the "Liza Jane" family.[1] Folklorist Benjamin Botkin includes the following line—"Swing Miss Liza single on a warm summer day"—as part of "Sweetheart A-Hunting" but does not connect the song to the "Liza Jane" family.[2] [2] The narrative of Alabama respondent Frank Menefee presents a couplet—"Dark cloud arising like gwine to rain / Nothing but a black gal coming down the lane"—that may refer to two traditions associated with "Liza Jane" songs.[3] These traditions would include the dual pathways of "the new cut road" and "the lane" as documented above, and in addition, rainstorm imagery that would later appear in "Liza Jane" songs such as "Rocky Island," recorded by Ralph Stanley."[4] [3] The narrative of Oklahoma respondent Lizzie Farmer offers lyrics and performance rituals for a "ring play" entitled "Miss Mary Jane." Farmer's report calls to mind the "Little Liza Jane" stealing partners game song traditions as well as the square dance calls reported by WPA respondent Lina Hunter, except for the name "Liza," which is lacking.[5]

Abraham Lincoln. Authors Kunigunde Duncan and D. F. Nickols assert that Lincoln knew a variant of "Liza Jane" but do not offer a citation or date stamp to support the claim.[6]

"Fanga Alafia." Some sources claim that the song "Fanga Alafia" precedes "Little Liza Jane" as an African song of welcome and that its melody transferred to "Little Liza Jane." Musician Robert Damm researched the history of "Fanga Alafia" and attributes its creation to either LaRocque Bey or Babatunde Olatunji in the late 1950s or early 1960s, in the United States, with the melody of "Little Liza Jane" transferring to it, instead.[7] Poet and Africanist scholar Gale Jackson presents additional viewpoints about "Little Liza Jane" and "Fanga Alafia" that are worth reviewing.[8]

Authorship/early appearances. Scattered sources claim that "Liza Jane" variants were first devised by Thomas "Daddy" Rice or Stephen Collins Foster. No citations or date stamps accompany these claims. Historian John M. Belohlavek avers that the Liza Jane character appeared in the song "Rose of Alabama" around the time of the Mexican-American War but did not offer a citation.[9]

Union soldiers in Mississippi. According to the oral history presented in *Lauderdale County, Mississippi, Four Families, 1835–1936*, Union soldiers marched away from the house of William Sheppard Smith in 1864 singing the chorus of "Little Liza Jane." Additionally, Smith's wife, Eliza Jane, is said to have "[cracked] a walking cane over the head of one of the Union soldiers."[10] Noting the name of Smith's wife, and the otherwise swashbuckling nature of the encounter, this story may be fictitious.

Mississippi soldiers in Virginia. Between 1914 and 1915, a contributor identified as Captain James Dinkins published several short articles in *Illinois Central Magazine* describing both his Civil War exploits and his experiences as an employee of the Illinois Central Railroad Company (the publisher of the magazine). During the Civil War, Captain Dinkins at one point served in the Eighteenth Mississippi Regiment. As a member of this Confederate unit, Dinkins indicates that he and his fellow soldiers sang "Go Long Liza Jane" on a march toward Winchester, Virginia in 1862. Unfortunately, he offers no information on the song beyond its title. While it is possible that Captain Dinkins sang the song as a soldier, there is not enough evidence to conclusively date his recollection.[11]

Alice Morgan Person. Musicologist Chris Goertzen published an interesting article about Person, who sold medical tonics in the nineteenth century and attracted customers by playing the piano. Person published arrangements of her songs in 1889, including music (but no lyrics) for an unusual rendition of "Liza Jane." While many of Person's songs have ties to the first half of the nineteenth century, Goertzen cannot date this rendition of "Liza Jane," which may not be a "Liza Jane" family member in the end.[12]

Pete Seeger and House Un-American Activities Committee. A version of the song "Li'l Liza Jane" credited to Seeger appeared in the *Congressional Record*, in 1953, as part of the transcript for testimony by Rev. Jack R. McMichael.[13] Its presence in the *Congressional Record* is somewhat mystifying, even as Seeger would be subpoenaed a couple of years later, beginning a long and painful saga for him.

Divorce in "slavery days." James Joseph McDonald claims in his book *Life in Old Virginia* that an enslaved man could divorce his wife by simply saying, "Goodbye Liza Jane." No citation or date stamp accompanies this claim.[14]

Countess Ada de Lachau. According to a July 25, 1916 article published in the *San Francisco Examiner*, Countess Ada de Lachau was born Ada Louise Metz in New York. She married Count Fabian Goudard de Lachau, said to be a French soldier, and was also known as Countess Goudard de Lachau.

APPENDIX 2: SHEET MUSIC OR NOTATED MUSIC OF MAJOR VARIANTS

This appendix displays sheet music or notated music for the four major "Liza Jane" branches described above—"Li'l Liza Jane," "Goodbye Liza Jane," "Liza, Poor Gal," and "Steal Miss Liza"—through the following examples:

1916 sheet music publication of "Li'l Liza Jane" by Countess Ada de Lachau.

1916 sheet music publication of "Li'l Liza Jane" by Countess Ada de Lachau.

1916 sheet music publication of "Li'l Liza Jane" by Countess Ada de Lachau.

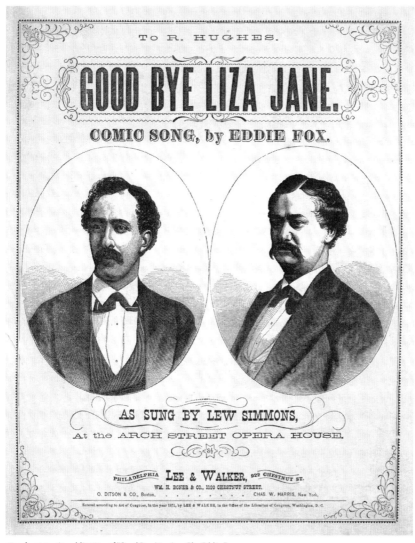

1871 sheet music publication of "Good Bye Liza Jane" by Eddie Fox.

1871 sheet music publication of "Good Bye Liza Jane" by Eddie Fox.

1871 sheet music publication of "Good Bye Liza Jane" by Eddie Fox.

1871 sheet music publication of "Good Bye Liza Jane" by Eddie Fox.

3.

Chickens and hens have gone to roost
  A hawk flew down and bit an old goose
Walk dad Lew Oh Mister Lew
  Ehe! Ehe! he! hear me now
Bit a young duck in the middle of the back
  Made the old drake go quack, quack, quack,
Walk dad Lew Oh Mister Lew
  Ehe! Ehe! he! hear me now.

CHORUS.

1871 sheet music publication of "Good Bye Liza Jane" by Eddie Fox.

1903 sheet music publication of "Good Bye Eliza Jane" by Harry Von Tilzer.

Good Bye Eliza Jane 4

1903 sheet music publication of "Good Bye Eliza Jane" by Harry Von Tilzer.

1903 sheet music publication of "Good Bye Eliza Jane" by Harry Von Tilzer.

Good Bye Eliza Jane 4

1903 sheet music publication of "Good Bye Eliza Jane" by Harry Von Tilzer.

The Missouri Play-Party   **317**

SHILOH

Scrapin' up sand in the bottom of the sea,
    Shiloh, Shiloh;
Scrapin' up sand in the bottom of the sea,
    Shiloh, Liza Jane.
Oh, how I love her! Oh, ain't that a shame!
Oh, how I love her! By-by, Liza Jane!

1911 publication of "Shiloh" in the *Journal of American Folklore* by L. D. Ames. (A "Goodbye Liza Jane" variant.)

Songs and Rhymes from the South.   129

SONGS AND RHYMES FROM THE SOUTH.

BY E. C. PERROW.

41. LIZA JANE.[3]

A.

(From East Tennessee; mountain whites; from memory; 1905.)

[1] An indigenous ballad that has many of the finer qualities of the older compositions.
[2] Compare this Journal, vol. xxiv, pp. 289, 354, 367.
[3] *Ibid.*, vol. iii, p. 290; vol. vi, pp. 131, 134.

1915 publication of "Liza Jane" in the *Journal of American Folklore* by E. C. Perrow. (A "Liza, Poor Gal" variant.)

Songs and Rhymes from the South.   179

Chorus.

CHORUS.

Chorus.
Pore little Liza, pore little gal!
Pore little Liza Jane!
Pore little Liza, pore little gal!
She died on the train.

B.

(From Kentucky; mountain whites; MS. of Mr. House; 1905.)

Go up on the mountain top
  To plant me a patch of cane
To make me a barrel of molasses
  To sweeten up Lizie Jane.

Standing on the platform,
  Waiting for the train;
"Get your old black bonnet,
  And let's go, Lizie Jane."

The hardest work that I ever done
  Was breaking on the train;
The easiest work that I ever done
  Was hugging Lizie Jane.

Her nose just like an old coffee pot;
  Mouth just like a spout;
Eyes just like an old fireplace
  With the ashes all took out.

My girl's name is Lizie;
  Her hair is very brown;
Face just like a thundercloud,
  And the rain come pouring down.

C.

(From Indiana; country whites; MS. of Mr. Davidson; 1908.)

Hoop-pole, Liza Jane,
  . Hoop-pole, Liza Jane.
Hoop-pole Liza, poly gal,
  And she rides on a train.

D.

(From Mississippi; country whites; MS. of Dr. Herrington; 1909.)

You go down the new cut road,
  And I'll go down the lane;

1915 publication of "Liza Jane" in the *Journal of American Folklore* by E. C. Perrow. (A "Liza, Poor Gal" variant.)

THE
AMERICAN
SONGBAG

Carl Sandburg

A Harvest Book
Harcourt Brace & Company
San Diego   New York   London

1927 publication of "Liza Jane" in *The American Songbag* by Carl Sandburg. (A "Liza, Poor Gal" variant.)

LIZA JANE

The mountains are friendly and homelike to many who live there. Gilbert R. Combs tells of men leaving for a year or two of "ranching it" on the western plains, and then straggling back saying of the flat prairies and level horizons, "It was too lonesome, too l-o-n-e-s-o-m-e." They have their own ways. Some are told of in these lines from men who are a law unto themselves. There are as many Liza songs in the Appalachian mountains as there are species of trees on the slopes of that range. The one in text A is called Liza Jane and the one in text B is known as Mountain Top.

Arr. A. G. W.

1927 publication of "Liza Jane" in *The American Songbag* by Carl Sandburg. (A "Liza, Poor Gal" variant.)

LIZA JANE

A

1 I'll go up on the mountain top,
  And plant me a patch of cane,
  I'll make me a jug of molasses,
  For to sweeten little Liza Jane.

  Refrain:
      O po' Liza, po' gal,
      O po' Liza Jane,
      O po' Liza, po' gal,
      She died on the train.

2 I'll go up on the mountain top,
  Put up my moonshine still,
  I'll make you a quart of old moonshine,
  For just one dollar bill.
  Refrain:

3 Head is like a coffee pot,
  Nose is like a spout,
  Her mouth is like an old fire-place,
  With the ashes all raked out.
  Refrain:

4 I went to see my Liza Jane,
  She was standing in the door,
  Her shoes and stockings in her hand,
  And her feet all over the floor.
  Refrain:

5 The hardest work that ever I did,
  Was a-brakin' on the train,
  The easiest work that ever I did,
  Was a-huggin' little Liza Jane.
  Refrain:

B

MOUNTAIN TOP

1 I'll go up on the mountain top
  And grow me a patch of cane,
  I'll make me a jug of molasses too,
  For to sweeten up Liza Jane.

2 Come along, sweet Liza Jane,
  Just come along with me,
  We'll go up on the mountain top,
  Some pleasures there to see.

3 I'll go up on this mountain top
  Put out me a moonshine still,
  I'll sell you a quart of old moonshine
  Just for a one dollar bill.

4 I will eat when I am hungry
  And drink when I am dry,
  If a tree don't fall on me
  I'll live until I die.

133

1927 publication of "Liza Jane" in *The American Songbag* by Carl Sandburg. (A "Liza, Poor Gal" variant.)

Steal Miss Liza

Traditional

2022 transcription of the traditional folk song "Steal Miss Liza" by Tucker Nance.

NOTES

INTRODUCTION: SLUDGE AND THEORY

1. William Christopher Handy, *Father of the Blues: An Autobiography*. New York, Macmillan, 1941, p. 142.

2. Handy, pp. 137, 146.

3. Anda Woods Slave Narrative. Rawick, George P., *The American Slave: A Composite Autobiography: Supplement, Series 1*. Westport, Conn., Greenwood Publishing Company, 1977, pp. 2388–92. [Also see: http://msgw.org/slaves/wood-xslave.htm.]

4. Handy, p. 137.

5. Howard W. Odum, "Folk-Song and Folk-Poetry as Found in the Secular Songs of the Southern Negroes." *Journal of American Folklore*, vol. 24, no. 93, 1911, p. 263.

6. Odum, p. 263.

7. Odum, p. 263.

8. Odum, p. 262.

9. Odum, p. 263.

10. Odum, p. 263.

11. Odum, p. 263.

12. J. H. Kwabena Nketia, *The Music of Africa*. W. W. Norton & Co. New York, 1974, p. 140.

13. V. Kofi Agawu, "The Rhythmic Structure of West African Music." *Journal of Musicology*, vol. 5, no. 3, 1987, p. 409.

14. Agawu, p. 412.

15. A. M. Jones, *Studies in African Music, Volume I*. Oxford University Press, 1959, p. 22.

16. Jones, p. 44.

17. Stephen Fleischman and Jonathan Donald, directors, *Anatomy of Pop: The Music Explosion*. New York, American Broadcasting Company, 1966. For the phrase "beyond category," also see: John Edward Hasse, *Beyond Category: The Life and Genius of Duke Ellington*. Boston, Da Capo Press, 1993.

18. Chris O'Leary, *Rebel Rebel: All the Songs of David Bowie from '64 to '76*. Winchester, United Kingdom, Zero Books, 2015, p. 11.

19. O'Leary, p. 22.

I. SNOTCHES OF SONGS: THE WPA *SLAVE NARRATIVE COLLECTION*

1. Clint Smith, "We Mourn for All We Do Not Know." *The Atlantic*, vol. 327, no. 2 (March 2021), p. 32.

2. Smith, p. 32.

3. Norman R. Yetman, "The Background of the Slave Narrative Collection." *American Quarterly*, vol. 19, no. 3, 1967, p. 535.

4. Yetman, pp. 535–36.

5. Ira Berlin, Marc Favreau, and Steven F. Miller, *Remembering Slavery: African Americans Talk about Their Personal Experiences of Slavery and Emancipation*. New York, The New Press, 2007, p. xvii.

6. Berlin, et al., p. xviii.

7. Berlin, et al., p. xix.

8. Berlin, et al., p. xx.

9. Berlin, et al., p. xx.

10. Berlin, et al., p. xx.

11. Berlin, et al., p. xxi.

12. Berlin, et al., p. xxii.

13. Berlin, et al., p. xxii.

14. Berlin, et al., p. xxii.

15. Robert B. Winans, "Black Instrumental Music Traditions in the Ex-Slave Narratives." *Black Music Research Journal*, vol. 10, no. 1, 1990, p. 43.

16. Winans, p. 51.

17. Winans, p. 43.

18. John W. Blassingame, "Using the Testimony of Ex-Slaves: Approaches and Problems." *The Journal of Southern History*, vol. 41, no. 4, 1975, p. 490.

19. Marshall Butler Slave Narrative, *Federal Writers' Project: Slave Narrative Project, Vol. IV, Georgia Narratives, Part 1, Adams-Furr*. Washington, DC, Library of Congress, 1941, pp. 161, 163.

20. Lawrence Evans Slave Narrative. Rawick, George P., *The American Slave: Mississippi Narratives, Part 4*. Westport, Conn., Greenwood Publishing Company, 1977, pp. 703–6. [Also see: http://msgw.org/slaves/evans-xslave.htm.]

21. Dosia Harris Slave Narrative, *Federal Writers' Project: Slave Narrative Project, Vol. IV, Georgia Narratives, Part 2, Garey-Jones*. Washington, DC, Library of Congress, 1941, pp. 103–4, 109–10.

22. Bryant Huff Slave Narrative, *Federal Writers' Project: Slave Narrative Project, Vol. IV, Georgia Narratives, Part 2, Garey-Jones*. Washington, DC, Library of Congress, 1941, pp. 238, 241.

23. Lina Hunter Slave Narrative, *Federal Writers' Project: Slave Narrative Project, Vol. IV, Georgia Narratives, Part 2, Garey-Jones*. Washington, DC, Library of Congress, 1941, pp. 254, 268.

24. Alice Hutcheson Slave Narrative, *Federal Writers' Project: Slave Narrative Project, Vol. IV, Georgia Narratives, Part 2, Garey-Jones*. Washington, DC, Library of Congress, 1941, pp. 282, 284.

25. Hannah Jameson Slave Narrative, Lankford, George E. *Bearing Witness: Memories of Arkansas Slavery Narratives from the 1930s WPA Collections*. University of Arkansas Press, 2006, pp. 163, 165.

26. Lydia Jefferson Slave Narrative. Cook, Charles Orson, and Poteet, James M., "'Dem Was Black Times, Sure 'Nough': The Slave Narratives of Lydia Jefferson and Stephen Williams." *Louisiana History: The Journal of the Louisiana Historical Association*, vol. 20, no. 3, 1979, pp. 283–84, 286–87.

27. Lucy Thurston Slave Narrative. Rawick, George P., *The American Slave: A Composite Autobiography: Supplement, Series 1*. Westport, Conn., Greenwood Publishing Company, 1977, pp. 2110–2120. [Also see: http://msgw.org/slaves/thurston-xslave.htm.]

28. Anda Woods Slave Narrative.

29. Anda Woods Slave Narrative.

30. Alisha J. Hines, *Geographies of Freedom: Black Women's Mobility and the Making of the Western River World, 1814–1865*. Doctoral dissertation. Department of History, Duke University, 2018, p. 111.

31. Hines, pp. 114–15.

32. Hines, p. 7.

33. Hines, p. 101.

34. Marion B. Lucas, *A History of Blacks in Kentucky: From Slavery to Segregation, 1760–1891*. Kentucky Historical Society, 2003, p. 31.

35. Lucas, p. 36. [The author cites a 1927 memoir by Robert Anderson, *From Slavery to Affluence: Memoirs of Robert Anderson, Ex-slave* (p. 26), but the Anderson book does not contain the cited reference. In his book, Anderson does refer to music, instrumentation, singing, and marching, but does not refer to a "Liza Jane" variant. Lucas also cites a 1940 book by J. Winston Coleman, *Slavery Times in Kentucky*, who on p. 76 presents one verse of "Eliza Jane," and attributes it to enslaved people, but does not offer a citation. Nevertheless, "Eliza Jane" may have been a song known to enslaved people in Kentucky.]

36. Dosia Harris Slave Narrative, pp. 107–8.

37. Jean Stearns and Marshall Stearns, *Jazz Dance: The Story of American Vernacular Dance*. Boston, Da Capo Press, 1994, p. 38.

38. Stearns and Stearns, p. 38.

39. Stearns and Stearns, p. 38.

40. Philip A. Jamison, "Square Dance Calling: The African-American Connection." *Journal of Appalachian Studies*, vol. 9, no. 2, 2003, p. 387.

41. Jamison, p. 389.

42. Jamison, p. 390.

43. Jamison, p. 391.

44. Jamison, p. 387.

45. *Check-list of Recorded Songs in the English Language in the Archive of American Folk Song to July, 1940: Alphabetical List with Geographical Index*. Washington, DC, Library of Congress, Music Division, 1942, p. 377.

46. James Alan McPherson, *Elbow Room*. New York, Little, Brown, 1977, p. 3.

47. McPherson, p. 4.

48. Margaret McKee and Fred Chisenhall, *Beale Black and Blue: Life and Music on Black America's Main Street*. Louisiana State University Press, 1993, p. 189.

49. T. DeWayne Moore, "The Mississippi Sheiks." *Fiddle Tunes from Mississippi: Commercial and Informal Recordings, 1920–2018*. Bolick, Harry and Russell, Tony, editors. University Press of Mississippi, Jackson, 2021, p. 386.

50. Alan Lomax, *Sam Chatmon: "Little Liza Jane."* (Film.) Hollandale, Mississippi, August 1978.

51. McKee and Chisenhall, p. 189.

52. Dorothy Scarborough and Ola Lee Gulledge, *On the Trail of Negro Folk-songs*. Harvard University Press, 1925, p. 226.

53. Scarborough, p. 227.

54. Smith, p. 33.

II. "LIZA JANE," YOU LITTLE ROGUE:
DR. ADONIS AND THE REGIMENTS

1. Dr. Adonis, "Affairs in Middle Tennessee." *Louisville Daily Journal*, February 23, 1864, p. 1.

2. Dr. Adonis, February 23, 1864.

3. Dr. Adonis, "Facts and Fancies from the Sunny South." *Louisville Daily Journal*, March 15, 1864, p. 1.

4. Dr. Adonis, *Louisville Daily Journal*, March 2, 1864, p. 1.

5. "Phases of Love in the Sunny South." *Chicago Daily Tribune*, March 5, 1864, p. 3.

6. "A Genuine Love Letter." *Portland Daily Press*, Maine, March 28, 1864, p. 4.

7. "A Rebel Loveletter." *Fremont Journal*, Ohio, November 11, 1864, p. 4.

8. Dr. Adonis, "Affairs in Northern Alabama." *Louisville Daily Journal*, February 29, 1864, p. 1.

9. Adam Goodheart, *1861: The Civil War Awakening*. New York, Vintage Books, 2012, p. 329.

10. Goodheart, p. 329.

11. Eileen Southern, *The Music of Black Americans: A History*. New York, W. W. Norton, 1971, p. 234.

12. Southern, p. 234.

13. Leander Winslow Cogswell, *A History of the Eleventh New Hampshire Regiment, Volunteer Infantry in the Rebellion War, 1861–1865*. Concord, NH, Republican Press Association, 1891, p. 267.

14. Cogswell, p. 267.

15. Cogswell, p. 267.

16. Cogswell, pp. 268–69.

17. Cogswell, p. 269.

18. Cogswell, p. 269.

19. Leander Winslow Cogswell, *History of the Town of Henniker, Merrimack County, New Hampshire*. Concord, NH, Republican Press Association, 1880.

20. Jeremiah M. Mickley, *The Forty-Third Regiment, United States Colored Troops*. Gettysburg, Penn., J. E. Wible, 1866, p. 71.

21. Mickley, p. 72.

22. Mickley, p. 72.

23. Cogswell. *A History of the Eleventh New Hampshire Regiment*, p. 267.

24. Mickley, p. 73.

25. Mickley, p. 73.

26. Mickley, p. 82.

27. Mickley, p. 82.

28. Mickley, p. 84.

29. William Blair, *Making and Remaking Pennsylvania's Civil War.* Pennsylvania State University Press, 2010, p. 146.

30. Blair, p. 146.

31. James R. Fuller, *Men of Color, to Arms! Vermont African-Americans in the Civil War.* Lincoln, Neb., iUniverse, 2001, pp. 93–100.

32. Mickley, pp. 21–62.

33. Andrew Atkinson Humphreys, *The Virginia Campaign of '64 and '65: The Army of the Potomac and the Army of the James.* New York, Charles Scribner's Sons, 1883, pp. 57–118.

34. Henry Clay Wall, *Historical Sketch of the Pee Dee Guards: (Co. D, 23d N. C. Regiment) from 1861 to 1865.* Raleigh, NC, Edwards, Broughton & Co., 1876, pp. 58–59.

35. Wall, p. 59.

36. Wall, p. 62.

37. Wall, p. 63.

38. Wall, p. 64.

39. Wall, p. 81.

40. Wall, p. 81.

41. Wall, pp. 97–98.

42. Reuben B. Scott, *The History of the 67th Regiment Indiana Infantry Volunteers: War of the Rebellion.* Bedford, Ind., Herald Book and Job Print., 1892, p. 9.

43. Scott, p. 9.

44. Scott, p. 9.

45. Scott, pp. 9–12.

46. Scott, p. 44.

47. Scott, p. 104.

48. Scott, p. 105.

49. Roger Pickenpaugh, *Captives in Blue: The Civil War Prisons of the Confederacy.* University of Alabama Press, 2013, pp. 57–73.

50. Scott, p. 105.

51. Scott, p. 106.

52. Scott, p. 111.

53. Scott, p. 111.

54. Scott, pp. 111, 114, 116.

55. John Otto, *History of the 11th Indiana Battery During the War of the Rebellion.* Fort Wayne, Ind., W. D. Page, 1894, p. 45.

56. William Worth Belknap, *History of the Fifteenth Regiment, Iowa Veteran Volunteer Infantry: From October, 1861, to August, 1865, when Disbanded at the End of the War.* Keokuk, Iowa, R. B. Ogden & Son, Printers, 1887, p. 241.

57. Dr. Adonis, "Department of the Gulf." *Chicago Tribune*, March 30, 1865, p. 2.

58. "The Funeral Escort." *Chicago Tribune.* April 22, 1865, p. 1.

59. "Dr. Byron Adonis." *Sunday Call*, San Francisco. August 1, 1892, p. 1.

60. *Semi-Weekly Wisconsin*, Milwaukee. November 14, 1863, p. 4.

61. John W. Storrs, *The "Twentieth Connecticut": A Regimental History.* Ansonia, Conn., Press of the Naugatuck Valley Sentinel, 1886, p. 276.

62. Storrs, p. 277.

63. Storrs, p. 277.

III. 1865

1. James Monaghan, *Civil War on the Western Border, 1854–1865*. University of Nebraska Press, 1984, p. 337.

2. Monaghan, p. 338.

3. Monaghan, p. 339.

4. Monaghan, p. 339.

5. Monaghan, pp. 340–45.

6. "Happy New Year." *Daily Monitor*, Topeka, Kansas. January 4, 1865, p. 2.

7. David Haward Bain, *Empire Express: Building the First Transcontinental Railroad*. New York, Viking, 1999, p. 227.

8. Stephen E. Ambrose, *Nothing Like It in the World: The Men Who Built the Transcontinental Railroad 1863–1869*. New York, Simon & Schuster, 2001, p. 138.

9. Ambrose, p. 138.

10. Brick Pomeroy, "Brick Pomeroy on Mosquitoes." *The Ashland Union*, Ohio. October 25, 1865, p. 1.

11. Billy Emerson, *Nancy Fat Songster*. New York, Dick and Fitzgerald, 1866, p. 15.

12. *The Weekly Review*, Crawfordsville, Indiana, November 4, 1865, p. 1.

13. *Christy's Negro Songster: containing the most popular melodies, as sung by Christy, Wood, White, Buckley, and other negro minstrels*. New York, Richard Marsh, 1856, p. 54.

14. William Francis Allen, *Slave Songs of the United States*. Bedford, Mass., Applewood Books, 1996, p. 88.

15. "Music Hall." *Gold Hill Daily News*, Nevada, November 23, 1865, p. 3.

16. Mark Knowles, *Tap Roots: The Early History of Tap Dancing*. Jefferson, NC, McFarland, 2002, p. 105.

17. *San Francisco Theatre Research, Vol. 13, Minstrelsy*. Works Progress Administration, Northern California, 1939, p. 119.

18. *San Francisco Theatre Research*, pp. 97–100.

19. *Carson Daily Appeal*, Nevada. October 24, 1875, p. 2.

20. "Crimes." *Worthington Advance*, Minnesota. November 5, 1875, p. 1.

21. *New York Herald*. April 2, 1871, p. 4.

22. *Los Angeles Daily Herald*. June 16, 1876, p. 2.

23. *Reno Gazette-Journal*, Nevada. August 8, 1876, p. 2.

IV. INTERMISSION NUMBER ONE:
THE POTENTIAL INFLUENCES OF ROBERT BURNS, "SUSAN JANE," AND OTHERS

1. James M. Montgomery, (1998) "How Robert Burns Captured America," *Studies in Scottish Literature*: vol. 30, no. 1, p. 237.

2. Montgomery, p. 238.

3. Montgomery, p. 239.

4. Montgomery, p. 239.

5. Fiddlin' John Carson & His Virginia Reelers, "Good-bye, Liza Jane." OKeh 45049, 1926. [Carson (vocals, fiddle), other musicians unknown] Discography: Russell and Pinson.

6. Bradley Kincaid, "Liza Up in the 'Simmon Tree." Gennett 6761, Champion 15687 and 45057, and Supertone 9362, 1929. [Kincaid (vocals, guitar)] Discography: Russell and Pinson.

7. John Grigg, *Grigg's Southern and Western Songster: Being a Choice Collection of the Most Fashionable Songs: Many of Which Are Original*. Philadelphia, Lippincott, Grambo, & Co., 1851, pp. 54–55. [A nineteenth-century American songster is cited here, to demonstrate Burns's appeal in the United States in the mid-1800s. According to several sources, the poem otherwise dates to 1786.]

8. Henry Thomas, "Run, Mollie, Run." Vocalion 1141, 1927. [Thomas (vocals, guitar)] Discography: Laird.

9. Simon J. Bronner, *Lafcadio Hearn's America: Ethnographic Sketches and Editorials*. University Press of Kentucky, 2014, p. 42.

10. Montgomery, p. 243.

11. Robert Burns, "Farewell to Eliza." *North Carolinian*, Fayetteville, June 3, 1848, p. 4.

12. Frank Williams, "Susan Jane or Dis child is by his Lub Forsaken as sung by Christy's Minstrels." Sheet music. Cincinnati, W. C. Peters & Sons, 1854, p. 5.

13. E. P. Christy, *Christy's Plantation Melodies*. Philadelphia, Fisher & Brothers, 1854, pp. 26, 48.

14. *White's New Ethiopian Song Book No. 3*. New York, H. Long & Brother, 1848, pp. 39, 55.

15. *White's New Ethiopian Song Book No. 3*, pp. 55–56.

16. *White's New Ethiopian Song Book No. 3*, p. 56.

17. *White's New Ethiopian Song Book No. 3*, p. 56.

18. "Truly Affecting." *Iowa Republican*, Iowa City. December 18, 1852, p. 4.

19. "To Lizzie Jane." *Loudon Free Press*, Tennessee. March 5, 1853, p. 3. "Dedicated to the 'Mountain Poet.'" *Loudon Free Press*, Tennessee. March 19, 1853, p. 2. "Dedicated to Lizzy Jane." *Loudon Free Press*, Tennessee. April 2, 1853, p. 3.

V. "LIZA JANE" MEETS THE MASSES:
POSTBELLUM MINSTRELSY, PART FIRST AND PART THIRD

1. Robert C. Toll, *Blacking Up: The Minstrel Show in Nineteenth Century America*. Oxford University Press, 1974, p. 52.

2. Jake Austen, and Yuval Taylor, *Darkest America: Black Minstrelsy from Slavery to Hip-Hop*. New York, W. W. Norton, 2012, p. 40.

3. Camille F. Forbes, *Introducing Bert Williams: Burnt Cork, Broadway, and the Story of America's First Black Star*. New York, Basic Civitas Books, 2008, p. 24.

4. Toll, p. 53.

5. Toll, p. 55.

6. Toll, p. 55.

7. Austen and Taylor, p. 40.

8. Forbes, p. 24.

9. Forbes, p. 24.

10. Toll, pp. 56–57.

11. Austen and Taylor, p. 40.

12. Austen and Taylor, p. 44.

13. Carl Frederick Wittke, *Tambo and Bones: A History of the American Minstrel Stage.* Duke University Press, 1930, p. 8.

14. Wittke, p. vii.

15. Wittke, p. vii.

16. Forbes, p. 24.

17. Forbes, p. 25.

18. Billy Emerson, *Billy Emerson's Nancy Fat Songster.* New York, Dick & Fitzgerald, 1866, p. 15.

19. John Strausbaugh, *Black Like You: Blackface, Whiteface, Insult & Imitation in American Popular Culture.* New York, Penguin, 2007, p. 126.

20. Strausbaugh, p. 126.

21. *Daily Dramatic Chronicle*, San Francisco, February 7, 1867, p. 1.

22. *Chicago Tribune*, April 28, 1867, p. 4.

23. William L. Slout, *Burnt Cork and Tambourines: A Source Book of Negro Minstrelsy.* Rockville, Md., Wildside Press, 2007, p. 29.

24. *Chicago Tribune*, May 1, 1867, p. 4.

25. Carl Sandburg, *Chicago Poems.* New York, Henry Holt, 1916, p. 3.

26. St. James Theatre, *Play Bill*, vol. 1, no. 156, June 7, 1868, San Francisco.

27. Emerson, Allen & Manning's Minstrels, Playbill. Tony Pastor's Opera House, New York. July 23, 1868. [Source for all minstrel playbills, unless otherwise noted: Harvard University, Houghton Library, Harvard Theatre Collection on Blackface Minstrelsy, Web]

28. Strausbaugh, p. 118.

29. *DeKalb Chronicle*, Illinois, March 27, 1931, p. 6.

30. *Chicago Tribune*, April 28, 1867, p. 4.

31. Southern, p. 147.

32. Southern, p. 147.

33. Southern, p. 148.

34. Strausbaugh, pp. 69–70.

35. Southern, p. 104.

36. Amiri Baraka (LeRoi Jones), *Blues People: Negro Music in White America.* New York, William Morrow, 1963, p. 84.

37. Baraka, p. 84.

38. Baraka, p. 84.

39. Baraka, p. 111.

VI. FROM THE *BOLD SOLDIER BOY'S SONGBOOK* TO THE CYLINDERS OF GEORGE W. JOHNSON: "OH, GOODBYE LIZA JANE"

1. *Daily Press and Herald*, Knoxville, Tennessee, February 16, 1868, p. 1.

2. Sandra Jean Graham, *Spirituals and the Birth of a Black Entertainment Industry.* University of Illinois Press, 2018, p. 126.

3. Edward Le Roy Rice, *Monarchs of Minstrelsy, from "Daddy" Rice to Date*. New York, Kenny Publishing Company, 1911, p. 198.

4. Rice, p. 195.

5. Rice, p. 126.

6. Rice, p. 195.

7. Rice, p. 198.

8. Eddie Fox, "Good Bye Liza Jane." Sheet music. Philadelphia, Lee & Walker, 1871.

9. Rice, p. 202.

10. *The New Negro Forget-Me-Not Songster*. Cincinnati, UP. James, 1859, p. 67.

11. *Jenny Lind Forget-Me-Not Songster*. Philadelphia, John B. Perry, 1853, pp. 338–39.

12. *White's New Illustrated Melodeon Songbook*. New York, H. Long & Brother, 1851, p. 75.

13. *New York Clipper*, December 30, 1871, p. 307.

14. Crockett, "The Carpet-Bagger's Departure: Good-Bye Liza Jane." *Staunton Spectator and General Advertiser*, Virginia, November 18, 1873, p. 4.

15. The Great California Minstrels, Playbill. Auckland, New Zealand, Reed & Brett Printers, 1874.

16. New York Minstrels, Playbill. Assinippi Hall, West Scituate, Massachusetts. February 11, 1874.

17. Moore & Burgess Minstrels, Playbill. St. James's Hall, London, England. October 25, 1876.

18. Duprez & Benedict's Minstrels, Program. 1871–1876 (estimated). [Source: Middle Tennessee State University, Center for Popular Music.]

19. Lafcadio Hearn, "Roustabouts: The Songs of the Longshoremen of the Mississippi—A Class of Men Whose Old Characteristics Are Departing." *Columbus Courier*, Kansas, April 6, 1876, p. 2.

20. Schoolcraft & Coes' Minstrels, Playbill. Howard Athenaeum, Boston, Massachusetts. 1877.

21. London Minstrels, Playbill. Durban, South Africa. 1879.

22. Billy Birch's San Francisco Minstrels, Program. San Francisco Minstrels Opera House, New York. October 1, 1883.

23. James Revell Carr, *Hawaiian Music in Motion: Mariners, Missionaries, and Minstrels*. University of Illinois Press, 2014, p. 170.

24. Schoolcraft and Coes' Minstrels, Playbill. Howard Athenaeum, Boston, Massachusetts. 1887 (estimated).

25. Madagascar Minstrels, Playbill. Music Hall, Boston, Massachusetts, 1889.

26. Rice, pp. 192–94.

27. *Henry De Marsan's New Comic and Sentimental Singer's Journal*. vol. 1, no. 65, p. 481. [This is given as a representative sample issue. All issues of the De Marsan journal are undated.]

28. Paul Charosh, "Studying Nineteenth-Century Popular Song." *American Music*, vol. 15, no. 4, University of Illinois Press, 1997, p. 470.

29. Charosh, p. 470.

30. *De Marsan*, vol. 1, no. 65, p. 481. Charosh, p. 470.

31. Charosh, p. 469.

32. Charosh, p. 475.

33. Emily Margot Gale, *Sounding Sentimental: American Popular Song from Nineteenth-Century Ballads to 1970s Soft Rock*. Doctoral Dissertation. University of Virginia, Department of Music, p. 61.

34. *Henry De Marsan's New Comic and Sentimental Singer's Journal*, vol. 2, no. 137, p. 291.

35. *De Marsan*, vol. 1, no. 65, p. 487.

36. *Henry De Marsan's New Comic and Sentimental Singer's Journal*, vol. 1, no. 86, p. 652.

37. Slout, p. 44.

38. "Flip flap." H. De Marsan, Publisher. 54 Chatham Street, NY Monographic. Library of Congress. "Jeremy Diddler." H. De Marsan, Publisher, 60 Chatham Street, NY. Monographic. Library of Congress. "Hop lite loo." H. De Marsan, Publishers, 54 Chatham Street, NY. Monographic. Library of Congress. [All three undated.]

39. *New York Clipper*, May 24, 1873, p. 64.

40. "Good-Bye, Liza Jane." Song sheet. Poet's Box, Glasgow, November 24, 1877.

41. *Buckley's Song Book for the Parlor*. New York, P. J. Cozans, 1855, p. 51.

42. *The New Negro Forget-Me-Not Songster*, p. 67.

43. *The Bold Soldier Boy's Song Book*. Richmond (?), West & Johnston (?),1861–1865, p. 62. [Accessed through the Internet Archive as well as the David M. Rubenstein Rare Book & Manuscript Library at Duke University. The Rubenstein Library estimates the dates of publication between 1861 and 1865, and inserts question marks after place of publication and title of publisher.]

44. Tim Brooks, *Lost Sounds: Blacks and the Birth of the Recording Industry, 1890–1919*. University of Illinois Press, 2004, p. 17.

45. Brooks, p. 18.

46. Brooks, p. 18.

47. Brooks, pp. 18–21.

48. Brooks, p. 23.

49. Brooks, pp. 24–25.

50. Brooks, p. 26.

51. Brooks, p. 27.

52. Brooks, p. 28.

53. Brooks, pp. 26, 29.

54. Brooks, p. 28.

55. Brooks, p. 30.

56. Brooks, pp. 31, 32.

57. Brooks, p. 43. Craig Martin Gibbs, *Black Recording Artists, 1877–1926: An Annotated Discography*. Jefferson, NC, McFarland, 2012, p. 20.

58. Brooks, p. 42.

59. *Delaney's Song Book, No. 13*. New York, William W. Delaney, 1896.

60. George W. Johnson, "The Laughing Coon." Edison 4005, 1898. [Johnson (vocals), possibly Frank Banta (piano)] Discography: Brooks; Gibbs.

61. Brooks, p. 41.

62. Brooks, p. 43. [Recordings posted to YouTube confirm these additional lyrics, as well as orchestral versions.]

63. *Discography of American Historical Recordings*. UC Santa Barbara Library. Web.
[A search of this site results in as many as eight recordings of the song between 1900 and 1905, on the Victor and Zonophone labels, including a ten-inch version]

64. *White's New Illustrated Melodeon Songbook*. New York, H. Long & Brother, 1851, p. 38.

65. Brooks, p. 43.

66. Brooks, p. 56.

67. Brooks, p. 67.

68. Daniel Webster Davis, *'Weh Down Souf: And Other Poems*. Cleveland, Helman-Taylor, 1897.

69. Joan R. Sherman, "Daniel Webster Davis: A Black Virginia Poet in the Age of Accommodation." *The Virginia Magazine of History and Biography*, vol. 81, no. 4, 1973, p. 470.

70. Sherman, p. 477.

71. Sherman, p. 477.

72. Davis, p. 49.

73. Davis, p. 103.

74. Davis, p. 76.

75. *Albion Journal*, December 16, 1897, p. 2.

VII. FROM THE NEW ORLEANS LEVEE TO THE
HAMPTON INSTITUTE: "LITTLE LIZA JANE" *AD INFINITUM*

1. "Personal." *Thomaston Herald*, Georgia, March 15, 1873, p. 1.

2. W. K. McNeil, "Lafcadio Hearn, American Folklorist." *Journal of American Folklore*, vol. 91, no. 362, 1978, p. 948.

3. McNeil, pp. 948–49.

4. McNeil, p. 952.

5. McNeil, p. 952.

6. Simon J. Bronner, *Lafcadio Hearn's America: Ethnographic Sketches and Editorials*. University Press of Kentucky, 2014, p. 37.

7. Bronner, p. 38.

8. Bronner, pp. 38–39.

9. Bronner, p. 39.

10. Bronner, p. 42.

11. *Henry De Marsan's New Comic and Sentimental Singer's Journal*, vol. 2, no. 137, p. 291.

12. Mississippi John Hurt, "Liza Jane (God's Unchanging Hand)." *Folk Songs and Blues*. Piedmont PLP 13157, 1963. [Hurt (vocals, harmonica)]

13. Angus S. Hibbard, *Chic; Or, Birds of a Feather: A Medley Operetta, in Three Acts*. Oakland, CA, Tribune Publishing Company, 1883, p. 9.

14. Hibbard, p. 10.

15. Hibbard, p. 14.

16. Hibbard, p. 14.

17. *Evening Star*, Washington, DC, October 22, 1945, p. A-8.

18. *Cedar Falls Gazette*, Iowa, December 2, 1870, p. 3.

19. *The Mercury*, Hobart, Tasmania, Australia, December 29, 1870, p. 3.

20. *The Stage*, "San Francisco Minstrels," vol. 12, no. 18, New York, Sept. 8, 1871.

21. *The Mercury*, Hobart, Tasmania, Australia, May 27, 1872, p. 1.

22. San Francisco Minstrels. Playbill. Brooklyn, New York, 1873.

23. *Daily Beacon*, Wichita, Kansas, August 1, 1873, p. 4.

24. Ethiopian Dramatic Society, Playbill, 1874.

25. Washington Minstrels, Playbill. Somerville, Massachusetts, 1874.

26. *South Australian Register*, Adelaide, December 18, 1874, p. 1.

27. *The Mercury*, Hobart, Tasmania, Australia, December 9, 1874, p. 2.

28. *Sydney Morning Herald*, New South Wales, Australia, May 15, 1875, p. 4.

29. Thomas Harper and George Stansill, *Harper & Stansil's Sweet June Rose Songster*. United States, A. J. Fisher, 1875, p. 19.

30. Emerson's California Minstrels, Playbill. New York, 1872–1876.

31. San Francisco Minstrels, Playbill. New York, 1877.

32. James Mass, "The Briar." *Henry De Marsan's Comic & Sentimental Singers' Journal*. New York, vol. II, no. 122, p. 173.

33. Megatherian Minstrels, Playbill. Boston, Massachusetts, 1880.

34. Female Minstrels, Playbill. Philadelphia, Pennsylvania, undated (thought to be no later than 1882).

35. Rice, pp. 68–70.

36. Natalie Curtis Burlin, *Hampton Series: Negro Folk-songs, Book I*. New York, G. Schirmer, 1918, p. 3.

37. Curtis Burlin, *Book I*, p. 3.

38. Curtis Burlin, *Book I*, p. 3.

39. Curtis Burlin, *Book I*, pp. 3, 4.

40. Curtis Burlin, *Book I*, pp. 3–4.

41. General S. C. Armstrong, "Report: Hampton Normal and Agricultural Institute." *Report of the Superintendent of Public Instruction of the Commonwealth of Virginia with Accompanying Documents*. Richmond, Va., Superintendent of Public Printing, 1886, p. 131.

42. Armstrong, p. 133.

43. Armstrong, p. 135.

44. Armstrong, p. 136.

45. Armstrong, p. 136.

46. Armstrong, p. 139.

47. Armstrong, p. 139.

48. Armstrong, p. 139.

49. Armstrong, p. 152.

50. Armstrong, p. 153.

51. Armstrong, p. 154.

52. Armstrong, p. 154.

53. Robert Francis Engs, *Educating the Disfranchised and Disinherited: Samuel Chapman Armstrong and Hampton Institute: 1839–1893*. University of Tennessee Press, 1999, p. 34.

54. Engs, p. 52.

55. Engs, p. 58.

56. Engs, p. xix.

57. Engs, p. 101.

58. Hale, Edward E., editor. *Lend a Hand*. Boston, J. S. Smith, vol. II, no. 1, 1887, p. 298.

59. Hale, p. 299.

60. Hale, p. 299.

61. Hale, p. 300.

62. Hale, p. 300.

63. *Music of the Ethiopian Serenaders: Nine Songs and a Set of Cotillions.* "Going Ober de Mountain." Sheet music. Philadelphia, E. Ferrett & Co., 1845, p. 72.

64. *The Bold Soldier Boy's Songbook*, p. 62.

65. *The Southern Workman and Hampton School Record*. Virginia, Hampton Normal and Agricultural Institute, vol. XXII, no. 5, May 1894.

66. *The Southern Workman and Hampton School Record*. vol. XXII, no. 5, May 1894, p. 68.

67. *The Southern Workman and Hampton School Record*. vol. XXII, no. 5, p. 69.

68. Engs, p. 159.

69. *The Southern Workman and Hampton School Record*. vol. XXII, no. 5, p. 84.

70. *The Southern Workman and Hampton School Record*. vol. XXII, no. 5, pp. 84, 85.

71. *The Southern Workman and Hampton School Record*. vol. XXII, no. 5, p. 85.

72. Natalie Curtis Burlin, *Hampton Series: Negro Folk-songs, Book II*. New York, G. Schirmer, 1918, cover.

73. Michelle Wick Patterson, *Natalie Curtis Burlin: A Life in Native and African American Music*. University of Nebraska Press, 2010, p. 7.

74. Patterson, p. 7.

75. Patterson, p. 7.

76. Patterson, p. 10.

77. Natalie Curtis Burlin, *Hampton Series: Negro Folk-songs, Book III*. New York, G. Schirmer, 1918, p. 8.

78. Natalie Curtis Burlin, *Hampton Series: Negro Folk-songs, Books I* (p. 6), *II* (p. 11), *III* (p. 7), *and IV* (p. 6).

79. Curtis Burlin, *Book IV*. New York, G. Schirmer, 1919, p. 5.

80. Curtis Burlin, *Book IV*, p. 41.

81. Curtis Burlin, *Book IV*, p. 41.

82. Curtis Burlin, *Book IV*, p. 7.

83. John Tinney McCutcheon, *Army Song Book*. Washington, DC, Commission on Training Camp Activities, 1918, p. 63.

84. Curtis Burlin, *Book IV*, p. 41.

85. Curtis Burlin, *Book IV*, p. 42.

86. Curtis Burlin, *Book IV*, p. 42.

87. Curtis Burlin, *Book IV*, p. 50.

88. Mary Olmsted Clarke, "Song-Games of Negro Children in Virginia." *Journal of American Folklore*, vol. 3, no. 11, 1890, p. 288.

89. Clarke, p. 288.

90. Clarke, p. 290.

91. Edmands, p. 131.

92. Edmands, p. 131.

93. Edmands, pp. 131–32.

VIII. INTERMISSION NUMBER TWO: THE LITERARY "LIZA JANE" OF
CHARLES CHESNUTT, JEAN TOOMER, AND MARGARET WALKER

1. *Minstrel Songs, Old and New: A Collection of World-wide Famous Minstrel and Plantation Songs, Including the Most Popular of the Celebrated Foster Melodies*. New York, Oliver Ditson, 1882, p. 112.

2. Harriet Beecher Stowe, *Uncle Tom's Cabin: Or, Life Among the Lowly*. Boston, John P. Jewett and Company, 1852, p. 100.

3. Stowe, p. 143.

4. Eric Lott, *Love & Theft: Blackface Minstrelsy and the American Working Class*. Oxford University Press, 2013, p. 218.

5. Charles Waddell Chesnutt, *The Wife of His Youth: And Other Stories of the Color Line*. New York, Houghton, Mifflin and Company, 1899, p. 1.

6. Chesnutt, p. 1.

7. Chesnutt, pp. 2–3.

8. Chesnutt, pp. 5–6.

9. Chesnutt, pp. 9–10.

10. Chesnutt, p. 10.

11. Chesnutt, p. 11.

12. Chesnutt, pp. 12–13.

13. Chesnutt, p. 13.

14. Chesnutt, pp. 14–15.

15. Chesnutt, p. 14.

16. Chesnutt, p. 17.

17. Chesnutt, p. 18.

18. Chesnutt, p. 21.

19. Chesnutt, p. 22.

20. Chesnutt, p. 23.

21. Chesnutt, p. 23.

22. Chesnutt, p. 24.

23. Janet Mohr, "Charles Chesnutt's Women." *CLA Journal*, vol. 49, no. 4, 2006, p. 433.

24. Mohr, p. 433.

25. Tanfer Emin Tunc. "The De(con)struction of Black/White Binaries: Critiques of Passing in Charles Waddell Chesnutt's "'The Wife of His Youth' and Other Stories of the Color Line." *Callaloo*, vol. 37, no. 3, 2014, p. 682.

26. Sandburg, *The American Songbag*, p. 133.

27. Chesnutt, p. 12.

28. Jean Toomer, *Cane*. New York, Boni and Liveright, 1923, p. 137.

29. Toomer, p. 134.

30. Toomer, p. 134.

31. Toomer, pp. 135–36.

32. Toomer, p. 137.

33. Toomer, p. 137.

34. Toomer, p. 138.

35. Toomer, p. 142.

36. Toomer, p. 144.

37. Toomer, pp. 144–45.

38. Toomer, p. 147.

39. Toomer, p. 147.

40. Robert Cooperman, "Unacknowledged Familiarity: Jean Toomer and Eugene O'Neill." *Eugene O'Neill Review*, vol. 16, no. 1, 1992, p. 44.

41. Cooperman, p. 44.

42. Toomer, pp. 149–50.

43. Toomer, p. 151.

44. Toomer, pp. 152–53.

45. Margaret Walker, *Jubilee*. Boston, Houghton Mifflin Harcourt, 2016, p. 11.

46. Lucy M. Freibert and Margaret Walker, "Southern Song: An Interview with Margaret Walker." *Frontiers: A Journal of Women Studies*, vol. 9, no. 3, 1987, p. 53.

47. *The Negro in Illinois: The WPA Papers*. Brian Dolinar, editor. University of Illinois Press, 2013, p. 259.

48. Walker, pp. 51–52.

49. Walker, pp. 52–53.

IX. YOU WENT A-DRIVING WITH MISTER BROWN: THE TIN PAN ALLEY PUBLISHING BONANZA

1. Rudi Blesh, *They All Played Ragtime*. New York, Oak Publications, 1971, p. 13.

2. Baraka/Jones, p. 86.

3. James Lincoln Collier, *Louis Armstrong: An American Genius*. Oxford University Press, 1985, p. 29.

4. Collier, p. 29.

5. Blesh, pp. 100–101.

6. Clayton W. Henderson, *On the Banks of the Wabash: The Life and Music of Paul Dresser*. Indiana Historical Society Press, 2003, p. 47.

7. Henderson, p. 153.

8. Paul Dresser, "I'se Your Nigger If You Wants Me Liza Jane." Sheet music. New York, Howley, Havilland & Co., 1896.

9. Henderson, p. 109.

10. James McKay, *The Films of Victor Mature*. Jefferson, NC, McFarland, 2013, p. 46.

11. G. M. Blandford, "Git Up Dar!" Sheet music. New York, Hamilton S. Gordon, 1897.

12. *Montpelier Daily Record*, Vermont, February 24, 1898, p. 2.

13. Silas Leachman, "Whoa Dar Mule." Victor A-801, 1901. Discography: Discography of American Historical Recordings. Web. [Leachman (vocals) and unknown piano]

14. The Stanley Trio, "Whoa! Mule." OKeh 40271, 1924. [R.M. Stanley (fiddle); Roba Stanley (guitar, vocal), William Patterson (guitar)] Discography: Russell and Pinson.

15. Charles Horwitz and Frederick Bowers, "I Needs You Very Badly, Liza Jane: Southern Love Plaint." Sheet music. Shapiro, Bernstein & Von Tilzer, New York, 1901.

16. David Freeland, *Automats, Taxi Dances, and Vaudeville: Excavating Manhattan's Lost Places of Leisure*. New York University Press, 2009, pp. 86–87.

17. Harry Von Tilzer and Andrew B. Sterling, "Won't You Roll Dem Eyes Eliza." Sheet music. New York, Von Tilzer Publishing Co., 1902.

18. Harry Von Tilzer and Andrew B. Sterling, "Good Bye Eliza Jane." Sheet music. New York, Von Tilzer Publishing Co., 1903. [Performers and editions include: Connolly Sisters (Library of Congress); Empire Comedy Four (Mississippi State University Library); Madge Fox (SUNY Fredonia Library); Artie Hall (Johns Hopkins University Library); Harold Kennedy (Indiana Historical Society); Arthur Klein (Baylor University Library); Zoa Matthews (Indiana Memory); Joe Maxwell (Indiana Historical Society); and Cecil Spooner (Digital Public Library of America.)]

19. Billy Murray, "Goodbye, Eliza Jane." Victor matrix A-890, 1904. Discography: *Discography of American Historical Recordings.* Web. [Murray (vocals) and unknown piano]

20. Bob Roberts, "Goodbye, Eliza Jane." Victor 2832, 1904. Library of Congress. [Roberts (vocals), other musicians unknown]

21. *Discography of American Historical Recordings.* UC Santa Barbara Library. Web. [The DAHR site lists as many as ten recordings of "Goodbye, Eliza Jane" by Roberts on the Victor, Columbia, and Zonophone labels]

22. Arthur Collins, "Goodbye, Eliza Jane." Victor matrix A-594, B-594, 1903. Web. [Collins (vocals), unknown piano] Discography: *Discography of American Historical Recordings.*

23. Joel Whitburn, *Joel Whitburn's Pop Memories, 1890–1954: The History of American Popular Music: Compiled from America's Popular Music Charts 1890–1954.* Menomonee Falls, Wisc., Record Research, 1986, p. 90.

24. Whitburn, p. 9.

25. Harry Von Tilzer and Andrew B. Sterling, "Hannah Won't You Open the Door." Sheet music. New York, Harry Von Tilzer Music Publishing Company, 1904.

26. Tim Gracyk with Frank Hoffman, *Popular American Recording Pioneers: 1895–1925.* New York, Routledge, 2012, pp. 65–66.

27. Henry Creamer and Turner Layton, "(I'm Waiting for You) Liza Jane." Sheet music. New York, Broadway Music Corporation, 1918.

28. Charlie Poole with the North Carolina Ramblers, "Good-Bye Sweet Liza Jane." Columbia 15601-D, 1930. [Poole (vocals, banjo), Odell Smith (fiddle), Roy Harvey (guitar)] Discography: Russell and Pinson.

29. Richard Carlin, *Folk.* New York, Facts on File, 2005, p. 159.

30. Patrick Huber, *Linthead Stomp: The Creation of Country Music in the Piedmont South.* University of North Carolina Press, 2008, p. 148.

31. Huber, p. 154.

32. Huber, p. 155.

33. Lead Belly, "Liza Jane." *Lead Belly's Last Sessions.* Folkways SFW40068, 1994. [Lead Belly (vocals)]

34. Sandburg, *The American Songbag,* p. 132.

X. POOR GAL

1. Rev. Hanford A. Edson, "North Carolina Mountain Songs." *Indianapolis Journal,* December 5, 1897, p. 13.

2. E. C. Perrow, "Songs and Rhymes from the South." *Journal of American Folklore*, vol. 28, no. 108, 1915, p. 178.

3. Perrow, p. 179.

4. Florence Truitt, "Songs from Kentucky." *Journal of American Folklore*, vol. 36, no. 142, 1923, p. 378.

5. K. J. Holzknecht, "Some Negro Song Variants from Louisville." *Journal of American Folklore*, vol. 41, no. 162, 1928, p. 575.

6. Sandburg, *The American Songbag*, p. 133.

7. Sandburg, *The American Songbag*, p. 308.

8. Sandburg, *The American Songbag*, p. 309.

9. Pete Seeger, "Oh! Liza, Poor Gal." *Goofing Off Suite*. Folkways FA 2045, 1955. [Seeger (vocals, banjo)].

10. Charles K. Wolfe, *Tennessee Strings: The Story of Country Music in Tennessee*. University of Tennessee Press, 1977, p. 46.

11. Wolfe, *Tennessee Strings*, p. 46.

12. Tenneva Ramblers, "Miss 'Liza, Poor Gal." Victor 21141, 1927. [Jack Pierce (fiddle), Jack Grant (banjo or mandolin), Claude Slagle (banjo), Claude Grant (guitar, vocal)] Discography: Russell and Pinson.

13. The Hill Billies, "Mountaineer's Love Song." Vocalion 15367, 5115, 1926. [Tony Alderman (fiddle), Charles Bowman (banjo), Elmer Hopkins (harmonica), Al Hopkins (lead vocals, piano), Joe Hopkins (guitar, vocals), John Hopkins (ukulele, vocals)] Discography: Russell and Pinson.

14. Norm Cohen, "The Hill Billies." *The Encyclopedia of Country Music*. Oxford University Press, 2012, p. 241.

15. Cohen, p. 241.

16. Kessinger Brothers, "Liza Jane." Brunswick 521, 1929. [Clark Kessinger (fiddle), Luches Kessinger (guitar)] Discography: Russell and Pinson.

17. Chares K. Wolfe, "Clark Kessinger: Pure Fiddling." *Mountains of Music: West Virginia Traditional Music from Goldenseal*. Lilly, John, editor. University of Illinois Press, 1999, p. 25.

18. Wolfe, "Clark Kessinger," p. 27.

19. Wolfe, "Clark Kessinger," p. 30.

20. See Intermission Number One, above.

21. Ernest Rogers, *Peachtree Parade*. Atlanta, Tupper and Love, 1956, pp. 86–87.

22. Wayne W. Daniel, *Pickin' on Peachtree: A History of Country Music in Atlanta, Georgia*. University of Illinois Press, 2001, p. 92. For more on Carson, also see: Wiggins, Gene. *Fiddlin' Georgia Crazy: Fiddlin' John Carson, His Real World, and the World of His Songs*. University of Illinois Press, 1987.

23. Daniel, p. 68.

24. Daniel, p. 69.

25. Daniel, p. 69.

26. *Discography of American Historical Recordings*. UC Santa Barbara Library. Web.

27. Joseph Murrells, compiler. *The Book of Golden Discs*. London, Barrie & Jenkins, 1978, p. 12.

28. Daniel, p. 88.

29. Daniel, p. 89.

30. Daniel, p. 90.

31. Steve Oney, *And the Dead Shall Rise: The Murder of Mary Phagan and the Lynching of Leo Frank*. New York, Pantheon, 2003, pp. 571–72, 580.

32. James Charles Cobb, *Redefining Southern Culture: Mind and Identity in the Modern South*. University of Georgia Press, 1999, p. 79.

33. Cobb, p. 80.

34. Cobb, p. 80.

35. Riley Puckett, "Liza Jane." Columbia 15014-D, Harmony 5140-H, Silvertone 3261, 1924. [Puckett (vocals, banjo), Gid Tanner (fiddle)] Discography: Russell and Pinson.

36. Daniel, p. 98.

37. Daniel, p. 101.

38. See Intermission Number One, above.

39. Charles K. Wolfe, *Kentucky Country: Folk and Country Music of Kentucky*. University Press of Kentucky, 1982, p. 50.

40. Wolfe, *Kentucky Country*, p. 51.

41. "The Old Persimmon Tree." *Florida Times-Union*, November 25, 1883, p. 4.

42. Wolfe, *Tennessee Strings*, p. 28.

43. Wolfe, *Tennessee Strings*, p. 28.

44. Wolfe, *Tennessee Strings*, pp. 28, 30.

45. Bob L. Cox, *Fiddlin' Charlie Bowman: An East Tennessee Old-Time Music Pioneer and His Musical Family*. University of Tennessee Press, 2007, p. 29.

46. Cox, p. 29.

47. Uncle Am Stuart, "Old Liza Jane." Vocalion 14841 and 5039, Brunswick (Canada) 1004, 1924. [Stuart (fiddle), Gene Austin (vocal), unknown piano] Discography: Russell and Pinson.

48. Norm Cohen, Carson Cohen, and Anne Dhu McLucas, editors. *An American Singing Heritage: Songs from the British-Irish-American Oral Tradition as Recorded in the Early Twentieth Century*. Middleton, Wisconsin, A-R Editions, 2021, p. 424. Russell and Pinson, p. 880.

49. Wolfe, *Tennessee Strings*, p. 28.

50. Cox, p. 29.

51. Felix Harcourt, *Ku Klux Kulture: America and the Klan in the 1920s*. University of Chicago Press, 2019, p. 140.

52. Harcourt, p. 140.

53. Sandburg, *The American Songbag*, p. 133.

54. Samuel A. Floyd, *The Power of Black Music: Interpreting Its History from Africa to the United States*. Oxford University Press, 1995, p. 49.

55. Floyd, pp. 49–50.

56. Lucinda Poole Cockrell, "Thomas Washington Talley." *Tennessee Encyclopedia*. Tennessee Historical Society, 2018. Web.

57. Thomas W. Talley, *Negro Folk Rhymes: Wise and Otherwise*. New York, The Macmillan Company, 1922, p. 3.

58. Talley, pp. 23–24.

59. Talley, pp. 31–32.

60. Talley, pp. 34–35.

61. Will S. Hays, "Oh! Sam." Sheet music. Philadelphia, Oliver Ditson & Co., 1872.

62. Talley, p. 56.

63. Talley, p. 63.

64. Thomas Washington Talley and Charles K. Wolfe, *Thomas W. Talley's Negro Folk Rhymes*. University of Tennessee Press, 1991, p. 49.

65. Talley, pp. 248–49.

66. Talley, p. 96.

67. Talley, p. 101.

68. Talley, p. 142.

69. Talley, p. 299.

70. Talley, p. 144.

71. Sandburg, *The American Songbag*, p. 309.

72. Perrow, p. 179. Edmands, p. 132.

73. Talley and Wolfe, p. 115.

74. Scarborough, p. 7.

75. Scarborough, pp. 7–8.

XI. I'SE GOT A GAL AND YOU GOT NONE: A COUNTESS-COMPOSER AND AN ACTRESS-AVIATRIX POPULARIZE "LI'L LIZA JANE"

1. "They're Dying Out." *Lexington Dispatch*, South Carolina, February 22, 1893, p. 1. [A similar article appeared in the *Atlanta Constitution*, August 22, 1892, p. 8.]

2. Anne Virginia Culbertson, *At the Big House: Where Aunt Nancy and Aunt 'Phrony Held Forth on the Animal Folks*. Indianapolis, Bobbs-Merrill Company, 1904, p. i.

3. Culbertson, p. ii.

4. Culbertson, p. 1.

5. Culbertson, p. 141.

6. Culbertson, p. 142.

7. Culbertson, pp. 142–43.

8. Culbertson, pp. 143–47.

9. *Evening Star*, Washington, DC, March 25, 1898, p. 7.

10. "At the Big House: Mr. Hare and Mr. Flint Rock." *Evening Star*, Washington, DC, March 25, 1905, Part 2, p. 15.

11. Culbertson, p. 72.

12. Harris Barrett, "Negro Folk Songs." *Southern Workman*, vol. XLI, no. 4, April 1912, p. 238.

13. Barrett, p. 238.

14. Barrett, pp. 238–39.

15. Barrett, p. 239.

16. Barrett, p. 239.

17. Barrett, p. 239.

18. Barrett, p. 241.

19. Barrett, p. 241.

20. Barrett, p. 243.

21. Barrett, p. 244.

22. Barrett, p. 244.

23. Barrett, p. 244.

24. Barrett, p. 244.

25. "A Business Man." *The Crisis*. New York, NAACP, vol. 11, no. 1., November 1915, pp. 13–14.

26. *The Crisis*. NAACP, vol. 11, no. 1., p. 221.

27. Suzanne Shelton, *Divine Dancer: A Biography of Ruth St. Denis*. Garden City, NY, Doubleday, 1981, p. 52.

28. Ruth St. Denis, *Ruth St. Denis, an Unfinished Life: An Autobiography*. London, George G. Harrap, 1937, p. 61.

29. Shelton, p. 134.

30. Shelton, p. 134.

31. John T. Galvin, *The Gentleman Mr. Shattuck: A Biography of Henry Lee Shattuck, 1879–1971*. Boston, Tontine Press, 1996, pp. 201–2.

32. St. Denis, p. 316.

33. St. Denis, p. 316.

34. St. Denis, p. 316.

35. St. Denis, pp. 22, 207.

36. St. Denis, p. 22.

37. *Theatre Magazine*. New York, Theatre Magazine Company, December 1917, p. 351.

38. Scott O'Brien, *Ruth Chatterton, Actress, Aviator, Author*. Albany, Ga., Bear Manor Media, 2013, p. 61.

39. O'Brien, pp. 61, 62.

40. *Harper's Bazaar*. New York, Hearst Corporation, vol. LI, no. 11, November 1916, p. 61. Albert Ellsworth Thomas, *Come Out of the Kitchen: A Comedy in Three Acts*. New York, Samuel French, 1921, p. 4.

41. Thomas, p. 5.

42. Thomas, p. 77.

43. Thomas, p. 124.

44. O'Brien, p. 62.

45. Gerald Martin Bordman, "Come Out of the Kitchen." *The Concise Oxford Companion to American Theatre*. Oxford University Press, 1987, p. 142.

46. Thomas, p. 57.

47. Countess Ada de Lachau, "Li'l Liza Jane." Sheet music. San Francisco, Sherman, Clay & Co., 1916.

48. Thomas, p. 5.

49. Thomas, p. 5.

50. O'Brien, pp. 265–66.

51. Earl Fuller's Famous Jazz Band, "Li'l Liza Jane—One-Step." Victor 18394, 1917. [Fuller (piano), Walter Kahn (cornet), Harry Raderman (tuba), Ted Lewis (clarinet), John Lucas (drums)] Discography: Rust and Shaw.

52. Samuel Charters, *A Trumpet Around the Corner: The Story of New Orleans Jazz*. University Press of Mississippi, 2010, p. 105.

53. Charters, p. 105.

54. *Talkmachine Talk.* Victor Talking Machine Company. Camden, NJ, vol. 3, no. 12, December, 1917, p. 14.

55. Harry C. Browne and the Peerless Quartet, "Li'l Liza Jane." Columbia A-2622, 1918. Discography: Rust and Brooks.

56. *Jacobs' Orchestra Monthly.* Boston, Walter Jacobs, vol. 9, no. 9, September 1918, p. 8.

57. *Songs of the Soldiers and Sailors, U.S.* Washington, DC, US. Government Printing Office, 1917, pp. 3–5.

58. John McCusker and Shane Lief, *Jockomo: The Native Roots of Mardi Gras Indians.* University Press of Mississippi, 2019, p. 138.

59. Countess Ada de Lachau, "Li'l Liza Jane." Sheet music. San Francisco, Sherman, Clay & Co., 1916–1918 [Expanded edition].

60. Bob Wills and His Texas Playboys, "Lil Liza Jane." OKeh 06371, Conqueror 9820, Columbia 376644 and 20263, 1941. Discography: Russell and Pinson.

61. Hugh McNutt and Karl Johnson, "Good-Bye Lil' Liza Jane (Hello, Alsace Lorraine)." Sheet music. St. Joseph, Missouri, Hugh McNutt Publishing Co., 1918.

62. "Marching Chants." *The Caduceus*, Camp Greene, NC, vol. 2, no. 2, November 30, 1918, p. 10.

XII. INTERMISSION NUMBER THREE: EFFIE LEE NEWSOME'S "CHARCOAL, LEDDY, CHARCOAL" AND BETTY VINCENT'S "PROBLEMS OF THE HEART"

1. Edith Wilson with Johnny Dunn's Original Jazz Hounds, "Vampin' Liza Jane." Columbia A3749, 1921. [Wilson (vocals) and Dunn (cornet). Possible musicians: Bud Aiken (trombone) and Garvin Bushell (clarinet). Unknown piano and violin] Discography: Gibbs.

2. Lynn Abbott and Doug Seroff, *The Original Blues: The Emergence of the Blues in African American Vaudeville.* University Press of Mississippi, 2017, p. 254.

3. Abbott and Seroff, p. 254.

4. Perry Bradford and Marion Dickerson, "Vampin' Liza Jane." Sheet music. New York, Perry Bradford Music Company, Inc., 1921.

5. William Davis, "In the Hotsy-Totsy Cabaret: Miss Edith Wilson in the Black Bottom Dance." (Photograph.) 1926. *New York Public Library.* Web.

6. Stearns and Stearns, p. 110.

7. Effie Lee Newsome, "Charcoal, Leddy, Charcoal." *The Crisis.* New York, NAACP, vol. 24, no. 4., August 1922, p. 158.

8. Newsome, p. 158.

9. Newsome, p. 159.

10. Newsome, p. 159.

11. Newsome, p. 159.

12. Newsome, p. 159.

13. Newsome, pp. 159–60.

14. Newsome, p. 160.

15. Honey, Maureen and Patton, Venetria K., editors. "Effie Lee Newsome." *Double-take: A Revisionist Harlem Renaissance Anthology.* Rutgers University Press, 2001, p. 243.

16. Honey and Patton, p. 244.

17. Jim Blanchard, *A Diminished Roar: Winnipeg in the 1920s*. Canada, University of Manitoba Press, 2019, p. 166.

18. Blanchard, p. 166.

19. Betty Vincent, "Problems of the Heart." *The Winnipeg Evening Tribune*, Tuesday, February 14, 1922, p. 8.

20. Paula S. Fass, *The Damned and the Beautiful: American Youth in the 1920's*. Oxford University Press, 1979, p. 25.

21. Fass, p. 25.

22. Vincent, p. 8.

XIII. "LIZA JANE" MEETS THE MEDIA:
FILM, ANIMATION, RADIO, TELEVISION

1. Sam Taylor, director. *Coquette*. United Artists, 1929.

2. Peggy Dymond Leavey, *Mary Pickford: Canada's Silent Siren, America's Sweetheart*. Toronto, Dundern, 2011, p. 143.

3. Charlene B. Regester, *African American Actresses: The Struggle for Visibility, 1900–1960*. Indiana University Press, 2010, p. 72.

4. Regester, p. 75.

5. Eileen Whitfield, *Pickford: The Woman Who Made Hollywood*. University Press of Kentucky, 2007, p. 262.

6. Whitfield, pp. 262, 263.

7. "Hearts in Dixie Heads Strand All-Talkie Week." *The Constitution-Tribune*, Chillicothe, Missouri, Saturday, July 6, 1929, p. 4.

8. Champ Clark, *Shuffling to Ignominy: The Tragedy of Stepin Fetchit*. Lincoln, Neb., iUniverse, 2005, pp. 19, 28.

9. McKay, p. 46.

10. Vernon Keays, director. *Blazing the Western Trail*. Columbia Pictures, 1945.

11. American Film Institute Catalog. *Blazing the Western Trail*. 1945. Web.

12. Bob Wills and His Texas Playboys, "Goodbye Liza Jane." *Blazing the Western Trail*. Columbia Pictures, 1945.

13. Bob Wills and His Texas Playboys, "Goodbye, Liza Jane." Columbia 20555, 1942. [Wills (fiddle, backing vocals), Louie Tierney (fiddle), Joe Holley (fiddle), Leon McAuliffe (lead vocals, steel guitar), Doyle Salathiel (guitar), Mo Billington (piano), Darrell Jones (bass), Bob Fitzgerald (drums)] Discography: Russell and Pinson.

14. Charles Townsend, *San Antonio Rose: The Life and Music of Bob Wills*. University of Illinois Press, 1986, p. 44.

15. Townsend, p. 45.

16. Townsend, p. 45.

17. Townsend, p. 45.

18. Townsend, p. 3.

19. Townsend, p. 3.

20. Townsend, pp. 3–4.

21. Townsend, p. 5.

22. L. D. Ames, "The Missouri Play-Party." *Journal of American Folklore*, vol. 24, no. 93, University of Illinois Press, 1911, p. 295.

23. Ames, pp. 295, 296.

24. Alan L. Spurgeon, *Waltz the Hall: The American Play Party*. University Press of Mississippi, 2005, p. 48.

25. Spurgeon, pp. 50, 51.

26. Spurgeon, p. 47.

27. Ames, p. 295.

28. Ames, p. 317.

29. David S. McIntosh, *Folk Songs and Singing Games of the Illinois Ozarks*. University of Southern Illinois Press, 1974, p. 68.

30. R. E. Dudley and L.W. Payne Jr., "Some Texas Play Party Songs." *Publications of the Folk-lore Society of Texas, No. 1*. Folk Lore Society of Texas, Austin, Tex. 1916, p. 31.

31. B. A. Botkin, *The American Play-Party Song*. Frederick Ungar Publishing Company, New York, 1963, p. 238. [This is a second edition of a book originally published in 1937.]

32. Leah Jackson Wolford, *The Play-Party in Indiana*. Indiana Historical Commission, Indianapolis, 1916, pp. 25–26.

33. Judy Henske, "Charlotte Town." Elektra, EKSN-45007-A, 1963.

34. Nora Brown, "Liza Jane." *Sidetrack My Engine*. Jalopy Records JR-009, 2021.

35. Irene L. Rogers, *Charlottetown: The Life in Its Buildings*. Charlottetown, The Prince Edward Island Museum and Heritage Foundation, 1983, p. 13. [Numerous newspapers in the United States and Canada reported the fire.]

36. Vance Randolph, "The Ozark Play-Party." *Journal of American Folklore*, vol. 42, no. 165, 1929, p. 201.

37. Randolph, p. 202.

38. Randolph, p. 202.

39. "The Rejuvenation of Liza Jane." *Motography*. Chicago, vol. 13, no. 2, March 20, 1915, pp. 467–68.

40. Henry T. Sampson, *That's Enough Folks: Black Images in Animated Cartoons, 1900–1960*. Lanham, Md., Scarecrow Press, 1997, pp. 132–33.

41. Sampson, p. 133.

42. Sampson, p. 133.

43. Van Beuren Studios, *Dixie Days*. 1930.

44. Sampson, p. 133.

45. Nicholas Sammond, "Gentlemen, Please Be Seated: Racial Masquerade and Sadomasochism in 1930s Animation." Johnson, Stephen, editor. *Burnt Cork: Traditions and Legacies of Blackface Minstrelsy*. University of Massachusetts Press, 2012, p. 164.

46. Sammond, p. 165.

47. Sammond, p. 169.

48. Walt Disney Studios, *Mickey Mouse Pioneer Days*. 1930.

49. *Catalog of Copyright Entries: Third series*. Washington, DC Copyright Office, the Library of Congress, 1949, p. 20.

50. *Nogales International*, Arizona, Friday, January 9, 1931, p. 6.

51. Timothy E. Wise, *Yodeling and Meaning in American Music*. University Press of Mississippi, 2016, p. 3.

52. Paul Tyler, "The Rise of Rural Rhythm." *The Hayloft Gang: The Story of the National Barn Dance*. Berry, Chad, editor. University of Illinois Press, 2008, p. 55.

53. Tyler, p. 55.

54. Tyler, p. 55.

55. Tyler, pp. 55–56.

56. Tony Russell, *Rural Rhythm: The Story of Old-Time Country Music in 78 Records.* Oxford University Press, 2021, p. 254.

57. Cackle Sisters, "Li'l Liza Jane." *Checkerboard Time* transcription disc, 1937–1941 (estimated).

58. John Biguenet, "The DeZurik Sisters: Two Farm Girls Who Yodeled Their Way to the Grand Ole Opry." *Best Music Writing 2006*. Gaitskill, Mary and Carr, Daphne, editors. Boston, Da Capo Press, 2006, p. 93. [The sisters also participated in a different Ralston Purina radio program in 1944, entitled *Checkerboard Funfest*.]

59. Biguenet, p. 95.

60. Russell, p. 254.

61. Barry Mazor, *Meeting Jimmie Rodgers: How America's Original Roots Music Hero Changed the Pop Sounds of a Century*. Oxford University Press, 2009, p. 310.

62. Biguenet, p. 96.

63. Mary A. Bufwack and Robert K. Oermann, *Finding Her Voice: Women in Country Music, 1800–2000*. New York, Crown Publishers, 1993, p. 98.

64. Bufwack and Oermann, p. 98.

65. Gary Poole, *Radio Comedy Diary: A Researcher's Guide to the Actual Jokes and Quotes of the Top Comedy Programs of 1947–1950*. Jefferson, NC, McFarland, 2001, p. 202.

66. Poole, p. 202.

67. William Young and Nancy K. Young, *The 1930s*. Westport, Conn., Greenwood Press, 2002, p. 214.

68. Clair Schulz, *Fibber McGee and Molly: On the Air 1935–1959*. Duncan, Okla., Bear Manor Media, 2013, p. 1465.

69. Schulz, pp. 1386, 1465.

70. Various sources suggest that *Fibber McGee and Molly* had a considerable market share during the early 1940s, including *Broadcasting Yearbook*, both 1940 and 1941 editions, as well as websites such as Old Time Radio Shows. Collectively, they depict the show as typically landing in the top three, nationwide, at that time. This would suggest between thirty and forty million listeners.

71. Ollie Shepard and His Kentucky Boys, "Li'l Liza Jane." Decca 7665, 1939. Discography: Dixon and Godrich.

72. Louise Massey & The Westerners, "Lil Liza Jane." Vocalion / OKeh 05561 and Conqueror 9682, 1940. Discography: Russell and Pinson.

73. Aljean Harmetz, *The Making of "The Wizard of Oz."* Chicago Review Press, 2013, p. 97.

74. Harmetz, p. 97.

75. Page Cook, "Introduction." *Hollywood Holyland: the Filming and Scoring of The Greatest Story Ever Told*, by Ken Darby. Lanham, Md., Scarecrow Press, 1992, p. xix.

76. "Gloria Lynne." *Ebony*, vol. 16, no. 6, April 1961, p. 43.

77. *Ebony*, p. 43.

78. June Bundy, "Belafonte Bunch in Set Smasher." *Billboard*, November 28, 1960, p. 14.

79. Bundy, p. 14.

80. Michael Shnayerson and Harry Belafonte, *My Song: A Memoir of Art, Race, and Defiance*. New York, Vintage Books, 2012, pp. 209–10.

81. Shnayerson and Belafonte, p. 210.

82. Harry Belafonte and Gloria Lynne, "Liza Jane." *New York 19*. CBS, 1960.

83. Shnayerson and Belafonte, p. 220.

84. Shnayerson and Belafonte, p. 220.

85. Judith E. Smith, *Becoming Belafonte: Black Artist, Public Radical*. University of Texas Press, 2014, p. 211.

86. Tim Brooks and Earle Marsh, *The Complete Directory to Prime-Time Network and Cable TV Shows, 1946–present*. New York, Ballantine Books, 1999, p. 1246.

87. Cynthia J. Miller and Tom Shaker, "Big Lessons from a Small Town: The Andy Griffith Show." Westengard, Laura and Barlow, Aaron, editors. *The 25 Sitcoms that Changed Television: Turning Points in American Culture*. Santa Barbara, CA, ABC-CLIO, 2017, pp. 39–40.

88. Douglas Martin, "Andy Griffith: America's Aw-Shucks Sheriff." McDonald, William, editor. *The Socialite Who Killed a Nazi with Her Bare Hands and 143 Other Fascinating People Who Died This Past Year: The Best of the New York Times Obituaries, 2013*. New York, Workman Publishing Company, 2012, p. 344.

89. Martin, p. 345.

90. David Fernandes and Dale Robinson, *The Definitive Andy Griffith Show Reference: Episode-by-Episode, with Cast and Production Biographies and a Guide to Collectibles*. Jefferson, NC, McFarland, 2012, pp. 35–36.

91. *The Andy Griffith Show*. "Cyrano Andy." CBS, March 6, 1961.

92. *Gunsmoke*. "Song For Dying." Season 10, Episode 21. February 13, 1965. CBS. [Theodore Bikel performed "Oh Liza, Little Liza Jane."] *Internet Movie Database*. Web.

93. *The Ed Sullivan Show*. Season 20, Episode 41. June 18, 1967. CBS. [Reuben Mitchell Trio performed "My Liza Jane."] *Television Database*. Web.

94. *Hee Haw*. Season 4, Episode 16. January 13, 1973. CBS. [Stringbean and Roy Clark performed "Little Liza Jane."] *Television Database*. Web.

XIV. THE LOMAXES

1. Nolan Porterfield, *Last Cavalier: The Life and Times of John A. Lomax, 1867–1948*. University of Illinois Press, 2001, p. 8.

2. Porterfield, p. 18.

3. Porterfield, p. 19.

4. John Lomax, *Cowboy Songs and Other Frontier Ballads*. New York, Macmillan, 1920, p. 377.

5. John Lomax and Alan Lomax, *American Ballads and Folk Songs*. New York, Macmillan, 1934, pp. 284–85.

6. John Lomax and Alan Lomax, p. 285.

7. Joshua Clegg Caffery, *Traditional Music in Coastal Louisiana: The 1934 Lomax Recordings*. Louisiana State University Press, 2013, p. 217.

8. Wilson "Stavin' Chain" Jones, Charles Gobert, and Octave Amos, "Liza Jane." Lafayette, LA, 1934. AFS 94B1, Library of Congress. [Jones (guitar, vocals), Gobert (fiddle), Amos

(banjo), ensemble vocals] Also see: Wilson "Stavin' Chain" Jones and String Band.
"(Little) Liza Jane." *Louisiana (Catch That Train and Testify!* Rounder Records 82161–830-2,
2004.

9. Caffery, p. 219.

10. Caffery, p. 220.

11. Caffery, p. 220.

12. Caffery, p. 220.

13. Caffery, p. 219.

14. Pete Harris, "Square Dance Calls." Richmond, Tex., 1934. AFS 78A1, Library of
Congress. [Harris (vocals, guitar)]

15. Pete Harris, "Square Dance Calls (Little Liza Jane.)" *Black Texicans: Balladeers and
Songsters of the Texas Frontier.* Rounder Records 11661-1821-2, 1999.

16. Johnny Mae Medlock, Gussie Slater, and Ruth Hines, "Steal Liza Jane." Raiford,
Florida, June 4, 1939. [Ensemble vocals] AFS 2718B2, Library of Congress.

17. Group of Little Negro Girls, "Steal Miss Liza Jane." Eatonville, Florida, 1935. AFS 349B2,
Library of Congress.

18. Group of Negro Girls, "Steal Miss Liza Jane." Frederica, Georgia, 1935. AFS 310A1,
Library of Congress.

19. Bessie Jones, "Steal Miss Liza, Steal Liza Jane." Association for Cultural Equity T979.
New York, 1961. [Jones (vocals)]

20. Willie Dean Andrews, "Negro Folk Games." *The Playground* vol. 21, no. 3. New York,
The Playground and Recreation Association of America, 1927, p. 132.

21. Andrews, p. 133.

22. Andrews, p. 133.

23. Kyra D. Gaunt, *The Games Black Girls Play: Learning the Ropes from Double-Dutch to
Hip-Hop.* New York University Press, 2006, p. 2.

24. Gaunt, p. 66.

25. Gaunt, p. 29.

26. Alan Lomax, *White Eagles Mardi Gras Indians: Little Liza Jane, Camera A.* (Film.)
Association for Cultural Equity. New Orleans, 1982.

27. Reid Mitchell, *All on a Mardi Gras Day: Episodes in the History of New Orleans
Carnival.* Harvard University Press, 2009, p. 114.

28. Mitchell, p. 114.

29. Oliver N. Greene, "The Aesthetic of Asé in the Black Masking Indians of New
Orleans: Musical Africanisms and Orisa Manifestations in the Big Chief." *Fire!!!*, vol. 6, no. 2,
Association for the Study of African American Life and History, 2020, p. 73.

30. Mary Unterbrink, *Jazz Women at the Keyboard.* Jefferson, NC, McFarland, 1983,
p. 18.

31. Alan Lomax, *Mister Jelly Roll: The Fortunes of Jelly Roll Morton, New Orleans Creole
and "Inventor of Jazz."* New York, Grove Press, 1950, p. 221.

32. Lomax, *Mister Jelly Roll*, p. 230.

33. Lomax, *Mister Jelly Roll*, pp. 149–52.

34. Jelly Roll Morton, "At the Cadillac Café, Los Angeles." *The Complete Library of Congress
Recordings.* Rounder, disc 7, 2005. [Morton (vocals)]

35. Jelly Roll Morton, "Little Liza Jane, continued / On the West Coast." *The Complete Library of Congress Recordings*. Rounder, disc 7, 2005. [Morton (vocals)]

36. Mountain Ramblers, "Little Liza Jane." Association for Cultural Equity T849, Lancaster County, Virginia, 1959.

37. Aunt Molly Jackson, "Commentary on Dan Hawk's songs / John Henry / Little Liza Jane." Association for Cultural Equity AFS2551. New York, 1939. [Jackson (vocals)]

38. Archie Green, *Only a Miner: Studies in Recorded Coal-mining Songs*. University of Illinois Press, 1972, p. 80.

39. Green, p. 78.

40. Shelly Romalis, *Pistol Packin' Mama: Aunt Molly Jackson and the Politics of Folksong*. University of Illinois Press, 1999, p. 103.

41. Romalis, p. 104.

42. Stephen Wade, *The Beautiful Music All Around Us: Field Recordings and the American Experience*. University of Illinois Press, 2012, p. 269.

43. Wade, p. 272.

44. Wade, p. 278.

45. Wade, p. 287.

46. Luther Strong, "Liza Jane." Association for Cultural Equity AFS1539. Perry County, Kentucky, 1937. [Strong (fiddle)]

47. Wade, p. 278.

48. D. K. Wilgus, *Anglo-American Folksong Scholarship Since 1898*. Rutgers University Press, 1959, pp. xvi, 162.

49. Matthew Barton, "The Lomaxes." *The Ballad Collectors of North America: How Gathering Folksongs Transformed Academic Thought and American Identity*. Spencer, Scott B., editor. Lanham, Md., Scarecrow Press, 2012, p. 167.

50. Rawlingson Hector, "Miss Eliza Jane / Dit-o Ça." Association for Cultural Equity T1107. Trinidad and Tobago, 1962. [Ensemble singing and percussion.]

XV. THE CONSTELLATION THAT CONNECTS LANGSTON HUGHES AND DAVID BOWIE, ANTONÍN DVOŘÁK AND NINA SIMONE

1. Langston Hughes and Arna Bontemps, editors. *The Book of Negro Folklore*. New York, Dodd, Mead, 1958, pp. xvii–xxv.

2. Hughes and Bontemps, pp. 211, 217.

3. Hughes and Bontemps, p. 33.

4. Hughes and Bontemps, pp. 424–25.

5. Hughes and Bontemps, p. 425.

6. Mary Johnson, Etherine Harris, and unidentified singers, "Miss Sue from Alabama / Who De Cat (Sail, Sail)." Association for Cultural Equity AFS6669. Coahoma County, Mississippi, 1942.

7. Hughes and Bontemps, p. 426.

8. *In Search of Our Past: Units in Women's History*. Washington, DC Women's Educational Equity Act Program, US Education Department, 1980, p. S-10.

9. Hughes and Bontemps, pp. 531–32.

10. Little Richard, "Steal Miss Liza." Manticore 7007, 1975. [Little Richard (vocals), Billy Preston (organ), remainder of musicians unknown.] Discography: White.

11. Jack Rummel and Dr. John, *Under a Hoodoo Moon: The Life of Dr. John the Night Tripper*. New York, St. Martin's Press, 1994, p. 186.

12. Rummel and Dr. John, p. 186.

13. Dr. John, "Little Liza Jane." *Dr. John's Gumbo*. Atco 7006, 1972. [Dr. John (vocals, piano), Lee Allen (tenor saxophone), Melvin Lastie (cornet), Freddie Staehle (drums), other musicians unknown.] Discography: see both Strong and Rummel.

14. Rummel and Dr. John, p. 186.

15. John Wirt, *Huey "Piano" Smith and the Rocking Pneumonia Blues*. Louisiana State University Press, 2014, p. 41.

16. Wirt, p. 41.

17. Huey "Piano" Smith and His Rhythm Aces, "Little Liza Jane." Ace Records 521, 1956. [Smith (piano, vocals), Lee Allen (tenor saxophone), Earl Palmer (drums), Dave Dixon and Issacher "Izzycoo" Gordon (lead vocals), Earl King (guitar), other musicians unknown.] Discography: Wirt.

18. Wirt, p. 46.

19. Wirt, p. 42.

20. Wirt, p. 69.

21. David Hurwitz, *Dvořák: Romantic Music's Most Versatile Genius*. Pompton Plains, NJ, Amadeus Press, 2005, p. xvii.

22. Hurwitz, p. 112.

23. Jean E. Snyder, *Harry T. Burleigh: From the Spiritual to the Harlem Renaissance*. University of Illinois Press, 2016, p. 75.

24. Snyder, p. 76.

25. Snyder, p. 77.

26. Snyder, p. 77.

27. Snyder, p. 78.

28. Snyder, p. 80.

29. Snyder, p. 80.

30. Maurice Peress, *Dvořák to Duke Ellington: A Conductor Explores America's Music and Its African American Roots*. Oxford University Press, 2004, p. 22.

31. Peress, p. 205.

32. Harry T. Burleigh, "The Negro and His Song." *Music on the Air*. Kinscella, Hazel Gertrude, editor. New York, Viking Press, 1934, pp. 188–89.

33. Burleigh, p. 187.

34. Burleigh, p. 187.

35. Burleigh, p. 188.

36. Peress, p. 24.

37. Peress, p. 24.

38. Peress, p. 24.

39. Peress, pp. 24–27.

40. Southern, p. 284.

41. Nadine Cohodas, *Princess Noire: The Tumultuous Reign of Nina Simone*. University of North Carolina Press, 2012, p. 97.

42. Cohodas, pp. 97–98.

43. Nina Simone, "Little Liza Jane." *Nina Simone at Newport*. Colpix CP-412,1960. [Simone (vocals, tambourine), Al Schackman (guitar), Bobby Hamilton (drums), Chris White (bass)] Personnel details from Cohodas.

44. Cohodas, p. 98.

45. Cohodas, pp. 5–6.

46. Nina Simone, "Little Liza Jane." Newport Jazz Festival, 1960.

47. All these recordings can be located through online discography sites such as 45cat, AllMusic, and Discogs.

48. Merle Travis, "Possum Up A Simmon Tree." *Back Home*. Capitol T-891, 1957.

49. Hank Thompson and His Brazos Valley Boys, "Li'l Lisa Jane." Capitol F3950, 1957.

50. Don Hager & The Hot Tots, "Liza Jane Bop." Oak O-358, 1957.

51. Smiley Lewis, "Lil Liza Jane." Imperial X5531, 1958.

52. Pete Seeger, Mike Seeger, and Rev. Larry Eisenberg, "Goodbye Liza Jane." *American Play Parties*. Folkways Records FC 7604, 1959.

53. Dale Hawkins, "Liza Jane." Checker 934, 1959.

54. Fats Domino, "Lil' Liza Jane." Imperial AI 103, 1959.

55. Ramsey Lewis, "Li'l Liza Jane." *Stretching Out*. Argo LPS 665, 1960.

56. Panama Francis, "Lil' Liza Jane." *The Beat Behind the Million Sellers*. ABC-Paramount 333, 1960.

57. Scotty McKay, "Little Liza Jane." Ace 603, 1960.

58. Slim Harpo, "Little Liza Jane." *Sting It Then!* Ace CDCHD 658, 1997.

59. Duane Eddy, "Big 'Liza." *Girls! Girls! Girls!* Jamie JLP-3019, 1961.

60. Coleman Hawkins, "Go Lil Liza." *Today and Now*. Impulse! A-34, 1962.

61. Don Reno and Red Smiley, "Goodbye Liza Jane." *Banjo Special*. King 787, 1962.

62. Wayne Cochran, "Liza Jane." Gala G-89, 1962.

63. New Lost City Ramblers, "Liza Jane." *Gone to the Country*. Folkways Records FA 2491, 1963.

64. O'Leary, p. 10.

65. O'Leary, pp. 8, 11.

66. O'Leary, p. 13.

67. O'Leary, p. 14.

68. O'Leary, p. 9.

69. O'Leary, p. 14.

70. O'Leary, p. 10.

71. Davie Jones with the King Bees, "Liza Jane." Vocalion Pop V.9221, 1964. [Jones (lead vocals, saxophone) George Underwood (guitar, backing vocals), Roger Bluck (guitar, backing vocals), Dave Howard (bass), and Robert Allen (drums)] Discography: O'Leary.

72. O'Leary, p. 11.

73. O'Leary, p. 14.

74. Various online discography sources credit the presence of Herb Hardesty and Dave Bartholomew on the Smiley Lewis release. (See recording information above.)

XVI. PORTRAIT OF A YOUNG ENSLAVED WOMAN STANDING STILL
IN THE CATHEDRAL SILENCE OF THE DEEP WOODS AFTER A DANCE

1. Carter Brothers & Son, "Liza Jane." OKeh 45202, 1928. [George Carter (fiddle, vocals), Andrew Carter (fiddle), Jimmie Carter (guitar)] Discography: Russell and Pinson.

2. Ditson, p. 140.

3. New Lost City Ramblers, [John Cohen (vocals, guitar), Mike Seeger (fiddle), Tracy Schwarz (fiddle)]. From Folkways liner notes; see endnote from previous chapter.

4. Michael Bourne, "Rahsaan Roland Kirk: Heavy Vibrations." *DownBeat—The Great Jazz Interviews: A 75th Anniversary Anthology*. Alkyer, Frank and Enright, Ed, editors. Milwaukee, Hal Leonard Books, 2009, p. 146.

5. Roland Kirk Discography, *JazzDisco*. Web.

6. John Kruth, *Bright Moments: The Life & Legacy of Rahsaan Roland Kirk*. New York, Welcome Rain Publishers, 2000, p. 93 [Kruth and Bourne establish Kirk's fondness for traditional Black music from New Orleans, but not necessarily what is known as "Dixieland."]

7. David Washington, "Roland Kirk." *Colby Echo*. vol. LXXIV, no. 17. April 9, 1971, p. 9.

8. Washington, p. 9.

9. Ty Davis, "About Rahsaan." *New York Times*, May 30, 1971, Section D, p. 22.

10. Ruth Rosen, *The Lost Sisterhood: Prostitution in America, 1900–1918*. Baltimore, Johns Hopkins University Press, 1982, p. 80.

11. Alan Lomax, *Mister Jelly Roll*, pp. 169–70. Rosen p. 80.

12. Joel R. Williamson, "Black Self-Assertion Before and After Emancipation." Nathan I. Huggins, Martin Kilson, and Daniel M. Fox, editors. *Key Issues in the Afro-American Experience, Volume I*. New York, Harcourt Brace Jovanovich, 1971, pp. 234.

13. Williamson, p. 234.

14. Williamson, p. 234.

APPENDIX 1: LOOSE ENDS

1. Eliza Overton Slave Narrative, *Federal Writers' Project: Slave Narrative Project, Vol. X, Missouri Narratives*. Washington, DC, Library of Congress, 1941, p. 267.

2. Botkin, p. 321.

3. Frank Menefee Slave Narrative, *Federal Writers' Project: Slave Narrative Project, Vol. I, Alabama Narratives*. Washington, DC, Library of Congress, 1941, p. 280.

4. Ralph Stanley, *A Man and His Music*. Rebel Records SLP-1530 REB-1530, 1974.

5. Lizzie Farmer Slave Narrative, *Federal Writers' Project: Slave Narrative Project, Vol. XIII, Oklahoma Narratives*. Washington, DC, Library of Congress, 1941, pp. 98–99.

6. Kunigunde Duncan and D.F. Nickols, *Mentor Graham: The Man who Taught Lincoln*. University of Chicago Press, 1944, p. 194.

7. Robert Damm, "Fanga Alafia: History and Meaning." *The Orff Echo*. Folk Music Issue, Winter 2011, pp. 21–25.

8. Gale P. Jackson, *Put Your Hands on Your Hips and Act Like a Woman: Black History and Poetics in Performance*. University of Nebraska Press, 2020.

9. John M. Belohlavek, *Patriots, Prostitutes, and Spies: Women and the Mexican-American War*. University of Virginia Press, 2017, p. 214.

10. William Sheppard Smith, *Lauderdale County, Mississippi, Four Families, 1835–1936: McLaurin, Simmons, Stevenson, and Smith*. United States, W.S. Smith, 2002, p. 88.

11. Captain James Dinkins, "Civil War Reminiscences." *Illinois Central Magazine*. Chicago, Illinois Central Railroad Company, vol. 3, no. 5, November, 1914, pp. 9–18.

12. Chris Goertzen, "Mrs. Joe Person's Popular Airs: Early Blackface Minstrel Tunes in Oral Tradition." *Ethnomusicology*, vol. 35, no. 1, University of Illinois Press, 1991, p. 40.

13. Hearings Regarding Jack R. McMichael. Hearings Before the Committee On Un-American Activities, House of Representatives, *Congressional Record*. Eighty-Third Congress, First Session. July 30 and 31, 1953, p. 2710.

14. James Joseph McDonald, *Life in Old Virginia*. Old Virginia Publishing Company, 1907, p. 96.

WORKS CITED

ARTICLES

Agawu, V. Kofi. "The Rhythmic Structure of West African Music." *Journal of Musicology*, vol. 5, no. 3, 1987, pp. 400–418.

Ames, L. D. "The Missouri Play-Party." *Journal of American Folklore*, vol. 24, no. 93, 1911, pp. 295–318.

Andrews, Willie Dean. "Negro Folk Games." *The Playground* vol. 21, no. 3, 1927, pp. 132–34.

Barrett, Harris. "Negro Folk Songs." *Southern Workman*, vol. XLI, no. 4, April 1912.

Blassingame, John W. "Using the Testimony of Ex-Slaves: Approaches and Problems." *Journal of Southern History*, vol. 41, no. 4, 1975, pp. 473–92.

Bundy, June. "Belafonte Bunch in Set Smasher." *Billboard*, November 28, 1960.

"A Business Man." *The Crisis*. New York, NAACP, vol. 11, no. 1., November 1915.

Charosh, Paul. "Studying Nineteenth-Century Popular Song." *American Music*, vol. 15, no. 4, University of Illinois Press, 1997, pp. 459–92.

Clarke, Mary Olmsted. "Song-Games of Negro Children in Virginia." *Journal of American Folklore*, vol. 3, no. 11, 1890, pp. 288–90.

Cockrell, Lucinda Poole. "Thomas Washington Talley." *Tennessee Encyclopedia*. Tennessee Historical Society, 2018.

Cooperman, Robert. "Unacknowledged Familiarity: Jean Toomer and Eugene O'Neill." *Eugene O'Neill Review*, vol. 16, no. 1, 1992, pp. 38–48.

Damm, Robert. "Fanga Alafia: History and Meaning." *Orff Echo*. Folk Music Issue, Winter 2011, pp. 21–25.

Edmands, Lila W. "Songs from the Mountains of North Carolina." *Journal of American Folklore*, vol. 6, no. 21, 1893, pp. 131–34.

Freibert, Lucy M., and Margaret Walker. "Southern Song: An Interview with Margaret Walker." *Frontiers: A Journal of Women Studies*, vol. 9, no. 3, 1987, pp. 50–56.

Goertzen, Chris. "Mrs. Joe Person's Popular Airs: Early Blackface Minstrel Tunes in Oral Tradition." *Ethnomusicology*, vol. 35, no. 1, University of Illinois Press, 1991, pp. 31–53.

"Gloria Lynne." *Ebony*, vol. 16, no. 6, April 1961.

Greene, Oliver N. "The Aesthetic of Asé in the Black Masking Indians of New Orleans: Musical Africanisms and Orisa Manifestations in the Big Chief." *Fire!!!*, vol. 6, no. 2, Association for the Study of African American Life and History, 2020, pp. 73–127.

Holzknecht, K. J. "Some Negro Song Variants from Louisville." *Journal of American Folklore*, vol. 41, no. 162, 1928, pp. 558–78.

Jamison, Philip A. "Square Dance Calling: The African-American Connection." *Journal of Appalachian Studies*, vol. 9, no. 2, 2003, pp. 387–98.

McNeil, W. K. "Lafcadio Hearn, American Folklorist." *Journal of American Folklore*, vol. 91, no. 362, 1978, pp. 947–67.

Mohr, Janet. "Charles Chesnutt's Women." *CLA Journal*, vol. 49, no. 4, 2006, pp. 423–45.

Montgomery, James M. (1998) "How Robert Burns Captured America," *Studies in Scottish Literature*: vol. 30, no. 1.

Newsome, Effie Lee. "Charcoal, Leddy, Charcoal." *The Crisis*. New York, NAACP, vol. 24, no. 4., August 1922.

Odum, Howard W. "Folk-Song and Folk-Poetry as Found in the Secular Songs of the Southern Negroes." *Journal of American Folklore*, vol. 24, no. 93, 1911, pp. 255–94.

Perrow, E. C. "Songs and Rhymes from the South." *Journal of American Folklore*, vol. 28, no. 108, 1915, pp. 129–90.

"The Rejuvenation of Liza Jane." *Motography*. Chicago, vol. 13, no. 2, March 20, 1915, pp. 467–68.

Randolph, Vance. "The Ozark Play-Party." *Journal of American Folklore*, vol. 42, no. 165, 1929, pp. 201–32.

Sherman, Joan R. "Daniel Webster Davis: A Black Virginia Poet in the Age of Accommodation." *Virginia Magazine of History and Biography*, vol. 81, no. 4, 1973, pp. 457–78.

Smith, Clint. "We Mourn for All We Do Not Know." *The Atlantic*, vol. 327, no. 2 (March 2021), pp. 28–41.

Truitt, Florence. "Songs from Kentucky." *Journal of American Folklore*, vol. 36, no. 142, 1923, pp. 376–79.

Tunc, Tanfer Emin. "The De(con)struction of Black/White Binaries: Critiques of Passing in Charles Waddell Chesnutt's "'The Wife of His Youth' and Other Stories of the Color Line.'" *Callaloo*, vol. 37, no. 3, 2014, pp. 676–91.

Washington, David. "Roland Kirk." *Colby Echo*. vol. LXXIV, no. 17. April 9, 1971.

Winans, Robert B. "Black Instrumental Music Traditions in the Ex-Slave Narratives." *Black Music Research Journal*, vol. 10, no. 1, 1990, pp. 43–53.

Yetman, Norman R. "The Background of the Slave Narrative Collection." *American Quarterly*, vol. 19, no. 3, 1967, pp. 534–53.

BOOKS AND SONGBOOKS

Abbott, Lynn, and Doug Seroff. *The Original Blues: The Emergence of the Blues in African American Vaudeville*. University Press of Mississippi, 2017.

Allen, William Francis. *Slave Songs of the United States*. Bedford, Mass., Applewood Books, 1996.

Ambrose, Stephen E. *Nothing Like It in the World: The Men Who Built the Transcontinental Railroad 1863–1869*. New York, Simon & Schuster, 2001.

Austen, Jake, and Yuval Taylor. *Darkest America: Black Minstrelsy from Slavery to Hip-Hop*. New York, W. W. Norton, 2012.

Bain, David Haward. *Empire Express: Building the First Transcontinental Railroad*. New York, Viking, 1999.

Baraka, Amiri (LeRoi Jones). *Blues People: Negro Music in White America*. New York, William Morrow, 1963.

Barrios, Richard. *A Song in the Dark: The Birth of the Musical Film*. Oxford University Press, 1995.

Belafonte, Harry, and Michael Shnayerson. *My Song: A Memoir of Art, Race, and Defiance*. New York, Vintage Books, 2012.

Belknap, William Worth. *History of the Fifteenth Regiment, Iowa Veteran Volunteer Infantry: From October 1861 to August 1865, when Disbanded at the End of the War*. Keokuk, Iowa, R. B. Ogden & Son, printers, 1887.

Belohlavek, John M. *Patriots, Prostitutes, and Spies: Women and the Mexican-American War*. University of Virginia Press, 2017.

Berlin, Ira, Marc Favreau, and Steven F. Miller. *Remembering Slavery: African Americans Talk about Their Personal Experiences of Slavery and Emancipation*. New York, The New Press, 2007.

Blair, William. *Making and Remaking Pennsylvania's Civil War*. Pennsylvania State University Press, 2010.

Blanchard, Jim. *A Diminished Roar: Winnipeg in the 1920s*. Canada, University of Manitoba Press, 2019.

Blesh, Rudi. *They All Played Ragtime*. New York, Oak Publications, 1971.

The Bold Soldier Boy's Song Book. Richmond, Va., West & Johnston, 1861–1865.

Botkin, B. A. *The American Play-Party Song*. Frederick Ungar Publishing Company, New York, 1963.

Broadcasting Yearbook. Washington, DC, Broadcasting Publications, 1940.

Broadcasting Yearbook. Washington, DC, Broadcasting Publications, 1941.

Bronner, Simon J. *Lafcadio Hearn's America: Ethnographic Sketches and Editorials*. University Press of Kentucky, 2014.

Brooks, Tim. *Lost Sounds: Blacks and the Birth of the Recording Industry, 1890–1919*. University of Illinois Press, 2004.

Brooks, Tim, and Earle Marsh. *The Complete Directory to Prime-Time Network and Cable TV Shows, 1946-present*. New York, Ballantine Books, 1999.

Buckley's Song Book for the Parlor. New York, P. J. Cozans, 1855.

Bufwack, Mary A., and Robert K. Oermann. *Finding Her Voice: Women in Country Music, 1800–2000*. New York, Crown Publishers, 1993.

Caffery, Joshua Clegg. *Traditional Music in Coastal Louisiana: The 1934 Lomax Recordings*. Louisiana State University Press, 2013.

Carlin, Richard. *Folk*. New York, Facts on File, 2005.

Carr, James Revell. *Hawaiian Music in Motion: Mariners, Missionaries, and Minstrels*. University of Illinois Press, 2014.

Catalog of Copyright Entries: Third series. Washington, DC, Copyright Office, the Library of Congress, 1949.

Charters, Samuel. *A Trumpet Around the Corner: The Story of New Orleans Jazz*. University Press of Mississippi, 2010.

Chesnutt, Charles Waddell. *The Wife of His Youth: And Other Stories of the Color Line*. New York, Houghton, Mifflin, 1899.

Christy, E. P. *Christy's Plantation Melodies*. Philadelphia, Fisher & Brothers, 1854.

Christy's Negro Songster: containing the most popular melodies, as sung by Christy, Wood, White, Buckley, and other negro minstrels. New York, Richard Marsh, 1856.

Clark, Champ. *Shuffling to Ignominy: The Tragedy of Stepin Fetchit*. Lincoln, Neb., iUniverse, 2005.

Cobb, James Charles. *Redefining Southern Culture: Mind and Identity in the Modern South*. University of Georgia Press, 1999.

Cohen, Norm, Carson Cohen, and Anne Dhu McLucas, editors. *An American Singing Heritage: Songs from the British-Irish-American Oral Tradition as Recorded in the Early Twentieth Century*. Middleton, Wisconsin, A-R Editions, 2021

Cogswell, Leander Winslow. *A History of the Eleventh New Hampshire Regiment, Volunteer Infantry in the Rebellion War, 1861–1865*. Concord, NH, Republican Press Association, 1891.

Cogswell, Leander Winslow. *History of the Town of Henniker, Merrimack County, New Hampshire*. Concord, NH, Republican Press Association, 1880.

Cohodas, Nadine. *Princess Noire: The Tumultuous Reign of Nina Simone*. University of North Carolina Press, 2012.

Coleman, John Winston. *Slavery Times in Kentucky*. University of North Carolina Press, 1970.

Collier, James Lincoln. *Louis Armstrong: An American Genius*. Oxford University Press, 1985.

Cox, Bob L. *Fiddlin' Charlie Bowman: An East Tennessee Old-Time Music Pioneer and His Musical Family*. University of Tennessee Press, 2007.

Culbertson, Anne Virginia. *At the Big House: Where Aunt Nancy and Aunt 'Phrony Held Forth on the Animal Folks*. Indianapolis, Bobbs-Merrill Company, 1904.

Curtis Burlin, Natalie. *Hampton Series: Negro Folk-songs, Book I*, New York, G. Schirmer, 1918.

Curtis Burlin, Natalie. *Hampton Series: Negro Folk-songs, Book II*, New York, G. Schirmer, 1918.

Curtis Burlin, Natalie. *Hampton Series: Negro Folk-songs, Book III*, New York, G. Schirmer, 1918.

Curtis Burlin, Natalie. *Hampton Series: Negro Folk-songs, Book IV*, New York, G. Schirmer, 1919.

Daniel, Wayne W. *Pickin' on Peachtree: A History of Country Music in Atlanta, Georgia*. University of Illinois Press, 2001.

Davis, Daniel Webster. *'Weh Down Souf: And Other Poems*. Cleveland, Helman-Taylor, 1897.

Delaney's Song Book, No. 13. New York, William W. Delaney, 1896.

Duncan, Kunigunde, and D. F. Nickols. *Mentor Graham: The Man Who Taught Lincoln*. University of Chicago Press, 1944.

Emerson, Billy. *Nancy Fat Songster*. New York, Dick and Fitzgerald, 1866.

Engs, Robert Francis. *Educating the Disfranchised and Disinherited: Samuel Chapman Armstrong and Hampton Institute: 1839–1893*. University of Tennessee Press, 1999.

Fass, Paula S. *The Damned and the Beautiful: American Youth in the 1920s*. Oxford University Press, 1979.

Fernandes, David, and Dale Robinson. *The Definitive Andy Griffith Show Reference: Episode-by-Episode, with Cast and Production Biographies and a Guide to Collectibles*. Jefferson, NC, McFarland, 2012.

Floyd, Samuel A. *The Power of Black Music: Interpreting Its History from Africa to the United States*. Oxford University Press, 1995.

Forbes, Camille F. *Introducing Bert Williams: Burnt Cork, Broadway, and the Story of America's First Black Star*. New York, Basic Civitas Books, 2008.

Freeland, David. *Automats, Taxi Dances, and Vaudeville: Excavating Manhattan's Lost Places of Leisure*. New York University Press, 2009.

Fuller, James R. *Men of Color, to Arms! Vermont African-Americans in the Civil War*. Lincoln, Neb., iUniverse, 2001, 93–100.

Galvin, John T. *The Gentleman Mr. Shattuck: A Biography of Henry Lee Shattuck, 1879-1971*. Boston, Tontine Press, 1996.

Gaunt, Kyra D. *The Games Black Girls Play: Learning the Ropes from Double-Dutch to Hip-Hop*. New York University Press, 2006.

Goodheart, Adam. *1861: The Civil War Awakening*. New York, Vintage Books, 2012.

Gracyk, Tim with Hoffmann, Frank. *Popular American Recording Pioneers: 1895–1925*. New York, Routledge, 2012.

Graham, Sandra Jean. *Spirituals and the Birth of a Black Entertainment Industry*. University of Illinois Press, 2018.

Green, Archie. *Only a Miner: Studies in Recorded Coal-mining Songs*. University of Illinois Press, 1972.

Grigg, John. *Grigg's Southern and Western Songster: Being a Choice Collection of the Most Fashionable Songs: Many of Which Are Original*. Philadelphia, Lippincott, Grambo, & Co., 1851.

Handy, William Christopher. *Father of the Blues: An Autobiography*. New York, Macmillan, 1941.

Harcourt, Felix. *Ku Klux Kulture: America and the Klan in the 1920s*. University of Chicago Press, 2019.

Harmetz, Aljean. *The Making of The Wizard of Oz*. Chicago Review Press, 2013.

Harper, Thomas, and Stansill, George. *Harper & Stansil's Sweet June Rose Songster*. United States, A.J. Fisher, 1875.

Hasse, John Edward. *Beyond Category: The Life and Genius Of Duke Ellington*. Boston, Da Capo Press, 1993.

Henderson, Clayton W. *On the Banks of the Wabash: The Life and Music of Paul Dresser*. Indiana Historical Society Press, 2003.

Hibbard, Angus S. *Chic; Or, Birds of a Feather. A Medley Operetta, in Three Acts*. Oakland, CA, Tribune Publishing Company, 1883.

Huber, Patrick. *Linthead Stomp: The Creation of Country Music in the Piedmont South*. University of North Carolina Press, 2008.

Hughes, Langston, and Arna Bontemps, editors. *The Book of Negro Folklore*. New York, Dodd, Mead, 1958.

Humphreys, Andrew Atkinson. *The Virginia Campaign of '64 and '65: The Army of the Potomac and the Army of the James*. New York, Charles Scribner's Sons, 1883.

Hurwitz, David. *Dvořák: Romantic Music's Most Versatile Genius*. Pompton Plains, NJ, Amadeus Press, 2005.

In Search of Our Past: Units in Women's History. Washington, DC, Women's Educational Equity Act Program, US Education Department, 1980.

Jackson, Gale P. *Put Your Hands on Your Hips and Act Like a Woman: Black History and Poetics in Performance*. University of Nebraska Press, 2020.

Jenny Lind Forget-Me-Not Songster. Philadelphia, John B. Perry, 1853.

Jones, A. M. *Studies in African Music, Volume I*. Oxford University Press, 1959.

Knowles, Mark. *Tap Roots: The Early History of Tap Dancing*. Jefferson, NC, McFarland, 2002.

Kruth, John. *Bright Moments: The Life & Legacy of Rahsaan Roland Kirk*. New York, Welcome Rain Publishers, 2000.

Leavey, Peggy Dymond. *Mary Pickford: Canada's Silent Siren, America's Sweetheart*. Toronto, Dundurn, 2011.

Lomax, Alan. *Mister Jelly Roll: The Fortunes of Jelly Roll Morton, New Orleans Creole and "Inventor of Jazz."* New York, Grove Press, 1950.

Lomax, John A. *Cowboy Songs and Other Frontier Ballads*. New York, Macmillan, 1920.

Lomax, John A., and Alan Lomax. *American Ballads and Folk Songs*. New York, Macmillan, 1934.

Lott, Eric. *Love & Theft: Blackface Minstrelsy and the American Working Class*. Oxford University Press, 2013.

Lucas, Marion B. *A History of Blacks in Kentucky: From Slavery to Segregation, 1760–1891*. Kentucky Historical Society, 2003.

Mazor, Barry. *Meeting Jimmie Rodgers: How America's Original Roots Music Hero Changed the Pop Sounds of a Century*. Oxford University Press, 2009.

McCusker, John, and Shane Lief. *Jockomo: The Native Roots of Mardi Gras Indians*. University Press of Mississippi, 2019.

McCutcheon, John Tinney. *Army Song Book*. Washington, DC, Commission on Training Camp Activities, 1918.

McDonald, James Joseph. *Life in Old Virginia*. Old Virginia Publishing Company, 1907.

McIntosh, David S. *Folk Songs and Singing Games of the Illinois Ozarks*. University of Southern Illinois Press, 1974.

McKay, James. *The Films of Victor Mature*. Jefferson, NC, McFarland, 2013.

McKee, Margaret, and Fred Chisenhall. *Beale Black and Blue: Life and Music on Black America's Main Street*. Louisiana State University Press, 1993.

McPherson, James Alan. *Elbow Room*. New York, Little, Brown, 1977.

Mickley, Jeremiah M. *The Forty-Third Regiment, United States Colored Troops*. Gettysburg, Penn., J. E. Wible, 1866.

Minstrel Songs, Old and New: A Collection of World-wide Famous Minstrel and Plantation Songs, Including the Most Popular of the Celebrated Foster Melodies. New York, Oliver Ditson, 1882.

Mitchell, Reid. *All on a Mardi Gras Day: Episodes in the History of New Orleans Carnival*. Harvard University Press, 2009.

Monaghan, James. *Civil War on the Western Border, 1854–1865*. University of Nebraska Press, 1955.

Murrells, Joseph, compiler. *The Book of Golden Discs*. London, Barrie & Jenkins, 1978.

The Negro in Illinois: The WPA Papers. Dolinar, Brian, editor, University of Illinois Press, 2013.

The New Negro Forget-Me-Not Songster. Cincinnati, U.P. James, 1859.

Nketia, J. H. Kwabena. *The Music of Africa*. New York, W. W. Norton & Co., 1974.

O'Brien, Scott. *Ruth Chatterton, Actress, Aviator, Author.* Albany, GA, Bear Manor Media, 2013.

O'Leary, Chris. *Rebel Rebel: All the Songs of David Bowie from '64 to '76.* Winchester, United Kingdom, Zero Books, 2015.

Oney, Steve. *And the Dead Shall Rise: The Murder of Mary Phagan and the Lynching of Leo Frank.* New York, Pantheon, 2003.

Otto, John. *History of the 11th Indiana Battery During the War of the Rebellion.* Fort Wayne, Ind., W. D. Page, 1894.

Patterson, Michelle Wick. *Natalie Curtis Burlin: A Life in Native and African American Music.* University of Nebraska Press, 2010.

Peress, Maurice. *Dvořák to Duke Ellington: A Conductor Explores America's Music and Its African American Roots.* Oxford University Press, 2004.

Pickenpaugh, Roger. *Captives in Blue: The Civil War Prisons of the Confederacy.* University of Alabama Press, 2013.

Poole, Gary. *Radio Comedy Diary: A Researcher's Guide to the Actual Jokes and Quotes of the Top Comedy Programs of 1947–1950.* Jefferson, NC, McFarland, 2001.

Porterfield, Nolan. *Last Cavalier: The Life and Times of John A. Lomax, 1867–1948.* University of Illinois Press, 2001.

Regester, Charlene B. *African American Actresses: The Struggle for Visibility, 1900–1960.* Indiana University Press, 2010.

Rice, Edward Le Roy. *Monarchs of Minstrelsy, from "Daddy" Rice to Date.* New York, Kenny Publishing Company, 1911.

Rogers, Ernest. *Peachtree Parade.* Atlanta, Tupper and Love, 1956.

Romalis, Shelly. *Pistol Packin' Mama: Aunt Molly Jackson and the Politics of Folksong.* University of Illinois Press, 1999.

Rosen, Ruth. *The Lost Sisterhood: Prostitution in America, 1900–1918.* Baltimore, Johns Hopkins University Press, 1982.

Rummel, Jack, and Dr. John. *Under a Hoodoo Moon: The Life of Dr. John the Night Tripper.* New York, St. Martin's Press, 1994.

Russell, Tony. *Rural Rhythm: The Story of Old-Time Country Music in 78 Records.* Oxford University Press, 2021.

San Francisco Theatre Research, Vol. 13, Minstrelsy, Works Progress Administration, Northern California, 1939.

Sandburg, Carl. *Chicago Poems.* New York, Henry Holt, 1916.

Sandburg, Carl. *The American Songbag.* New York, Harcourt, Brace and Co., 1927.

Scarborough, Dorothy, and Ola Lee Gulledge. *On the Trail of Negro Folk-songs.* Harvard University Press, 1925.

Schulz, Clair. *Fibber McGee and Molly: On the Air 1935–1959.* Duncan, Okla., Bear Manor Media, 2013.

Scott, Reuben B. *The History of the 67th Regiment Indiana Infantry Volunteers: War of the Rebellion.* Bedford, Ind., Herald Book and Job Print., 1892.

Shelton, Suzanne. *Divine Dancer: A Biography of Ruth St. Denis.* Garden City, NY, Doubleday, 1981.

Slout, William L. *Burnt Cork and Tambourines: A Source Book of Negro Minstrelsy.* Rockville, Md., Wildside Press, 2007.

Smith, Judith E. *Becoming Belafonte: Black Artist, Public Radical*. University of Texas Press, 2014.

Smith, William Sheppard. *Lauderdale County, Mississippi, Four Families, 1835–1936: McLaurin, Simmons, Stevenson, and Smith*. United States, W. S. Smith, 2002.

Snyder, Jean E. *Harry T. Burleigh: From the Spiritual to the Harlem Renaissance*. University of Illinois Press, 2016.

Songs of the Soldiers and Sailors, U.S. Washington, DC, US Government Printing Office, 1917.

Southern, Eileen. *The Music of Black Americans: A History*. New York, W. W. Norton, 1971.

Spurgeon, Alan L. *Waltz the Hall: The American Play Party*. University Press of Mississippi, 2005.

St. Denis, Ruth. *Ruth St. Denis, an Unfinished Life: An Autobiography*. London, George G. Harrap, 1937.

Stearns, Jean, and Marshall Stearns. *Jazz Dance: The Story of American Vernacular Dance*. Boston, Da Capo Press, 1994.

Storrs, John W. *The "Twentieth Connecticut": A Regimental History*. Ansonia, Conn., Press of the Naugatuck Valley Sentinel, 1886.

Stowe, Harriet Beecher. *Uncle Tom's Cabin: Or, Life Among the Lowly*. Boston, John P. Jewett and Company, 1852.

Strausbaugh, John. *Black Like You: Blackface, Whiteface, Insult & Imitation in American Popular Culture*. New York, Penguin, 2007.

Talley, Thomas W. *Negro Folk Rhymes: Wise and Otherwise*. New York, the Macmillan Company, 1922.

Talley, Thomas W. and Charles K. Wolfe. *Thomas W. Talley's Negro Folk Rhymes*. University of Tennessee Press, 1991.

Thomas, Albert Ellsworth. *Come Out of the Kitchen: A Comedy in Three Acts*. New York, Samuel French, 1921.

Toll, Robert C. *Blacking Up: The Minstrel Show in Nineteenth-Century America*. Oxford University Press, 1974.

Toomer, Jean. *Cane*. New York, Boni and Liveright, 1923.

Townsend, Charles R. *San Antonio Rose: The Life and Music of Bob Wills*. University of Illinois Press, 1986.

Unterbrink, Mary. *Jazz Women at the Keyboard*. Jefferson, NC, McFarland, 1983.

Wade, Stephen. *The Beautiful Music All Around Us: Field Recordings and the American Experience*. University of Illinois Press, 2012.

Walker, Margaret. *Jubilee*. Boston, Houghton Mifflin Harcourt, 2016.

Wall, Henry Clay. *Historical Sketch of the Pee Dee Guards: (Co. D, 23d N. C. Regiment) from 1861 to 1865*. Raleigh, N.C., Edwards, Broughton & Co., 1876.

Whitburn, Joel. *Joel Whitburn's Pop Memories, 1890–1954: The History of American Popular Music: Compiled from America's Popular Music Charts 1890–1954*. Menomonee Falls, Wisc., Record Research, 1986.

White's New Ethiopian Song Book No. 3. New York, H. Long & Brother, 1848.

White's New Illustrated Melodeon Songbook. New York, H. Long & Brother, 1851.

Whitfield, Eileen. *Pickford: The Woman Who Made Hollywood*. University Press of Kentucky, 2007.

Wilgus, D. K. *Anglo-American Folksong Scholarship Since 1898*. Rutgers University Press, 1959.

Wirt, John. *Huey "Piano" Smith and the Rocking Pneumonia Blues.* Louisiana State University Press, 2014.

Wise, Timothy E. *Yodeling and Meaning in American Music.* University Press of Mississippi, 2016.

Wittke, Carl Frederick. *Tambo and Bones: A History of the American Minstrel Stage.* Duke University Press, 1930.

Wolfe, Charles K. *Kentucky Country: Folk and Country Music of Kentucky.* University Press of Kentucky, 1982.

Wolfe, Charles K. *Tennessee Strings: The Story of Country Music in Tennessee.* University of Tennessee Press, 1977.

Wolford, Leah Jackson. *The Play-Party in Indiana.* Indiana Historical Commission, Indianapolis, 1916.

Young, William and Nancy K. Young. *The 1930s.* Westport, Conn., Greenwood Press, 2002.

CHAPTERS OF BOOKS, ENTRIES IN ANTHOLOGIES

Armstrong, General S. C. "Report: Hampton Normal and Agricultural Institute." *Report of the Superintendent of Public Instruction of the Commonwealth of Virginia with Accompanying Documents.* Richmond, Va., Superintendent of Public Printing, 1886.

Barton, Matthew. "The Lomaxes." *The Ballad Collectors of North America: How Gathering Folksongs Transformed Academic Thought and American Identity.* Spencer, Scott B., editor. Lanham, Md., Scarecrow Press, 2012.

Biguenet, John. "The DeZurik Sisters: Two Farm Girls Who Yodeled Their Way to the Grand Ole Opry." *Best Music Writing 2006.* Gaitskill, Mary, and Carr, Daphne, editors. Boston, Da Capo Press, 2006.

Bordman, Gerald Martin. "Come Out of the Kitchen." *The Concise Oxford Companion to American Theatre.* Oxford University Press, 1987.

Bourne, Michael. "Rahsaan Roland Kirk: Heavy Vibrations." *DownBeat—the Great Jazz Interviews: A 75th Anniversary Anthology.* Alkyer, Frank and Enright, Ed, editors. Milwaukee, Hal Leonard Books, 2009.

Burleigh, Harry T. "The Negro and His Song." *Music on the Air.* Kinscella, Hazel Gertrude, editor. New York, Viking Press, 1934.

Cohen, Norm. "The Hill Billies." *The Encyclopedia of Country Music.* Oxford University Press, 2012.

Cook, Page. "Introduction." *Hollywood Holyland: the Filming and Scoring of The Greatest Story Ever Told.* Ken Darby. Lanham, Md., Scarecrow Press, 1992.

Dudley, R. E., and L.W. Payne Jr., "Some Texas Play Party Songs." *Publications of the Folk-lore Society of Texas, No. 1.* Folk Lore Society of Texas, Austin, Tex. 1916.

Harrison, Daphne Duval. "Edith Wilson." *Harlem Renaissance Lives from the African American National Biography.* Gates, Henry Louis and Higginbotham, Evelyn Brooks, editors. Oxford University Press, 2009.

Hearings Regarding Jack R. McMichael. Hearings Before the Committee on Un-American Activities, House of Representatives. *Congressional Record.* Eighty-Third Congress, First Session. July 30 and 31, 1953.

Honey, Maureen and Venetria K. Patton, editors. "Effie Lee Newsome." *Double-take: A Revisionist Harlem Renaissance Anthology*. Rutgers University Press, 2001.

Martin, Douglas "Andy Griffith: America's Aw-Shucks Sheriff." *The Socialite Who Killed a Nazi with Her Bare Hands and 143 Other Fascinating People Who Died This Past Year: The Best of the New York Times Obituaries, 2013*. McDonald, William, editor. New York, Workman Publishing Company, 2012.

Miller, Cynthia J., and Tom Shaker. "Big Lessons from a Small Town: The Andy Griffith Show." *The 25 Sitcoms that Changed Television: Turning Points in American Culture*. Laura Westengard and Aaron Barlow, editors. Santa Barbara, CA., ABC-CLIO, 2017.

Moore, T. DeWayne. "The Mississippi Sheiks." *Fiddle Tunes from Mississippi: Commercial and Informal Recordings, 1920–2018*. Harry Bolick and Tony Russell, editors. University Press of Mississippi, 2021.

Sammond, Nicholas. "Gentlemen, Please Be Seated: Racial Masquerade and Sadomasochism in 1930s animation." *Burnt Cork: Traditions and Legacies of Blackface Minstrelsy*. Stephen Johnson, editor. University of Massachusetts Press, 2012.

Sampson, Henry T. "Dixie Days." *That's Enough Folks: Black Images in Animated Cartoons, 1900–1960*. Lanham, Md., Scarecrow Press, 1997.

Tyler, Paul. "The Rise of Rural Rhythm." *The Hayloft Gang: The Story of the National Barn Dance*. Berry, Chad, editor. University of Illinois Press, 2008.

Williamson, Joel R. "Black Self-Assertion Before and After Emancipation." Nathan I. Huggins, Martin Kilson, and Daniel M. Fox, editors. *Key Issues in the Afro-American Experience, Volume I*. New York, Harcourt Brace Jovanovich, 1971.

Wolfe, Chares K. "Clark Kessinger: Pure Fiddling." *Mountains of Music: West Virginia Traditional Music from Goldenseal*. John Lilly, editor. University of Illinois Press, 1999.

DISCOGRAPHY—RECORDINGS

Most of these songs can be heard on streaming apps, YouTube, or CDs. As described in the Endnotes, some recordings can be found on the Association for Cultural Equity and Library of Congress websites. See additional categories below for sources of discographic information as well as information on film, radio, and television performances.

Brown, Nora. "Liza Jane." *Sidetrack My Engine*. Jalopy Records JR-009, 2021.

Browne, Harry C., and the Peerless Quartet. "Li'l Liza Jane." Columbia A-2622, 1918.

Carson, Fiddlin' John, & His Virginia Reelers. "Good-bye, Liza Jane." OKeh 45049, 1926.

Carter Brothers & Son. "Liza Jane." OKeh 45202, 1928.

Cochran, Wayne. "Liza Jane." Gala G-89, 1962.

Collins, Arthur. "Goodbye, Eliza Jane." Victor matrix A-594, B-594, 1903.

Domino, Fats. "Lil' Liza Jane." Imperial AI 103, 1959.

Dr. John. "Little Liza Jane." *Dr. John's Gumbo*. Atco 7006, 1972.

Earl Fuller's Famous Jazz Band. "Li'l Liza Jane—One-Step." Victor 18394, 1917.

Eddy, Duane. "Big 'Liza." *Girls! Girls! Girls!* Jamie JLP-3019, 1961.

Francis, Panama. "Lil' Liza Jane." *The Beat Behind the Million Sellers*. ABC-Paramount 333, 1960.

Hager, Don, & The Hot Tots. "Liza Jane Bop." Oak O-358, 1957.

Harpo, Slim. "Little Liza Jane." *Sting It Then!* Ace CDCHD 658, 1997.

Harris, Pete. "Square Dance Calls (Little Liza Jane.)" *Black Texicans: Balladeers and Songsters of the Texas Frontier*. Rounder Records 11661-1821-2, 1999.

Hawkins, Coleman. "Go Lil Liza." *Today and Now*. Impulse! A-34, 1962.

Hawkins, Dale. "Liza Jane." Checker 934, 1959.

Hector, Rawlingson. "Miss Eliza Jane / Dit-o Ça." Association for Cultural Equity T1107. 1962.

Henske, Judy. "Charlotte Town." Elektra, EKSN-45007-A, 1963.

The Hill Billies. "Mountaineer's Love Song." Vocalion 15367, 5115, 1926.

Hurt, Mississippi John. "Liza Jane (God's Unchanging Hand)." *Folk Songs and Blues*. Piedmont PLP 13157, 1963.

Jackson, Aunt Molly. "Commentary on Dan Hawk's songs / John Henry / Little Liza Jane." Association for Cultural Equity AFS2551. 1939.

Johnson, George W. "The Laughing Coon." Edison 4005, 1898.

Johnson, Mary, Harris, Etherine, and unidentified singers. "Miss Sue from Alabama / Who De Cat (Sail, Sail)." Association for Cultural Equity AFS6669. 1942.

Jones, Bessie. "Steal Miss Liza, Steal Liza Jane." Association for Cultural Equity T979. 1961.

Jones, Davie, with the King Bees. "Liza Jane." Vocalion Pop V.9221, 1964.

Jones, Wilson "Stavin' Chain," and String Band. "(Little) Liza Jane." *Louisiana (Catch That Train and Testify!)* Rounder Records 82161-830-2, 2004.

Kessinger Brothers. "Liza Jane." Brunswick 521, 1929.

Kincaid, Bradley. "Liza Up in the 'Simmon Tree." Gennett 6761, Champion 15687 and 45057, and Supertone 9362, 1929.

Leachman, Silas. "Whoa Dar Mule." Victor A-801, 1901.

Lead Belly. "Liza Jane." *Lead Belly's Last Sessions*. Folkways, 1953.

Lewis, Ramsey. "Li'l Liza Jane." *Stretching Out*. Argo LPS 665, 1960.

Lewis, Smiley. "Lil Liza Jane." Imperial X5531, 1958.

Little Richard. "Steal Miss Liza." Manticore 7007, 1975.

Massey, Louise, & The Westerners. "Lil Liza Jane." Vocalion / OKeh 05561 and Conqueror 9682, 1940.

McKay, Scotty. "Little Liza Jane." Ace 603, 1960.

Medlock, Johnny Mae, Slater, Gussie, and Hines, Ruth. "Steal Liza Jane." AFS 2718B2, Library of Congress. 1939.

Morton, Jelly Roll. "At the Cadillac Café, Los Angeles." *The Complete Library of Congress Recordings*. Rounder, disc 7, 2005.

Morton, Jelly Roll. "Little Liza Jane, continued / On the West Coast." *The Complete Library of Congress Recordings*. Rounder, disc 7, 2005.

Mountain Ramblers. "Little Liza Jane." Association for Cultural Equity T849. 1959.

Murray, Billy. "Goodbye, Eliza Jane." Victor matrix A-890, 1904.

New Lost City Ramblers. "Liza Jane." *Gone to the Country*. Folkways Records FA 2491, 1963.

Poole, Charlie, with the North Carolina Ramblers. "Good-Bye Sweet Liza Jane." Columbia 15601-D, 1930.

Puckett, Riley. "Liza Jane." Columbia 15014-D, Harmony 5140-H, Silvertone 3261, 1924.

Reno, Don, and Red Smiley. "Goodbye Liza Jane." *Banjo Special*. King 787, 1962.

Roberts, Bob. "Goodbye, Eliza Jane." Victor 2832, 1904.

Seeger, Pete. "Oh! Liza, Poor Gal." *Goofing Off Suite*. Folkways FA 2045, 1955.

Seeger, Pete, Mike Seeger, and Rev. Larry Eisenberg. "Goodbye Liza Jane." *American Play Parties*. Folkways Records FC 7604, 1959.

Shepard, Ollie, and His Kentucky Boys. "Li'l Liza Jane." Decca 7665, 1939.

Simone, Nina. "Little Liza Jane." *Nina Simone at Newport*. Colpix CP-412,1960.

Smith, Huey "Piano," and His Rhythm Aces. "Little Liza Jane." Ace Records 521, 1956

Stanley, Ralph. "Rocky Island." A Man and His Music. Rebel Records SLP-1530 REB-1530, 1974.

The Stanley Trio. "Whoa! Mule." OKeh 40271, 1924.

Strong, Luther. "Liza Jane." Association for Cultural Equity AFS1539. 1937.

Stuart, Uncle Am. "Old Liza Jane." Vocalion 14841 and 5039, Brunswick (Canada) 1004, 1924.

Tenneva Ramblers. "Miss 'Liza, Poor Gal." Victor 21141, 1927.

Thomas, Henry. "Run, Mollie, Run." Vocalion 1141, 1927.

Thompson, Hank, and His Brazos Valley Boys. "Li'l Lisa Jane." Capitol F3950, 1957.

Travis, Merle. "Possum Up A Simmon Tree." *Back Home*. Capitol T-891, 1957.

Wills, Bob, and His Texas Playboys. "Goodbye, Liza Jane." Columbia 20555, 1942.

Wills, Bob, and His Texas Playboys. "Lil Liza Jane." OKeh 06371, Conqueror 9820, Columbia 376644 and 20263, 1941.

Wilson, Edith, with Johnny Dunn's Original Jazz Hounds. "Vampin' Liza Jane." Columbia A3749, 1921.

DISCOGRAPHY—SOURCES

As detailed in the Endnotes, these sources were used to document many of the older recordings. Additional sources included websites such as 45cat, AllMusic, Association for Cultural Equity, Discogs, JazzDisco, Library of Congress, and Wikipedia. In some cases, liner notes or labeling on the records themselves provided useful information.

Check-list of Recorded Songs in the English Language in the Archive of American Folk Song to July, 1940: Alphabetical List with Geographical Index. Washington, DC, Library of Congress, Music Division, 1942.

Discography of American Historical Recordings. UC Santa Barbara Library.

Dixon, Robert, and John Godrich. *Blues & Gospel Records 1902–1943*. Chigwell, Essex, United Kingdom, Storyville Publications, 1982.

Gibbs, Craig Martin. *Black Recording Artists, 1877–1926: An Annotated Discography*. Jefferson, NC, McFarland, 2012.

Laird, Ross. *Brunswick Records: A Discography of Recordings, 1916–1931. Volume 3: Chicago & Regional Sessions*. Westport, Conn., Greenwood Press, 2001.

Russell, Tony, and Bob Pinson. *Country Music Records: A Discography, 1921–1942*. Oxford University Press, 2004.

Rust, Brian, and Tim Brooks. *The Columbia Master Book Discography, Vol. II: Principal U.S. Matrix Series, 1910–1924*. Westport, Conn., Greenwood Press, 1999.

Rust, Brian, and Malcolm Shaw. *Jazz and Ragtime Records (1897–1842): Volume 1, A-K.* Denver, Colo., Mainspring Press, 2002.

Strong, Martin C. *The Great Rock Discography.* New York, Canongate, 2004.

White, Charles. *The Life and Times of Little Richard.* Harmony Books, New York, 1984.

DISSERTATIONS

Gale, Emily Margot. *Sounding Sentimental: American Popular Song from Nineteenth-Century Ballads to 1970s Soft Rock.* Doctoral Dissertation. University of Virginia, Department of Music, 2014.

Hines, Alisha J. *Geographies of Freedom: Black Women's Mobility and the Making of the Western River World, 1814–1865.* Doctoral dissertation. Department of History, Duke University, 2018.

FILMS, PHOTOGRAPHS, RADIO SHOWS, AND TELEVISION SHOWS

Many of these performances can be found on YouTube, Vimeo, other media sites that maintain archives of radio and television shows, and the Association for Cultural Equity website. Additional information can be found online at the American Film Institute, Internet Movie Database, and Television Database websites.

Anatomy of Pop: The Music Explosion. (Television.) ABC, 1966.

Beavers, Louise, and uncredited guitar player. "Little Liza Jane." *Coquette.* (Film.) United Artists, 1929.

Belafonte, Harry, and Gloria Lynne. "Liza Jane." *New York 19.* (Television.) CBS, November 20, 1960.

Bikel, Theodore. "Oh Liza, Little Liza Jane." *Gunsmoke.* "Song For Dying." (Television.) CBS, Season 10, Episode 21. February 13, 1965.

Cackle Sisters. "Li'l Liza Jane." (Radio.) *Checkerboard Time,* 1937–1941, or 1944 (estimated).

Chatmon, Sam. *Sam Chatmon: "Little Liza Jane."* (Film.) Association for Cultural Equity, 1978.

Clark, Roy, and Stringbean. "Little Liza Jane." *Hee Haw.* (Television.) CBS, Season 4, Episode 16. January 13, 1973.

Davis, William. "In the Hotsy-Totsy Cabaret: Miss Edith Wilson in the Black Bottom Dance." (Photograph.) 1926. *New York Public Library.*

Griffith, Andy, Don Knotts, Elinor Donohue, and Betty Lynn. "Little Liza Jane." *The Andy Griffith Show.* "Cyrano Andy." (Television.) CBS, March 6, 1961.

The King's Men. "Little Liza Jane." *Fibber McGee and Molly.* "Back From Vacation in Alaska." (Radio.) NBC. September 30, 1941.

Mitchell, Reuben, Trio. "My Liza Jane." *The Ed Sullivan Show.* (Television.) CBS, Season 20, Episode 41. June 18, 1967.

Uncredited performers. "Little Liza Jane." *Dixie Days.* (Cartoon.) Van Beuren Studios, 1930.

Uncredited performers. "Little Liza Jane." *Mickey Mouse Pioneer Days.* (Cartoon.) Walt
Disney Studios, 1930.
White Eagles Mardi Gras Indians. *White Eagles Mardi Gras Indians: Little Liza Jane, Camera A.*
(Film.) Association for Cultural Equity, 1982.
Wills, Bob, and His Texas Playboys. "Goodbye Liza Jane." *Blazing the Western Trail.* (Film.)
Columbia Pictures, 1945.

NEWSPAPERS

Burns, Robert. "Farewell to Eliza." *North Carolinian*, Fayetteville, June 3, 1848.
Crockett. "The Carpet-Bagger's Departure: Good-Bye Liza Jane." *Staunton Spectator and
General Advertiser*, Virginia, November 18, 1873.
Davis, Ty. "About Rahsaan." *New York Times*, May 30, 1971, Section D, Page 22.
Dr. Adonis. "Affairs in Middle Tennessee." *Louisville Daily Journal*, February 23, 1864.
Dr. Adonis. "Affairs in Northern Alabama." *Louisville Daily Journal*, February 29, 1864.
Dr. Adonis. "Department of the Gulf." *Chicago Tribune*, March 30, 1865.
Dr. Adonis. "Facts and Fancies from the Sunny South." *Louisville Daily Journal*, March 15,
1864.
Dr. Adonis. *Louisville Daily Journal*, March 2, 1864.
Edson, Rev. Hanford A. "North Carolina Mountain Songs." *Indianapolis Journal*, December 5,
1897.
Hearn, Lafcadio. "Roustabouts: The Songs of the Longshoremen of the Mississippi—A Class
of Men Whose Old Characteristics Are Departing." *Columbus Courier*, Kansas, April 6,
1876.
Pomeroy, Brick. "Brick Pomeroy on Mosquitoes." *The Ashland Union*, Ohio. October 25, 1865.
Vincent, Betty. "Problems of the Heart." *Winnipeg Evening Tribune*, Tuesday, February 14,
1922.
"At the Big House: Mr. Hare and Mr. Flint Rock." *Evening Star*, Washington, DC, March 25,
1905.
"Crimes." *Worthington Advance*, Minnesota. November 5, 1875.
"Dedicated to the 'Mountain Poet.'" *Loudon Free Press*, Tennessee. March 19, 1853.
"Dedicated to Lizzy Jane." *Loudon Free Press*, Tennessee. April 2, 1853.
"Dr. Byron Adonis." *Sunday Call*, August 1, 1892.
"The Funeral Escort." *Chicago Tribune*. April 22, 1865.
"A Genuine Love Letter." *Portland Daily Press* (Maine) March 28, 1864.
"Happy New Year." *Daily Monitor*, Topeka, Kansas, January 4, 1865.
"Hearts in Dixie Heads Strand All-Talkie Week." *Constitution-Tribune*, Chillicothe, Missouri,
Saturday, July 6, 1929.
"Marching Chants." *The Caduceus*, Camp Greene, NC, vol. 2, no. 2, November 30, 1918.
"Music Hall." *Gold Hill Daily News*, Nevada, November 23, 1865.
"The Old Persimmon Tree." *Florida Times-Union*, November 25, 1883.
"Personal." *Thomaston Herald*, Georgia, March 15, 1873.
"Phases of Love in the Sunny South." *Chicago Daily Tribune*, March 5, 1864.
"A Rebel Loveletter." *Fremont Journal* (Ohio) November 11, 1864.

"They're Dying Out." *Lexington Dispatch*, South Carolina, February 22, 1893.

"To Lizzie Jane." *Loudon Free Press*, Tennessee. March 5, 1853.

"Truly Affecting." *Iowa Republican*, Iowa City, December 18, 1852.

Carson Daily Appeal, Nevada. October 24, 1875.

Cedar Falls Gazette, Iowa, December 2, 1870.

Chicago Tribune, April 28, 1867.

Chicago Tribune, May 1, 1867.

Daily Beacon, Wichita, Kansas, August 1, 1873.

Daily Dramatic Chronicle, San Francisco, February 7, 1867.

Daily Press and Herald, Knoxville, Tennessee, February 16.

DeKalb Chronicle, Illinois, March 27, 1931.

Evening Star, Washington, DC, March 25, 1898.

Evening Star, Washington, DC, October 22, 1945.

Los Angeles Daily Herald. June 16, 1876.

The Mercury, Hobart, Tasmania, Australia, December 29, 1870.

The Mercury, Hobart, Tasmania, Australia, May 27, 1872.

The Mercury, Hobart, Tasmania, Australia, December 9, 1874.

Montpelier Daily Record, Vermont, February 24, 1898.

New York Clipper, December 30, 1871.

New York Clipper, May 24, 1873.

New York Herald. April 2, 1871.

Nogales International, Arizona, January 9, 1931.

Reno Gazette-Journal, Nevada. August 8, 1876.

Semi-Weekly Wisconsin, Milwaukee. November 14, 1863.

South Australian Register, Adelaide, December 18, 1874.

The Stage. "San Francisco Minstrels." Vol. 12, no. 18, New York, Sept. 8, 1871.

Sydney Morning Herald, New South Wales, Australia, May 15, 1875.

Weekly Review, Crawfordsville, Indiana, November 4, 1865.

PLAYBILLS AND PROGRAMS

As described in the endnotes, most materials can be found at the Harvard Theatre Collection on Blackface Minstrelsy, with exceptions noted.

Billy Birch's San Francisco Minstrels. Program. San Francisco Minstrels Opera House, New York. October 1, 1883.

Duprez & Benedict's Minstrels. Program. 1871–1876 (estimated).

Emerson, Allen & Manning's Minstrels. Playbill. Tony Pastor's Opera House, New York. July 23, 1868.

Emerson's California Minstrels. Playbill. New York, 1872–1876.

Ethiopian Dramatic Society. Playbill, 1874.

Female Minstrels. Playbill. Philadelphia, Pennsylvania, undated.

George Christy's Minstrels. Playbill. Lowell, Massachusetts, January 12, 1863.

Great California Minstrels, The. Playbill. Auckland, New Zealand.1874.

London Minstrels. Playbill. Durban, South Africa. 1879.

Madagascar Minstrels. Playbill. Music Hall, Boston, Massachusetts, 1889.

Megatherian Minstrels. Playbill. Boston, Massachusetts, 1880.

Moore & Burgess Minstrels. Playbill. St. James's Hall, London, England. October 25, 1876.

New York Minstrels. Playbill. Assinippi Hall, West Scituate, Massachusetts. February 11, 1874.

San Francisco Minstrels. Playbill. Brooklyn, New York, 1873.

San Francisco Minstrels. Playbill. New York, 1877.

Schoolcraft & Coes' Minstrels. Playbill. Howard Athenaeum, Boston, Massachusetts. 1877.

Schoolcraft and Coes' Minstrels. Playbill. Howard Athenaeum, Boston, Massachusetts. 1887
    (estimated).

St. James Theatre *Play Bill*, San Francisco, vol. 1, no. 156, June 7, 1868.

Washington Minstrels. Playbill. Somerville, Massachusetts, 1874.

SERIAL PUBLICATIONS

The Billboard. April 9, 1949.

Dinkins, Captain James. "Civil War Reminiscences." *Illinois Central Magazine*. Chicago,
    Illinois Central Railroad Company, vol. 3, no. 5, November, 1914.

Hale, Edward E., editor. *Lend a Hand*. Boston, J. S. Smith, vol. II, no. 1, 1887.

Harper's Bazaar. New York, Hearst Corporation, vol. LI, no. 11, November 1916.

Henry De Marsan's New Comic and Sentimental Singer's Journal. New York, vol. 1, no. 65.

Henry De Marsan's New Comic and Sentimental Singer's Journal. New York, vol. 1, no. 86.

Henry De Marsan's New Comic and Sentimental Singer's Journal. New York, vol. 2, no. 137.

Jacobs' Orchestra Monthly. Boston, Walter Jacobs, vol. 9, no. 9, September, 1918.

Mass, James. "The Briar." *Henry De Marsan's Comic and Sentimental Singers' Journal*. New
    York, vol. II, no. 122.

The Southern Workman and Hampton School Record. Virginia, Hampton Normal and
    Agricultural Institute, vol. XXII, no. 5, May 1894.

Talkmachine Talk. Victor Talking Machine Company. Camden, NJ, vol. 3, no. 12, December,
    1917.

Theatre Magazine. New York, Theatre Magazine Company, December 1917.

SHEET MUSIC AND SONG SHEETS

Blandford, G. M. "Git Up Dar!" Sheet music. New York, Hamilton S. Gordon, 1897.

Bradford, Perry, and Marion Dickerson. "Vampin' Liza Jane." Sheet music. New York, Perry
    Bradford Music Company, Inc., 1921.

Creamer, Henry, and Turner Layton. "(I'm Waiting For You) Liza Jane." Sheet music. New
    York, Broadway Music Corporation, 1918.

de Lachau, Countess Ada. "Li'l Liza Jane." Sheet music. San Francisco, Sherman, Clay & Co.,
    1916.

de Lachau, Countess Ada. "Li'l Liza Jane." Sheet music. San Francisco, Sherman, Clay & Co.,
    1916–1918 [Expanded edition].

Dresser, Paul. "I'se Your Nigger If You Wants Me Liza Jane." Sheet music. New York, Howley, Havilland & Co., 1896.

"Flip flap." Song sheet. H. De Marsan, Publisher. 54 Chatham Street, NY.

Fox, Eddie. "Good Bye Liza Jane." Philadelphia, Lee & Walker, 1871.

"Good-Bye, Liza Jane." Song sheet. Poet's Box, Glasgow, November 24, 1877.

Hays, Will S. "Oh! Sam." Philadelphia, Oliver Ditson & Co., 1872.

"Hop lite loo." Song sheet. H. De Marsan, Publishers, No 54 Chatham Street, NY.

Horwitz, Charles, and Frederick Bowers. "I Needs You Very Badly, Liza Jane: Southern Love Plaint." Sheet music. Shapiro, Bernstein & Von Tilzer, New York, 1901.

"Jeremy Diddler." Song sheet. H. De Marsan, Publisher, 60 Chatham Street, NY.

McNutt, Hugh, and Karl Johnson. "Good-Bye Lil' Liza Jane (Hello, Alsace Lorraine)." Sheet music. St. Joseph, Missouri, Hugh McNutt Publishing Co., 1918.

Music of the Ethiopian Serenaders: Nine Songs and a Set of Cotillions. "Going Ober de Mountain." Sheet music. Philadelphia, E. Ferrett & Co., 1845.

Von Tilzer, Harry, and Andrew B. Sterling. "Good Bye Eliza Jane." Sheet music. New York, Von Tilzer Publishing Co., 1903.

Von Tilzer, Harry, and Andrew B. Sterling. "Hannah Won't You Open the Door." Sheet music. New York, Harry Von Tilzer Music Publishing Company, 1904.

Von Tilzer, Harry, and Andrew B. Sterling. "Won't You Roll Dem Eyes Eliza." Sheet music. New York, Von Tilzer Publishing Co., 1902.

Williams, Frank. "Susan Jane or Dis child is by his Lub Forsaken as sung by Christy's Minstrels." Sheet Music. Cincinnati, W. C. Peters & Sons, 1854.

WPA NARRATIVES (MENTIONING "LIZA JANE" SONGS)

Marshall Butler Slave Narrative. *Federal Writers' Project: Slave Narrative Project, Vol. IV, Georgia Narratives, Part 1, Adams-Furr.* Washington, DC, Library of Congress, 1941, pp. 160–67.

Lawrence Evans Slave Narrative. Rawick, George P. *The American Slave: Mississippi Narratives, Part 4.* Westport, Conn., Greenwood Publishing Company, 1977, pp. 703–6. [Also see: http://msgw.org/slaves/evans-xslave.htm.]

Dosia Harris Slave Narrative. *Federal Writers' Project: Slave Narrative Project, Vol. IV, Georgia Narratives, Part 2, Garey-Jones.* Washington, DC, Library of Congress, 1941, pp. 104–14.

Bryant Huff Slave Narrative. *Federal Writers' Project: Slave Narrative Project, Vol. IV, Georgia Narratives, Part 2, Garey-Jones.* Washington, DC, Library of Congress, 1941, pp. 238–43.

Lina Hunter Slave Narrative. *Federal Writers' Project: Slave Narrative Project, Vol. IV, Georgia Narratives, Part 2, Garey-Jones.* Washington, DC, Library of Congress, 1941, pp. 253–72.

Alice Hutcheson Slave Narrative. *Federal Writers' Project: Slave Narrative Project, Vol. IV, Georgia Narratives, Part 2, Garey-Jones.* Washington, DC, Library of Congress, 1941, pp. 281–88.

Hannah Jameson Slave Narrative. Lankford, George E. *Bearing Witness: Memories of Arkansas Slavery Narratives* from the 1930s WPA Collections. University of Arkansas Press, 2006, pp. 163–66.

Lydia Jefferson Slave Narrative. Cook, Charles Orson, and Poteet, James M. "'Dem Was Black Times, Sure 'Nough': The Slave Narratives of Lydia Jefferson and Stephen Williams."

Louisiana History: The Journal of the Louisiana Historical Association, vol. 20, no. 3, 1979, pp. 281–92.

Lucy Thurston Slave Narrative. Rawick, George P. *The American Slave: A Composite Autobiography: Supplement, Series 1.* Westport, Conn., Greenwood Publishing Company, 1977, pp. 2110–2120. [Also see: http://msgw.org/slaves/thurston-xslave.htm.]

Anda Woods Slave Narrative. Rawick, George P. *The American Slave: A Composite Autobiography: Supplement, Series 1.* Westport, Conn., Greenwood Publishing Company, 1977, pp. 2388–2392. [Also see: http://msgw.org/slaves/wood-xslave.htm.]

WPA NARRATIVES (MENTIONING SONGS RELATED TO THE
"LIZA JANE" FAMILY)

Lizzie Farmer Slave Narrative. *Federal Writers' Project: Slave Narrative Project, Vol. XIII, Oklahoma Narratives.* Washington, DC, Library of Congress, 1941, pp. 97–101.

Frank Menefee Slave Narrative. *Federal Writers' Project: Slave Narrative Project, Vol. I, Alabama Narratives.* Washington, DC, Library of Congress, 1941, pp. 278–81.

Eliza Overton Slave Narrative. *Federal Writers' Project: Slave Narrative Project, Vol. X, Missouri Narratives.* Washington, DC, Library of Congress, 1941, pp. 266–68.

INDEX

ABOUT THE AUTHOR

Dan Gutstein is author of eight books and chapbooks, including *Metacarpalism* (poems), *Buildings Without Murders* (novel), and *non/fiction* (stories). His writing has appeared in *Ploughshares, American Scholar, Prairie Schooner, The Penguin Book of the Sonnet*, and *Best American Poetry,* among many other publications. He is coproducer of a forthcoming documentary film devoted to "Liza Jane" and was the vocalist for the 2022 punk album *States of America,* released by rock band Joy on Fire. A recipient of grants and awards from the Maryland State Arts Council, Arts & Humanities Council of Montgomery County (Maryland), and Women in Film & Video, Dan is presently nomadic, having lived most recently in the Washington, DC area. More information can be found at www.dangutstein.com.

Made in United States
North Haven, CT
25 February 2024

49176747R00190